JEFFERSON DAVIS

PRESIDENT
OF THE
CONFEDERATE STATES
OF
AMERICA

NOTABLE SOUTHERN FAMILIES

VOLUME II

COMPILED BY

ZELLA ARMSTRONG

JANAWAY PUBLISHING, INC.
Santa Maria, California

Notice

In many older books, foxing (or discoloration) occurs and, in some instances, print lightens with wear and age. Furthermore, this reprint's original printing was, by today's standards, of mediocre quality and included uneven type with numerous unintended ink markings throughout the text. Reprinted books, such as this, often duplicate these flaws, notwithstanding efforts to reduce or eliminate them. The pages of this reprint have been digitally enhanced and, where possible, the flaws eliminated in order to provide clarity of content and a pleasant reading experience.

Notable Southern Families. Volume II

Copyright © 1922, by Zella Armstrong

Originally published
Chattanooga, Tennessee
1922

Reprinted by:

Janaway Publishing, Inc.
732 Kelsey Ct.
Santa Maria, California 93454
(805) 925-1038
www.janawaygenealogy.com

2018

ISBN: 978-1-59641-396-2

Made in the United States of America

FOREWORD

In compiling this book of valuable family records I am indebted to scores of people. In many cases some of them contributed only a few names and dates but all of great value, while others gave time to the preparation of extended family data which could not otherwise have been obtained.

Among those to whom credit must be given for valuable assistance are:

Robert A. J. Armstrong, S. G. Heiskall, Richard Lee Kelton who prepared the Kelton data and a portion of the Wear article; John A. Kelly, Mrs. Anna Belle Hardwick Brown, who prepared the Hardwick and Montgomery data; Mrs. J. P. Stephenson, who prepared the Donelson data; Mrs. C. R. Greer, who prepared the Rhea record; Mrs. Sally Strother Hollingsworth who prepared the Hollingsworth line; Mrs. Louise Wilson Reynolds who wrote the Bean, Magill, Carter and Williams, and a part of the Wear; Mrs. Alice Vance Robinson who wrote the Vance record; Mrs. Bernis Brien who prepared the Brien and Holliday data; Mrs. Charles Polk McGuire who prepared the Shelby story; Miss Lucy M. Ball, Mrs. C. L. Hardwick, Mrs. J. E. Johnston; the late Oscar K. Lyle, the late James A. Caldwell, Mrs. Robert Houston Stickley, Mrs. Metta Andrews Green. Mrs. A. S. Bowen, C. K. Hill, Mrs. Joseph C. Vance and others.

Hundreds of histories, court records, Bibles and family documents have also been consulted.

ZELLA ARMSTRONG

CONTENTS

BEAN
BOONE
BORDEN
BRYAN
CARTER
DAVIS
DONALDSON
HARDWICK
HAYWOOD
HOLLIDAY
HOLLINGSWORTH
HOUSTON
JOHNSTON
KELTON
MAGILL
RHEA
MONTGOMERY
SHELBY
VANCE
WEAR
WILLIAMS

Notable Southern Families

BEAN

Let us visualize the present Tennessee as it was about the year 1770—not an unknown wilderness where any man might go and build his cabin if not intimidated by the Indians, but as an area jealously watched by both France and England. Where the boats of the Frenchman du Bois glided side by side with the Indian canoe, and French adventurers were made welcome in the wigwam; where, on the other hand, traders and explorers from Virginia, Pennsylvania and the Carolinas traversed valley and mountain trails to the Indian towns unmolested, and carried away rich peltries on their pack-horses.

Before Fort Loudon was erected in East Tennessee, French traders had built a fort near the present site of Nashville, and Frenchmen were operating silver mines upon the tributaries of the Cumberland.

Dating possibly as far back as the erection of Fort Louden and Long Island, Watauga had been the mecca for traders. Two, if not more cabins were erected there for their convenience before the year 1769, the date of its first settlement.

These traders played no little part in the early events on the Watauga. Through friendship for the people, some lost goodwill of the Indians and became victims of their animosity.

While it is possible that an interesting, if not bulky, volume might be written of the days before Tennessee is generally supposed to have attained the dignity of swaddling clothes, our history begins with the coming of one William Bean to Boone's Creek, in 1769.

All historians speak of William Bean as an "intrepid man," and it is doubtful if any other word could so well describe him.

Other men had gone into the wilderness alone or in companies, but William Bean came encumbered with wife and children.

NOTABLE SOUTHERN FAMILIES

A few years ago the writer came into possession of the bold autograph of Russell Bean, and looking at it felt a desire to know more about the Bean family in general, and more particularly concerning the parents of, so far as is known, the first baby born in Tennessee of English parentage.

The result of the research was a little disappointing in that so many of the traditions were contradictory or unauthentic, but there were compensations. And I became convinced that when Tennessee gets the habit of building monuments, the memory of William Bean will mean as much to Tennesseeans as that of Daniel Boone to Kentucky, and the state will erect a monument to William Bean and to his wife who was the first heroine mentioned in the pioneer history of Tennessee.

Captain William Bean, of Watauga, is believed to have been descended from John Bean, who in 1660 came from Ireland and settled in Exeter, Massachusetts. The Beans were worthy people who boasted a coat-of-arms and who contributed to the educational and social development of Exeter. William was a favorite name with the Exeter family, and one William at least drifted out upon the big Pennsylvania frontier.

While Captain William Bean came from Pittsylvania County of Virginia, to Watauga, he was born in Pennsylvania, and had possibly lived in North Carolina. There is a tradition that he had spent his honeymoon at Fort Loudon and that through the intervention of Nancy Ward, the daughter of a British adventurer, and the granddaughter of Oconostoto, he and his wife were saved from the massacre. The tradition possibly originated through the efforts of some writer to corrupt historical facts to meet the demand of popular fiction.

Mrs. William Bean was before her marriage Lydia Russell, daughter of James Russell, of Virginia, and a member of that pioneer family of the name who furnished so many well-known frontier soldiers and statesmen. When Mrs. Bean accompanied her husband to Watauga she was the mother of five children, William, Robert, George, Sarah and Jane. It is possible that there were other children whose names are not known. Before building his cabin, William Bean and his wife kept house in the shanty erected by Bean and Daniel Boone on a hunting expedition in that region; Russell Bean, so says tradition, was born in this rude habitation.

It was July 1, 1776, that the memorable Indian attack was made upon Fort Watauga. It had been seven years

BEAN

since the Beans came to Watauga, and the Watauga and Holston settlements numbered about six hundred people.

Forewarned by Isaac Thomas, a trader, to whom Nancy Ward had confided the plans of the coming uprising, the families surrounding Watauga had taken refuge in the fort, but although her husband was on military duty, Mrs. Bean had for some reason failed to do so, and was taken captive by the Indians under the Cherokee chief, Old Abraham. The Indians, on retreating, carried Mrs. Bean with them to their camp on the Nollichucky River. Here, at the point of a gun, she was forced to witness the torture and death of a neighbor. Mrs. Bean was questioned concerning the strength and provisions of the garrison at the fort. Although facing death, she retained her composure and answered in a manner that would lead her questioners to conclude that the fort was well defended and possessed of provisions sufficient to withstand a long siege.

Later Mrs. Bean was told "she would not be put to death but be taken to the the Indian towns, where she should teach the Indian squaws how to make butter". Subsequently she did accompany them to their town, where she remained some time in captivity before being ransomed.

It is said she was saved by Nancy Ward who said that the Magic Powers had revealed to her that the Nation would be destroyed if they burned Mrs. Bean.

William Bean was one of the first patentees of the land leased from the Indians by Charles Robertson as trustee for the settlers and later secured by treaty. His name is found to the petition for annexation to North Carolina, which is in the archives at Raleigh, and was received by messenger August 22, 1776. He was one of the earliest captains of militia, and his name is given as one of the captains when in response to Governor Rutherford's requisition the commissioned officers met for the purpose of dispatching troops for the relief of South Carolina.

From the beginning, the Watauga and Holston settlements had been troubled with a few undesirable citizens, who, with the idea of obtaining more license, openly avowed their Tory sentiments. In reality they were but the renegades such as are found in all isolated and frontier settlements.

As the depredations of these men increased, two military companies seem to have assumed, or to have been delegated the duty of driving them out of the neighborhood—a task not so easy because of the wide area and mountainous nature of the country.

The captains of these two companies were William Bean and Robert Sevier (a brother of Colonel John Sevier who was mortally wounded later at the battle of Kings Mountain).

Captain Sevier had recently located in the Nollichucky settlement near the present Green and Cocke County line. William Bean in this year, 1778, when the depredations of the Tories became serious, settled Bean Station in Grainger County; this station was the foremost frontier post. It is now known as Tate.

The worst of the Tory desperadoes was Grimes, or "Captain" Grimes, as he is called by the historians Haywood and Ramsey. His real name was Henry Grimes, and he had at one time possessed a sort of respectability and was one of the original patentees at Watauga.

Grimes had gathered together a banditti whose crimes ranged from horse stealing to murder. Their lairs in the mountains for a time seemed inaccessible. They killed a Mr. Milliban (Millican in Washington County), and a Mr. Grubbs who lived on the Nollichucky, had been carried to a high cliff of the river, and with threats of throwing him off, forced to purchase his life with the promise to convey all of his property to the Tory band. Mr. James Roddy, prominent during the State of Franklin, and representative of Green County in the North Carolina Assembly of 1785, was also captured by Grimes, but later effected his escape.

Captain Bean's company, having succeeded in driving Isham Yearley, a seditious Tory, from the Nollichucky, determined to penetrate the Watauga mountains and drive out Captain Grimes and his men. Grimes, though wounded, managed to escape to North Carolina. Here he joined Ferguson. After the battle of Kings Mountain he was taken prisoner, and again falling into the hands of the overmountain men, the latter saw that he paid in full the penalty for all of his crimes. He was one of the nine Tories convicted and hanged after the battle.

Serving under Captain William Bean in the expedition that pursued Captain Grimes was his brother, John Bean, a man of education, and a delegate to the convention of Franklin from Washington County, and also Captain Bean's son, George Bean, and Edmond Bean, probably a son of John Bean.

The Beans were all famous as riflemen, and history chronicles more than one instance of their marksmanship.

It is not generally known that at one crucial period during the Revolution the Watauga settlement became a

BEAN

haven of refuge not only for the hard-pressed little Whig bands from both Georgia and North Carolina, but for the families as well of the bold leaders who might suffer persecution at the hands of the British and Tories. So welcome were these refugees and so hospitable the people of the over-mountain settlements, that following the Revolution many were glad to take up their permanent residence among them.

Ramsey relates that "when Colonel Clark returned to Georgia after exile in the Watauga and Holston settlements he was accompanied by many recruits from this section".

One of these recruits was Robert Bean, the son of Captain William Bean. Colonel Clark with his small army in Georgia was forced to use the same strategic methods of warfare practiced by Marion and Sumpter in South Carolina. On one occasion he approached a British camp, and posted his men, among whom were many of the new recruits, in ambush, and sent a small detachment to draw the enemy within the ambuscade. The ruse was successful. The unerring riflemen killed several British, with the loss of only one Georgian. The commanding officer of the British camp was shot down by Robert Bean. The behavior of the mountain soldiers on this occasion is said to have done much to perpetuate the friendship Clark already felt for the people of the western settlements.

Another historic incident is that which occurred on Sevier's expedition in 1782, when he invaded as far as Chickamauga. Much of the trouble with the Indians had long been attributed to the activities of British spies in the Indian towns. The disaffection among the Indians of the lower towns seemed to radiate from towns of the Chickamaugas, and in September Colonel John Sevier and Colonel Joseph Anderson, of Sullivan County, marched into the hostile country, killed the warriors and burned their towns.

The spy to whom the trouble was attributed was discovered at Coosa. He had assumed the name of Clements and was living with an Indian woman by the name of Nancy Coody. Papers were found on his person which proved him to be a British sergeant. "Bean, one of the soldiers, shot him dead". This member of the Bean family may have been Jesse Bean, one of Sevier's captains, and who also participated in the battle of Kings Mountain. Jesse Bean accompanied Captain William Bean to Bean Station and owned land near the fort: whether he was a son of Captain William Bean, or a son of John Bean of Washington County, has not been ascertained.

Like Daniel Boone, his old friend and companion, Captain Bean "did not like to be crowded". He had helped blaze the Boone trail and watched emigrants settle upon the Watauga and Holston until they numbered perhaps a thousand people, then he began to look around for a home with more latitude, and where game was more plentiful. It is a family tradition that he selected the site of Bean Sattion because of the gap in the mountain, and because of the sulphur springs, and salt licks, which latter attracted deer and other game.

Captain Bean erected Bean Station about the year 1778. Since he had grandchildren at this date, he could no longer be considered a young man, but as this is the year of his activities against the Tories it will be seen that he was still very active in frontier military affairs. The fort is said to have been strongly built and well defended, when occasion necessitated, by the few families who settled in its proximity.

The number of years that pioneer families lived in fear and suffered the atrocities from the Indians is shown by the massacre of Jane Bean, a daughter of Captain William Bean, twenty-one years after the family had moved to Bean Station.

Jane Bean had gone to a nearby spring for the purpose of doing a washing when Indians hidden in a cedar thicket jumped out, killed and scalped her. The grave may yet be seen in the rear of a barn near the public road, and is marked with a rough stone bearing the inscription, "Jane Bean, Nov. 12, 1799," now on the place of Mr. Ethelbert Williams, once part of the estate of the Cobbs at Tate.

The only remaining daughter of Captain Bean of whom we have record is Sarah, who became the wife of John Bowen, brother of the brave Lieutenant Reece Bowen, whose death is so graphically described by Mr. Draper in "Kings Mountain and It's Heroes".

There are many interesting traditions extant in this branch of the family of the early days at Bean Station.

The story goes that "on the day preceding the marriage of Sarah Bean, when all plans had been made for the celebration, John Bowen was called away to assist in quelling an Indian uprising, and the wedding had to be postponed". Two weeks later, however, the wedding took place and after the culmination of the ceremony the groom took his bride to his cabin five miles distant from the station.

The honeymoon was spent in continuous trepidation and fear of the Indians, who at this particular time either through real or imaginary grievances against encroachments and broken faith of the settlers, were stealing into every settlement, massacreing and plundering.

In the early morning Sarah Bowen would take her pail, and while her husband stood guard in the doorway with his gun, hasten to the spring for water.

One night Sarah and John Bowen were awakened by a stealthy and suggestive tapping outside the door. They arose, armed themselves with hatchet and gun and awaited the moment of attack.

Moments and hours passed and nothing more alarming transpired than the same suggestive Tap! Tap! Tap!

With dawn the mystery of the delayed attack was solved. While dipping candles on the doorstep, Mrs. Bowen had spilled some of the tallow, which had attracted a gander one of several that Mrs. William Bean had brought her daughter the same day that she might collect feathers for a new feather tick!

When Indian danger threatened and Mr. Bowen was off on duty, one of Sarah Bean's brothers would hasten for her, force her to jump astride the horse behind him, a feat shocking to the modesty, but necessary in the emergency, and dash away with her to the protection of the fort.

Mrs. Bowen was a true daughter of the frontier, and lived to be ninety-three years old. After the death of her husband she accompanied a son on a flat-boat to Texas and lived and died near the present city of Dallas.

Russell Bean was the youngest child of Captain William Bean and Lydia Russell Bean, and his name has been immortalized as "the first white child born in Tennessee". If tradition is to be believed, he grew up to be a handsome youth with black, curly hair and fine physique. He married a daughter of Captain Charles Robertson, a man of culture, an emigrant from South Carolina and trustee of the Watauga settlers until their lands were purchased outright from the Indians. He was sometimes called "Black Charles Robertson," either because of his swarthiness of complexion or to distinguish him from another Charles Robertson of the settlement.

Russell Bean early developed a propensity for adventure, often leaving his wife in Washington County, he acted as pilot for convoys down the river from Knoxville to the Cumberland settlements. Later in the same capacity he traveled between Memphis and Natchez.

On one occasion Russell Bean remained away for so long that his wife, believing him dead, married again. On his return, finding her married, he proceeded to take the law in his own hands in a manner which placed him in a position to be presecuted by the Robertson family.

After this unfortunate incident, Russell Bean left East Tennessee, going to Nashville, where he married again, and it is said became one of the first police of that city, a position offered him no doubt because of his unusual size and strength.

The sequeal to the story of Russell Bean, if true, is one in which "Old Hickory's" eloquence reunited Russell Bean with his first wife, death in the course of years having claimed the other participants in matrimony.

On his way to be inaugurated in Washington, Andrew Jackson was dining at the hotel in the old town of Jonesboro. As a dinner was being served Mr. Jackson saw Russell Bean on the veranda of the hotel. It is true that the domestic felicity of the two men had been disrupted in a manner not dissimilar in character, but Jackson had been the state's prossecuting attorney against Bean, and Russell Bean's presence at this time may not have indicated enthusiasm or good will toward the new President.

However, Mr. Jackson greeted him cordially, engaged him in conversation, eventually secluding him in a corner of the hotel, were oblivious of dinner and waiting guests, he talked long and eloquently. As a result of this meeting it is said Russell Bean sought a reconciliation with his wife.

Of course there may be doubting Thomases who will disbelieve this tradition, but who does not wish the first little babe born in the hunter's shanty on the banks of the Watauga the culmination of a happy romance?

The one tradition that can safely be denied is that whch states "That Captain William Bean in his will disinherited Russell, because of his treatment toward his wife". Russell Bean's domestic troubles occurred about the year 1796, fourteen years after the death of Captain Bean.

Captain William Bean's will was proved at the May term of the Washington County court in the year 1782.

The next year, by the formation of a new county, Bean Station was thrown into Greene County. It is now in Grainger County.

Russell Bean, the first white child born in what is now Tennessee, married first Rosamund Robertson, daughter of Charles Robertson, as before stated.

Ther children as given by Draper, were: Baxter Charles, James, Joseph, Robert and Camilla. She married a Garland.

Early records show that Robert Bean, son of William, resided near the town of Greeneville in the year 1874. He

BEAN

later moved to Bean Station. "Jacob Bean" owned land on the south side of the Nollichucky River in 1788-99. David Bean, in 1790, lived on the French Broad in Jefferson County. Russell Bean was prosecuted in the courts of Greeneville in 1796; he was an inhabitant of the County in 1799, although Grainger County was formed from Hawkins and Knox Counties in the year 1796.

All of the early Beans are supposed to have descended from Captain William Bean and his brother John, of Washington County.

I have been told that all of the family of Captain Bean had left the neighborhood of Bean Station shortly after the year 1800.

Of the last days of Captain Bean there is no tradition. In 1780 he was one of the captains of the militia when reinforcements were sent into South Carolina, and the writer is certain that some time she has seen a record of his served while under Marion in that state.

There seems to be no certainty of his burial place.

A few years ago a pile of rock near the grave of Jane Bean was supposed to mark his grave, and perhaps other members of the family. It is probable that this is true; such monuments were common in the days when Indians violated the graves of those who were their sworn enemies.

There was a day when Bean Station, located on the main stage road at the gap in the mountain, promised to be somewhat of a metropolis. That day is past, but it is still often visited by the lover of historical spots. The springs visited by many deer in Captain Bean's time are today annually visited by many seekers after health and pleasure. Tate Springs is typically a Tennessee resort. The site of Bean Station, where the first man who brought his family to reside in Tennessee lived and died, as did his wife, who in the face of an Indian rifle dared to quibble with the truth, hoping by so doing that she might save her neighbors, gathered in the little fort of Watauga, is surely worthy of a monument.

BOONE

The family of Daniel Boone (who is best known of the name), begins apparently with one George Boone, born in England about 1625 or earlier. He married in England and died in England. There are four George Boones in a direct line, showing that George was an established family favorite before Daniel made the name Boone a household word.

The first George Boone, born about 1625 or earlier, had a son George Boone, born about 1646 or earlier. He was a blacksmith. He married Sarah Uppen in England about 1665. He died at the age of sixty years. Sarah Uppen Boone lived to be eighty years of age. They had at least one son whom they named George and who is the George Boone the Third in this chronicle. He was born in 1666 at Stoak, near Exeter, Devonshire England. He was a weaver and when he came to maturity he went to a neighboring town to pursue his calling. There he married Mary Maugridge. They were Quakers. They had nine children and emigrated to America after three of the nine children had emigrated to the new country. George Boone the Third died in America in 1744 in Pennsylvania. His wife, Mary Boone, born 1669 in Brandnich, England, married about 1688 in Bradnich, died in Pennsylvonia, Feb. 2, 1740.

Their nine children were born in Bradnich, England, the birth place of the mother, and the marriage place of George and Mary. The three eldest children preceded their parents to America and in August 1717 the parents sailed from England accompanied by the remaining members of the family. Eight of the nine children, all save John, married and raised families.

The nine children were:

I George Boone the fourth.
II Sarah Boone married Jacob Stover, a German.
III Squire Boone born November 25, 1696, married Sarah Morgan (1720) at Gwynedd Meeting House with a Quaker ceremony.
IV Mary Boone married James Webb.
V John Boone died unmarried.
VI Joseph Boone.
VII Benjamin Boone married Sussanah ———.
VIII James Boone married Mary Foulks.
IX Samuel Boone.

NOTABLE SOUTHERN FAMILIES

I GEORGE BOONE

George Boone, fourth of the name and one of the nine children of George and Mary Maugridge Boone was one of the emigrants that landed at Philadelphia, October 10, 1717.

George Boone, the Fourth was born in Bradnich, England, July 13, 1690, died Nov. 20, 1753 in America. Early traditions say that when he was about twenty-two or three he, his sister Sarah and his brother Squire Boone, were sent by the family to America and that he returned with a favorable report and that remaining members of the family then accompanied him on his second journey to America, landing at Philadelphia October 10, 1717. He married Deborah Howell, 1713. She was born August 1691, died January 26, 1759.

Their children were:

1 George Boone, Fifth, in a direct line, born 1713 or 1714; died unmarried in 1730.

2 Mary Boone, born 1716, married Isaac Lee.

3 Hannah Boone, born 1718, died 1753; married George Hughes and had three children: Boone Hughes, Jen Hughes and Samuel Boone Hughes, born 1766, and perhaps had other children.

4 Deborah Boone, born 1720.

5 Dinah Boone, born 1722, married, first. ——— Williams, and had Abner Williams, and married, second, ——— Cotes, and had Solomon Cotes.

6 William Boone, born 1724, married Sarah Lincoln and had eight children: Jeremiah, William, George, Thomas, Hezikah, Abigail (who married Adin Pancost), Mary and Mordicai.

7 Joseph Boone, born 1726, married ——— and had at least one son, George Boone, and perhaps others.

8 Jeremiah Boone, born 1728.

9 Abigail Boone.

10 Hesekiah Boone, born 1743.

Another record gives also:

11 Sarah Boone, married David Wilcoxen.

II SARAH BOONE

I have been unable to find any record of Sarah Boone subsequent to her marriage to Jacob Stover, a German, or Jacob Stuber, March 15, 1715. She was born in Brandnich, England, February 18, 1691.

III SQUIRE BOONE

Squire Boone, son of George and Mary Maugridge Boone, was born in Brandnich, England, November 26,

BOONE

1619. He was one of the three eldest children of the family who were sent to America preceding the family emigration in 1717. He married Sarah Morgan, July 23, 1720, at the Gwynedd Meeting House, according to the Quaker ceremony. She was a daughter of John Morgan. The name Squire is not just a corruption of Esquire or a title but seems to have become a family cognomen because of some previous connection and it descends for several generations. Squire Boone was dismissed from the Quaker Church in 1748 because he gave his approval to his son, Israel Boone, for marrying "out of the church". Squire Boone moved for this reason to Holman's Ford, North Carolina, on the Yadkin River during or before the year 1750. It is to this circumstance that his son, Daniel Boone, most famous of the name, became a pioneer of the North Carolina, Tennessee and Kentucky Mountains.

Squire and Sarah Boone had twelve children, namely:

1 Sarah Boone, born April 7. 1724; died 1824; married John Wilcoxen.

2 Israel, born May 20, 1729; married about 1748 "out of the Church" for in that year Squire Boone is dismissed from the Quaker congregation for approving his son's marriage.

3 Samuel Boone, born May 3, 1878; died 1815. He was in the Revolution. Married Sarah Day, who was alive October 19, 1730.

4 Jonathan Boone, born December 17, 1730.

5 Elizabeth Boone, born February 16, 1732; married William Grant, born 1720 and died 1864, in Fayette County, Kentucky. He was among the Virginians who emigrated to Kentucky in 1779 and built a fort at Bryan's Station with his brother-in-law, Daniel Boone. He is mentioned in histories of Kentucky. It is said that Elizabeth after his death, married Bouton Fletcher and another record says she married John Turner.

6 Daniel Boone, born —, 1734. His record will follow.

7 Mary Boone, born November 14, 1736, married, first William Bryan (see Bryan family), and married, second, General Charles Smith.

8 George Boone, born January 13, 1738 or 1739.

9 Edward Boone, born November 30, 1740 or 1742.

10 Squire Boone, Second.

11 Hannah Boone, born August 1, 1746, died 1820; married, first, John Stuart, who died 1770. They had four children. She married, second, Richard Pennington and had a fifth child whose name was Richard Pennington, and she perhaps had other Pennington children.

NOTABLE SOUTHERN FAMILIES

12 Nathan Boone.

Of the foregoing twelve children of Squire Boone the First, and his wife, Sarah Morgan Boone, the record of each is well established, but the story of Daniel Boone, the Pioneer and Revolutionary hero, rather overshadows all his brothers and sisters and their families.

DANIEL BOONE

Daniel Boone was the sixth child of Squire Boone and Sarah Morgan Boone. He was born 1734 in Bucks County, Pennsylvania, and came to Holman's Ford, Yadkin River, North Carolina some time during or before 1750 (some records say 1749) while he was still quite young. He died in 1820 in St. Charles, Missouri, at the home of his grandson, Nathan Boone. His body and his wife's were reintered in Frankfort, Kentucky.

He married Rebecca Bryan in 1755, his father Squire Boone, then a Justice of the Peace in Rowan County officiating. Rebecca was a daughter of Morgan Bryan (see Bryan history). She died in Missouri in 1813. His meeting with Rebecca when he thought she was a deer, or at least a wild creature—she had gone out to the Spring to bring in water—his leveling his gun at her and later following the supposed deer into her father's house to meet her there and fall in love with her, is all a part of his romantic history which is all deeply enmeshed in the history of the three states: North Carolina, Tennessee and Kentucky. This record however is briefly a genealogical story and has not space for his remarkable history no matter how interesting it is.

There were born to Daniel Boone and Rebecca Bryan Boone children, namely:

1 James Boone, born May 5, 1757; killed by Indians October 10, 1775.

2 Israel Boone, born 1759; killed by Indians.

3 Susannah Boone, born November 2, 1760; married William Hays.

4 Jemima Boone, born October 4, 1762 (Kentucky history says she was born 1775); married Flanders Calloway.

5 Lavina Boone, born March 13, 1776; married Joseph Echoll.

6 Daniel Morgan Boone, born 1768, said to be the first settler in Kansas; married Sarah Lewis.

7 Rebecca Boone, born 1770; married Phillip Goe.

8 Jesse Bryan Boone, born 1773; married Chloe Van Bibber, daughter of Captain John Van Bibber.

9 William Boone, born June 1775; died young.

BOONE

10 Nathan Boone, born 1781; married Olive Van Bibber; buried at Ash Grove, Missouri.

Rebecca Bryan Boone was probably the first white woman in Kentucky and with her husband must be called one of the founders of Boonsborough, the second oldest settlement in Kentucky. The first woman to own a piece of land in Kentucky was Susannah, daughter of Daniel and Rebecca Boone, who at an early date obtained a patent for a tract in Madison County. Daniel kept on exploring all his life and his wanderings were many, finally taking him to the present state of Missouri where he died.

Susannah Boone, third child of Daniel and Rebecca Bryan Boone, married William Hays. They went to Kentucky with Daniel and Hartley's Life of Daniel Boone speaks of his living with his daughter, Susannah Hays, in Platte County, Missouri. Among her children were: Lucy Hays, who married ——— Lancaster, and had Ramson M. Lancaster,(who married Sarah A. Roberts) and Lucy Lancaster, (who married ——— Jenkins); and Susan Hays who married Isaac Van Bibber and had Fannie Van Bibber who married Cyrenius Cox and had Missouri Cox and James M. Cox..

Jemima Boone, daughter of Daniel Boone and Rebecca Bryan Boone was born October 4, 1762. She was captured by the Indians when she was a child but was rescued. She married Flanders Calloway and had ten children, namely: John B. Calloway (who married Elizabeth Cotton); Larkins Calloway (who married Susan Howell); Captain James Calloway (who married Nancy Howell); Susannah Calloway (who married Thomas Howell); Frances Calloway; Daniel Boone Calloway; Sallie Boone Calloway; Tabitha Calloway; Betsy Calloway and Minerva Calloway.

BORDEN

The founder of the Borden family in America was Richard Borden, a son of Matthew Borden, church warden of Hedcorn Parish, County Kent, England, and his wife, Joan. Matthew Borden is traced back to Henry Borden of Hedcorn Parish who was born about 1375, and his wife, Robergia. The Borden family is of Norman-English origin; the original spelling of the name was Bourdon. There have been many variants on the name Borden, the most frequent being, at least in the American family, the form Burden.

Richard Borden, the immigrant, was born at Hedcorn and was baptized September 22, 1595. On September 28, 1625, he was married in Hedcorn church to Joan Fowle. In 1628 Richard and Joan (Fowle) Borden removed from the parish of Hedcorn to the neighboring parish of Cranbrook, thence in 1635 to New England, settling in Boston Neck, near Roxbury, Massachusetts. In the spring of 1638, they became members of the first colony of settlers of Rhode Island. Richard Borden was one of the three men who laid out the original town of Portsmouth, Rhode Island, and according to Mussell (American Ancestry, Vol. VII), he was elected in 1654 treasurer of the United Colonies. The first five children of Richard and Joan (Fowle) Borden were born in England; the sixth, Matthew, born May 16, 1638, was the first white child born on Rhode Island. In all there were twelve children. From the seventh, John, the Southern Bordens are descended. During the last century his descendants have greatly outnumbered those of all his brothers, and now they may be found in almost every state of the Union. He married Mary Earle, daughter of William and Mary (Walker) Earle, and granddaughter of Ralph and Jona Earle, who were also among the original setters of Rhode Island.

John and Mary (Earle) Borden had nine children. Of these the sixth son and youngest child, Benjamin, born in Portsmouth 1692, inherited 5,000 acres of land in Pennsylvania and also acquired a large estate in New Jersey, where he settled. It is said that he first went to Virginia in 1732. By a grant dated July 12, 1734, 1,122 acres of land "on the western side of the Shenandoah River in the county to be called Orange" were patented to Benjamin Borden, Andrew Hapton and David Griffith. The county court of Orange

NOTABLE SOUTHERN FAMILIES

was opened January 12,1734,and the justices included in the "Commission of Peace", were James Barbour (grandfather of Governor James Barbour and Phillip Pendleton Barbour), Zachary Taylor (grandfather of President Taylor), Joist Hite, Morgan Morgan, Benjamin Borden, and the ubiquitous John Smith.

Benjamin Borden deserves to have his name remembered chiefly on account of the part he played in settling up the valley of Virginia, he obtained from Governor Gooch, October 3, 1734, patent for a tract of land in Frederick County which was called Borden's Manor. At the same time he was promised 100,000 acres (according to Peyton's History of Augusta County (500,000),on the waters of the James River, as soon as he should locate one hundred settlers on the tract. Borden's Manor was south of Beverly's Manor, and it embraced the whole upper part of Augusta and Rockbridge Counties, the famous Natural Bridge being located on the tract. Neither Borden nor the proprietors of Beverly's Manor (William Beverly, John Randolph, Richard Randolph and John Robertson) tired in their efforts to secure immigrants. Borden made at least two trips to Europe for this purpose. He returned from the first one in 1737 with a number of colonists. The first settlers on Borden's Manor were Ephriam McDowell and his family. They were soon followed by Archibald Alexander, John Patton, Andrew Moore, Hugh Telford, John Matthews, the Prestons, Paxtons, Lyles, Grigsbys, Stewarts, Wallaces, Wilsons, Caruthers, Campbells, McClungs, McRaes, and others who became the founders of some of Virginia's distinguished families.

Benjamin Borden died November. ———, possessed of 130,000 acres of land in Virginia and New Jersey. He was survived by his wife, Jerusah, who soon returned to New Jersey to reside, and by ten children, as follows: (1) Benjamin, who married Mrs. Magdalene (Woods) McDowell (they had only one child who grew to maturity, a daughter, Martha, who married, first Benjamin Hawkins, and had four children:: (1) Sarah, who married William Mitchell, (2) Magdalene, who married Colonel Harvey, (3) William and (4) James. Martha (Borden) Hawkins married, second, Robert Harvey); (2) Hannah, who married Edward Rogers (their son, Edward, was a Revolutionary soldier); (3) Mercy, who married William Fearnley; (John (see below); (5) Abigail, who married, first, Jacob Worthington (they had a son, William, who married Elizabeth Machir), and, second, James Pritchard; (6) Rebecca, who married Thomas Bronson, and had two sons, Levi and Eli,

BORDEN

(7) Deborah, who married Thomas Henley; (8) Lydia, who married Jacob Peck (see below); (9) Elizabeth, who married, first Nichols and had a son, William, born 1747, and, second, Patton and left Patton descendants in Tennessee, and (10) Joseph, who removed to Tennessee.

John Borden, son of Benjamin, Sr., died in 1875 in Covington, Kentucky, leaving eight children: (1) Joseph, of Knoxville, Tennessee, (see below), and William, who settled in White County, Tennessee, and later removed to Washington County, Arknasas, where he left three sons, John, Joseph and William; (3) Benjomin, who married and had several daughters; (4) John, who died in Hardeman County, Tennessee, leaving several daughters; (5) Rebecca, who married Overstreet, of Overton County, Tennessee; (6) Margaret, who married Judge Keither, of Knoxville; (7) Nancy, who married John McWilliams, of Bledsoe County, Tennessee, and (8) Sarah, who married Alexander McCoy, of Knoxville.

Joseph Borden of Knoxville, married Mary Echols. They had five children: (1) Eli, who married Marcha Wheeler; (2) Hawkins, who settled in Walker County, Alabama; (3) John, who married, first, Catherine Matlock, and second, Catherine Sevier, a grandaughter of Governor Sevier (see Sevier family); (4) Joseph, who settled in 1818 in Calhoun County, Alabama, and (5) Ann, who married Moses Johnson and had one son, Allan.

I think it probable that Borden's first wife, Catherine Matlock, was also of the Sevier family and that she was a daughter of William and Polly Sevier Matlock, the latter a sister of Governor John Sevier, and named Catherine for the governor's other sister.

Lydia Borden, daughter of Benjamin, Sr., (born 1720, died 1801), married Jacob Peck, a native of Wurttemberg, Germany, who settled 1738 in Pennsylvania. This name was written Beck, but in southern Germany was pronounced Peck. All of the sons of Jacob used the form Peck, with the possible exception of Joseph, whose last reference found in 1785, is under the name Beck. Joseph probably settled in Northern Alabama; Hardesty (Historical and Geographical Encyclopedia) says that Jacob settled in Alabama, but this doubtless incorrect, as he was still living at Staunton, Virginia, at the age of 71). Jacob and Lydia (Borden) Peck had eight children: (1). Benjamin (see below); Jacob, who married , first, Mary Abney, and second, Elizabeth Dashkam; (3) John H., of Botecourt County, Virginia, who married Mary McCreary; (4) Adam, who settled in East Tennessee, and left a number of descendants, including

NOTABLE SOUTHERN FAMILIES

Judge J. Peck, one of the founders of Emory and Henry College; (5) Mary, who married Jacob Carper; (6) Joseph, who married Hannah Thomas (Joseph was a soldier of the Revolution, as some of his brothers are said to have been; (7) Hester (see below), and (8) Hannah who married Peter Holm.

Benjamin, son of Jacob and Lydia (Borden) Peck, was born in 1746. He married Margaret Carper and settled in what is now Craig County, Virginia. They had five sons: John, Jacob, Adam, Benjamin and Joseph. John, the eldest son, was born September 10, 1772. He settled in Giles County, Virginia, and in 1806 was appointed one of the first Justices of the Peace of that county. He married Elizabeth Snidow, daughter of Colonel Christian Snidow and his wife, Mary Burke, a granddaughter of Captain James Burke, who in 1753, discovered the picturesque valley in Tazewell County, Virginia, known as Burke's Garden. Their Children were: (1) Mary Burke, who married her cousin, Benjamin Borden Peck; (2) Margaret Carper, who married Charles Lewis Pearis, son of Colonel George and Rebecca (Clay) Pearis (their only child, Electra, married Dr. Charles W. Pearis, son of Samuel P. and Rebecca (Chapmab) Pearis); (3) Christian Lewis, who married Susan Price and left descendants in Giles County; (4) Clara S., who married John H. Vawter (they had several children, among them a son, Captain Charles E. Vawter, for many years principal of the Miller School, of Albermarle County, Virginia, who married Virginia Longley); (5) Joseph Addison, who married Eellen Baker and settled in Texas; (6) Sarah S., who married Edwin Amos (they had a daughter, Sarah, who married Colonel William Palmer, of Richmond and Blacksburg, Virginia. Their daughter, Sarah, married Robert Preston Reams and their only child is Mrs. Valentine Nesbit, of Birmingham. Another daughter, Elizabeth Palmer, married Frank Christian, a third, Lelia, married Egbert Leigh, of Richmond, and the fourth, Claudia, is Mrs. William Ormond Young, of Richmond); (7) William Henry, who married Elizabeth Amos, a sister of Edwin, and settled in Logan County, West Virginia; (8) Rebecca R., who died young; (9) Charles Decatur, who married Rachel Hoge Thomas, a daughter of Colonel William Thomas and wife, Rachel Montgomery Hoge, who was a granddaughter of James and Elizabeth (Howe) Hoge, pioneer settlers of what is now Pulaski County, Virginia; (10) Dr. Erastus Watson Peck, who married first, Mary Mason, of Lynchburg, second Ann Handley, and third Martha Hobbs; (11) Elizabeth E., who married Dr. Robert B

BORDEN

McNutt (they had several sons and two daughters (1) Mary, who married Colonel James Barbee Peck and had several children among them a daughter, Josephine, who married Dr. S. D. Long, president of Martha Washington College, and Juanita, who married Judge George B. Sinclair, formerly of Charlottesville, Virginia, now of New York); (12) Martha M, who married Judge John Alexander Kelly, son of Vincent Howell and Ann Simmons (Alexander) Kelly (one of their sons, Francis Alexander Kelly, married Eliza Patton (see Gaines family, Volume I Notable Southern Families); another, Judge L. Kelly, of Virginia Court of Appeals, married Mary Hull, daughter of Captain D. D. Hull, of Marion, Virginia), and (13) Josephine E., who married Dr. Richard Phillips and settled in Alabama.

Jacob, the second son of Benjamine and Margaret (Carper) Peck, married Malinda Givens. They had eleven children: (1) Benjamin Borden, who married Mary Burke Peck (they had six sons, Pembroke, Charles, Lewis, James H., Jacob A., Erastus H. and Borden Wallace, who was killed in the battle of Gettysburg); (2) William Givens, who died unmarried; (3) Elisha G., who married Margaret Peters; (4) Daniel R., who died unmarried; (5) George Harrison, who married Sarah J. Handley; (6) James Preston, who married Elizabeth Scott; (7) Jacob H., who married Ann Hendley; (8) Margaret Carper, who married Archibald Peck, son of John and Jane (Hutcheson) Peck; (9) Rhoda E., who married James McClaugherty; (10) Louisa S., who married Lewis Payne and (11) Rebecca, who married John A. Calfee.

Benjamine, son of Benjamin and Margaret (Carper) Peck, married Rebecca Snidow, sister of his brother's wife, and settled in Monroe County, West Virginia. Their children were: (1) William H., (2) Christian, (3) Francis, (4) John S., who married Mary Burke Snidow, daughter of John and Rachel (Chapman) Snidow. (They had the following children: James P., who was killed in 1864 in the battle of Cold Harbor; Hugh T., who lives in Maryland, Chapman J., of Giles County, John, Ann, who married John P. Peck, and Elizabeth, who married Harvey Snidow); (5) Martha Hobbs; (11) Elizabeth E., who married Dr. Robert B. who married John A. Chalfee.

Hester Peck, daughter of Jacob and Lydia (Borden) Peck, married Isaac Van Meter. They had eight children: (1) Hannah, who married McFerrin; (2) Mary, who married Charles Hedrick; (3) Elizabeth, who married Benjamin Carper (they had three sons, James, George and Joseph, who married Ann West and had four children: Elizabeth, who married ——— Echols, Robert who was killed near Williamsburg, Virginia, in the War Between the States; Wyndham, and Ariana Williamson, who married William B. Bean—Dr. Robert Bennet Bean, of the University of Virgnia, is their son); (4). Placentia, who married ——— McFerrin; (5) Jacob, who married Patsy Ushur Shrewsbury (see below); Joseph, of Marion, Virginia, who married Damaris Lockland, of Hagerstown, Maryland. (They had seven children, none of whom left descendants; (7) Sarah Hawkins, who married Dr. Eleazer Sweetland and settled in Greenup County, Kentucky (see below).

Jacob and Patsy (Shrewbury) Van Meter had eight children: (1) William Steel, who married Mary Shrewsberry; (2) Mary, who married William Cooke; (3) Julia, who married Atwood G. Hobson; (4) Caroline E., who married George Bradley Adams, of Bowling Green, Kentucky; (5) Samuel Kirk, who married Jane Sharp; (6) Charles Joseph, who married Mrs. Catherine(Moss)Overall; (7) Sarah, who married M. P. Clarkson and (8) Clinton Clay, who died unmarried.

Dr. Eleazer and Sarah Hawkins (Van Meter) Sweetland had ten children: (1) Elizabeth, who married Thomas Jefferson Obenchain, of Wythville, Virginia; (their eldest son, Dr. William Alexander Obenchain, president of Ogden College, Bowling Green, Kentucky, married Eliza Calvert, the novelist, whose nom de plume is Eliza Calvert Hall. They have four children: Margery, William, Thomas Hale and Cecilia Calvert); (2) Mary Hester, who married George Walter Strickland; (3) Charles Gould, who died in Strickland, California, unmarried; (4) Samuel McFerrin, who married first Martha Abernethy and second, Mary Abernethy; (5) Martha, who married Elijah Walker; (6) Isaac Van Meter, who married Martha Russell; (7) Henry Pettit, who married Augusta Ladd; (8) Captain William A., who was killed in the battle of Gettysburg; (9) Sarah, who married Luke Powell, and (10) James Otis, who married Martha Scott.

William Borden, fifth son of John and Mary(Earle) Borden married Alice Hull, daughter of John and Alice (Teddeman) Hull, and settled in 1733 in Beaufort County, North Carolina, on the river which he named Newport River. They had three daughters and one son, William, who married Mrs. Comfort (Lovett) Small. They had six children, as follows: (1) John, who died young; (2) William, married Ann Delaney, and had one son, Barcley; (3) Alice who married Colonel David Ward; (4) Benjamine,

BORDEN

who married, first Nancy Wallace, and second, Rebecca Staunton; (5) Hope, who married Asa Hatch, of Jones County, North Carolina, and (6) Joseph, who married Mrs. Esther (Wallace) Easton, daughter of David and Mary (Willis) Wallace. Joseph and Esther (Wallace) Borden resided in Carteret County, North Carolina. They had nine children: (1) William, who married Elizabeth Dickson. (They had two children, Eleanor Hull, who died unmarried, and Martha Webb, who married, John S. Telfair; (2) Benjamin, who married, first Margaret Hill and second, Mrs. Martha (Cocke) Gray, of Lynchburg, Virginia. (They had seven children, as follows: Joseph who married Frances Scott Gray; Thomas J., who married Elizabeth Byrn; Miranda, who married Major Thomas Crawford Clark; William A., who married Alice G. Moore; Mary, who married, first William T. Cheney and second Edward Fenwick Campbell; Benjamin Clayborn, who married Robert Moore, and James Pennington, who married Melissa Parham. (3) David Wallace, who married his cousin, Hope Ward (their children were Elizabeth Graham, who married George Lovic Pierce, Mary James, who married David Grace of Birmingham, Hannah War, who married, first George Lovic Pierce and second, William Kirk Wallace, and Joshua A., who died young). (4) Joseph, of Borden, California, who married Juliet Rhodes; (they had eight children: Thomas Pennington, Mary, Judge Rhodes Borden, of the Supreme Court of San Francisco, Nathan Lane, who married Minnie Lee Borden, Sheldon, who married Frances Burnett, Ivey Lewis, who married Hetty Thompson, and Ann Helen). (5) Thomas Richardson, who married Ann M. Jones; (6) Judge James Wallace Borden, who married Emma Griswold (their children are Esther, who married George H. Aylesworth, Mary, Rebecca, Kenyon, who married Charles E. Grover, Joseph, William, who married Lavinna Fielding, Brigadier-General George Pennington Borden, who married Elizabeth Reynolds; Emiline, who married Captain Charles E. Hargous and David H. who married Mary Nelson); (7) Mary Wallace, who married Israel Sheldon; (they had one daughter, Mary, who married, first William Watson Woolsey and second, Colonel Woolsey Rogers Hopkins). (8) Isaac Pennington, who married Elizabeth Marset and (9) Hannah G., who died young.

A third branch of the Borden family that settled in the South is descended from Arnold Borden, (born September 3, 1795), a grandson of Joseph, the third son of John and Mary (Earle) Borden. Arnold Borden married Ann Brown-

NOTABLE SOUTHERN FAMILIES

rigg and moved to Goldsboro, North Carolina, and also purchased an estate in North Alabama. They had seven children: (1) Harriet, who married Dr. Charles F. Dewey, uncle of Admiral Dewey; (2) James Cole, a captain in the Confederate Army, who married Mary Caruthers; (3) Edwin Brownrigg, who married Georgia Whitefield; (4) Louisa, who married Frances W. Kornegay; (5) Sarah, who married Dr. John Miller; (6) Eugenia Arnold, who died in infancy, and (7) William Henry, who married, first Susan Edmondson, second, Julia Edmondson, and third Harriet Kennedy.

The founder of a fourth branch of the Borden family was Gail Borden II, who married Philadelphia Wheeler, a descendant of Roger Williams. This Gail Borden was a grandson of John, who was the second son of John and Mary (Earle) Borden. Gail and Philadelphia (Wheeler) Borden settled in 1841 in Kentucky. They had four sons: (1) Gail III (see below); (2) Thomas Henry, who married, first Dennis Woodward and second Louisa A. Graves, and settled in Galveston, Texas; (3) Paschal Pavolo, who married Mary S. Hatch and settled in Weimar, Texas. The eldest of these four brothers was born November 6, 1801. He was an important figure in the early history of Texas, where he was intimately connected with Stephen F. Austin. He was the inventor of pemmican meat biscuits and an excellent beef extract and in 1856 he patented his celebrated condensed milk. Texas commomorates his name in Borden County, of which the principal town is Gail. He married Penelope Mercer, and had seven children: (1) Henry Lee, who was head of the Borden Condensed Milk Company of Chicago; (2) Morton Quinn, who died young; (3) Philadelphia Wheeler, who married Judge Jehu Warner Parker of Clarksburg, West Virginia; (4) Stephen Austin, who died young; (6) Mary, who married Mills S. Munsill of Connecticut; (5) John Gail of Ormond, Florida, who married Ella L. Graves. He succeeded to the presidency of the New York Condensed Milk Company at the death of his father.

Thomas Henry and Louisa (Graves) Borden had two sons, John who married Mary McKee and James Cochran, who married Palmyra Atkinson, daughter of Dorsey and Mary (Patton) Atkinson, of Williamson County, Tenn.

Parschal Pavolo and Martha (Stafford) Borden also had two sons, Milan, who married Ella Underwood, and William, who married Emma Graves.

John Pettit and Mary (Hatch) Borden, had four children: Thaddeus H., who was killed in the War Between the States; Sidney G., who married Mary Sullivan; Fielda, who

BORDEN

married William J. Duffel and Lee deWitt, who married Mary A. Green, of Louisville, Kentucky.

The Borden coat of arms is as follows: The field azure, a chevron engrailed, ermine, two bourbons, or pilgrim's staves proper in chief; and a cross-crosslet in base, or Crest; a lion rampant above a scroll (argent) on his sinister foot: Motto Palma Virtuti: and above the crest, Excelsior.

BRYAN

It has been said that the family tree of the O'Briens bends beneath the weight of its royal ancestry. "On every branch hangs a monarch" was almost too true at one time. Kings of Thomound, of Munster and Limrick, Earls of Ichquin and Barons of Tadcaster are of this line.

The Monarch, Brien Boru, killed at the battle of Cloutart in 1014, is said to be responsible for the name Bryan as the surname, the "O" meaning the son of, or descendant of Brien, and no matter what the spelling of the name, they are all the same family, from Machias O'Brien of Maine with his six fighting sons to Joseph Bryan, the English planter, who settled in South Carolina prior to 1700.

Pennsylvania, Virginia and North Carolina received their quota of emigrants of the name, three main lines all add to the same story of political intrigue in the old country, showing a common ancestor. Many believe this to be William Smith Bryan, "deported to the colony of Virginia in 1650, as an undesirable citizen, with his family goods and chattles, consisting of a shipload (McKenzie Colonial Families, Vol. VI).

He was the son of Sir Francis Bryan, a prominent man of Ireland about the middle of the 16th century.

One authority makes Francis Bryan the son of William Smith Bryan and places William Smith Bryan's arrival in Virginia, in 1615, with the statement that between the years 1623 and 1666 there were twenty-one Bryans, sons and grandsons of William Smith Bryan, who took up lands in Virginia. Certain it is that in 1631, January 2, John Bryan, aged 25, was transported to Virginia in boat "Bonaventure"

William Smith Bryan is said to be the ancestor of Sir Edward O'Brien, of William Smith O'Brien and Lord Ichquin. The Edward O'Brien line settled in North Carolina. "Edward was the eldest of five brothers, and brought with him the coronet which was his birth-right".

NOTABLE SOUTHERN FAMILIES

Needham Bryan, born in Virginia in 1690, settled in North Carolina, "urged by relatives already there". William Smith Bryan, the first in Virginia, son of Sir Francis Bryan, settled in Gloucester County, Virginia, and had eleven sons. We are only sure of one, Francis, the eldest, altho Morgan Bryan in Norfolk County in 1693 is thought to be a son. Perhaps also James Bryan a land owner in Isle of Wight County and his brother, William Bryan (father of Needham) who settled in Isle of Wight County in 1688, Richard in King George County, 1694 and John the father of five O'Briens who settled in North Carolina (Edward, William, John, Council and Hardy). In Vol. VI, Virginia Colonial Records, page 12, the will of Thomas Wight, Sept. 20, 1672, of Moratico Creek, mentions sons-in-law Thomas and Robert Bryan.

Francis Bryan, eldest son of William Smith Bryan, born about 1630, returned to Ireland in 1667 and endeavored to recover his hereditary titles and estates, but was so persecuted by the English Government that he sought refuge in Denmark where he married Sarah Brinker or Brunker. He later returned to Ireland, where he died in 1694. His son, Morgan, was born in Denmark in 1681 and William in Ireland in 1685.

THIRD GENERATION

"After Morgan Bryan (Francis, William Smith) came to years of maturity, he left his parents in Ireland and came to America, to Pennsylvania. The record shows that Morgan Bryan lived in Chester County, where in 1719 he married Martha Strode". Several children were born in Pennsylvania. Then in 1728 or 1730, he with Alexander Ross and others received a grant of one thousand acres of land on the Potomac and Opequan Rivers in Virginia, and settled near the present site of Winchester. Here the rest of his children were born, and Martha Strode Bryan died in 1747. After her death he sold his interest in Virginia and in the fall of 1748 moved his family to North Carolina and settled in the forks of the Yadkin River, then Anson County, later (1753) Rowan. About two years later Squire Boone moved from Pennsylvania to North Carolina, and became a near neighbor. Here Daniel Boone and Rebecca Bryan were were married in 1755 and William Bryan and Mary Boone the same year. All family records say that Martha Strode Bryan died 1747 in Virginia. but in Augusta County Records, Vol. III. p. 340, we find that on September 27, 1753, Edward Hughes, Squire Boone and James Carter, of Roane County, were appointed to take acknowledgement of

BRYAN

Martha, wife of Morgan Bryan.
Morgan Bryan died in 1763, aged 92 years. (This would make his birth 1671) and was buried in Rowan County. His will on file at Salisbury County, North Carolina, Will Book A, p. 13, gives unto my beloved son, Thomas, my mansion house and plantation; unto my beloved daughter, Elinor Linville, all my wife's apparel. I give and bequeath, Joseph, Samuel, Morgan, John, Willam, James and Thomas and daughter Elinor Linville, etc.

The children of Morgan and Martha Strode Bryan were:
1 Joseph, born 1720; married Hester Hampton (second wife) or name Alice and Hester.
2 Samuel, married Masmilla Simpson.
3 James, born 1723-1802; married 1756, Rebecca Knox.
4 Morgan Jr., born May 20, 1729; married Mary Forbes.
5 John, married Frances Battle.
6 Elinor, married William Linville.
7 Mary, married Forbes.
8 William, died 1781; married 1755, Mary Boone.
9 Thomas, born 1736, died 1789; married ——— Hunt.
10 Sarah.
11 Rebecca, married 1755, Daniel Boone.

Of these, James, Morgan and William and some records say Joseph, went to Kentucky with Boone and built the fort known as Bryan's Station.

1 Joseph, the eldest, remained in Virginia, while the others moved to North Carolina with their father. He is found in many deeds in Augusta County, and his wife Alice as late as 1754 and 1755, ["Alice, wife of Joseph Bryan, has a private examination". They had three sons: William, Morgan and John.

2 Samuel was the only son of Morgan Bryan who did not serve in the Revolution. He raised an army of eight hundred men and tendered them with himself to the Governor of North Carolina to fight for the King. After the war he was courtmarshalled and his property was confiscated. No record of descendants.

3 James Bryan, son of Morgan and Martha (Strode) Bryan, was born in 1723, died in 1802. He married in 1756, Rebecca Knox. They had the following children:
David Bryan, born Oct. 29, 1757, who married Mary Poor and had ten children: James, Morgan, Elizabeth, Mary, Willis, John, Susan, Hrizella, Samuel and William.

NOTABLE SOUTHERN FAMILIES

Jonathan, born July 15, 1759, married Mary Hughes Coshon and had ten children: Parthenia, Phoebe, Nancy, Elijah, Abner, Mary, Alsey, James, Delilah and Lavinia.

Henry, born Jan. 15, 1759; married Elizabeth Sparks and had eight children: Susan, Joseph, Rebecca, Elizabeth, Cynthia, Johannah, John W. and Polly.

Susannah, born April 11, 1763; married Israel Grant and had three children: James, William and Israel B. Grant.

Mary, born December 13, 1765.

Rebecca, born March 1, 1767; married first Hugh Logan, and married second, James Smith. Her seven children were: William, Alexander, Hugh, Henry and Mary Logan and Susan and James Smith.

4 Morgan Bryan, Jr., died May 2, 1729; married Mary Forbes; was one of the committee of Public Safety for Rowan County, North Carolina. Morgan also went to Kentucky. His son, George Bryan, (died 1758) married in the Fort, Elizabeth Neal Rogers, in May, 1780, the first marriage solemnized in Kentucky. George Bryan served in the Revolution and is on the pension list of 1840 from Bourbon County, Kentucky. He married second, Mrs. Cassandra Miller, in 1830, and died November 22, 1845, in Springfield, Illinois. Only record of one son, William Smith, died March 17, 1785, at Bryans Station; married Judith Field, January 25, 1814. They had three sons and one daughter:

1 William Smith, married Miss Bartlett, of Louisville.
2 George W., born August 23, 1815, married Elizabeth Miller.
3 Robert T., married first, Miss Kenny; married second, Mary Offutt.
4 Eliza, married Frank Tucker; no issue.

5 John Bryan, married Frances Battle. He was a Catpain in the Revolution and while home on a furlough, the first or second morning, was killed at his own door by Colonel Flanning, a British officer with a squad of men, who had by some means learned of his presence. They called him to the door and demanded that he take oath to support the King's cause and shot him upon his refusal to do so. He is said to have had a large family. One son, Lewis Bryan, married Elizabeth White and had six children:

1 Sarah, married Jesse Salts.
2 Annie, married Isaac Rebber.
3 Polly, married Peter Barnes.
4 Fannie, married James Davis.
5 Battle, married Rebecca Miller.

BRYAN

6 John Gilson, married Pollie Morris.
John Gilson Bryan lived to be 98 years old. Battle Bryan and Rebecca Miller had twelve children: Polly, Susan, John Gilson, Henry M., William, Lewis, Nancy, Elizabeth, Joseph D., Sally, Jane, Caroline and Ann.

William Lewis Bryan married Sallie Hayes; had eight children: Julia C., James H., Cora L., George A., Carrie H., Robert K., Bartlett R. and Lewis L.

6 Elinor Bryan, daughter of Morgan, senior, married William Linville. Name appears in many deeds of Augusta County. They later went to North Carolina and both are said to have been killed by Indians.

7 Mary (daughter of Morgan), probably married a Mr. Forbes, as Morgan in his will leaves "to my granddaughter, Mary Forbes, my great pot of five shillings". This could not be Mary, daughter of his son, Thomas, as she was not born until 1769, although she did marry a Mr. Forbes.

WILLIAM BRYAN AND MARY BOONE BRYAN

8 William Bryan, 1733-1781, married 1755, Mary Boone, sister of Daniel Boone.

William Bryan was also one of the Kentucky pioneers, and was killed by the Indians in 1781, while defending the Fort. William and Mary Boone Bryan had issue:

1 Samuel married 1775, Isabella Hunt, daughter of Jonathan and Isabella Hunt. Samuel served in the Revolution (Pension Department, Washington).
2 Daniel Boone, married Elizabeth Turner.
3 Sarah, married Col. William Chinn; moved to Missouri.
4 William.
5 Phoebe.
6 Hannah.
7 John.
8 Abner.
9 Elizabeth.
10 Mary

The children of Samuel Bryan and Isabella Hunt Bryan were: (1) Anne, (2) Phoebe, (3) William, (4) Abner, (5) Luke, (6) Thomas, (7) Sarah, (8) Mary, (9) Daniel, (10) and (11) Samuel. Luke Bryan, born November 22, 1784, married Mary Sanders (daughter of Capt. John Sanders and wife Sarah), had twelve children: Alphonse H., John, Samuel, Mary Boone, Elbert W., Dorcas, Armilda, Jesse, Joseph McM., William S., James L., and Thomas N.

Daniel Boone Bryan (William, Morgan), born Feb. 10, 1758, in Rowan County, North Carolina, died Feb. 27, 1845; married Elizabeth Turner, and had issue:
1 Joseph Bryan.
2 Thomas Bryan, married Mary (Polly) Kay.
3 Louis Bryan.
4 William Bryan.
5 Samuel Bryan.
6 Daniel Bryan, Elizabeth Bryan (Twins).
7 Sallie Bryan, married William Barr.
8 Phoebe Bryan, married John Womack.

Thomas Bryan (Daniel, William, Morgan), born ———, died 1872, in Fayette County, Kentucky; married 1830 and had issue:
1 Thomas Bryan, married Mary Barton, of Kansas City.
2 Phoebe Elizabeth Bryan (Thomas, Daniel, William, Morgan), born 1841, died 1880, in Jessamine County Kentucky; married John J. Cassell, and had issue:
1 Robert Bryan Cassell, married Pearl Hill.
2 Henry Bryan Cassell, married Flora Lillard.
3 Joseph Bryan Cassell, married Etta Gray.
4 Allie Bryan Cassell, married Frances Gibson.

Robert Bryan Cassell, who married Pearl Hill, had issue:
1 Margaret Bryan Cassell, unmarried;
2 Henry Bryan Cassell, who married Etta Gray.
had issue:
1 John Cassell, unmarried.
2 Frances Cassell, unmarried.
3 Flora Lewis Cassell, unmarried.

Allie Bryan Cassell, married Frances Gibson and had issue:
1 John Cassell, unmarried.
2 Tom Cassell, unmarried.
3 Margaret Cassell, unmarried.
4 Frances Gibson Cassell, unmarried.

9 Thomas Bryan, born 1736, died 1789; served as a surgeon in the Revolution. He married —— Hunt, daughter of the Rev. Jonathan Hunt. After the Revolution he practiced medicine in Mississippi; later returned to North Carolina; had issue:
1 Jesse Bryan, born Nov. 1757, died Jan. 18, 1834.
2 Jonathan, born Oct. 1766, died 1830.
3 Mary, born April 1796, married Mr. Forbes.
4 Martha, born Aug. 1772, died 1848; married Stephen Gano.

BRYAN

5 Morgan Hunt, born Dec. 16, 1774, died Sept. 17, 1843; married Jan. 17, 1805 Sallie Hunt, born Dec. 15, 1786; daughter of John Hunt and Margaret Wilson, a sister of James Wilson, the singer.

6 Thomas, born Jan 6, 1776; never married.

7 William, born Jan. 6, 1776; never married.

The widow of Dr. Thomas Bryan is said to have married for her second husband the Rev. John Gano, "Fighting Chaplain of the Revolution". She moved to Kentucky, with him in 1792, and was killed by a fall from her horse. The children of Morgan Hunt Bryan and Sallie Hunt were:

1 Milton E., born Dec. 1805, died 1892.
2 John H., born July 1807
3 Cordelia, born March 1810.
4 William W., born Jan. 1811, died 1886.
5 James, born March 1813.
6 Thomas, born Sept. 1815.
7 Martha, born Sept. 1817.
8 Mary, born March 1821.

10 Sarah (daughter of Morgan), married Francis Puisen. Deed, Augusta County Records, Vol. III, p. 318, July 26, 1753, Frances Puisen (Puisen and Sarah of Rowan County, North Carolina, to John Hinton, 236 acres on Muddy Creek. Test, Joseph and John Bryan).

11 Rebecca Bryan, married Daniel Boone. Their descendants will be found in the Boone article. Two sons were killed by Indians; James while on the way to Kentucky, and Israel later in a battle with the Indians. One daughter, Jemma, was carried off by the Indians, but rescued by her father. She later married Mr. Calloway.

Dr. J. D. Bryan, in his Boone-Bryan History, says: "After the death of James Bryan's wife, his children were raised by his sister, Rebecca, wife of Daniel Boone, and married from their home". He also says that James and Morgan Bryan were both with the forces at King's Mountain, 1780.

WILLIAM BRYAN LINE

Line of William Bryan, brother of Morgan Bryan. In following this (William Bryan line we must always keep in mind the County Divisions made at different times.

Spotsylvania was the original Western County of Virginia formed in 1721 by an act of Virginia Legislature "to extend to the river (Shenandoah) beyond the high mountains". It has one Parish called St. George's. In 1730, this was divided into St. George's and St. Mark's. The latter lying in the upper part of the County became in 1734 Orange County. In 1738, Augusta County was taken from Orange, also Culpepper and Madison, Rappahanock from Culpepper in 1832. Rockbridge, Botetourt and Roanoke were all at one time part of Augusta.

Old William Bryan is in one of the first deeds of Spotsylvania County, but always spoken of as Orange County. His son, William, lived in then Augusta County, though his home was down on the Roanoke near Salem (now Roanoke County), and his will is now on file in Botetourt County.

First Generation in America

In McKenzie's Colonial Families, Vol. VI, we find:
William Smith Bryan 1, a landholder in Ireland, probably County Clare, at the time of the British invasion under Cromwell, and for taking the side of Ireland was transported as a rebellious subject in 1650 to American Colonies with his family, goods and chattels, consisting of a ship load. He settled in Gloucester County, Virginia; had eleven sons; Morgan Bryan in Norfolk County in 1693, thought to have been a son.

Francis Bryan 2, the oldest son, had Morgan, born 1671, died 1763, age 92 years; William, born 1685; wife Margaret.

Third Generation

William Bryan 3, and wife, Margaret, lived at Ballyconey, County Down, Ireland. They were Presbyterians. The town of Bryansford near by is said to have been named for some of this family. William and Margaret Bryan sent their little son John, into the woods to cut a stick to make a handle for a hook used in weaving, and he was arrested for poaching. After much trouble and expense, his father got him clear, and immediately sailed for America, where, as he said, "timber was free and there were no constables". This was in the year 1718. They first settled in New Jersey or Pennsylvania. Morgan Bryan (his brother), was in Chester County, Pennsylvania, as early as 1719, where he married Martha Strode.

About 1745, William Bryan and his sons, James and David, either a son or a brother but thought to be a brother, died 1767, wife Elizabeth, removed to the Staunton River in (present) Roanoke County. They with others, were the

BRYAN

first white settlers in that locality.

William Bryan settled at the place called Lake Springs, where he died at the age of 104 years (1685-1789), and David at Big Lick, both near Roanoke City.

Prior to the Staunton River settlement, William Bryan lived in the part of Spotsylvania County that in 1730 was called Orange County. Here in 1733, March 5, he gives to Philip Bush eight hundred pounds of tobacco and 102 acres in St. Mark's Parish.

David Bryan also witnesses a will, March 11, 1733, and David's wife, Elizabeth, witnesses deed, 1733, Aug. 2.

William Bryan's daughter, Mary, married Philip Bush (he died 1772, son of John and Margaret Bush), and their son William, born 1746, went to Kentucky with the Bryans and Boones. David Bryan moved to North Carolina on account of being troubled with the Indians. The children of William and Margaret Bryan were:

1 John Andrew, born prior to 1717, died 1799; married Mary Morrison.
2 James.
3 William, married Margaret Watson.
4 Mary, married Philip Bush; died 1772. Philip Bush kept tavern near Winchester.

Fourth Generation

William Bryan and wife, Margaret Watson, also settled on Roanoke River soon after. He was known as 'William Bryan of Roanoke'. Their children were:

1 William, died 1806.
2 John.
3 James, married Elizabeth Vineyard: had Andrew and Alexander.
4 Catherine, married Samuel Cole.
5 Daughter married Andrew Lewis. (See Deed).
6 David.
7 Daughter, married, first, Martin; second, Boyd.

William, James and David Bryan were in the Revolution. William was a Captain. He came into possession of David Bryan's place at Big Lake, while James inherited his father's place at Lake Springs.

Some of the descendants of William Bryan settled in Mason County, West Virginia. The Post office of Bryan was doubtless named for some of them.

James moved to North Carolina then to Kentucky, and his son, Alexander and wife, Elizabeth Parker moved from Montgomery County to Putnam County, Indiana, in 1834. Had the following children:

NOTABLE SOUTHERN FAMILIES

1 George, married Eliza.
2 James.
3 Harvey.
4 Barton.
5 Nancy, married Jacob Cox.
6 Ellen, married Parker Coffmon.
7 Alexander S., born Sept. 24, 1824, in Montgomery County, Kentucky, married Jane Farrow.
Augusta County Records, Vol. III, p. 97.
Will of Darrick Bryan, of Roanoke, Dec. 13, 1776. Ex. wife, and Brother William.
Daughter, Mary.
Son, William.
Son, David.
Proved March 18, 1767, by Barnes and William Bryan. Elizabeth (her mark).
Augusta County Records, Vol. 1, p. 135.
Elizabeth Bryan, Ex. of David Bryan, May 25, 1767. In 1771, widow had married John Bowman.
Augusta County Records, Vol. II, p. 223. Prior to 1771. William Bryan owned 400 acres on Roanoke River near Salem, divided between sons William and James. James sold to Andrew Lewis, and moved to Mason County. William Bryan, junior, died 1806. James had a son, Andrew.
Will of William Bryan, of Roanoke, in Botetourt County, wife Elizabeth (second wife), sons, William, James and John; daughter, Catherine Cole.
Augusta County Records, Vol. I, p. 61.
Road ordered, William Bryan, overseer, from William Carravans plantation to William Bryan's on Roan Oak. Workers: William Bryan, junior, and John Bryan, same p. 123.
1765, Willam Bryan exempt from County Levy (which means he was an old man), Oct. 11, 1765. William Bryan, senior, to William Bryan, junior, son of William, senior, 133 acres on Roanoke River, adjoining James Love.
John Andrew Bryan, and wife Mary Morrison, moved to Burden County, near Fairfield, Rockbridge County (which was founded in 1737), about the same time that William and Margaret Watson Bryan moved to Staunton River settlement. This John Bryan is thought to have been at the battle of Great Meadows, 1754, Captain Peter Hogg's Company. (Virginia County Records, Vol. II, p. 111, Augusta County. 'After Battle of Great Meadows, returned to Captain Stobo's Company, 1754. Men fit for duty, John Bryan').
After living a few years at the Borden Colony, John

BRYAN

Andrew and Mary and family proceeded to the Staunton River, where he became owner of land upon a part of which Salem is now situated. He left the Staunton River in 1863-4, traded his land for a pair of cart-wheels, and moved with his family to (present) Campbell County, Va., Here he bought 329 acres of Richard Stith and 439 acres of Benjamin Arnold. On the last named tract, he at once erected a bark hut about two miles Southeast of Rustburg, and later built a house farther down on the other branch (Molly's Creek). A lot on the place was used as a muster ground for many years after the Revolution).

The children of John Andrew and Mary Morrison Bryan were:

1 William, born 1774, married Mary.
2 Andrew Morrison, born April 25, 1748, died April 20, 1821; married Mary Akers.
3 Mary, born May 27, 1750, died young.
4 Margaret, born March 14, 1752, married first, Daniel Mitchell; second, Patrick Gibson.
5 John, married Catherine Evans.
6 Jane, born May 16, 1761, married John Davison.
7 Agnes, born August 9, 1763, married first, John Akers; second, Reuben Bagby.
8 Catherine, born Oct. 21, 1765.

Fifth Generation

William Bryan, son of John Andrew, received from his father the tract of 320 acres on Molly's Creek, but in 1779 sold his land and moved to Bedford County, where he died without issue.

Andrew Morrison, married Mary Akers, received from his father, John A. Bryan, in 1773, 156 acres of land. He probably sold his land on Molly's Creek to his brother, John, and he and his wife were living in North Carolina when their youngest son, David, was born, Oct. 24, 1793. A few years later they returned to Campbell County, Virginia. It is thought he was in the war of the Revolution.

Daniel and Margaret Bryan Mitchell kept tavern near Bedford County line. After Margaret married Patrick Gibson they moved to Rockbridge County.

John, son of John Andrew, married Catherine Evans, was a large man; weighed at death about 350 pounds. He was in the Revolutionary War in Battles of Eutaw Springs, Guilford Court House, Waxham and Yorktown. He owned and lived on his father's place in Campbell County; was prosperous for the times.

NOTABLE SOUTHERN FAMILIES

Jane Bryan married John Davidson. They were well off and owned slaves.

Sixth Generation

The children of Andrew Morrison Bryan and Mary Akers were:
1. John, married Rebecca.
2. Elizabeth, married John Page.
3. William Akers, married.
4. Morrison, married 1805, Rhoda Johnson. Rhoda J. Bryan married second, Peyton Short.
5. James, married Mary Johnson.
6. Mary, married George Evans.
7. Thomas, married Mary Bryan.
8. David, born North Carolina, Oct. 24, 1793, married Mildred Johnson.

The children of John Bryan (son of John A. Bryan) and Catherine Evans, were:

1. Rees, married first, Bridget Evans; second, Mrs. Elizabeth Jasper.
2. Mary, married Thomas Bryan (cousins).
3. Bridget, married Robert Russell.
4. Agnes, married Ephriam Gardner.
5. John, married Elizabeth Richardson George.
6. Catherine, married Henry Robinson.
7. Nancy, married William Walthall Dinwiddie.

O'BRIEN, OF NORTH CAROLINA

"At the time Ireland was divided into small monarchies Munster was the house of the O'Briens, and one competitor for the crown was John O'Brien. (It is said an account of him is found in Grimshaw's History of England). Some time during the latter part of the Seventeenth Century, his five sons, who were under political proscription on account of the rebellion, left their native land for America. Their names were Edward, John, William, Hardy and Council, who died at sea. Edward was the eldest, and brought with him the coronet, which was his birthright. They landed at New Berne, prior to 1700. They soon dropped the 'O' and wrote the name 'Bryan' ".

They worked with tar, and before many years had purchased slaves and invested in sea-going vessels.

Edward, the eldest, married Anne, widow, and died in 1746. His will is dated Jan. 28, 1745, proved May 9, 1746. Gives son, John Bryan 220 acres of land; gives son William,, 300 acres of land; gives son, Edward, a lot in New Berne; gives wife, Ann Bryan, one plantation. Ex. wife

BRYAN

Anne, Brother Hardy and Lewis Bryan.
Family records give his children as:
1 John, married Rebecca Martin.
2 Penelope, married first, Levin Lane; second, Daniel Yates.
3 Edward, never married.

1 John Bryan, eldest son of Edward and Ann Hand Bryan, married Rebecca Martin, "an amiable, good woman, of high family". John Bryan was a Colonel in the Revolution (D. A. R. Lineage Book, Vol. IX, p. 320), died May 25, 1801, in Jones County, North Carolina. Issue:
1 John, married first, Mary Tootle; second, Ann Zilpah, daughter of William and Susan Bryan.
2 Edward, married Elizabeth Ellington.
3 James, married Widow Exum; no issue.
4 William, married Martha Hodges.
5 Joseph, married Eleanor Evans.
6 Susan, never married.
7 Mary Bush, maried Richard Grice, Jr.
8 Elizabeth, married Elijah Bryan, a cousin on the mother's side. Their fathers had the same name and same Irish descent (probably cousins).

2 John Hill Bryan, married Elizabeth Harrison (daughter of William) Nov. 27, 1782. He was born 1761; was a member of the House of Commons from Jones County, North Carolina, 1788. Took part in the Revolution, Captain Jones Company Militia. Moved to Georgia about 1801, where he died in 1826. Issue:
1 Penelope, born 1784; married John Coffee.
2 Edward, born 1786; married Susan Horn.
3 John, born 1788; no record.
4 Mary, born 1790; married Shadrach Atkinson.
5 William, born 1792, died infancy.
6 James, born 1790, died infancy.
7 Joseph, born 1795; married Lucy Warner; son, Lucius E., married Mrs. Emma Bryan Dabney.
8 Susan, born 1797, married Hiran Atkinson.
9 Fred, born 1798, died infancy.
10 Elizabeth, born 1798, died infancy.
11 Hardy, born 1799, married first, Martha Wyche; second, Maria Wyche.

3 Penelope, daughter of John and Rebecca Martin Bryan, married first, James Montford. Issue:
1 Bryan Montford.

NOTABLE SOUTHERN FAMILIES

  2 Elizabeth Montford.
  3 Rebecca Montford.
  4 James Montford.
She married second, Fred Hargate, and had issue:
  5 John Hargate, married Elizabeth Zilpah Bryan, daughter of Joseph.
  6 Penelope.
  7 Frederick.
  8 Penie.
  9 Durant.
Married, third, Bothwick Gillespie. No issue.
  4 William (3), married Susan Harrison, sister of Mrs. John Hill Bryan. Issue:
  1 John.
  2 William.
  3 Edward.
  4 Frederick.
  5 Joab.
  6 Nancy.
  7 Elizabeth.
  8 Zilpah, married John Bryan.
  9 Penelope, married Joseph Green.
10 Rebecca.

  5 Frederick, married Susan Hargate. Issue:
  1 Elizabeth.
  2 John Council.

  6 Ann Zilpah, married first, Richard Grice (son of Richard Grice and Mrs. Anna Hill Slade, widow). Issue:
  1 Nancy Grice, married Bryan Grimes, of Pitt County, a cousin.
  2 Richard, married Mary Bush Bryan, daughter of Edward, a cousin. She married, second, John Bryan, son of Edward and Susannah.
  7 Joseph Bryan, married, first, Elizabeth Hargate. Issue:
  1 Zilpah, married John Hargrave.
  2 Elizabeth.
  3 Louis.
Joseph married second, Susan Hargate, cousin of first wife. Issue:
  4 Nancy, married Isaac Hathway.
  5 John.
  6 Polly.
  7 Edward.

BRYAN

8 Peter.
9 William.
10 Joseph.
Married third, a widow, Mrs. Parsons. Issue:
11 Frederick.
2 Penelope Bryan, daughter of Edward and Anne Hand Bryan, married first, Levin Lane. Issue:
1 Levin.
2 Ezekiel.
3 Polly.
4 Penelope, married first, William Bush (son of Hardy Bush and Katherine Frank); married second, Needham Whitfield. (Fourth wife).
5 Elizabeth, married second, Daniel Yates. Issue:
6 Nancy Yates.
8 Leach Yates.

Fourth Generation—Children of Edward and Susannah

1 John Bryan (Edward, John, Edward), son of Edward and Susannah Blackshear Bryan, married first, Mary Tootle; married second, Ann Zilpah Bryan, his cousin, daughter of William and Susan Harrison Bryan; only record one son.
1 John T, married Mary Armistead.
2 Edward (son of Edward and Susannah), married Eliza Ellington. Issue:
1 Susan, married David Blackshear, son of Gen. David Blackshear of Georgia.
2 John (given as marrying Zilpah Bryan).
3 Mary Harriet, died infancy.
4 Fanny, married first, Henry King; second Washington Chapman.
5 Mary, married Dr. L. L. Newsom.
6 Louisa.
7 Ellington B.
8 James Wm., died infancy.
3 William Bryan (son of Edward and Susannah), married Martha Hodges. Issue:
1 Elizabeth, married W. J. Robinson.
2 Mary, married C. W. Davis.
3 Blackledge, never married.
4 Martha, married John W. Pooser.

5 Josephine, married Dr. J. O. Lewis.
4 Joseph Bryan (son of Edward and Susannah), married Eleanor Evans. Issue:

NOTABLE SOUTHERN FAMILIES

  1 James, married Marcissa Hayes.
  2 Susan P., married Dr. Frank Wakefield.
  3 Mary, married Dr. Wm. Standifer.
  5 Mary Bush (daughter of Edward and Susannah), married her cousin, Richard Grice (son of Ann Zilpah Bryan Grice, sister of Edward). Issue:
  1 Frederick Grice, married Mary Wardlaw.

After death of Mary Bush Bryan, Richard Grice married Martha Cook. Issue: Two daughters.

  6 Elizabeth Bryan (daughter of Edward and Susannah), married Elijah Bryan, a first cousin through their mothers (Blackshear). Their fathers had the same name. Edward Bryan, born 1759, Elijah's father, was a son of Col. Joseph Bryan and Sarah Maule. He married Penelope Blackshear (sister of Susannah).
  1 Harriet, married James E. Heam.
  2 Joseph, married Harriet Hamister.
  3 Hamilton, married Christiana Baemes.
  4 Frank.
  5 Penelope, married J. M. Erwin.
  6 Georgia, married Erwin.
  7 Annie Laura.
  8 Lizzie.
  9 Robert.
10 Elijah.
11 Emily, married Louis H. Smith.

Col. Joseph Bryan was a son of either William or John, the two brothers of whom we have no record.

Fourth Generation—Children of John Hill Bryan

  1 Penelope Bryan, born Sept. 23, 1784, daughter of John Hill Bryan and Elizabeth Harrison, married Gen. Joshua Coffee, born in Virginia 1780. Issue:
  1 Sarah Ann, married Mark Wilcox.
  2 Joshua, married Emily Church.
  3 Peter Harrison, married Susana A. Rodgers.
  4 John married first, Rebecca Wilcox; second, Marcella Griffin; third, Mary E. Warmack.
    Christopher C., married Mary Rodgers.
  6 Susah, married John Bryan, a cousin.
  7 Andrew J., married Susah Church.
  8 Hill Bryan, married Mary Church.

  10 Hardy Bryan, born Dec. 1799 (youngest son of John Hill and Elizabeth Bryan) married first, Martha Wyche; married second, Maria Wyche, Aug. 5, 1824—(sisters: daughters of Col. Littleton Wyche and Susannah Mitchell.

BRYAN

Wyche). Issue by second wife:
1. Leon, born 1825, died 1857; unmarried.
2. Caroline, married first, Mr. Hall; second, Gillespie.
3. Magnolia E., married George M. Brannon.
4. Iredelle E., married Mary Edwards.
5. Hardy, Jr., never married.
6. Courtland.
7. Louise B., married William Galahin.
8. Rudolph, never married.
9. Baltimore, died young.
10. Idella, married Needham Bryan Whitfield.

Family records say that Edward Bryan, son of Edward, Sr., never married, and no mention is made of the son, William, who received 300 acres of land. The will of one William Bryan has been found in Bertie County (North Carolina History and Genealogy Register, Vol. III, p. 167), dated December 12, 1746, proved June Court, 1747, mentions wife Anne; sons William, Lewis, John, Jesse, daughter Elizabeth and Ann. Ex., Ann Bryan, wife, Joseph Bryan, brother and William Bryan, son. This William could not have been one of the five brothers, as he mentions a brother, Joseph. These two are probably sons of either William or John, of whom we have no record.

Joseph, or Col. Joseph Bryan, born about 1730, married about 1753, Sarah Maule, daughter of Dr. Patrick Maule. Had issue:
1. George.
2. William.
3. Edward, born 1759, died 1825; married Penelope Blackshear; moved to Twigs County, Georgia. His tombstone says he served in the Revolution at the age of sixteen.
4. Lewis.
5. Mary, died unmarried.
6. Sarah.
7. Elizabeth, married Mr. Grist.
8. Gennett, married Mr. Dawson.
9. Ann, married William Grimes.

The line of Hardy Bryan, one of the five brothers, is given in McKenzie's Colonial Families, Vol. I, p. 53, as follows:

"The Bryan family is Irish in origin. Col. Hardy Bryan emigrated to America at the beginning of the Eighteenth Century from Munster, Ireland. Settled near New Berne, North Carolina; married Mrs. Bonner Worsely (other records give her name as Mrs. Reynolds, formerly Sarah Bonner). Had issue:

NOTABLE SOUTHERN FAMILIES

1 William (of whom below), born 1730, died 1810.
2 Mary, married first, Mr. Hatch; second, Mr. Tooley.
3 Thomas, died 1760; married Mrs. Rachel Lavender.
4 Hardy, married Mrs. Hatch.
5 Nathan, married 1773; first, Winifred Bryan (daughter of Needham); married second, Nancy Reynolds.
6 Isaac, married first, Mrs. Cox; second, Mrs. Herritage (Rachel Whitford—her fourth husband).
7 Lewis, married first, Mrs. Saper; second, Mrs. Hatch Bryan.

Wheeler, p. 221, says: "Hon. Nathan Bryan was a man of piety and usefulness. In 1799, represented this County (Jones, from Cravan), in House of Commons, in 1794 he represented New Berne District in Congress. He died in Philadelphia, 1798, while in Congress, and was buried in the Baptist Meeting House Yard".

William Bryan, born 1730, died 1810 (see D. A. R. Lineage Book, Vol. XLIX, p. 446); married three wives; first, Miss Green; second, Mrs. Respas; third, Mrs. McKay. He was a large land owner and prominent patriot. Represented Craven County in the Hillsboro Assembly of 1775; representative to Provisional Congress, 1776; Lieut-Co. of Minutemen; appointed Brig-Gen. 1776, by Continental Congress. Gen. William Bryan was a member of the House of Assembly from Craven County 1780-83. Issue:

1 Holland, married Mr. Mastin.
2 Sarah, married Mr. Green.
3 Nancy, married, first, Allen; second, Lane; third, Mastin.
4 Elizabeth, married Frederick Lane.
5 Green, married Nancy Blackledge.
6 Hardy, married Mrs. Swan.
7 Eleanor, married Mr. Wadsworth.
8 Susan, married first, Armstrong; second, Mince.
9 Margaret, died unmarried.

Other records give a son, John, who married 1796-7, Elizabeth Oliver, and had a son, James, who married Rachel Heritage, of Needham-Bryan line.

NEEDHAM BRYAN

That there were Bryans in North Carolina before the five O'Briens or Bryans landed at New Berne, has been proven by early records. In the History of Halifax County (W. C. Allen), we find a list of the early land holders whose descendants are still living in the County, and among them is Thomas Bryan, whose grant was between 1720-30. This may have been a son of the Thomas Bryan whose will is dated March 13, 1709-10, and gives his friend as Benjamin West.

Also we find (Habersham Col. Ga., Vol II), that "John Gray, from Scotland, married Anne Bryan, in Bertie County, North Carolina," and their grand-daughter, Elizabeth Gray, married William Bryan, grandson of Needham Bryan.

These early Bryans were the cause of Needham Bryan leaving Virginia in 1722 and settling in Bertie County, North Carolina. They are said to have been living in North Carolina as early as 1653

Two Bryans, brothers, William and James (some records give John), settled in Isle of Wight County. James was a large land owner, in 1683 he had a grant of 315 acres, in 1689-, 762 acres and in 1702, 100 acres more. No record of descendants.

The fact that no record of the arrival of this William Bryan can be found in early records, makes it seem possible that he was one of the eleven sons of William Smith Bryan, in Virginia 1650.

William Bryan, married in Ireland, Alice Needham, said to be a daughter of the Lord of Kilmorey. They were living in Isle of Wight County in 1688, and their son, Needham, was born there Feb. 11, 1690.

Needham Bryan, born 1690, in Virginia, married Nov. 16, 1711, Annie Rambeau, and in 1722 moved to North Carolina and settled on a farm on Albemarle Sound, Bertie County, where he died in 1770, at the age of 80 years.

Annie Rambeau Bryan died March 16, 1730, and Needham married a second wife, Susannah Horrell, and a third wife in 1752, Sarah Woodward, who survived him.

Issue by first wife, Annie Rambeau:

1 Rachel, born June 10, 1723; married William Whitfield.

2 William, born Oct. 31, 1724, died 1785; married 1744 Elizabeth Smith.

3 Needham, born 1726, died 1784; married 1749, Nancy Smith.

Elizabeth and Nancy Smith were daughters of John Smith (the Smiths were in Isle of Wight County in 1622) and Elizabeth Whitfield, married 1700. She was the daughter of Matthew Whitfield. His son, William Whitfield, born about 1690, married Elizabeth Goodman, and their son, William, born May 29, 1715, in Bertie County, North Carolina, was the husband of Rachel Bryan.

NOTABLE SOUTHERN FAMILIES

1 William, born June 1743, died March 1817; married Hester Williams.
2 Elizabeth, born 1745; married 1765, Alexander Smith.
3 Sarah, born April 16, 1747; married 1769, Col Joseph Greer.
4 Bryan, born Feb. 19, 1754, died Jan. 3, 1817; married first 1780, Nancy Bryan (daughter of Needham, Jr); second, 1798, Winifred Bryan (daughter of Hon. Nathan Bryan.
5 Charity, born April 1756, died 1818; married 1771, David Smith.
6 Needham, born Feb. 20, 1758, died April 6, 1812.
7 Rachel, born April 16, 1760; married first, McCabe; second, James Whitfield; third, John Hentage; fourth, Isaac Bryan (son of Col Hardy Bryan).
8 Mary, born May 8, 1763, married 1785-6, Kedar Bryan, second wife (son of Needham).
9 Rev. Lewis, born June 23, 1765, married first, Charlotte Moore Bryan (daughter of Needham Bryan, Jr.); married second, Tabitha Atkinson; married third, Patsy Hinton Bryan and widow of John Bryan (son of William Bryan and Elizabeth Smith).

William Bryan, second child of Needham Bryan and Annie Rambeau, born in Bertie County, North Carolina, Oct. 31, 1724, died 1785; married in Johnston County, 1744, Elizabeth Smith, daughter of John Smith and Elizabeth Whitfield. Issue:

1 Louis Bryan, born Nov. 4, 1745, Johnston County, North Carolina; married about 1769, Nancy Hinton (daughter of Maj. John Hinton and Sally Smith). No record.
2 William Bryan, born July 1747, died Sept. 1800, in Bertie County; married Elizabeth Gray (daughter of William Gray and Frances Lee. William Gray's mother was Anne Bryan of the Colony, 1653).
3 Arthur, born May 12, 1749.
4 Elizabeth, born May 28, 1751.
5 Hardy, born June 4, 1753 (the name Hardy shows some connection with the O'Brien line).
6 Blake, born June 12, 1759.
7 Esther, born June 22, 1760
8 Susannah, born Nov. 25, 1763.
9 John, born Jan. 14, 1765.

William Bryan was a member of the Provincial Congress 1775, was among the officers appointed by the Convention which organized the militia.

BRYAN

2 William Bryan (William-Needham), born Juy 1747, died Sept. 1800; married Elizabeth Gray. Issue:
  1 Francis Lee Bryan, born 1779, died at Windsor, North Carolina, 1850.
  2 William Bryan, born March 5, 1781, died young.
  3 Elizabeth, born March 26, 1783, died July 30, 1840.
  4 Ann Gray, born Dec. 5, 1784, died Oct. 12, 1864.
  5 Jane Smith, born April 24, 1786, died Feb. 18, 1818.
  6 Susannah Bush, born April 11, 1791.
  7 John Gray, born 1796, died Oct. 31, 1830.
  8 John Stevens, born April 1797, died 1848, in New York.
  9 James Louis, born Aug. 6, 1799, died Nov. 26, 1856.

Ann Gray Bryan married 1808, Sam Hyman, of Bertie County, had Francis Lee, Elizabeth, John, Samuel, Susan and William.

Jane Smith Bryan married 1812, Peter Boyd Martin; issue: Robert C., Elizabeth G., Susan B., and Mary.

John Stevens Bryan, married Lucy Haywood, of Raleigh; issue: Janet, Lucy, Eleanor, Elizabeth, William and John S., Jr.

3 Arthur Bryan (William-Needham), born May 12, 1749; married about 1780, Miss McCullen, of Johnstown County; moved to Twiggs County, Georgia, 1800. Issue: Only one son:
  1 John Arthur Bryan.

4 Elizabeth Bryan (William-Needham), born May 28, 1751; married Dec. 20, 1770, Col. Josiah Sasser. Issue:
  1 Lewis Sasser.
  2 Blake Sasser.
  3 William Sasser.
  4 Mary Sasser, born 1775; married Aug 28, 1792, William Stevens. Issue:
    1 Henry, born 1793; married Mary Bass.
    2 Josiah, born 1795; married Margaret Melton.
    3 Edmund, born 1798.

Mary Sasser Stevens, married second, her cousin, Benjamin Bryan, son of Needham III, and Sally Hinton. They moved to Georgia in 1818. Issue:
  4 Benjamin Bryan, Jr., born North Carolina, 1801.
  5 William Bryan.
  6 Rose Bryan married William Boynton.
  7 Louis.
  8 Penelope Bryan, married Joseph Boynton.
  9 Algernon S., married Sarah Oliver.

Elizabeth Bryan Sasser, widow of Col. Josiah Sasser,

NOTABLE SOUTHERN FAMILIES

married 1783, Col. William Blackman; had:
  5 Elizabeth B. Blackman, born 1784, died 1811; married Isaac Williams.
  5 Hardy Bryan (William-Needham), born June 4, 1753; married 1777, Winifred McCullers of Johnston County. Issue:
  1 William, born Sept. 10, 1779.
  2 Hardy, born Aug. 10, 1781
  3 Matthew, born Dec. 1783.
  4 Gen. Harry, born May 7, 1786.
  5 David, born Dec. 1790.
  6 John Gray, born 1792.
  Gen. Harry Bryan, born 1786, married 1815, Susan Blackman; had William Hardy, Susan, Joseph, John and James. David Bryan, born 1790, married the widow of Edwin Smith; had: Washington, Needham and Harry.
  6 Blake Bryan (William-Needham), born June 12, 1759; married 1790, Elizabeth Blackshear of Jones County, North Carolina (she was born Sept. 16, 1765, daughter of Joseph Blackshear and Catherine Franks; widow Bush). Issue:
  1 Mary Bryan, born 1792; married 1814 Maj. Ezekiel Wimberley.
  2 Elizabeth, born Dec. 9, 1795; married in Georgia, 1814, Joel Walker.
  3 Joseph, born 1798, married in Georgia, 1819, Mary Walker.
  4 Blake, Jr., died young.
  7 Esther Bryan (William-Needham), born North Carolina, 1760; married about 1780, Jonathan Smith, her cousin. Issue:
  1 Elizabeth, born 1787, married 1802, Nathaniel Lane.
  2 Esther B., never married.
  8 Susannah Bryan (William-Needham), born 1763; married John Bush, of Jones County, moved to Georgia. Issue:
  1 David, 1784.
  2 Elizabeth, born 1785; married 1805, James Tooke.
  3 Zilpah, married Mr. Baker.
  9 John Bryan (William-Needham), born Jan. 1765; married 1795, Patsy Hinton (daughter of Col. Sam Hinton and Delilah Hunter. Col. Sam Hinton was a brother of Col. John Hinton). She was born July 25, 1775.
  1 Bythan, born 1796; married 1825, Julia Smith, daughter of Maj. Sam Smith, Jr.
  2 Nancy, born 1798; married 1827, James Hinton Smith, son of Edward Smith and Temperance Hinton.

BRYAN

After John Bryan's death, Patsy Hinton Bryan married Rev. Lewis Whitfield, son of Rachel Bryan and William Whitfield.

3 Needham Bryan, Jr., third and last child of Needham Bryan and Annie Rambeau, born Bertie County, 1726, died 1784; married Nancy Smith (daughter of John Smith and Elizabeth Whitfield). Issue:
1 Needham III, born 1750.
2 Kedar, born 1752.
3 Winifred, born 1754.
4 Nancy, born 1756.
1 Needham (Needham-Needham), born 1750, died 1798; married 1768, when 19 years of age, Sallie Hinton (daughter of Maj. John Hinton and Sallie Smith). Had Issue:
1 Leonard, born 1769; married Elizabeth Green, daughter of Col. Joseph Green and Sarah Whitfild. Had:
1 Needham Green Bryan, born 1795, died 1837.
2 Elizabeth Green Bryan.
3 Daughter.
Sallie Hinton Bryan, married second, Probest Collier.
2 Clement, born Oct. 13, 1770, died 1839; married Edith Smith, born Dec. 1772 (daughter of Col David Smith and Charity Whitfield). Issue:
1 Sarah Hinton Bryan, born 1793.
2 Mary S. Bryan, born 1795.
3 Charity Bryan, born April 30, 1798, died 1841; married 1816, O. P. Cheatham.
4 Polly Bryan, born 1800; married John Rains.
5 Edith Bryan, born 1802, died 1843; married Martin Brown.
6 Judge Leonard Bryan, born Oct. 13, 1804, died Aug. 15, 1887; married Eliza Wyche.
7 Needham Bryan, born Aug 27, 1806, died 1841; Married Martha Battle.
8 Ann Bryan, born Dec. 1808; married William Ingraham.
9 Grazella, born 1811; married Jefferson Hines.
10 Emmeline, born 1814; married Mr. Watts.
11 David, born 1816; married Nancy Battle.
3 Benjamin Bryan, born North Carolina 1771; married June, 1800, Mary Sasser Stevens, widow of William, Stevens. Issue:
1 Benjamin Bryan, Jr., born North Carolina, 1801.
2 William Bryan.
3 Rose Bryan; married William Boynton.
4 Louis Bryan.

5 Penelope Bryan; married Joseph Boynton.
6 Algernon S Bryan; married Sarah Oliver.
4 Sallie Bryan, born 1773; married 1793, Jack Hinton.
Needham Bryan, married second, 1780, Charlotte Moore, daughter of Col. Joseph Moore. Had:
5 Charlotte Moore Bryan, born April 1785, died 1808; married Louis Whitfield (his first wife).
2 Kedar Bryan (Needham-Needham), born 1752; married about 1781, Elizabeth Smith (daughter of Alexander Smith and Elizabeth Whitfield). Issue:
1 John, born 1784; married Eleanor Torrence. Had: Eliza, Eleanor, Susan, Thomas K., John A. and Kedar.
Kedar Bryan married second, 1786, Mary Whitfield. Issue:
2 Rachel, born 1781; married 1805, Gibson Sloane.
Kedar Bryan, married third, 1793, Betsy Jones. No issue; married fourth, 1800, Nancy Dickson. Had issue:
3 Needham.
4 Kedar.
5 Robert.
6 Nancy.
7 Catherine.
8 Elizabeth.
3 Winifred Bryan (Needham-Needham), born 1754; married 1773, Hon. Nathan Bryan (son of Col. Hardy Bryan). He died in Philadelphia while attending Congress. Issue:
1 Mary, born 1774; married Gen. William Croom.
2 John, born 1776; married Miss Hatch.
3 Nathan, born 1777; married Rachel Whitfield, daughter of Gen. Bryan Whitfield and Nancy Bryan. second wife.
4 Winifred, born 1778; married 1797, Gen. Bryan Whitfield, second wife.
5 Needham, born 1781..
4 Nancy Bryan (Needham-Needham), born 1756; married 1780, Gen. Bryan Whitfield. Issue:
1 Bryan Whitfield, Jr., born 1782; married 1810, Elizabeth Turner.
2 Needham Whitfield died young.
3 Rachel, married first, Nathan Bryan; second, William Herring.
4 Nancy, married 1815, John Cobb.
5 Patsy, married William Coom.
General Bryan Whitfield, married second, Winifred Bryan, daughter of Winifred Bryan and Hon. Nathan Bryan.

BRYAN

6 Nathan Bryan Whitfield, born Sept. 1779; married Betsy Whitfield.
7 Louis Whitfield.
8 George Whitfield.
9 James Bryan Whitfield, married Sally Wooton.
10 Winifred Whitfield, married Richard Croom.
11 Mary Ann Whitfield, married Gains Whitfield.

BRIEN—TUBB OF TENNESSEE

William Bryan was a native of Cumberland County, Pennsylvania. He moved to North Carolina before the Revolution; married Jane Clarke, either in Pennsylvania or North Carolina. He lived with his family in Orange County, near Hillsboro. Their children were:

1 James, married Anne Lytle, May 11, 1779; moved to Logan County, Kentucky, 1798; died Oct. 31, 1815. Served in the Revolution.
2 Elijah, married Miss Marshall.
3 William, died in Virginia, 1835.
4 Thomas, married Polly Baker, Nov. 20, 1794.
5 David, married Miss Rany.
6 Sallie, married William Clark, moved to Logan County, Kentucky.
7 Hannah, married Joseph White.
9 Nancy, married Samuel Scott.
9 John, had five children, only two known; John and Cynthia.

James Bryan and Ann Lytle Bryan had issue:

1 Robert, born Feb. 28,1780, died Jan. 15, 1834; married Mary Guder, of Warren County, Kentucky.
2 William, born Oct. 1, 1781, died ——
3 Daniel, born Aug. 26, 1783.
4 Jane, born Aug. 9, 1785; married Mr. Mitchell; moved to Illinois.
5 Lytle,
6 James, Jr., born June 25, 1792; served in War of 1812; was State Senator, and the town of Briensburg, Marshall County, is named for him.
7 Archie, born Oct. 2, 1794.
8 John, born Dec. 16, 1796; married Eliza Marshall; lived in Louisville.
9 Hannah, born Jan. 22, died Jan. 26, 1813.
10 Joseph H, born Aug. 4, 1802, died Aug. 23, 1823.
11 Fruis E., born Aug. 4, 1802, died Aug. 23, 1823.
12 Alfred McG., born Aug. 19, 1805; Presbyterian minister.

13 Sally, born ——, married Mr. Riggs, moved to Springfield, Illinois.

One of the sons of William and Jane Clark Bryan had a son, Elisha. Who his father was he failed to tell, but he spelled the name Brien. We find his marriage to Ann Milner took place in Campbell County, Virginia, in 1806, and in 1810 he sold his property to John Hancock, and moved to Smith, now DeKalb County, Tennessee, where he died about 1834, and is buried near Alexandria.   1

The father of Elisha Brien is said to have come to Tennessee also, and his family were the twelfth to settle at Lebanon, Tennessee.

Elisha Brien had brothers, Elijah, William and David. David settled in Illinois; William was an old bachelor. He fought in the Creek Wars under Gen. Jackson, and died about 1864, while on a visit to his brother, David.

The children of Elisha Brien and Ann Milner were born in Tennessee, except the two oldest.

1 John Smith, 1807-1868, by first wife had issue: Carleton, William and John. By second wife, Rochie, Howard. One daughter, Rochie, who married Gen. Don Carlos Buell.

2 Paschel Winston, born May 8, 1809, died Feb. 20, 1881; married first Oct. 16, 1828, Narcissa Purnell Duncan, five children, all died young but Martha Ann, born Aug. 8, 1829, who married Eliel Tubb, son of Col. James Tubb. Paschal W. Brien, married second, Evelyn Trigg Jackson, July 26, 1842; no issue.

3 Manson Milner, 1811-1886, married Polly Tubb, daughter of Col. James Tubb. She died Oct. 1892. Their children were, Manson Milner, Jr., lawyer of Nashville; married Virginia K. Shoup, James, William A., Robert, John, Mary and Alice.

4 Alfred Watson, born Feb. 14, 1814, died Feb. 28, 1884, married first, Oct. 27, 1835, in Tennessee. Mary P. Stewart, one daughter, Mary, 1836-1869, married Dr. Joseph Warren Maybie. Alfred Watson Brien, married second, in Mississippi, June 1841, Amanda Cowan; no issue.

5 Martha, married Joseph Stuart, died 1863, had four daughters and one son.

All these sons of Elisha Brien were lawyers. John Smith Brien was Judge of the circuit court and chancellor of the state of Tennessee. Hon. Manson Milner Brien was Circuit Judge of Davidson County, later lived in Nashville. Alfred W. Brien was one of the most successful criminal lawyers of his time. Also served in the Revolution.

After the death of Ann Milner Brien, Elisha married in

BRYAN

Tennessee, Sarah Elizabeth Johnston, and had: (1) Elisha, (2) James, (3) Livingston, born March 5, 1820, died May 17, 1904, married Sarah Elizabeth Billingslea, (4) Ellen, (5) Susan.

TUBB—SOUTH CAROLINA-TENNESSEE

James Tubb of South Carolina married Polly Fisher, and had eleven children.
1 Abe Tubb, married Polly Lancaster.
2 John Tubb, marrid Polly Benson.
3 Nicholas Tubb, married Rhoda Lancaster.
4 George Tubb, married Patsy Corley.
5 Samuel Tubb, married Polly Terry.
6 Thomas Tubb, Jr, married Malinda Decker.
7 James Tubb, Jr., married Elizabeth Reynolds.
8 William Tubb, married Minerva ———
9 Polly Tubb, married ——— Lancaster.
10 Didame Tubb, married Isaac Bates.
11 Peggy Tubb, married ——— Barnett.

All these children with their families, except James, Jr., moved to Mississippi and to Texas, before the War Between the States.

James Tubb, Jr., born March 18, 1788, died July 18, 1868, was one of the pioneers and one of the best known men of DeKalb County, Tennessee. He lived on Smith's Fork Creek, east of Alexandria. He owned hundreds of acres of fine land. He was a colonel in the war of 1812. His military record and commission are given in Will S. Hale's History of DeKalb County.

Their children were:
1 Narcissa Tubb, married Mr. Simpson.
2 Julia Tubb, married Mr. Ashworth.
3 Helen Tubb, married Mr. Shurer.
4 Monroe Tubb.
5 John B. Tubb.
6 Caroline Tubb, married Mr. Fite.
7 Eliel Tubb, married Martha Ann Brien, daughter of P. W. Brien, had Livingston, James, Brien, Harry and Callie.
8 James Tubb.
9 Polly Tubb, married Manson Milner Brien, (son of Elisha), had M M., Jr., James, William A., Robert, John, Mary, Elizabeth and Alice.
10 Adelia Tubb.

CARTER

The history of the Virginia Carters begins with John Carter, who is supposed to have been a Cavalier and to have emigrated to Upper Norfolk about the year 1649. John Carter removed to Lancaster County, which he represented in the House of Burgesses, and from whence he was appointed a member of the Governor's Council. He also received a commission as Colonel Commandant of the Lancaster Militia, and as such is said to have entirely exterminated the Rappahannock Indians.

John Carter built his home on the Rappahannock and called it by the Indian name "Crotoman". Bishop Meade relates that when he was a boy the ruins of this old mansion, together with its ancient walls and fortress, could be seen amid the tanglewood.

John Carter also built the original Christ Church, which, rebuilt by his son, is the oldest religious edifice in Virginia. It is here that the first generations of Carters are buried. Unfortunately, by the time the "preservation and restoration movement" reached Virginia, decadence and vandalism had run rife for years. A tourist visiting the old church of Lancaster some fifty years ago, writes:

"The walls of dull red brick are little discolored by time. Entering by one of the massive doors, which are never locked, we discover an interior with which our modern figures seem altogether out of keeping. The cruciform aisle, flagged with stone, is bordered by high, square pews over the tops of which the occupants could behold only the parson in his lofty cock-pit pulpit well up under the eaves. Three of the aisles terminate in the doorways, and the fourth leads to the chancel which is panneled all around almost half way up to the groined ceiling. Above the communion table are two framed tablets of black canvas with the Lord's Prayer, Creed and Commandments painted in queer letters thereon. The baptismal font of

NOTABLE SOUTHERN FAMILIES

white marble has become separated from its pedestal by the rusting of the iron dowel which joined them and now rests upon the table, its cherub-bedight brim giving it a fanciful resemblance to Holmes' ancient punchbowl'."

At this date the inscriptions on the Carter gravestones, which have been preserved to history through Bishop Meade, himself a descendant of John Carter, seem to have been legible. The epitaph of the first Colonel John Carter in quaint phraseology informs all who might perchance be interested that this "Colonial Nat Goodwin" took unto himself five wives: Jane, daughter of Mr. Morgan Glynn; Elinor, ye widow Brocas; Anne, ye daughter of Mr. Cleve Carter; Sarah, ye daughter of Mr. Gabriel Ludlow; and lastly, the wife who survived him, Elizabeth Shirley.

The will of Colonel John Carter is still preserved in Lancaster County, Virginia, as is also the inventory of his estate. There is a traditon that the tomb of Colonel Carter originally bore a carved and mysterious "coat-of-arms," and that the family silver and linens were marked with unidentified monograms. Notwithstanding, "Cleave" was one of the beautiful family estates of the Carters, posterity has not been able to place in the family tree, "Ye Mr. Cleve Carter" whose daughter became the third wife of Colonel John, the founder of the Carter family in Virginia. It would seem that during the lifetime of the latter the Carters must have been already pretty well established in the colony, and that the first John formed the unfortunate precedent of marrying into his own family and beginning the tangle of intermarriages that is almost impossible to unravel.

Although so many times married, Colonel John Carter of "Crotoman" only left one son from whom there is any known issue, Robert Carter, the "King Carter" of romance and history. Robert Carter was carefully trained and educated from the age of five years as befitted the son of one of Virginia's wealthiest planters.

As agent for Lord Fairfax for the Northern Neck, and by land speculation and tobacco, King Carter trebled his fortune until his wealth is supposed to have exceeded that of any other planter of Colonial Virginia.

The epitaph of King Carter was done in Latin, and his tomb is said to have been wilfully defaced by those who resented his overbearing dispositon and arrogance displayed during his lifetime. This tradition may be taken with the proverbial grain of salt since there is no proof extat   As a member of the King's Council he seems to have displayed good statesmanship, and during an interregnum of governors, filled the position for the colony

CARTER

The Gentlemen's Magazine in London for November, 1732, contains the following notice of his death. "Robert Carter, Esq., August 4th in Virginia. He was president of the Council and left to his children about one thousand negroes and ten thousand pounds".

King Carter was married in 1668 to Judith Armistead. After the death of Judith, in 1701, he again married, his second wife being a widow, Elizabeth Willis, but before marriage Elizabeth Langdon, the beautiful daughter of Thomas Langdon, of Middlesex County, Virginia

Of the four sons of Robert Carter, John, of Crotoman the eldest, will be the only one mentioned in this sketch since it is through him the Tennessee family traces its line of descent from the Virginia Carters.

John of Crotoman inherited his grandfather's plantation on the Rappahannock, but through his marriage with Elizabeth Hill he came into possession of what was then the most renowned plantation in Virginia, that of Shirley, which Sir Edward Hill had purchased for his bride, a Welsh heiress and court beauty.

John Carter "the second," studied law in London at the Inner Temple. In 1722 he was appointed secretary of Virginia and is known in Carter genealogy as "Secretary Carter".

As secretary he seems to have resided mostly at Williamsburg and at Shirley. Crotoman was a tobacco mart, and records show that at one time he upheld one Joseph Carter as inspector despite the accusations against him and the protestations of Corbin, Receiver of Customs, and other officials.

Death came to Secretary Carter July 31, 1742. After the prescribed period of mourning expired, Elizabeth Carter married a certain Browler Cocke of whom little is known except that he held Shirley until the year 1771, at which date Charles Carter of Crotoman came into the estate of Shirley.

All family records handed down, and famous paintings of both Byrds and Carters have been preserved through the lines of Charles Carter, of Crotoman and of Shirley. There are no traditions or records of deaths or missalliances or of domestic upheavals in the family of Secretary Carter.

However, there is food for thought in the observation that although Secretary Carter married in 1723, Charles, the supposed eldest son of Secretary Carter, was not born until ten years later. Elizabeth Hill, who was but one year older than her brother, became the wife of "William Byrd III" of Westover. There was a difference of six years between the birth of Charles and the younger and only remaining son, Edward of Blenheim. It would seem also that the eldest son would, as was the custom usually observed, have borne the name of John, since that was the name of both the Secretary and his father. One would suppose, too, that Charles as the eldest son received the paternal estate of Crotoman, that Edward would have been entitled to the estate Shirley, since he was christened the namesake of Edward Hill, the brother from whom his mother inherited Shirley.

Why too, we muse, was the step-father permitted to usurp Shirley so long after Charles became of age? It could not have been indifference on the part of the Carters, for of all Colonial homes Shirley was the most to be desired.

One could imagine a missing heir, eccentricities on the part of Secretary Carter, and irregularities on the part of Charles of Shirley, to concoct a book of fiction. But it would be fiction. There is nothing in history, written records or traditions to uphold such a supposition.

Charles Carter of Shirley, is said to have been a man of splendid character and renowned for his charity. He was twice married (1) Mary, the daughter of his uncle, Charles Carter of Cleve, (2) Mary Butler Moore. He was the father of twenty-three children. John Hill Carter, eldest son, born 1750, is given in the family tree of the Byrds as having been a member of the House of Delegates from Lancaster County in 1780, and as dying unmarried. Charles, the second son, also died unmarried. The third son, George Carter, married a daughter of Sir Peyton Skipworth. Mary Carter, the eldest daughter, married George Braxton. Elizabeth Carter married Colonel Robert Randolph. Charles Carter married Nancy Carter of Sabine Hall. Edward Carter married Jane Carter of Sudley. Landon Carter died unmarried. Robert Carter, the eldest son by the second marriage (to Mary Moore), died unmarried; the next daughter, Anne Hill Carter, married General Henry Lee of Stratford. Robert Carter (2) married Mary, daughter of Governor Nelson. Bernard Carter married a daughter of General Henry Lee of Stratford (whose wife was daughter of Philip Ludwell Lee). Anne Lee Carter (born 1773, died 1829) was the mother of Robert E. Lee. Calphurnia Carter of Shirley was born as late as 1796.

The tradition that the Pioneer John Carter, of Tennessee, was a member of the same family as Anne Carter Lee is evidently unfounded. The eldest of this large family of

CARTER

twenty-three children, John Hill Carter, who is said to have died unmarried, was born in 1750, and John Carter of Tennessee had grown sons and probably grandsons in 1775.

Anne Carter Lee, however, was not only a daughter of Charles Carter of Shirley, but she was granddaughter of Charles, "Uncle Charles of Cleve".

Charles Carter of Cleve, son of King Carter, married (1) Mary Walker, (2) Anne Byrd, (3) Lucy Taliaferro. The only John of this family was the son of Anne Byrd, who married in Philadelphia in 1771, the daughter of Colonel Claiborne.

Landon Carter, brother of Charles Carter of Cleve by his second wife, Maria Byrd, had a son, known as John of Sudley who married Janet Hamilton.

By glancing over the names by the early Carter family line both in the male and female lines, in Tennessee, it would seem that the Tennessee family were descended from Robert Carter of Nomoni and his wife, Pricilla Bladen of Maryland. Robert Carter was the second son of William (King) Carter. Robert died a few months before his father, and his brother, Secretary Carter was guardian for his two children, Robert and Elizabeth. Robert was married in 1727 and his death occurred in 1732. In 1736 or prior to this date, Pricilla Bladen Carter married Colonel John Lewis of Warner Hall. The expense accounts for the children, Robert and Elizabeth, have been kept, and they seem to have been provided for in a manner befitting the grandchildren of King Carter.

Robert Carter, junior, one of the most famous Carters, known as "Chancellor Robert," inherited his father's estate. He was born in 1728 and died in 1804. He married Frances Tasker of Maryland. The most prominent Virginia family in this line is descended from a son, George Carter, of Oatlands.

The first children of Robert and Pricilla Carter, viz: Benjamin, Robert, John, Sophia, Harriet, Mary, all are given in the family tree as dying unmarried, which after all seems an easy and effective method of disposing of surplus progeny in family genealogy. Pricilla married a Mr. Mitchell. Frances married a Major Thomas Jones, of Essex County.

Betty Landon married Spencer Ball. Anna Tasker married John Mound. Sarah, the fourteenth and last child of Robert and Frances Tasker Carter, married —— Chinn.

Elizabeth Carter, daughter of Robert Carter and Pricilla Bladen, and sister of the Councillor, at the age of seventeen married, Francis Willis of Gloucester.

NOTABLE SOUTHERN FAMILIES

Again it is a temptation to let the imagination run riot and conjecture another offspring, a younger child of Pricilla Bladen Carter, but here again tradition and family record refuse to support any such claim.

Colonel John Carter, the founder of the Tennessee Carters, is precluded from being the son of Chancellor Carter, and a grandson of Robert Carter and Pricilla Bladen, if family records are correct. However, the writer believes that sons of the Chancellor and allied and collateral families of Jones, Lewis, Willis and Balls, were among those who chose to follow their kinsmen to the North Carolina frontier.

Having traveled around "Robin Hood's Barn" and back to the starting place the writer must confess that in all published records and genealogies of Virginia families of Carters, there is no mention—and apparently no place—for Colonel John Carter, of Tennessee. His history is not unlike that of the first Colonel John Carter of Crotoman, who built and fortified his home upon the Rappahannock and who despite efforts to attach him to different ancestral trees, still remains "John the Founder".

The Carters of Tennessee

Concerning the fort built at Long Island in 1759 we are told that it covered a goodly area on a smooth green level, was built strong, fortified with small cannon, and the heavy gates spiked with nails "so that the wood was all covered".

We may well imagine that there were gentlemen adventurers among the soldiers and surveyors who spent that memorable winter with Colonel Byrd at Long Island.

Following in the footsteps of the hunters and traders, allied families of the Byrds whose names are associated with Colonial Virginia, settled upon the banks of the Watauga Holston. John Carter and Amos Byrd were pioneers, and ere the Revolution was commenced we find families of Hills, Loyds, Harrisons, Randolphs, Nelsons and Carters residing in Washington County, Tennessee.

Colonel John Carter of Virginia

Fifteen years subsequent to the date of its first settlement there were several branches of the Carter family in Tennessee, each of whom is supposed to have had as head a son or grandson of Colonel John Carter.

The year of Colonel John Carter's birth is not known. He came to Watauga at about the same time that the Sevier family came, or earlier, and selected for his home a spot about one-half mile distant from the present town of Elizabethton.

The Watauga Association was composed of thirteen Commissioners, in whom all power was vested. It is probable that the Articles of the Association were outlined by Colonel Carter. Concerning his activities at this time Mr. Ramsey writes:

"Intelligent and patriotic, he was soon a leader in the Watauga Association, and became the Chairman of its Committee, and its Court—which for several years combined the legislative, the judicial, and the executive functions of the infant government west of Allegheny. His administration was wise and popular".

The Association, which assembled in 1772, is said to have had the first written laws west of the Allegheny Mountains.

Four years later Colonel Carter was Chairman of the Convention which framed the petition to North Carolina for annexation. The signature of Colonel Carter is referred to by Mr. Ramsey as being written "in a palsied hand".

Notwithstanding this supposed old age Colonel Carter seems to have led rather a strenuous life during the two years following. In response to the Watauga settlers' petition, North Carolina created Washington District and John Carter, John Sevier and Charles Robertson were appointed to represent the District in the North Carolina Assembly at Halifax, November, 12, 1776. It was one year later that John Carter received his commission from Governor Alexander Martin as Colonel Commandant of the Militia at Washington County.

In 1778 the strength of the settlements was depleted through the enlistment of the younger men, in the North Carolina and Virginia service. Beside Indian depredations, Tories dribbled into the settlement and seem to have gathered in some numbers in "Brown's Settlement" on the Nollichucky.

Colonel Carter sent to Virginia for reinforcements, marched to Browns, where he forced upon all British sympathizers the Test Oath which they had hoped to escape by fleeing to Virginia and North Carolina.

In some manner, we are told, officers acting under the orders of General Rutherford, interfering with his authority, Colonel Carter dispatched the following laconic epistle to the Governor:

"Your Excellency may be assured that I will do everything in my power for regulating the militia for the defense of our frontier, and for the benefit of the United States;

but if my dignity is to be sported with under those circumstances, I have no need of your commission as Commanding Officer of Washington District".—Ramsey's Annals of Tennessee).

When the first court for Washington County was held February 3, 1778, Colonel Carter was appointed not only chairman of the court, but entry taker for Washington County.

In 1780 when a meeting of military officers was held for the purpose of sending recruits into South Carolina, Colonel John Sevier had succeeded Colonel Carter as Colonel of the Washington County militia.

Also in October of this same year when Colonel Sevier was in need of money for provisioning the expedition to King's Mountain, John Adair was the entry-taker who furnished the money and whose patriotic reply to Colonel Sevier on his request for the same has gone down in history.

Landon Carter, Soldier and Statesman

While not the oldest of the sons of Colonel John Carter of Watauga, Landon Carter is the only one whose name has gone down in historical annals. The name "Landon" no doubt received from his paternal grandmother, Elizabeth Landon, second wife of Robert (King Carter) was also borne by a Virginia Statesman of the Revolution, Landon Carter of Sabine Hall, of whom it was written, "That when a member of the King's Council, he favored the Colonists and not the King in all things".

Tennessee's pioneer, Landon Carter, reached maturity during the rough and constructive days of the frontier. Possessing inherited ability, and a better education than the average frontiersman, his talents were not unrecognized and he served with equal devotion North Carolina, Franklin, the Territorial government and Tennessee.

The name, Landon Carter, is found on the petition of Watauga settlers to North Carolina for annexation.

He was a lieutenant of militia in 1780 and is thought to have been at King's Mountain, and served with the recruits who were sent into South Carolina.

He participated in the Battle of Boyd's Creek, after which he was commissioned Major. Later as a Colonel he was conspicuous in the Indian wars.

Landon Carter's sympathies were with the State of Franklin. Because of judicial training, personality and popularity he was chosen by Governor Sevier as an am-

CARTER

bassador to the North Carolina Assembly to inform it of the secession of the over-mountain counties.

During the existence of Franklin he served as a member of its Council, Secretary of State, and Speaker of the Senate.

Under Governor Blount and the Territorial regime, Colonel Carter held the important position as treasurer for Washington District, a position he retained after the formation of the state. In 1796 he was a member of the Convention which framed the Constitution for the State of Tennessee.

Colonel Landon Carter had been educated at old Liberty Hall, North Carolina. He was an able lawyer, practicing in all of the early courts of the state. His character was such as to make him loved and respected by all of his family and associates.

When a new county was taken from Washington County in 1796, it was named Carter County in his honor; and its county seat, Elizabethton, was so called for his wife.

Beside a son, William B. Carter, Landon Carter had a daughter, Eliza, who became the wife of George Gillespie, and a daughter Mary, who married the eminent lawyer, James P. Taylor, grandfather of the late Hon. Robert Love Taylor, of Tennessee.

Mary Carter, Wife of General Nathaniel Taylor

The Taylors and Carters were no doubt related before the emigration to Tennessee. Nathaniel Taylor is said to have built the first mill on the Watauga. His wife was Mary, daughter of Colonel John of Watauga and sister of Landon Carter. The writer has no record of other daughters of Colonel Carter.

John Carter, Son of Colonel John of Watauga

John Carter is thought to have been the eldest of at least five sons of Colonel John Carter of Watauga, Washington County, Tennessee. It was he who with the exception of the French trading post near Nashville owned and operated the first store for the selling of merchandise in the present state of Tennessee.

John Carter was one of the first patentees of Watauga. With Joseph Parker he operated a store, which is located by the historians Haywood and Ramsey as about "fifteen or eighteen miles from Rodgersville". According to tradition it was at Carter's Station, now Albany in Greene County, where descendants of the family have kept a store on or near the spot since pioneer days.

The primary object of this store was no doubt to do a profitable trade with the Indians, and it seems to have prospered to such an extent that when it was plundered by a marauding party, the owners did not attempt to retaliate. But at the Treaty of Sycamore Shoals at which time Daniel Boone, Colonel Henderson, and Charles Robertson secured titles to their land by purchase, Carter and Parker likewise were present and demanded damages, "an extension of their lands from Chimney Top Mountain to Cloud's Creek".

In order to meet the conditions of the Indians, it was necessary for Carter and Parker to take Robert Lucas as a partner in the business. The latter's interest was probably purchased by one or more of John Carter's brothers since Robert Lucas accompanied General James Robertson to the Cumberland, and later met his death at the attack on Freeland's Station.

The Carters may have had ambition to become landed Barons, but the land they had settled upon thinking it in Virginia, was in North Carolina and the latter state did not recognize the validity of lands purchased from the Indians The Carters and Parkers did secure their improvements and grants from North Carolina, which placed the former among the largest landowners in Greene and Hawkins Counties.

John Carter died in the year 1812.

Daniel Carter and Other Carters

Daniel Carter was one of the largest landowners among the early Carters, and owned 2,000 acres in Greene County. He was either the son or brother of John Carter and was the executor of his estate. He was a magistrate in 1788, and again in 1798. In the year 1803 he was one of the commissioners to lay off the boundary line between Greeneville and Hawkins County. A daughter, Sophie, married a son of John Pogue, one of the early settlers from Augusta County, Virginia. A son, Elisha, married Margaret Anderson, and had a son, Benjamin, who married Peggy Foster in 1824. Daniel was no doubt the father of a large family, including sons Daniel and John and Benjamin, of whom there are several of the names in the early records.

One of the oldest mills in Greene County was one built by Philip Rabb, on the road from Greeneville to Rodgersville. This mill seems to have been the nucleus around which a number of Virginia families, who evidently came through Carter's Valley, settled. Prior to 1800 the Carters who re-

CARTER

sided in this section were numerous, and no doubt were the sons and grandsons of Colonel John Carter, of Watauga.

Some of the families with whom they intermarried were the Templeton, Harrison, Pogue Keller, Jones, Weems, Corbin, Newman, Hardin Loyd, Hill, Lane and Parker.

Abraham Carter, perhaps one of the sons of Colonel Carter, was a large landowner and resided between Babb's Mill and Rodgersville. His son, Ekial, was the father of a large family.

Joseph also lived on the Babb's Mill road. He was a magistrate in 1805 and 1807; he died in 1811, and a son, Joseph, was the administrator of his estate. Joseph Carter, senior, was a brother of Daniel.

Jacob Carter was overseer of the Babb's Mill Road in 1804. His name is found on the tax receipts of 1783. His marriage to Sally Edmonds, possibly a second wife, is recorded in 1819.

Levi Carter died in 1811.

Hugh Carter, Senior, had a son, Hugh, who married Rebecca Babb, 1814.

Francis J. Carter sold his land in 1801, and is supposed to have emigrated elsewhere. (See next page.)

James Carter moved to Jackson County in 1814.

Jesse Carter resided on the Babb Mill Road near Rodgersville, 1798.

Pricilla Rebecca Carter married Jesse Morrison, 1819.
David Carter married Agnes Jones, 1795.
Polly Carter married Wesley Harrison, 1815.
Sarah Carter married P. Edmonds, 1819.
Rachel Carter married Havely, 1789.
William Carter married Elisabeth Jones, 1790.
Ann Carter married Andrew McFarland, 1825.
Lewis Carter married Elisabeth Parker, 1820
Hugh, 1789.

There were many Benjamins to be found among the Carters. It is possible Benjamin, senior, was one of the older sons of Colonel John Carter of Watauga. Benjamin had a son Nathaniel Carter, perhaps a namesake of Nathaniel Taylor, who died prior to 1796. His son, Nathaniel or Nathan, lived near the Sherrills in the Cove Creek Settlement. Another Carter, who lived on Cove Creek, was Samuel, the father of James and Anderson Carter.

The foregoing are only a few among the many of the early Carters found in Greene and Hawkins County. They were numerous notwithstanding the fact that Alabama,

NOTABLE SOUTHERN FAMILIES

Georgia and Mississippi received representatives of these same families.

Concerning Joseph Parker, who, with John Carter, established the first store. He is believed to have had sons, William, George and John.

One son was a Captain of militia in 1793.

George Parker probably married a daughter of Caleb Carter; he had a son Caleb, who lived on "Landon Churn," Camp Creek. This land had evidently at one time been in the Carter family.

The village of Ottway, some distance removed from the county seat of Greeneville, in Stage Coach days, was not without its aspirations. Now an educational, and progressive farming center it was in pioneer days the cradle of many of the best families of Washington, Greene and Hawkins counties. The Ottways of Virginia were a collateral family of the Byrds, and were also allied with the Carters.

A son of Colonel William Byrd and Elisabeth Carter Byrd was educated and resigned his commission in the British army to accept a place on the staff of General Henry

Ottway was perhaps intended as a family seat of the Carter family such as possessed by their ancestors in England and later planted on Virginia soil, but which could not materialize in the new and democratic frontier, which is now Tennessee.

Francis Jackson Carter, born ———, married February ———, died 1857, said to be a son of John Carter of Hawkins County, and brother of Landon Carter, settled in Sweetwater Valley, Tennessee. He married Esther Crockett, a kinswoman of Davy Crockett. The marriage took place February 17, 17—. She was born ——— and died July 9, 1870.

Mr. W. B. Lenoir in the History of Sweetwater Valley, says this Francis Jackson Carter, was a son of John Carter of Hawkins County, and a brother of Landon Carter, and as he must have known Francis Jackson Carter's widow well, the evidence is convincing.

Among the several children of Francis J. and Esther Crockett Carter were:

1 Theresa Newell Carter, who married John Scruggs. She was born near Newport, Tennessee, October 8, 1806. She was married September 7, 1824, and died November 9, 1888. She had fourteen children, among them (a) Richard Francis Scruggs, who married Elizabeth Ramsey Heiskell;

CARTER

and they had (1) Martha, died young. (2) Frank Heiskell; married Lowry. (3) John Frederick, married May Williams. (4) Daniel Pope, married Eva Dulaney Rodgers. (5) Arthur Bruce, married Belle Heabler. (6) Susan Newman. (7) Joseph. (8) Katherine, married Henry Hardey. (9) Annie Nelson, married Ross Owen. (10) Richard Abjah.

Elizabeth Esther Scruggs, daughter of John Scruggs, married September 30, 1847, Horace Burton Yearwood. She died October 25, 1905. Their children were: William C. G.; John Scruggs; Richard J.; Lavina Ida; Horace Burton; Daniel Boone; James Bennie; Francis Carter; Charles; Hugh. Of the foregoing. John Scruggs Yearwood married Mary Bell Fitzgerald, and had seven children: Pearl; Ida Zoe; Sadie Ethel; James Horace; Ella Hortense; Mack Fitzgerald, and Hugh Gaines. Francis Carter Yearwood married Mattie Moulton, and their children were: Esther, died young, and Francis C. Yearwood, junior.

Richard Jarnigan Yearwood married Jennie Walker. Their children are: Maude, married John Staub Fouche, (they have one son, John Staub Fouche, junior); Fawn Yearwood. and Richard Horace Yearwood.

OTHER TENNESSEE CARTERS

Pascal Carter, married Betsey Durett, and had four children:

1 Serena Carter, married John Shadden, and had one child, Margaret.

2 John G. Carter, married twice; first, Darthula Ann Inman, and had six children: (a) Annie Elizabeth Carter, who married W. F. Hutchenson. W. F. Hutcheson and Anne Elizabeth (deceased) had one child, Samuel Carter Hutcheson (who married Katherine Andrews).

(b) James Inman Carter, who married Samuella Childress. James Inman and Samuella Childress Carter have five children, namely: John Garnett (who married Freida Uttermoehlen—no children); Mary Lane (who married Richard Stites—one child, Richard junior); Paul, unmarried Lucile (who married James Glascock and has Ann and Lou Glascock), and Dorris Inman (who married Edward Young Chapin, junior).

(c) John Bowie Carter, married Elizabeth Flinn, and has three children: John, James and Frank.

(d) Rhoda Inman Carter, died in childhood.

(e) Mae Carter, married William Albert Jones, and

has four children: Anne Mae, who married, first, Richard Garner Watkins (deceased), and second, James Nihill Condon); Margaret Inman (who married Robert Winthrop Barr, junior, and has one child: Margaret Jones Barr); Ensign Hal Carter Jones, unmarried; Barbara Lea Jones, unmarried.

(f) Hugh Lea Carter; died in infancy.

2 John Goodley Carter, married second, Myra Inman, and had three children: (a) August Jarnagin, who first married Blanche Crossland (deceased), one child, John Allen; second, Marie Burguine (no issue); (b) Peyton Lea, who married Rowell; (c) Darthula (deceased), who married Oscar McLain, and had one child, Della Carter (deceased).

3 Pascal Carter, who married ―――――.
4 Peyton Carter; unmarried.

Another well known Tennessee branch of the Carter family is that of Mathew Carter, born in Greeneville, South Carolina, December 15, 1829. He moved to Jonesboro, Tennessee, when a young man and married Mary Emma Brown, daughter of Captain Enoch Brown of Jonesboro. They moved to Cleveland, Tennessee, in 1857. Mary Emma Brown born October 17, 1831, died May 29, 1906. Mathew Carter, born December 15, 1829, in Greenville, South Carolina, died April 1885. Their children were:

1 Edgar V. Carter, married Kate Robeson, daughter of A. C. Robeson, of Athens, Tennessee, and now lives in Atlanta. Their children are Robeson Carter, Edgar V. Carter, junior, Frank Carter and Katherine Carter.

2 Robert Lafayette Carter married Viola Cleveland.

3 Andrew P. Carter, married first, Pauline Gray, of Atlanta, and had one child, Andrew P. Carter, junior, and married second, Eva Wintersmith, had one child, Richard Carter.

4 Walter Bland Carter married Pearl Linch and had Afton W. Carter, Walter Carter, junior, and Pearl C. Carter.

5 Fred A. Carter married first Josephine King, daughter of A. S. King, and had two daughters, Josephine and Mary Craig Carter; married second, Belle Jones, daughter of John M. Jones, of Sweetwater, Tennessee.

6 May Carter, married Frank Y. Jackson. Their children are: Mary, Frank Y., Margaret and Mansfield Jackson.

DAVIS

Davis is one of the oldest Welsh family names. The line can be traced for many centuries and is said to include Kings Cole and Cadwaldar. The motto of the family is "With God as a Leader and a Sword as a Comrad".

Of the many Davis emigrants to America the family which later became most notable is that of Evan Davis, Samuel Davis and Joseph Davis; three brothers who emigrated from Cardiff, Wales, about 1730. Evan Davis and Samuel Davis landed at Philadelphia: Joseph Davis was drowned on the voyage. Samuel Davis went to what was then the Middle West.

Some time after 1761, the exact date not being known, Evan Davis emigrated from Pennsylvania to Georgia. He married while still in Pennsylvania, Mrs. Mary Emory Williams, a widow. Her father was Joseph Emory. By her first marriage this lady had two sons, Daniel Williams and Isaac Williams, both of whom were soldiers in the Revolution. It was due to their participation in the war that their young half-brother, Samuel Davis also joined the forces of the Revolution, being sent by their mother to join them.

Evan Davis and his wife (Mary Emory Davis), had at least one son, Samuel Davis, mentioned above, who was born in Pennsylvania in 1756. This Samuel Davis, who was in the Revolution, was the father of President Jefferson Davis of the Confederate States of America.

Mrs. Metta Andrews Green, the well-known historian of Georgia, has made close study of the life and residence of Evan Davis. She writes: "Evan Davis moved to Georgia from Pennsylvania and settled about forty miles above Augusta, so says Mrs. Davis in the life of her husband.

"The place forty miles above Augusta' is in Wilkes County four miles south of Washington. It belongs to the estate of Mr. Gabriel Toombs. Before Mr. Toombs died

I had a long talk with him. I was at this time writing something of Jefferson Davis' ancestry. Mr. Toombs told me that he himself was the third owner of the place from Samuel Davis, the father of Jefferson Davis. The deeds are all recorded here in our court house.

"I also found that Samuel Davis fought at the Battle of Kettle Creek: His name is certified to by General Elijah Clarke. Evan Davis died and is buried on the place now owned by the estate of Gabriel Toombs. The spot was pointed out to me. I have visited it many times. There is a large Indian mound near by. The place I speak of is on Beaver Dam Creek, near the Washington branch of the Georgia railroad.

"If records filed in the court house and human testimony count for anything, there can be no doubt of these facts. I wrote to Mrs. Davis about the matter and I have her letter agreeing with my statement. I also visited her in her apartment in New York. I was at the time very interested in collecting names of those who fought at Kettle Creek, and when I found Samuel Davis' name, I began to study the Davis' family history, also the genealogy.

The Kettle Creek battle alluded to was fought February 14, 1780, at War Hill. General Toombs used to speak of Wilkes County as the "Hornets Nest" of the Revolution. It was more than that. Like the battle of King's Mountain, it was a turning point.

Savannah had been captured and the British commanders were making plans to aid the Tories in possessing Georgia. To this end Colonel Boyd, a British officer, was secretly employed to organize the Tories in South Carolina and had crossed the Savannah River and entered Wilkes on his way to the British army, expecting to join the British forces which had possession of Augusta. This would have given the British commanders a sweep of the Southern country. The Royal Governor had been restored to power in Savannah. Thus the importance of the Kettle Creek battle.

Samuel Davis was at the siege of Savannah, and as he had raised and was captain of a Georgia company during the war, it is more than probable that he had, with him under General Clarke at Kettle Creek a portion of his company. As his father, Evan Davis, lived in Wilkes, the Samuel Davis company must have enlisted most of its men from the "Hornets Nest" and were "Wilkes boys".

Col. Elijah Clarke lived to realize his fond hopes to see Augusta again under the American colors. The State of Georgia as a reward for his services, gave him a commission as a major-general and a handsome grant of land. And South Carolina gave large land grants to Samuel Davis.

CAPTAIN SAMUEL DAVIS

Samuel Davis, the Revolutionary soldier, son of Evan Davis the Emigrant, and his wife Mary Emory Davis, was born in 1756, in Pennsylvania. He died in 1824 in Mississippi. As stated in foregoing paragraphs, he was a Captain in the Revolution, having raised a company of Volunteers in Georgia. Later he joined the Continental Army and served in South Carolina as well as Georgia. He was in the Battle of Kettle Creek and in the Siege of Savannah. For his services the State of South Carolina granted him a thousand acres of land (in what is now Kentucky) and he moved to settle upon that property. There his famous son Jefferson Davis was born. From Kentucky Samuel Davis moved to Louisiana, and again in 1811 he moved to Mississippi where in 1824 he died.

Captain Samuel Davis married in 1782, Jane Cook, a daughter of Mrs. Sarah Simpson Cook, who was herself a daughter of Samuel Simpson, said to have been assistant Quartermaster of the Pennsylvania Regiment during the Revolution. His father was Thomas Simpson and his father was John Simpson, who emigrated from Scotland to Ireland and from Ireland to America, settling in Pennsylvania as did many of the Scotch-Irish people.

Samuel Davis and his wife, Jane Simpson Cook Davis, had ten children, namely:

1 Joseph Emory Davis.
2 Benjamin Davis.
3 Samuel Davis, Second.
4 Isaac Davis.
5 Anne Davis.
6 Amanda Davis.
7 Lucinda Davis.
8 Matilda Davis.
9 Mary Anne Davis.
10 Jefferson Davis.

JOSEPH EMORY DAVIS

1 Joseph Emory Davis, born 1784, died 1870; was a lawyer and planter in Mississippi. His young brother, Jefferson Davis, spent much time with him and in the splendid library of the home absorbed much of the wealth of knowledge for which he was noted in after years. Joseph Emory

NOTABLE SOUTHERN FAMILIES

Davis married Elizabeth Van Benthysen and had one daughter, Mary Lucinda Davis, who married in 1837, Dr. Charles Jouett Mitchell, of Vicksburg, as his first wife.

2 Benjamin Davis, Second, was a planter. He married Cynthia Campbell (Moably) and died leaving children.

3 Samuel Davis, Second, was a planter. He married Lucy Throckmarton. They had one daughter, Helen Davis, who married —— —— Keary, and had Robert Keary, Samuel Keary, Pauline Keary and Ellen Keary.

4 Isaac Davis married Susan Guerthy. They had one son who was General Joseph Emory Davis, Second.

5 Anne Davis married Luther Smith, and had a daughter, Anne Davis Smith.

AMANDA DAVIS

6 Amanda Davis, married David Bradford. They had four children, namely: (a) Jefferson Davis Bradford (who was an enginer in the United States Army; (b) Lucy Bradford (who married Dr. Charles Jouett Mitchell, of Vicksburg, her first cousin's widower, as his second wife and had at least one daughter —— —— Mitchell, who married Eli Joseph Ganier. They had two sons, Lincoln Mitchell Ganier, who is unmarried and lives in Chattanooga, and Albert Francis Ganier who lives in Nashville and married Ann Eastman, daughter of Mr. and Mrs. Roger Eastman of Nashvile. Their two sons are: Albert Francis Ganier, junior, and Roger Eastman Ganier.

(c) Elizabeth Porter Bradford, who married Mansell II, son of Mansell White I, in the United States. Their children were Mansell White, III, who is unmarried; Lucy White, who married Clement Penrose Wilkerson and has four children; Mary Bradford White, who married Ringgold Brouspears and had five children; Carl White (who married Mary Mitchell of Cincinnati, and had seven children, namely: Carl White, Second, who is unmarried, Elizabeth White who is a nun in the convent of the Sacred Heart, Nancy Miles White who married Charles Earl Johnson, junior, of Raleigh, North Carolina, and has a son, Charles Earl Johnson, Third, Charlotte White who married Robert Swepson Cowan, Second, and has a son Robert Swepson Cowan, junior, Mansell White, Fourth, Lincoln Mitchell White and Richard White who are unmarried); Albert Sidney Johnson White who married Ellen Tobin and has five children; (d) Elizabeth Parker Bradford White who married Edwin Rodd,, Nancy Miles White who married Thomas Helms Anderson and has two chil-

DAVIS

dren); and David Bradford, Second, (who served in the Confederate Army. He married in 1838, Ada Eliza Pottenger).
7 Lucinda Davis, married William Stampes of Woodville, Mississippi.
8 Matilda Davis, died unmarried.
9 Mary Anne Davis, married Robert Davis of South Carolina.

JEFFERSON DAVIS, PRESIDENT OF THE CONFEDERATE STATES OF AMERICA

10 Jefferson Davis was the tenth child and the fifth son of Captain Samuel Davis and Jane Cook Davis. He was born in Christian County, Kentucky, June 3, 1808. He died in New Orleans, December 8, 1889. His father and mother removed from Wilkes County, Georgia, to Kentucky, shortly after the revolution owing to a grant of six thousand acres of land, a reward for distinguished Revolutionary service.

Captain Samuel Davis, when his distinguished son was still small, moved again, this time to Mississippi. Jefferson Davis attended schools in Mississippi, St. Thomas College Kentucky, Transylvania University, at Lexington, Kentucky and he graduated from West Point in 1828, with high honors and served in the Indian Wars. In 1825 while an officer in the army he married Sarah Knox Taylor, daughter of General Zachary Taylor and Margaret Mackall Smith Taylor. Upon his marriage, Lieutenant Davis resigned from the army and retired to Briarfield, the plantation in Mississippi, which had been given him by his brother, Joseph Emory Davis.

There his young wife died within a year. He devoted himself to study in the years succeeding her death and in the library of his brother, Joseph Emory Davis, then probably the largest and most extensive in Mississippi, he acquired a profound knowledge of history and literature that in after public life served him well. In 1845 he was elected to congress. Upon the breaking out of the Mexican War he resigned from Congress, volunteered, and was Colonel of the First Mississippi Rifles. He won great distinction, and was acclaimed as the Hero of Buena Vista where he saved the Amercan Army from complete disaster. He was severely wounded in the engagement. He declined the rank of Brigadier-General and once again retired from Military service. In 1847 he was appointed United States

Senator and later was elected to the same office. While in the Senate he was Chairman of Military affairs. In 1851 he decided to become a candidate for Governor of Mississippi and therefore resigned his seat in the Senate. He did not win the election however and retired to Briarfield. In 1853 President Pierce appointed him Secretary of War, an office he was eminently fitted to occupy by his natural gifts and attainments and he ranks as the greatest Secretary of War. Among the achievements of his administration were the survey made for the route of the Pacific Railway; the extension of the Capitol; the building of the aqueduct which supplies Washington with water; the building of Cabin Johns Bridge, a remarkable engineering feat which was solely his design. His name as Secretary of War was cut from the tablet on the bridge and has only recently been restored after fifty years of effort on the part of the Daughters of the Confederacy, the Confederate Veterans and the Confederate Memorial Association.

He was again elected to the Senate at the close of President Pierce's term and was the leader in that body when the question of secession began to be discussed. Colonel Davis as he was called only approved secession as a last resort, but in 1861 when Mississippi seceded he returned to his State and was almost immediately made a Major-General of the Mississippi troops. His election to the Presidency of the Confederate States of America soon followed.

An interesting incident of his inauguration in Montgomery was the famously eloquent introduction of Mr. Davis to the assembled people by William Yancey. The seven words are classic in their simplicity:

"The hour and the man have met".

Col. Davis himself was a brilliant speaker and shared with Yancey the reputation of being the greatest orator in the United States. His voice was purest melody and he could move any audience to his will. Except for the war and his election to the Presidency of the Confederate States, he would probably have been President of the United States, as he was immensely popular throughout the North. His keen political power as an orator made him a popular candidate for the office for which he was being widely discussed throughout the North as well as the South.

In the formation of the Confederate Government however he hoped for military rank and his genius and accomplishment in military affairs entitled him to expect it. He was instead, given the greatest office in the gift of Southern people.

He was reluctant to talk war and hoped for reunion. His history for four years is identified with that of the Confederate States and need not be given in detail here. When the Confederacy fell he was imprisoned and kept in close confinement, much of the time manacled, for many months.

In 1876 he was admitted to bail, but the indictment was never dismissed and Jefferson Davis died still under indictment, though he and his friends continually implored for trial. It is said that the Attorney-General of the United States advised against trial as treason could not be proved, the states having the right previous to 1861 to withdraw and also because every West Point student was instructed (until 1861) that in the event of any state withdrawing, allegiance was due to the state. This was in Rawl's Constitution which was a text book at West Point until 1861, when the books were destroyed. Only a few are now in existence.

Returning from prison, when bail was admitted, to his beloved Mississippi to the home of his brother, Joseph Emory Davis, who had been a father and older brother to him, he was received by his people with adoration that must have softened somewhat the sorrow of suffering. His niece, Mrs. Lucy Mitchell, of Vicksburg, who lived until a short time since, the daughter of a favorite sister, Amanda Davis, recently told the writer, of the affecting scenes when the people would come for miles to see him, to kneel by his chair where his thin form half reclined, to weep over him and to kiss the wrists that had been manacled so long.

His health was shattered by his long and arduous confinement and he traveled for three years in Canada and Europe. In 1879 he settled at Beauvoir, Mississippi, and wrote his "Rise and Fall of the Confederacy". During his last years he was beloved by his people and worshipped wherever he went. "He lived a dignified life to a dignified close." "He was a statesman with clean hands and a pure heart, who served his people faithfully from budding manhood to hoary age, without thought of himself with unbending integrity, and to the best of his ability".

Dr. Henry E. Shepperd, of Baltimore, said of Jefferson Davis:

"The marked versatility of intellectual power revealed in Mr. Davis' character suggested a parallel between him and Thomas Jefferson. A failure in the sphere of oratory, in the richness and amplitude of his knowledge, Jefferson stood without a peer until the advent of Mr. Davis.

" 'The Prison Life of Jefferson Davis', by his attending physician, Dr. Craven, recalls to memory the exuberant wealth of acquirement illustrated in the lives of three foremost lights of modern statesmanship—Jefferson, Gladstone, and the late Lord Salisbury. The Prometheus of the Confederacy in the gloom of his cell at Fortress Monroe, took all human knowledge for his province, discoursed upon art, literature, philosophy, strategy, economic problems, political issues until the darkness of his casement was radiant with the light of the Baconian ideal, unfolded to his prophetic vision, and interpreted to a single listener. His mastery over language and gift of illuminating whatever theme he touched, displayed its power in every relation, personal or official, in the executive station when he stood on Fortune's crowning slope, or later when he enjoyed the sweet aloofness of social converse".

The work of Dr. Craven holds a unique place in our literary record. It was published by the Neal Company, New York. Rarely has so marvelous a narative of heroic endurance been presented to the world.

It is a matter of regret that so small a portion of Mr. Davis' speeches associated with the Confederacy, have been preserved. Particularly it is regretted that the one to General Lee delivered in Richmond in November, 1870, is not preserved; "An oration", says Dr. Shepperd,"worthy of Pericles has vanished and it is but one of a select company upon which a seal of immortality should be wrought in strongest relief".

"In all Mr. Davis' writings and speeches, art grace, fervor, patriotism blend into a golden harmony".

Jefferson Davis married for his second wife, February 28, 1845, Varina Banks Howell (born 1828, died 1908), daughter of William Burr Howell, of New Jersey, and his wife Margaret Louisa Kemp Howell. William Burr Howell was a son of Major and Governor Richard Howell (born 1752, died 1802), of New Jersey and his wife Keziah Burr Howell. Margaret Louisa Kemp's father was Colonel James Kemp, an Irish gentleman who came to America after the Emmett Rebellion.

Varina Banks Howell was born May 7, 1828. She was

DAVIS

named in honor of her mother's friend, Mrs. George Banks (Varina Staunton Banks), of Natchez, Mississippi.

She married Jefferson Davis, February 28, 1845, at Briarfield, which is still standing about a mile south of Natchez on a bluff overlooking the river. The marriage records show the names Jefferson Davis, William B. Howell, Varina Howell and the name of the officiating minister.

Mrs. Davis, after the death of her husband, often signed her name "V. Jefferson Davis", the "V", being the initial of "veuve", the French word for widow. This is a custom in the South, in New Orleans and Mobile regions and in the Lower Mississippi country. Her signature when so shown means "Widow Jefferson Davis" and not Varina Jefferson Davis as many historians state. One historian says her name was Varina Jefferson Howell. This is manifestly a mistake. It is a very singular fact that the records the Chancery Court of Vicksburg, Mississippi, show that she signed her will as Varina Jefferson Davis which must have been an inadvertance and could not have been correct. The proper legal signature for such a document would have been Varina Banks Howell Davis if she had signed her full name.

Jefferson Davis and Varina Howell Davis had six children, namely:

1 Samuel Emory Davis, who died in infancy.
2 Margaret Howell Davis.
3 Jefferson Davis, who died unmarried.
4 Joseph Evan Davis, who died young..
5 Varina Ann Howell Jefferson Davis, died unmarried.

Samuel Davis died in infancy. Jefferson Davis, junior, born 1858, died unmarried in 1878, in Memphis, Tennessee, a hero of the yellow fever epidemic which afflicted the South in 1878.

Joseph Evan Davis, died in infancy.

Varina Ann Howell Jefferson Davis was born in the White House in Richmond, in 1864. She was called Winnie and was adopted as the daughter of the Confederacy. She died unmarried in 1898.

Margaret Howell Davis married in 1877 Joel Addison Hayes and had five children, namely:

1 A son who died in infancy.
2 Varina Howell Davis Hayes.
3 Lucy White Hayes.
4 Jefferson Davis Hayes.
5 William Davis Hayes.

NOTABLE SOUTHERN FAMILIES

Of the foregoing Varina Howell Hayes married Dr. Gerald Bertram Webb. Their children are: Varina Margaret Webb, Gerald Bertram Webb, junior, Frances Robina Webb, Eleanor Leila Constance Webb, Joel Addison Hayes Webb.

Lucey White Hayes married George Bower Young. Their children are: Margaret Josephine Young, Harvey Young, George Oliver Young.

Jefferson Davis Hayes, born 1884, was the first living son of Margaret Howell Davis Hayes and Joel Addison Hayes. He was five years old when his grandfather, the Great Southernor died. Standing by his grandfather's bier he heard some one say that the dead statesman left no one to bear his name. The boy proudly claimed that he was his grandfather's namesake, which was of course quite true. The whole circumstance was explained to him and he insisted that he wanted to be named for his grandfather. The Bishop of Mississippi, who was present was deeply touched and in the presence of the family and close friends, he laid his hands, one upon the boy's head, the other upon the cold forehead of President Davis and said:

"I christen thee Jefferson Davis".

The change of name was subsequently legalized by legislative enactment in three states: Louisiana, Missssippi and Virginia. He uses his father's name with his own, Jefferson Hayes-Davis. He graduated from Princeton, 1907, and from Columbia as a mining engineer in 1911. He followed this profession in the West for several years, and then settled at Colorado Springs as assistant cashier of the First National Bank of which his father was president.

His first military experience was with the National Guard on the Mexican border, as a gunner in a battery of field artillery; and before his company was mustered out he was promoted to the rank of First Lieutenant. On the following August the battery entered the Federal service, and after a period of training was ordered abroad. The vessel on which he crossed the Atlantic was with the Tuscania when that illfated ship met disaster; but it reached an Irish port in safety, and First Lieutenant Davis and his comrades crossed over to France in safety. As observation officer for his battery, it was his duty to go aloft in an anchored

DAVIS

balloon, watch the fire of his guns, and signal orders to the gunners.

He married Doree Dewitt. They have two children: Jefferson Addison Hayes-Davis, and Harriet Adele Hayes-Davis.

William Davis Hayes, son of Joel Addison Hayes and Margaret Howell Davis Hayes, married Elizabeth ———. They have two children, Elsie Hayes and William Davis Hayes, junior.

DONALDSON
DONELSON

The Donaldson family came from Scotland where the name was spelled Donaldson. The name came from the Christian name, Donald. (Family Names and their Story, S. Baring Gould). In the early generations in this country it was variously spelled Donaldson, Donalson, Donelson, Doneldson, Donolson and Donilson. (Virginia Militia in the Revolution, J. T. McAllister). Stockley, a son of Col. John Donelson, spelled his name several ways in signing legal documents. (Ramsey's Annals of Tennessee).

The brothers, Col. John Donelson and William Donaldson, founders of the family in Tennessee, used different spellings. Most of the descendants of the former continue to use his spelling, Donelson, while the descendants of William use the original spelling, Donaldson, as used by him. In this article the compiler will endeavor to use the spelling adopted by the individual.

The Donaldson Coat-of-Arms, dated 1312, has the single word, "Promtus", as its motto. (Burke's General Armory).

The emigre, John Donaldson, (whose father was John Donaldson of Scotland), came to America in 1716, and settled near Delaware Bay. At this time he owned his vessel and was engaged in the shipping business between America and London. It is said that his father and grandfather had been shippers. He married Catherine Davies, daughter of David Davies and Martha Thomas Davies of Virginia, (a sister of Samuel Davies, D. D., LL. D., third President of Princetown College, (1761-1766) after its reorganization). They had children:
I John Donelson II.
II William Donaldson.
III Andrew Donaldson.
IV A daughter (name unknown), married —— Henry.

NOTABLE SOUTHERN FAMILIES
I JOHN DONELSON II.

I John Donelson II (1720-1785) is said to have been born in Pittsylvania County, Virginia. He married Rachel Stockley, of Virginia, and had children:
I Alexander Donelson, never married.
II Catherine Donelson.
III John Donelson III.
IV Mary Donelson.
V Jane Donelson.
VI William Donelson
VII Stockley Donelson.
VIII Samuel Donelson.
IX Severn Donelson.
X Levin Donelson, never married.
XI Rachel Donelson.
XII Elizabeth Donelson.

Colonel John Donelson II was a man of education and achieved prominence in Virginia. "He was a burgess from Pittsylvania County in assemblies of May 1769, 1769-1771, 1772-1774". (Virginia Biography. Tyler). Prior to the Declaration of Independence he was made colonel of his regiment of militia. (History of Tennessee. Putnam). He was appointed several times to negotiate treaties with Indian tribes, and in each case was successful. He, with three other men, surveyed the boundary between Georgia and North Carolina, which, at that time, ran west to the Mississippi River. (History of Tennessee. Haywood. History of Kentucky. Butler).

One of the most remarkable adventures undertaken in the settlement of the West was the voyage of the company of pioneers with Col. John Donelson as commander, which left the Watauga Settlement, (Dec. 22, 1789), traversed the Holston, Tennessee, Ohio and Cumberland Rivers to French Lick, now Nashville, arriving on April 24, 1780. Nearly two hundred persons made this remarkable voyage on flat boats, dugouts and scows, traversing dangerous rapids and constantly surrounded by hostile Indians. In this company were his family and the families of a number of men who, under James Robertson, had preceded them going overland through the wilderness.

DONALDSON

Col. Donelson's journal of the good boat, Adventure, forms an important chapter in all the histories of early Tennessee. Theodore Roosevelt says, in his Winning of the West, "Robertson's special partner was a man named John Donelson. The latter went by water and took a large party of immigrants, including all the women and children, down the Tennessee, and thence up the Ohio and Cumberland to the Bluff, or French Lick, a distance of more than two thousand miles. Among them were Robertson's entire family and Donelson's daughter, Rachel, the future wife of Andrew Jackson, who missed by so narrow a margin being mistress of the White House... The settlers who came by water passed through much greater peril and hardship (than the party, under Robertson which went overland). By a stroke of good fortune the journal kept by Donaldson, the leader of the expedition, has been preserved. As with all the other recorded wanderings and expeditions of these back-woods adventurers, it must be remembered while this trip was remarkable in itself, it is especially noteworthy because, out of many such, it is the only one of which we have a full account. . . . Donelson's flotilla, after being joined by a number of other boats, consisted of some thirty craft all' told—flat boats, dug-outs, and canoes. There were probably two or three hundred people, perhaps many more, in the company. The chief boat, the flagship of the flotilla, was the Adventure, a great scow, in which there were over thirty men, besides the families of some of them". Ramsey, in his Annals of Tennessee, says, "The distance traveled on this inland voyage, by Col. Donelson, the extreme danger in every respect marks the expedition as one of the greatest achievements in the settlement of our western country".

Finding French Lick surrounded by hostile Indians Col. Donelson moved to Kentucky, where he had large interests in land, and resided there for a few years. Then, returning to Tennessee, he located on a farm near what now is Nashville, where he lived until 1785, when he was shot from ambush, by an Indian, and killed.

II Catherine Donelson

Catherine Donelson was born in Pittsylvania County, Virginia. She married Col. Thomas Hutchings and had children: (1) John Hutchings (married Mary Smith); (2) Stockley Hutchings (married Elizabeth Atwood and had

NOTABLE SOUTHERN FAMILIES

chilren: (a) Mary Catherine Hutchings who married James Murdack; (b) Elizabeth A. Hutchings who married Andrew J. Coffee). (3) Lemuel Hutchings (married ——— Owen and had children: Alexander, Arthur, Stockley Donelson and two daughters. names unknown); (4) Christopher Hutchings (married (1829) Louisa Ann Edwards and had children: (a) Mary Hutchings who married John H. Cross; (b) Elizabeth Cooke Hutchings; (c) John Hutchings; (d) Frank Hutchings, killed in Civil War; (e) Jackson Hutchings; (f) Fannie A. Hutchings; (g) John Hutchings; (h) Stockley Hutchings; (i) William Hutchings); (5) Rachel Donelson Hutchings (married James Smith Rawlings); (6) Mary Hutchings (married ——— Small) (7) Jennie Hutchings; (8) Thomas Hutchings; (9) Elizabeth Hutchings.

III John Donelson III

III John Donelson III (1755-1840), married (1779) Mary Purnell (1763-1848). Captain John Donelson III was born in Virginia, and his wife in Snow Hill, Maryland. They as bride and groom, made the trip from Watauga Settlement to French Lick, in 1779, on the "Adventure" in the Company commanded by his father, Colonel John Donelson. They had children:

1 Chesed, died in infancy.
2 Tabitha Donelson,
3 Alexander Donelson,
4 John Donelson IV, (1787-1840), married (1823) Eliza Butler.
5 Lemuel Donelson,
6 Rachel Donelson,
7 Mary Donelson, marrid John Coffee,
8 William Donelson,
9 Elizabeth Donelson,
10 Catherine Donelson,
11 Chised Donelson, died in infancy,
12 Stockley Donelson,
13 Emily Donelson,

2 Tabitha Donelson (1781-1854), married (1854) George Smith (1876-1849), and had children: (1) Mary Smith (1798-1853), who married (1826) Lafayette Saunders, and had children: Augusta Saunders (1827-1898), (married (1845) John King (jurist). Children: (a) Lafayette Saunders

DONALDSON

King (married twice: First, Helen Ingersol; Second, Josephine Strickland); (b) Mary Saunders King (married (1890) L. P. Lastrapse. Children: Helen Lastrapse, who married Valentine King Irion, and had children: Mary Caroline, Alfred King, Alice and Albert; Augusta Lastrapse, who married (1894) Walter Webb Duson, M. D., and had children: Walter, Caroline and Donald McNaughton); (c) Nannie M. King; (d) Augusta Saunders King, (married Lindsay Dunn Beale, (jurist). Children: Lindsay Dunn Beale II; Augusta Beale, who married William Mercer Hall, and had children: William Mercer Hall II, Lindsay, and Minnie; Anna Mariah Beale, who married (1911) Gordon Bakewell Golson, and had children: Lindsay and Gordon Bakewell Golson II; Thomas Buffington Beale, who married(1911) Jennie Munson, and had a child, William Ruffin; John E. K. Beale; Robert George Beale; Phoebe L. Beale; Helen Beale; Lafayette Saunders Beale); Tabitha Saunders, married (1852) Andrew S. Herron. Child: Mary Saunders Herron, who married Charles Cecil Bird, and had children: Andrew Herron, Charles Cecil Bird II, Thomas Buffington and Mary); (2) Sallie Smith (1801-), who married Thomas Watson, and had children: (a) Winifred Scott Watson, (married ―― Schofield); (b) Harriet Watson married twice: First, Orville Cage; Second, James Douglas. Children by second husband: Noel and Lula); (c) George Smith Watson, (married twice: Children Thomas and Mary Jane); (d) Tabitha Watson, (married twice: First, ―― Gordon; Second, ―― Miller. Three Children by first husband); (e) Margaret Watson, (married ―― Dunn. Children: Mary Lee, Harry Smith and Sallie); (3) Tabitha Smith (1803-1849), who married (1821) Anselm D. Bugg, and had children: (a) George S. Bugg; (b) Samuel Bugg; (c) Mary Saunders Bugg, (married (1850) William Murray. Children: Rufus Saunders Murray, who married Minnie Mills, and had children: Samuel, Mary, (who married James Smith, and had children: Minnie Lou (married ―― Phillips), another daughter and two sons); John Dean, Cloe Mills and William; Anslem Bugg Murray, who married Theda Bland Fitzhugh, and had children: Mary Etta, Theda Bland, Fitzhugh and Katie Trousdale; William Murray; George Smith Murray; John Armfield Murray; Anna Murray, who married M. T. Cartwright, and had children: Murray Anslem, Mary Armfield and Myra Eugenia); (d) Emily Don-

NOTABLE SOUTHERN FAMILIES

elson Bugg; (4) Harry Smith (1806-1888), who married (1859) Sallie Sypert, and had children: (a) Tabitha Donelson Smith; (b) Nannie Smith, (married (1880) Horatio Berry. Children: Harry Smith Berry, who married Georgia Knox, and had children: Katherine Knox and Nancy; Jane E. Berry, who married Charles E. Buntin, and had children: Charles Erwin, Rachel Craighead, Horatio Berry and William; Emma Horatio Berry, who married W. A. Bryan, M. D., and had children: Ann, Elizabeth and Allen; Sarah Crosby Berry; Julius Trousdale Berry, who married Grod Cornell); (5) Elizabeth Smith; (6) Jane Smith (1818-), who married John J. Wherry, and had children: (a) Tabitha Wherry, (married Alexander Cowan (a minister of the Gospel), and had children: Sarah, and Jane who married David C. Kelly); (b) John Wherry; (c) Emily Wherry; (d) William Wherry; (e) Harry Wherry, (married Celia Willis); (f) George Wherry; (g) Augusta Wherry, (married William Hamilton); (h) Daniel Wherry, (married Susie Knox).

5 Lemuel Donelson (1789-1832) married Elizabeth White, (daughter of Judge Hugh Lawson White) and had children: (1) John Donelson V (married Kate Allen. Children: John Donelson VI and Lemuel Donelson II); (2) Pheriba White Donelson (married Harper Sheppard).

6 Rachel Jackson Donelson (1794-), who married (1809) William Eastin, and had children: (1) Mary Eastin, who married (1832) Lucius Polk, and had children: (a) Sarah Rachel Polk, (married (1855) Robina Cadwallader Jones. Children: Mary Polk Jones, who married (1877) Duncan Brown Cooper, and had children: Sarah (married Lucius Burch, M. D. Child, John C.), William, Robin Jones (married Eva Lee Smith), Mary Polk, (married Beverly R. Wilson. Children: Mary and Beverly) and Duncan Brown Cooper II (married Dorothy Crowe); Rebecca Edward Jones; Robin Jones; Sarah Polk Jones, who married (1888) James C. Bradford, and had children: Sarah Polk and Thomas; Lucy Green Jones, who married (1888) Stanley Bell Herndon, and had children: Robin C. Jones, Virginia, Rebecca and Lucy); (b) Mary Brown Polk, Married (1858) Henry Clay Yeatman. Children: Mary Eastin Yeatman, who married Thomas Shepherd Webb, Henry Clay, Russell Houston, Trezevant Player,

DONALDSON

Jane and Lucia Polk); (c) Emily Donelson Polk, (married (1860) J. Minnick Williams. Children: Harry, who married Louise Pitcher, Emily, Lucius Polk, Minnick, Anna Fassman, Eliza Polk and Pricilla Shelby Williams, who married G. W. Briggs, and had a son, George Shelby); (d) William Polk, (married Rebecca Mays); (e) Eliza Eastin Polk; (f) Frances Ann Polk, (married (1866) Edward Dillon. Children: Edward Dillon, who married Susan S. Pendleton, and had children: Edward, Edmund P., Mary Unity, William Polk and Susan; James Royal Dillon; Lucius Polk Dillon, who married Mary Evelyn Morton, and had a child, Lucius Polk Dillon II; John Cunningham Dillon, who married May McClung Childress; Eliza Polk Dillon, who married Robert Scott Spillman, and had children: Frances Polk and Robert Scott (twins), and Edward D.;Frances Polk Dillon; Frances Cunningham Dillon); (g) Susan Rebecca Polk, (married (1866) George Campbell Brown. Children: Lucius Polk Brown, who married twice: First, Jessie Roberts; Second, Susan Katherine Massey. Child by first wife, Jesse Roberts; Second, Susan Katherine Massey. Child by first wife, Campbell Huxley Brown. Children by second wife: Susan Massey Polk, Lazinka and Lucia; Ewell Richard Brown, who married Mabel Lee; George Campbell Brown II; Percy Brown, who married Gertrude Plunket, and had a son, James Plunkett; Lazinka Campbell Brown); (h) George Washington Polk, (married (1885) Jane Jackson. Children: Kate, George, Jane and Harry;) (2) Eliza Eastin; (3) Susie Eastin; (4) Rachel Eastin, who married (1842) Richard O. Currey, M. D., and had children: Robert, and Mary who married William Whorton, and had children: Sadie, Mary, William, Richard and Annie; (5) John Donelson Eastin (1820-), who married (1848) Amanda Galloway, and had children: (a) Rosa Eastin, (married (1875) Hyder Ali Bedon, M. D. Children: Eva, (who married Frank Pittman, and had one child, Rosa), Susie, Tulia D., (married William Hunt Burress, M. D. Children, Sarah and Susan), Hyder and Richard); (b) James Eastin; (c) Mary Polk Eastin, (married (1868) William Littlefield. Children: Elizabeth, (who married Bruce Buckner, and had children: Mary, Sadie, Bruce, Elizabeth, Henry and Isabelle), John, Preston, William and Frank); (d) Susan Amanda Eastin, (married George E. Purvis. Children: Rachel (married Richard Snyder, M. D.), Mary (married G D. Andrews, and had children: George and Walter), Eastin, Susie and Emily).

NOTABLE SOUTHERN FAMILIES

7 Mary Donelson (1793-1871), married (1809) John Coffee (1772-1833). (General John Coffee took part in the Creek War and was in the Battle of New Orleans). They had children: (1) Mary Donelson Coffee (1812-1839), who married Andrew Hutchings, and had children: Mary, John Coffee, Coffee, and Andrew; (2) John Donelson Coffee (1815-1837), who married Mary Narcissa Brahan, and had one child, John Donelson Coffee II, who married Sallie Ruffin Tucker, and had children: (a) Mary Percy Coffee, (married Frederick H. Long. Child, Harry Long); (b) Sarah Donelson Coffee; (3) Elizabeth Graves Coffee; (4) Andrew Jackson Coffee (1819-1891), who married Elizabeth Hutchings, and had children: (a) Kate Coffee, (married Charles J. McDougal. Children: Katherine Coffee McDougal, who married Carpenter Gorgas, had child, Mary; Elizabeth Coffee McDougal, who married Stuart Cooper, and had children: Elizabeth, Stuart, Kate and Elizabeth Stuart; Caroline Marian McDougal, who married John Land Neilson, and had children: Caroline McDougal and Mary Charlesworth; Douglas Cassel McDougal, who married Sabina Wood Watts, and had children: Douglas and David Stockton); (b) Susan Coffee, (married Lewis C. Heilner. One child, Katherine, who married Ray Strath McDonald, and had one child, Ray Strath McDonald II); (c) Frank Larned Coffee, (married twice: First, Posey Beauregard Green; Second, Blanch Marie Elizabeth Pitard. Children by first wife: Andrew Jackson Coffee and Elizabeth Hutchings Coffee who married Robert Navarre Corbalay. Children: Carroll Douglas Marion and Robert Navarre Corbalay, and had children: Carroll Douglas Marion and Robert Navarre Corbalay II and had children: Theadore, Robert and Carroll. Children by second wife: Blanche Marie, Catherine Copley, Dorothy Pitard and Evelyn Mercedes; (d) John Coffee; (e) Andrew Jackson Coffee; (f) Mary Elizabeth Coffee; (g) Stockley Hutchings Coffee; (h) Ellen Posey Coffee; (i) Andrew Jackson Coffee, (married twice: First, Edith Hinton: Second, Ellen Lenore Muffley. Child by first wife, Luen Pope. Child by second wife, Lenore Jackson); (5) Alexander Donelson Coffee (1821-1901), who married twice: First, Ann Eliza Sloss; Second, Mrs. Camilla Madden Jones. Child by first, Mary Coffee, married twice: First, Edward Asbury O'Neal; Second, William Parke Campbell. Child by first husband, Edward, who married Julia Camper, and had children: Edward, Camper and Amelia; (6) Rachel Jackson Coffee (1823-1892), who married Alexander Jackson Dyas, and had children: Robert Dyas, and Alexander

DONALDSON

Jackson Dyas who married Annie Lamar Curry, and had children: Rachel Jackson, Hammond Curry, Alexander Jackson Dyas II and John Coffee; (7) Katherine Harriet Coffee; (8) Emily Coffee; (9) William Coffee (1830-1903), who married Virginia Malone, and had one child, Mary Donelson who married Charles Albert Nye, and had children: (a) Virginia Coffee Nye, (married ——— Irvine); (b) Anna Rogers Nye; (c) Charles Albert Nye II; (10) Josua Coffee.

9 Elizabeth Donelson (1796-) married John C. McLemore, and had children: (1) Mary McLemore (married Monroe Walker, M. D. Child: Elizabeth Walker, who married Andrew Jackson Hays, a cousin); (2) Catherine McLemore (married ——— Gholston. Child: Josephine Gholston, who married Robert Butler Hays, a cousin, and had children: Andrew, William, Joseph and Willoughby); (3) John C. McLemore II (married Sallie Lane. Had several children, one of whom is John C. McLemore III).

10 Catherine Donelson (1799-1836), married James Glasgow Martin, and had children: (1) Elizabeth Martin, who married twice. No descendants; (2) James Glasgow Martin II, (1823-1904), who married (1851) Mary Donelson, (daughter of Daniel Smith Donelson and Margaret (Branch) Donelson). They had children: (a) Margaret Branch Martin, (married twice: First, James M. Griffice; Second, Andrew Watson. Children by first husband: James H. Griffice II, who married (1907) Estelle McLaughlin, and had children: James Martin, and Branch Gordon and Violine (twins); Branch Donelson Griffice, who married Gena Sollum; David Dismukes Griffice, who married (1903) Maidie Lemuman, and had children; Ruth, David, Lawrence and Marrin; John Shute Griffice, who married (1900) Lucy Vance Harmon, and had children: John Fay and Ada; Anrew Jackson Griffice, who married (1907) Jennie Bruner; Mary E. Griffice; Hillman Griffice); (b) Daniel Donelson Martin, (married (1886) Fanny Level Spears. Children: William Lee, Mary Woodfalk, Isla Victoria and Charles Spears); (c) Katherine Martin; (d) Elizabeth Martin; (e) Nannie Greenway Martin, (married (1885) William Leslie Franklin. Children: Mary Donelson Franklin, who married (1906) William Hugh Blackwood, and had children: William Hugh Blackwood II and Mary Leslie; Lucelia Douglas Franklin, who married (1905) Joseph E. Johnson and had children: William Richard and Joseph E. Johnson

NOTABLE SOUTHERN FAMILIES

II; Emily Currey Franklin, who married (1915) Walker Pendleton; Isaac Douglas Franklin; William Leslie Franklin; Rebecca Donelson Franklin); (f) James Glasgow Martin III, (married (1898) Jane Woodruff. Children: Annie May, Mary Donelson and Jane Elizabeth); (3) Catherine Donelson Martin; (4) Mary Donelson Martin ((1818-1860), who married Robert Brownlee Currey, and had one child, Mary Elizabeth Currey, (married William Fox. Children: Mary Elizabeth, Trescott, Robert B., Lewis, Marion, Albert and Henry); (5) Emily Donelson Martin (1825-1892), who married (1846) George Washington Currey and had children: (a) Martin Currey, (married (1879) Dora Sawyers); (b) Mary Clementina Currey, (married (1870) Duncan Robertson Dorris. Children: Duncan Robertson Dorris II, who married (1899) Elizabeth Bryan, and had one child, Catherine Hardy; George Preston Dorris, who married (1899) Edith Jenkins, and had children: Emma May, George Preston Dorris II and Duncan Krenning; Lewis Randolph Dorris, who married (1905) Augusta Donelson, and had children: Margaret and Lewis Randolph Dorris II; Andrew Currey Dorris); (c) Robert Brownlee Currey, (married (1884) Elizabeth Norton. Children: Robert Brownlee Currey II, Bradley Norton, George Washington, Elizabeth (married Charles LeSueur Cornelius), Jennie Gray, Sarah Elmira and Brownlee); (d) Jennie Gray Currey; (e) Andrew Donelson Currey; (f) Kate Sumpter Currey; (g) George Ringold Currey, (married Lillie McCarthy); (h) Preston Currey; (6) Rachel Jackson Martin; (7) John Donelson Martin, who married (1857) Rosalie Adella White, and had children: (a) John Donelson Martin II, (married (1882) Mary Walker Hull. Children: John Donelson Martin III, who married (1909) Savilla Driver, and had a son, John Donelson Martin IV; Mary Clayton Martin, who married (1909) Faris R. Russell); (b) Clark White Martin; (8) Andrew Jackson Martin, who married three times: First, Elizabeth Fristoe; Second, Anna Harris; Third, (1869) Rosalie Adella Martin, nee White, the widow of his brother, John Donelson Martin. By his first wife he had children: (a) Thomas Fristoe Martin, M. D., (married Lola Long. Children: Hazel, Martina and Venoy); (b) Robert Martin; (c) Catherine Martin. Children by his third wife: (d) Mary Martin, (married (1898) William F. Frost. Children: Walker E. and William P.); (e) Andrew J. Martin; (f) Shelton White Martin; (g) Rosadella Martin, (married (1907) Heiskell Weatherford. Children: Mary and Joseph Heiskell); (9) Ann Hardy Martin.

DONALDSON

12 Stockley Donelson (1805) married (1828) Phila Ann Lawrence (1809-1852), and had children: (1) John Purnell Donelson; (2) Laura Ann Donelson (1833-1894), married W. J. Wade. Children: (a) Mary Emily Wade, (married Robert W. Thompson. Children: Laura and Mathew Neil); (b) Matilda Henderson Wade, (married Albert Hadley. Children: Albert, Wade, Caroline, Laura and Howard; (c) Caroline Wade (twin of Matilda Henderson, married David Burke Dismukes. Children: David, Susie and Stockley); (d) Stockley Donelson Wade, married Nettie Turnley. Children: Ednelia, William James, Nettie and Susie); (e) Levi Lawson Wade, (married Lizziedean Kennedy. Children: Lizziedean, Laura and Caroline); (f) Laura Medora Wade, (married John Boyd Hayes. Children: John Boyd Hayes II, Susie, Laura, and Lawrence); (g) John Lawrence Wade, (married Octavia Weaver. Child: John); (h) Susie Wade; (i) William James Wade II); (3) William Stockley Donelson (1835-1895) (married twice: First, Alice Ewin; Second Medora Wade Smith. Children: (a) Mary Elizabeth Donelson (1882-), who married Edward R. Dabney, (b) John Donelson VII (1874-), who married Bettie M. Hooper; (c) Alice E. Donelson (1876-1891); (d) Wena E. Donelson (1880-), who married Thomas Goodall; (e) Phila Ann Donelson (1887-), who married Nisbet Hambaugh); (4) Mary Emily Donelson (1837-), (married twice: First, Joseph E. Boddie; Second, William B. Walton. Child by first husband; (a) Laura Annie Boddie, (married (1880) Mora Hammond Sharpe. Children: Mary, Catherine, Mora and Laura). Children by second husband: (b) Emily Walton, (married Joseph Mann Ford. Children: Charles, William, Lewis, Lucien, Eugene, Joseph and Ida); (c) Caroline Walton (married Andrew Arthur Adams. Child, Arthur Adams); (d) Alice Walton; (e) Fannie Walton; (f) Daisy Walton, (married William Miller Dismukes. Child. John Dismukes)); (5) Lawrence Donelson (1845-65); (6) Caroline Minerva Donelson, who married Alfred Gibson Merritt, and had children: Annie Lawrence, Alfred Gibson Merritt II (married Bonida Turner), Stockley Donelson (married Maude Logue), Ida Johnson and Lawrence.

13 Emily Donelson (1807-1836) married Andrew Jackson Donelson. son of Samuel Donelson and Mary (Smith) Donelson. Children under the father, Andrew Jackson Donelson.

After the death of his wife Andrew Jackson, President-

NOTABLE SOUTHERN FAMILIES

elect appointed Major Andrew Jackson Donelson his private secretary, and invited Mrs. Donelson to officiate as Mistress of the White House.

"She was born in Davidson County, Tennessee, and educated at the old Academy, in Nashville. Of rare personal loveliness and splendid intellect, no expense or care was spared to fit her for the high position she was destined to fill in society. Though her childhood was spent in what was then called the 'backwoods', it was not passed in obscurity for her close relationship with Mrs. Andrew Jackson, the public prominence of her near relations, Generals Smith, Coffee and Hays, and the wealth and high standing of her father, early made her familiar with camps and crowds, and developed that courtly grace and ease of manner for which she was afterwards so preeminent.... Her tact and grace contributed much to render General Jackson's term such a brilliant epoch in American history". (The Ladies of the White House, Holloway).

IV Mary Donelson

IV Mary Donelson married John Caffrey. They lived in New Orleans, Louisiana, and had children: (1) Jefferson Caffrey, (2) Donelson Caffrey who married Lydia Murphey, and had one son, Donelson Caffrey II, who married (1869) Bethia Richardson, and had children: (a) Donelson Caffrey III, (married Martha Taylor. Children: Katherine, Martin, Bethia Donelson Caffrey IV. Mary Louise, Emma, St. John Liddell and John Taylor); (b) Frank Richardson Caffrey; (c) Ralph Earle Caffrey (married Letice Deenir. Children: Letice Eulalie, Frank Richardson and Earle Deenir); (d) John Murphy Caffrey, (married Mary Frere. Children: John Murphy Donelson Thomas and Mary); (e) Gertrude Caffrey, (married Henry Haywood Glassie. Children: Donelson Caffrey, Gertrude and Henry Haywood Glassie II); (f) Bethia Caffrey; (g) St. John Liddell Caffrey; (h) Charles Smith Caffrey, (married Cora Nell Hunt. Child, Cora Nell); (i) Edward Caffrey; (3) Jane Caffrey; (4) ——— Caffrey, who married ——— VanDorn, and had children: (a) Earle VanDorn, (General in Confederate Army during War Between the States); (b) Aaron VanDorn; (c) Jane VanDorn, (married ——— Vertner. Child, ——— who married M. D. Leonard;) (d) ——— VanDorn, (married ——— Lacy); (5) Nancy Caffrey, who married John Jenkins, M.

DONALDSON

D., and had children: Elizabeth Majors, Mary Donelson, John Jenkins II (had a son John Jenkins III), Nancy Rachel, Sophia VanDorn (married —— McCarrell), William Banks and Donelson Caffrey; (6) —— Caffrey (a daughter who married —— Walker, and had a son, T. C. Walker; (7) Mary Caffrey, who married John Knox, and had children: William L. Knox and Sarah Knox, who married George Washington Sevier (see Sevier Family, Notable Southern Families, Vol. I, p. 201) and had children: (a) Mary Kate Sevier, (married Robert Joseph Shields Dunbar. Children: Nannie Bell who married Charles P. Kanning, and Robert Shields Dunbar II); (b) Andrew Jackson Sevier, (married Columbia Elizabeth Dobyns. Children: Sallie Knox, Columbia Simpson (who married William H. Utz, and had one child, Merrick), Andrew Jackson Sevier II (married Mary Day, and had one child, Andrew Jackson Sevier III), Annie Champe (married Joseph Agee, and had a child, Curtis), Jennie Vertner (married T. Fred Young, and had one child, Elizabeth), Mary Kate (married W. T. Ward. Children, William Henry, Kathryn and Louise) and Ada E. (married A. C. Williamson)); (c) Jane Vertner Sevier. (married twice: First, George Clark; Second, Adolphus Watson Harris. Child by first husband, George Sevier Clark; Child by second husband, Sadie Knox Harris, who married George Henry Sager); (d) Eliza Sevier, (married William E. Jeffries. Children: Evan Shelby, Mary Dunbar, William T. Jefferies II and George Sevier.

V Jane Donelson

V Jane Donelson married (1787) Colonel Robert Hays, who was born in Scotland. On coming to America he located at Nashville, later at Haysville, Tennessee. They had children: (1) Stockley Donelson Hays (1788-1831), who married Lydia (Lyda) Butler, and had a child named Richard Jackson Hays (1822-1899), who married (1847) Sarah Ann Ballon, and had one child, Stockley Donelson Hays (1852-1905), who married (1876) Ida Gertrude Stovall, and had children: (a) Katherine Stovall Hays (1877-), (married (1898) James Ernest Edenton. One child, James Ernest Edenton II (1909)); (b) Richard Hartwell Hays; (c) Sarah Ballon Hays (1884-), (married (1903) Edwin Smithson Rogers. One child, Edwin Smithson Rogers II (1905-)); (d) Margaret Angelyn Hays, married (1911) James P. McMillin; (e) Ida Gertrude Hays (1889-), (married (1911)

NOTABLE SOUTHERN FAMILIES

Reuben H. Scott); (f) Eleanor Donelson Hays (1891-), (married (1919) Elbert S. Stegall. One child, Elbert S. Stegall II (1920-)); (g) Stockley Donelson Hays; (h) Henry Donelson Hays (1897-); (2) Martha Hays (1791-1856), who married William Butler, M. D.; (3) William Hays; (4) Samuel Jackson Hays (1800-1865), who married (1829) Frances Middleton, and had children: (a) Andrew Jackson Hays (1830-1878), (married Elizabeth Walker, a cousin. Children: Samuel Jackson Hays II; James Walker Hays (-1862), (married Minnie Bolster, and had children: James Walker Hays II, Mary, Daniel S., Frances, Mildred and George); John McLemore Hays, (married Mary Gregory, and had children: Joseph Gregory, Ida Myrtle (married James E. M. White. One child, Dorris White), John McLemore Hays II)); (b) Mary Hays; (c) James Hays; (d) Rachel Jackson Hays; (e) Elizabeth Hays; (f) Frances La Motte Hays(-1891),married twice: First, Walter Preston, no issue. Second, Lucius Battle, M. D., and had children: Walter Preston and Pickney); (g) Robert Butler Hays (1840-1909), (married Josie Gohlston. Children: Andrew William, Joseph and Willoughby); (h) John Middleton Hays (1843-), (married (1869) Sallie Parker Caruthers. Children: John Middleton Hay II. Frances Caruthers (married (1892), James Caruthers, Samuel J. (married (1904), Musidora McCorry (married (1902), Stoddert, Mary Caruthers, Florence Parker (married (1902), Elinor Virginia (-1909) and Trimble Middleton); (i) Samuel Jackson Hays; (j) Martha Hays; (k) Rebecca Hays; (l) Lydia Hays; (m) Patricia Hays; (5) Rachel Hays, who married Robert Butler; (6) Narcissa Hays; (7) Mary Hays; (8) Elizabeth Hays, who married Robert I. Chester.

VI William Donelson

VI William Donelson married (1796) Charity Dickinson, and had children: (1) Mary Donelson, (married Dr. ———— Hamblen); (2) Severn Donelson, (married Mary Sampson, and had children: George, William and Rachel); (3) Jacob Donelson (1801-), who married (1825) Agnes Sampson, and had children: (a) Martha Donelson (1826-1871), (married six times. By second husband, Thomas Patton, she had one child, William; By her fifth husband, Edward Littlebridge, she had children: Edward Littlebridge II and William Terry); (b) William Alexander Donelson (1828-1882), (married (1850) Laura Beaty. Children; David Agnes, Robert, Mary Adelaide); (c) Micajah Terryl Donelson; (d)

DONALDSON

John Coffee Donelson; (e) George Sampson Donelson; (f) Agnes Charity Donelson (1835-1875), (married Dewitt Clinton Thompson. Children: Odeneal, who married Joseph H. Bishop, and had Sarah); (g) Jacob Dickerson Donelson (1837-), (married Mary Smith; (h) Andrew Jackson Donelson; (i) James K. Polk Donelson; (j) Robert M. Burton Donelson; (4) Martha Donelson (1809-1873), who married twice: First, Robert M. Burton; Second, Paul Anderson. Children by first husband: (a) Elizabeth Charity Burton (1827-), (married Ralph Martin. Children: Robert Martha, William Burton, Sallie Walker (married J. P. Eastman, and had one child, Marion), Temple O. Harris (married Bessie Williamson, and had children: Marguerite Kirkpatrick and Temple O. Harris II). Minnie Nelson (married Judge W. A. Roane, grandson of Governor Roane, of Tennessee, and had children: Bessie Donelson, Temple, Ralph, Archibald, Ena Alice, Mary Frost, Minnie, Gladys, James and Evelyn); Martha Donelson Martin (married Henry E. Williams, and had children: Percy Warner, Henry E. Williams II, Ralph Martin, Burton Heath, Thelma Burton, William and Robert Burton), Ralph Martin, (married Alexander Wythe Whitaker, and had children; Alexander Wythe Whittaker II and Ralph)); (b) William Donelson Burton (1829-), married Minnie (or Mary) Nelson Children: John Nelson Burton, who married Daisy Wade; Sallie Burton, who married W. E. Drake; Robert Burton; William Donelson Burton;) (c) Andrew Jackson Burton (1831-1862), (married Caroline (or Fanny) Smith. One child, George Washington); (d) Robert Montgomery Caruthers Burton (1834-), (married Jennie Vogeine. Children: Beulah, Cornelia, Robert Montgomery and Nora); (5) Elizabeth Hays Donelson, who married Robert A. Burton, and had children: (a) Martha Burton; (b) Mary M. Burton, (married (1867) John M. Williams. Children: Josiah Burton Williams, who married Kittie C. Cunningham, and had children: John Maxey, Walton, Mary Burton and Josiah Burton Williams II; Robert Percy Williams, who married Mary Phillips, and had one child, Robert Percy Williams II); (c) Alfred M. Burton; (d) William Burton; (e) Emma C. Burton; (f) Ellen S. Burton (married Hugh M. McAdoo. Children: Mary Elizabeth (married F. E. Gullick. One child), Hugh, Porter (married A. Anderson), Alfred H. and Mary Burton); (6) Milberry Donelson, (married John McGregor. Children: (a) Martha McGregor, who married Temple O. Harris, no issue; (b) Mary Mc-

NOTABLE SOUTHERN FAMILIES

Gregor (1826-1904) who married Colonel Patrick Anderson, and had children: Times Anderson; Lovie Anderson; (married Carmott Cobb, and had children: Lila Cobb who married Seth Gordan, Joe Cobb, and Carmott Ashley Cobb); Berry Anderson; Paul Anderson; Edgar Poe Anderson; Donelson Anderson; Lady Anderson, (married Temple Bowling. Children: Temple Bowling and Ellie Bowling who married ——— Barnes, and had two sons); Sallie Erskine Anderson; (c) Flowers McGregor, who married Fannie Roane, no issue; (d) Donelson McGregor, who never married. He was a colonel in the Confederate Army and was killed at the Battle of Murfreesboro; (e) Andrew McGregor, who served in the Confederate Army as Captain of the Fourth Tennessee Cavalry, married Eudora Anderson, and had children: John McGregor; Horde McGregor who married D. A. McKnight, and had one child, Paul; Andrew McGregor; Paul Britton McGregor; Leonard McGregor who married Edward A. Barbour and had children: McGregor, Edward and Mary Ellis; Temple Harris McGregor who married Nellie Herndon, and had children: Douglass McGregor, and Marietta; Eudora McGregor; Graeme McGregor who married Rutledge Smith and had children: Albert Perrine, McGregor and Dollie; Sallie Ashe McGregor, Frank Monroe McGregor and Dewitt McGregor, M. D.; (f) Milberry McGregor, (married ——— McKissack, and had a daughter, Mollie); (8) Andrew Jackson Donelson (1815-), who married twice: First, ——— Nelson; Second, ——— Nelson. He had children: (a) Catherine Donelson, (married ——— Ellis); (b) Alice Donelson, (married ——— McFadden); (c) Louisa Donelson, (married ——— Crichlow. Children: James and a daughter who married Jake Boyles); (d) William Donelson; (e) John Donelson; (f) Andrew Donelson, (married Mrs. Robert Burton. Children: Andrew Jackson Donelson II, and a daughter who married ——— Crutchert, and had a son, Andrew J. Donelson); (g) Elizabeth Donelson, married ——— Lewen); (h) Mamie Donelson, (married ——— Breau. One child, Allie); (i) Sallie Donelson; (9) Rachel Donelson; (10) Alexander S. Donelson; (11) William Donelson II.

VII Stockley Donelson

VII Stockley Donelson married Elizabeth Martin, nee Glasgow, widow of John Martin. No issue.

DONALDSON

VIII Samuel Donelson

VIII Samuel Donelson (-1802) married (1797) Mary (or Polly) Smith, and had children:
1. Andrew Jackson Donelson,
2. Daniel Smith Donelson,
3. John Donelson, died young.

1 Andrew Jackson Donelson (1799-1871) married twice: First, Emily Donelson, daughter of John Donelson and Mary (Purnell) Donelson; Second, Elizabeth Anderson Randolph nee Martin, (daughter of James Glasgow Martin and Katherine (Donelson) Martin), a niece of his first wife.

Andrew Donelson graduated at the U. S. Military Academy. While Second Lieutenant, Engineers, he served as Aid-de-Camp to General Andrew Jackson, while the latter was Territorial Governor of Florida ((1821-1823). "On Jackson's election to the Presidency he became his confidential adviser and private secretary, continuing in that capacity until the close of his second administration. He was Minister to the Republic of Texas in 1845. In 1846 he was appointed Minister to Prussia, and, in 1848, to the Federal Government of Germany, which office he resigned in 1849. In 1856 he abandoned the Democrats and joined the American party, receiving the nomination of Vice-president on the ticket with Millard Fillmore". (Cyclopedia of American Biography, Appleton).

(1) Andrew Jackson Donelson; (2) Mary Emily Donelson (first child born in the White House) (born in 1829, and died 1905), married (1852) John Alexander Wilcox (was a member of the Confederate Congress). They had children: (a) Andrew Donelson Wilcox, (married Ida R. Seymour. Children: Cadmus Marcellus and Pauline Seymour); (b) Mary Rachel Wilcox; (3) John Samuel Donelson; (4) Rachel Jackson Donelson; Children by second wife: Daniel S. Donelson; Andrew Jackson Donelson by his second wife, Elizabeth Anderson Randolph, had no children; (5) Daniel Smith Donelson II; (6) Martin Donelson (1846-1889) (was born in Berlin, Germany. He married Eliza Glenn, (-1888) and had children: (a) Glenn Donelson, who married Louise Ginon, and had one child, Louise; (b) Martin Donelson, who was a sergeant in the U. S. Navy); William A. Donelson (1848-1901) (was born at Frankfort-on-the-Main, Germany. He married Bettie Mizell, and had one child, William A. Donelson II); (8) Vinet Donelson (1854-1913) (married Mary Brown, daughter of Gov. Neil S.

Brown, of Tennessee); (9) Katrene Donelson (died young); (10) Lewis Randolph Donelson (1856-) (married (1880) Louisa DeSaules McAllister (1856-) (see Rhea family). Children: (a) Lewis Randolph Donelson II,(1881) who married Katherine Campbell, and had children: Lewis Randolph Donelson III and William Campbell Donelson; (b) Elsie Donelson (1883-) who married Donald White McKeller, and had children: Lady Carolyn, Elsie and Marion Crawford); (11) Rose Donelson (died in infancy); (12) Andrew Jackson Donelson III (1861-1914) (married Sallie Taylor, and had children: (a) Harry Donelson; (b) Andrew Jackson Donelson IV, who married Nancy Busby; (c) Frank Donelson; (d) Helen Donelson, who married ——— Powell; (e) Anna Donelson; (f) Eliza Donelson).

2 Daniel Smith Donelson, married Margaret Branch, (daughter of John Branch, who was Governor of North Carolina, Secretary of the Navy, and twice Governor of Florida). They had children: (1) Elizabeth Branch Donelson (1831-), who married (1849) William Williams, and had children: (a) Margaret Branch Williams, (married (1871) Walter Scott Davis. Children: William Henry and Bessie) ; (b) Mary Elizabeth Williams; (c) Evander McIver Williams, (married Lizzie Bates. Children: William Bates and Elizabeth); (d) Sallie Phillips Williams, (married Nicholas Love. Children: William McIver and Donelson); (e) William Henry Williams; (f) Emma Horton Williams, (married William Louis Dismukes); (g) Eula Ramsey Williams, (married Robert Vaughn. Children: Bessie Donelson and Emma Baxter); (2) Mary Ann Donelson (1834-), who married (1851) James Glasgow Martin II. (The children are given under the father); (3) Sarah Smith Donelson (1836-1869), who married (1856) William Henry Bradford, and had children: (a) Nannie Bradford, (married William Phelps. Children. Sarah Bradford, Robert and Bradford); (b) Emily Bradford; (4) Emily Donelson (1838-), who married (1860) James E. Horton, and had children: (a) Daniel D. Horton; (b) Lucy Horton; (c) Margaret Donelson Horton, (married twice: First, John Tanner; Second, McA Lewis. Children by second husband: James Edward, and William G.); (d) Sarah B. Horton; (e) Mary Rebecca Horton;(f)Emily Donelson Horton, (married (1894) Thomas McClelland. One child, Robert); (g) Jessie Donelson Horton, (married (1900) Jack Wright Frost. One child, Jack Wright Frost II); (h) James Edwin Horton; (5) Rebecca Williams Donelson; (6) James Branch Donelson

DONALDSON

(1843-1912), who married (1867) Josephine Evans, and had children: (a) Daniel Smith Donelson; (b) John Evans Donelson, (married twice: First, Katie Lee Cole; Second, Helen Eichelberg. Child by first wife, John Lee); (c) Susan Hopkins Donelson; (d) Augusta Frances Donelson, (married (1906) Lewis Randolph Dorris. Children: Margaret Dorris and Lewis Randolph Dorris II); (e) Margaret Branch Donelson; (f) James Branch Donelson III; (g) Emily Hillman Donelson, (married Albert Edward Whalley. One child, Albert Edward Whalley II); (7) Samuel Davis Donelson; (8) Martha Bradford Donelson, (1847-1893), who married (1867) John M. Shute, and had children: (a) Margaret Lee Shute, (married Gilbert G. Bradbury. Children: Gilbert, Robert Clark and Ruth); (b) Mary Donelson Shute, (married Henry Smith Dunn. Children: Louise Hamilton Dunn, who married Woodford Hall Dunn, and had children: Mary Louise and a son; Harry Smith Dunn); (c) John Branch Shute, (married Lizzie Dunn. Children: Mary, Elizabeth Branch and John Donelson); (d) Martha Bradford Shute, (married Edward Dunn. Children: John Donelson, Edward, Martha Donelson, Margaret Lee and William); (9) Susan Branch Donelson (1848-1871), who married (1866) Marcus L. Dismukes, and had children: Daniel Donelson, James D., and Marcus L. Dismukes II; (10) John Branch Donelson, who married Jennie Alexander; (11) Daniel Smith Donelson II (1853-1914), who married (1890) Florence Hood, and had children: Margaret Susan Donelson, and Samuel Donelson who married (1913) Florence Diehl.

IX Severn Donelson

IX Severn Donelson was born in Virginia, in 1773, and died October 1818. He married Elizabeth Rucker, who was born June 8, 1782, and died March 31, 1828. They had children:

1 John Donelson II
2 Samuel Donelson
3 Andrew Donelson, later Andrew Jackson
4 Thomas Jefferson
5 Alexander Donelson
6 Rachel Donelson
7 Lucinda Rucker Donelson

1 John Donelson II (1807-1879), married twice: First, (1833) Laura Matilda Lawrence (1815-1844); Second, (1849) Delia Catherine Waters (1824-). Children: by first

wife: (1) Caroline Minerva Donelson (1834-1895), who married (1856) Alexander Whyte Whitaker, and had children: (a) Laura Maude Whitaker, (married J. William Berry); (b) William Henry Whitaker, (married (1887) Eva Hall. Child, William Whyte); (c) Alexander Whyte Whitaker II, (married (1890) Ralph Martin. Children: Alexander Whyte Whitaker III, and Ralph Martin Donelson); (d) Leven Donelson Whitaker, (married Mrs. Bettie Jackson; (e) George Campbell Whitaker; (2) Leven Donelson; (3) Benjamin Risley Donelson; (4) Elizabeth Ann Donelson. Children by second wife: (5) Laura Elma Donelson (1849-1903), who married (1868) James Hudson, and had children: (a) Virginia Grace Hudson, (married H. P. Pearson. Children: Edna Grace, Wilber Preston, Benjamin Donelson, Sarah Elma, Macaja Lyle, Henry Lawrence and Chester Alan); (b) Donelson Hudson, (married Agatha Jones. Child, Andrew Jackson); (c) Lena Rembert Hudson; (d) Marion Emmett Hudson, (married Rella Shire. Children: Marion Douglas, Marjorie and Ruth Elma); (e) Delia Waters Hudson, (married Shelly Blackwood. Children: Jessie Lee (married Henry W. Jett), Nellie D., Mollie Ida, James Hudson, Risley, Nona Catherine, Louise Florence and Mary Corinne); (f) Risley Zenonia Hudson; (g) Benjamin Wallace Hudson; (h) James Rembert Hudson, married Eva Clark); (i) Charles Talbot Hudson, (married Carrie Brown. Children: Rembert Carlisle, Charles Talbot Hudson II, James Davidson and Marion Brown); (j) Elma Donelson Hudson, (married T. B. Shoemaker. Children: Crystal Wannita and James Rembert); (6) Delia Corinne Donelson; (7) William Severn Donelson; (8) Daniel Smith Donelson; (9) Rachel Donelson; (10) Mary Waters Donelson, who married twice: First, E. B. Kelly; Second, William Wood.

2 Samuel Donelson (1810-), married twice: First Elizabeth Eastin; Second, Jane Royster. Children by first wife: John, Samuel and Alexander. Child by second wife: Linnie Donelson, who married —— Crews, and had one child, Linnie.

3 Andrew Donelson (Andrew Donelson and Thomas Jefferson Donelson were twins, born December 4, 1804). His aunt, Rachel (Donelson) Jackson took Andrew, when he was a few days old, to her home, the Hermitage, for the purpose of relieving his mother. After a few days she and General Jackson requested that the child be given to them. This request being granted General Jackson went before

DONALDSON

the Legislature and formally adopted the child, changing his name to Andrew Jackson, Jr. (For his family see under his adopted mother, Rachel (Donelson) Jackson).

4 Thomas Donelson (twin of Andrew Donelson, later Andrew Jackson. Born December 4, 1804), married Emma Farquar. They had children: (1) Fannie Donelson, who married ——— Gatzy; (2) Eliza Yorke Donelson, who married Bernard Adolphus Hoopes, and had one child, Elizabeth Yorke, who married Josiah Bedon II.

5 Alexander Donelson (1816-1887), married (1841) Kate Royster, and had children: (1) Helen Donelson, who married (1866) William McLean, and had children: Donelson, Helen, Katie and Durell; (2) Richard Donelson, who married (1874) Fannie Bragg, and had children: (a) Mary Donelson; (b) Richard Sampson Donelson, (married Mary Armistead. Children: Elizabeth Armistead, Richard Sampson Donelson II, and Fannie Rosalie); (c) Alexander Donelson; (d) Armistead Donelson; (e) Kate Donelson; (3) Alexander Donelson; (4) Sarah Jackson Donelson, who married Winchester Lake, and had one child, Henry, who married Nettie Wilson.

7 Lucinda Rucker Donelson (1812-), married (1830) George W. Martin. They had children: (1) Jackson Martin, who married Mary Barr Warfield, and had children: Marie Griffith, George Washington (married Olive Graves Ellis), Harriet Elizabeth (married Charles Meadowcroft), and William Pollock; (2) George Martin; (3) Elizabeth Donelson Martin, who married Jacob Melchoir Hoffa, and had children: (a) Stella McKnight Hoffa, (married Richard Pinkney Lake. Children: Richard Henry, Estelle Hoffa, Elizabeth Donelson (married Lee Dameron Jones. Children: Elizabeth Donelson and Lee Dameron Jones II), Robert Pinkney Lake II, Edith Read, Adele Dorothy, Donelson Martin, Alice Maury and Charles Hoffa); (b) George W. Hoffa; (c) May Hoffa, (married (1888) George Read. Children: Mary, George Reed II and Philip Courtney; (d) Charles Bell Hoffa; (e) William Brand Hoffa, (married Velma Cloud. Children: Louisa, Elizabeth Martin and William Brand Hoffa II); (f) Adele Donelson Hoffa; (g) Henry Hoffa.

XI Rachel Donelson

XI Rachel Donelson was born in Virginia, in 1777, and died at the Hermitage, near Nashville, Tennessee, Dec. 22, 1828. She married twice: First Capt. Lewis Robards, of Kentucky. Second Gen. Andrew Jackson. She had no children but she and Gen. Jackson adopted Andrew, a son of Severn Donelson, (q.v.).

Rachel Donelson's first marriage proved a most unfortunate alliance and, after her friendship and marriage to Gen. Andrew Jackson, was used as an excuse for the vent of fierce party spirit for, in those days, political animosity respected neither sex nor the most sacred relationships of life. Holloway, in Ladies of the White House, says, "The cruel misrepresentations of her husband's political opponents had crushed her heart, and ended her days before he took possession of the home of the Presidents. She was denied the gratification of accompanying him to Washington. and of gracing the White House, but she was, even in death, the President's wife, and as such is ranked". Continuing, she gives a full and just history of the important events in this woman's life, and shows her to have been of noble character and superior sense, beloved by all who came in contact with her, and the adored wife of a distinguished husband whose honors and responsibilities she shared. It was for her that Gen. Jackson built the Hermitage.

Dying, as before said, a few weeks after her husband's election to the Presidency, she was denied the privilege of sharing the honors of that position with him, but it was her niece whom he selected as the presiding Mistress of the White House, and it was her nephew whom he had previously adopted as his son and heir. giving to him his name, Andrew Jackson, (born the son of Severn-Donelson and Elizabeth (Rucker) Donelson.)

Andrew Jackson II married (1831) Sarah Yorke (daughter of Peter Yorke, of Philadelphia, whose grandfather, Judge Yorke, held an appointment under the crown of Great Britain, prior to the Revolution). Marrying soon after the inauguration of President Jackson, Mrs. Jackson Jr. made her entree to the White House as a bride. "To settle a question of precedence between Mrs. Jackson. Jr. and Mrs. Donelson, who were both inmates of the President's house, he said to Mrs. Jackson, 'you, my dear, are Mistress of the Hermitage, and Emily is Hostess of the White House.' Both were satisfied with this decision"). (Ladies of the White House, Holloway).

After the retirement of President Jackson to private life she assumed the arduous duties of the Mistress of the Hermitage, where she lived until her death at an advanced age.

DONALDSON

Children of Andrew Jackson II and Sarah (Yorke) Jackson: (1) Rachel Jackson (1832-)), who married (1853) John Marshall Lawrence, the official custodian of the Andrew Jackson Historical Home, The Hermitage), and had children:(a)Sarah Yorke Lawrence, married Charles Winn, M. D. Child, Lawrence, who married Minnie Henderson and had a child, Marion); (b) Annie Lawrence (married Joshua Smith. Children: William Walton and Rachel Jackson); (c) Andrew Jackson Lawrence, (married twice: First, Emma George; Second, Julia Millican. Children by first wife: Andrew Jackson Lawrence II (married Sarah Schell) and Marie Lawrence. Children by second wife: Mary Louise, James Walton and Edward Montgomery); (d) Carrie Lawrence, (married William D. Bradfield, a minister. Children: Florence, Landon, James Lee and John Lawrence); (e) Samuel Jackson Lawrence, (married Maude V. Johnson. Children: Samuel Jackson Lawrence II, Maude Wanda, John Marshall and Clifton Hyde); (f) John Marshall Lawrence; (g) Marion York Lawrence, (married John Cleaves Symmes II, Sue Rae, and Marion Yorke); (h) William Walton Lawrence, (married Mary Fisher. Child, Edith Eudora); (i) Thomas Jefferson Lawrence; (2) Andrew Jackson III (1834-), (served in the War Between the States as Colonel in the Confederate Army). He married Amy Rich (1920), of Ohio, and had children: (a) Andrew Jackson IV, (married Marion Caulkins. One child, Amy Lee); (b) Albert Marble; (3) Samuel Jackson; (4) Thomas Jefferson Jackson; (5) Robert Jackson.

Andrew Donaldson

Andrew Donaldson is said to have been born in Virginia and moved to middle Tennessee where he resided until his death, in 1870. He was a descendant of Colonel John Donelson, said to be a grandson. He married Isabella Luckey, of middle Tennessee. After his death his widow and her sons moved to Coryelle County, Texas. They had children: (1) John Marshall Donaldson (married Harriet ———, and had children: Andrew and Isabella;) (2) Jasper Donaldson (never married); (3) Harriett Donaldson (married Arthur Williams, no issue); (4) Mary Donaldson (1826-1902), (married, in Tennessee, Masterson Coleman McCormick Abernathy, and moved to Texas. Children (a) John Sterling Abernathy (1848-), who married Rosa Beckham, no issue; (b) Charles Edgar Abernathy(1850-), who married Benjamin Smith; Pink

NOTABLE SOUTHERN FAMILIES

Abernathy who married Amanda Bell; Isabella Abernathy who married John Reese; Etta Abernathy who married Mike Laxton; Susan Abernathy; Luther Abernathy; (c) Frances Aline Abernathy (1852-), who married George Riser, and had one child, Gem Riser who married John Petty; (d) Mary Florence Abernathy (1854-), who married June L. Cogdelle, and had children: Lena Cogdelle who married Lucien Suttle; Bertha Cogdelle who married James Atkins, and had children, Florence, Tad, Guy, Bertha and Rhea; Lillian Cogdelle who married William Erskin; Marvin Cogdelle who married Olga ———; Wyatt Cogdelle who married Mary Alexander; Starley Cogdelle who married Alma Bounds; Beulah Cogdelle who married Samuel Scott; Ella Cogdelle who married Eugene Acock; Catherine Cogdelle who married Stuart Odelle; Dougless Cogdelle; (e) Orpha Dorin Abernathy (1856-), who married Frederick Stith Jackson, and had children: Walker G. Jackson, who married Elizabeth Stroud; Mary Pearl Jackson; John Gillman Jackson, who married Rue Bertha Roberts; Zulette Jackson who married Duwaine Hughes, and had children: Loring, Jackson, Katherine, and Frances; (f) Isabella Andella Abernathy (1858-), who married Peter S. Kauffman, and had children: Mary Lawrence Kauffman; Philip Sterling Kauffman, who married Margaret Mabel Harper; Ethel Rhea Kauffman, who married Bell Stephen Huey, and had children: John Peter and Phillip; (g) Lora Isabella Abernathy (1860-), who married John Adolphus Rhea, and had children: John Rhea, Mary Rhea and William Rhea (1882-1904) who married Daisy Hasson. (see Rhea famiy); (h) Masterson Coleman McCormick Abernathy II (1862-), who married Winnie Pool and had children: Mary, Joseph, Martha, Gertrude, Marvin, Wendell, Irene and Lora; (i) Zulette Abernathy, died young; (j) Martha Elizabeth Abernathy, died young; (k) Isaac Luckey Abernathy (1868-), who married Minnie Stuck, and had children: Gladys and Gertrude); (5) Martha Donaldson (married Arthur Williams and had one child: Alice); (6) Elizabeth Donaldson (married John Gabbert and had one child: Elizabeth); (7) John Donaldson (married Frances Harper, and had children: Abigail, Andrew, John and Mary).

II WILLIAM DONALDSON

II William Donaldson was born April 25, 1738, in Virginia, and died March 19, 1819. He was the son of John Donaldson and Catherine (Davies) Donaldson, who was

DONALDSON

married near Philadelphia, Pennsylvania, to Mary Sweeney (1748-1839). They moved, about 1766, to the Holston Country, then a part of North Carolina, now Tennessee, and located on a farm where their children were born.

"William Donaldson enlisted as a private in Colonel Wood's Company of Eighth Virginia Regiment of Foot, Revolutionary War. He was enlisted, March 6, 1777, to serve three years and his name last appears on the roll of the company, dated Morristown, Tennessee, December 9, 1779. (War Dept. and Pension office Record).

Listed in Virginia Militia in the Revolution, by J. T. McAllister, as "Ensign, June 22, 1778, William Donaldson".

William Donaldson and Mary (Sweeney) Donaldson had children:
I Elizabeth Donaldson,
II Andrew Donaldson,
III Mary Donaldson,
IV Ann Donaldson,
V John Donaldson,
VI Rebecca Donaldson,
VII Jane Donaldson

I Elizabeth Donaldson

I Elizabeth Donaldson (1767-1847) married (about 1784) Joseph Rodgers (-1833). She moved to the Holston Country, where they married. They went at once to Knox County, Tennessee, at that time a part of North Carolina, and located on Big Sinking Creek, three miles from Campbell's Station. Their home was surrounded by a vast forest. Joseph Rodgers was a soldier in the Revolutionary War, was in the Battle of Cowpens and served as Wagonmaster in the War of 1812. He was stationed at Mobile during the Battle of New Orleans. His wife is said to have been a beautiful woman of commanding personality. They had children:
1 James Rodgers, married (1815) Elizabeth Bond, moved to Texas (1850).
2 William Rodgers.
3 Joseph Rodgers, married Adaline Scott of Virginia.
4 Thomas Rodgers, married Parthena Clark, moved to Texas (1850).
5 Mary Rodgers,
6 Elizabeth Rodgers, married Jacob Lowe,
7 Sarah Rodgers, married James Erwin,
8 Rebecca Rodgers, married Martin Lowe,

NOTABLE SOUTHERN FAMILIES

9   Margaret Rodgers, married Stephen Lowe.

2   William Rodgers was born February 13, 1794, and died January 29, 1866, at Concord, Tennessee. He married, March 30, 1816, Mahala Lowe (1798-1873) (a daughter of Abram Lowe and Mary (Martin) Lowe, and a sister of Martin and Stephen Lowe who married Rebecca and Margaret Rodgers). She was born at Lov 's Ferry (Campbell's Station) on the Tennessee River, in Knox County, in the ancestral home of the Lowes. This home was located on a highway and became noted for its generous hospitality as they welcomed travelers of all degrees. One, by the name of Farragut, coming down the River, with his family, stopped at this farmstead to avoid traveling by flatboat, in winter, and remained several months. Abram Lowe gave them the use of a log cabin and his wife assisted in providing a layette for the little baby who was born to the travelers while there. This baby became Admiral Farragut. In 1900 The Daughters of the Revolution erected a monument to Admiral Farragut on the spot that was formally the sight of the old Lowe home. Among the many distinguished guests of this home, in those early days, was the eminent English philanthropist and minister, William Forester, who sickened and died while there cared for by his host, General Samuel D. W. Lowe, a son of Abram Lowe.

William Rodgers was a man of large means, benevolent, and a leader in his community. He was progressive and did much to introduce fine stock into his section. He brought the first iron plow into east Tennessee (about 1825). He made several trips to Kentucky, by barges, down the rivers carrying stock and grain for sale, and returning overland—a perilous journey at that time. He served in Major Child's Brigade, under General Jackson, in the War of 1812. Enlisted as a private, promoted to lieutenant, was in Mobile during the Battle of New Orleans.

William Rodgers and Mahala (Lowe) Rodgers had children:
(1)   James Martin Rodgers,
(2)   Joseph Nelson Rodgers,
(3)   Abram Wiley Rodgers,
(4)   George Donnel Rodgers,
(5)   Semira Ann Amanda Rodgers
(6)   Samuel Andrew Rodgers,
(7)   William Donaldson Rodger

(1) James Martin Rodgers (1818-1901) married twice: lrst, Martha Gourley, no issue, second (1846) Malvina

DONALDSON

Galbraith (1828-1904). He with his brothers, Joseph, Wiley and George, traveled from St. Louis, in 1853, across the plains, by wagon. He moved to Watsonville, California, (1865), with his family and remained there until his death. He had children: (a) Arthur Rodgers (1848-1903), (married (1895) Mrs. Elizabeth Montgomery, and had one child: Millie Lucile Rodgers (1896-), who married (1921) Frank J. Jones. Arthur Rodgers was an eminent lawyer of San Francisco and was a member of the Board of Regents of the University of California); (b) Lee Omar Rodgers, M. D., (1851-), (married (1873) Emma Jones, and had one child: Walter Rodgers (1876-), who married Julia Burt, and had one child, Lee Walter Rodgers (1918-). Lee Omar Rodgers was a practicing physician in SanFrancisco until he retired, in 1904 to Palo Alto); (c) Mary Rodgers (1853-), (married (1881) Horace Cowles. Children: Florence Bell Cowles (1883-), who married (1905) George Webb, and had children: Arthur (1906-), Mildred (1908-), Earl (1911-), Gordon (1913-), and Evelyn (1915-); Herbert James Cowles (1885-), who married (1906, Edna Mann, and had children: George (1908-), Eloise (1909-), and Hazel (1911-); Lillie May Cowles (1888-); Ethel Malvina Cowles (1891-), who married (1918) Frederick Hudson, and had one child, Frederick Rodgers Hudson (1919-); Gertrude Emily Cowles (1894-), who married (1921) Harlow Brenner Ford); (d) Luther Rodgers (1856-); (e) Charles H. Rodgers (1858-1912), (married (1890) Josephine Jacobsen. Children: Carrol James (1894-), Harold Marion (1895-), Florence Malvina (1897-), and Margaret Amelia (1899-i); (f) Maggie Rodgers (1860-), (married Lee Shideler, no issue); (g) Julia Rodgers, (died young); (h) Elizabeth Rodgers (1866-), (married (1892) Fred Nohrden. Children: Elmer (1894-), Chester (1898-), and Olive Elizabeth (1902-)); (i) Alice Rodgers (1871-), (married (1895) John S. Brown. Children: Kenneth (1905-), and Dorris (1908-)).

(2) Joseph Nelson Rodgers (1819-1887), married Mary Ann Rankin (1825-1910), and had children: (a) Laura Ann Rodgers (1846-1917), (married Samuel Pride Brown. Children: Lena D. Brown (1862-), who married William A. Doughty, and had one child: Fred who married Adra Smith and had children: Fred Doughty II and Billie; Victor Brown; Mary E. Brown (1865-), who married (1909) Robert Longbottom; Spencer C. Brown (1867-), who married Sallie Bell Preston; Luther L. Brown (1870-), who married Nellie Palmer; Nell Brown (1872-), who married J. G. Young; Minnie Lee Brown (1875-), who married

NOTABLE SOUTHERN FAMILIES

William G. West; Frances May Brown (1877-), who married George E. Knox; Stella Fay Brown (1880-), who married Charles Ray Calloway; Dora Reid Brown (1884-), who married Hal Doggett; Joe Rodgers Brown (1887-); (b) Ellen Jane Rodgers (1850-), (married twice: First (1868) J. M. Smith; Second, (1884) Benjamin Longbottom. Children by first husband: Spencer C. Smith (1869-), who married ———, and had children: Alfratta, Frank, Ellen Clifford, Bessie, Annie and J. D.; Ida May Smith (1875-), who married David Nelson Fox; Annie Laura Smith (1877-). Children by her second husband: Lassie Ellen Longbottom (1885-), who married William David Peters; Bessie Lee Longbottom (1890-), who married Joseph Melvin Porter, and had one child, Mildred Virginia (1916-); Edgar B. Longbottom (1887-1920)); (c) Tennessee Rodgers (1852-), (married (1868) Henry C. Anderson. Children: Joseph W. Anderson (1871-), who married Frances Chamness, and had children: Carl (1907-), Mildred (1909-), and Joseph Willis (1914-); Cora Pearl Anderson (1875-), who married John F. Hinton, and had children: Thelma (1902-), Iva (1904-), Helen (1911-), Harry (1918-), and John F. Hinton II (1909-); Daisy Anderson (1878-), who married Charles David Hughes, and had children: Ralph (1900-) and Mary Louise (1910-); Jennie Grace Anderson (1879-), who married Charles Bell; Ophelia Rankin Anderson, who married Robert Taylor Gammon, and had children: Mary Eleanor (1909-), Robert Taylor Gammon II (1911-), and Virginia (1920); Omar Rodgers Anderson); (d) Spencer Clay Rodgers, M. D. (1848-), (married (1874) Cordelia Virginia Haun (1853-1920). He moved from Tennessee (1890) to Watsonville, California, where he attained eminence as a physician and progressive citizen. They had children: Frank Rodgers (1876-), who married (1905) Mabel Grimer, and had children: Kathryn (1907-) and Arthur (1909-); Clara Rodgers (1879-), who married (1903) Frank Silliman, and had children: George (1905-), twins—Floyd and Frances (1908-), and Mildred (1910-); Floyd Rodgers (1884-), who married Alma Yale; Grace Rodgers (1887-), who is teaching in a school for soldiers in Manilla, P. I. (1921); Iva Rodgers (1901-); (e) Alice Belle Rodgers (1859-), (married John W. Alexander. Children: Lena, Lucy, Cora Jane, Austin, Floyd Rodgers, Ann and Irene); (f) Samuel Arthur Rodgers (1862-), (married Elizabeth Wells, no issue); (g) Elizabeth Malvina Rodgers (1866-1898), (married (1884) Albert Addison Woods. Children: Roy

DONALDSON

Woods (1886-); Mabel Woods (1888-), who married Fred Hobbs, and had children: James, Raymond and Clara; Alma Woods (1895-), who married Robert Singleton, and had children: Mabel, Helen and Nelly; Lida Elizabeth Woods (1893-), who married Calvin Davenport, and had children: Harry and Wilma; (h) Rufus Donald Rodgers (1870-), (married (1894) 'Lida Potts, and had one child; Elizabeth Rodgers (1896-), who married Lewis Stanley Adcock, and had children: Josephine (1917-), and Jack (1918-)).

(3) Abram Wiley Rodgers (1823-1883), married twice: First, Mary Ellen Wallace (1830-1867); Second, Mrs. Isabella Scruggs, nee Saffel, a niece of his first wife. Abram Wiley Rodgers while in the shipping business died at Mazatlan while on a trip to Mexico. His widow was a beautiful cultured woman of fine sense and character, capable of assuming the responsibilities of rearing her large family, which she did with success. Children by first wife: (a) Charles Craig Rodgers, died young; (b) Lucy Bell Rodgers (1858-1908), (married (1881) William Abraham Stingley. Children: Raymond, Sarah (1888-) and Leroy (1891-), who married Julia ——— and had one child, Maud Leone (1913-); (c) William Rodgers; (d) Mary Amanda Rodgers (1862-), (married Otto Damcke. Children: Emily and Rodgers); (e) Sarah Tennessee Rodgers (1864-), (married Daniel S. Stewart. Children: Evelyn, Marie, Daniel and Mildred); Children by second wife: (f) George Rodgers; (g) Frank Rodgers (-1905), (died in China. He married and had one child); (h) Viola Rodgers (who distinguished herself in newspaper work); (i) Rosa Rodgers, (died young); (j) Harry Rodgers (-1914), (married and had one or more children).

(4) George Donnel Rodgers (1825-1894) married Julia Lenoir Browder (1834-1907). They were born and married in Tennessee, and moved to Watsonville, California. They had children: (a) Henry Browder Rodgers (1873-), (married (1908) Anna Bieth); (b) George Floyd Rodgers (1875-), (married (1904) Helen Smith; (c) Blanche Lenoir Rodgers (1879-), married (1899) Edward Wilkinson. Had one child: Catherine (1900-); (d) Minnie Arthur Rodgers (1880-).

(5) Samira Ann Amanda Rodgers (1827-1904) married (1846) Samuel Love Russell (1822-1903), and had children: (a) Alice Donnel Russell (1847-), (A woman of rare character who devoted the chief efforts of her life to the advancement of education); (b) William P. Russell (1849-

NOTABLE SOUTHERN FAMILIES

1920), (married (1874) Fannie R. Wheeler (1849-). Children: Bessie Rodgers Russell (1876-); Mary A. Russell (1877-); Lucy Norvell Russell (1879-), who married (1904) William Elbert Andrews, and had children: Frances Adelene (1905-), Dorothy Alice (1906-), Marjory Norvell (1908-), William Elbert Andrews II (1909-), Thomas Russell (died young), and Robert Andrews (1918-); Bertie Virginia Russell (1881-); Annie Wheeler Russell (1883-), who married (1913) Will Tucker Banks, and had one child, Anne Russell (1914-); Willie Frances Russell (1886-), who married (1913) Frank Elliott Barnard, and had one child: Frank Elliott Barnard II (1914-)); (c) Robert Wiley Russell (1852-), (married (1885) Rena Gertrude Scott ((1859-). Children: Roberta Gertrude Russell (1885-), who married (1918) Walter Franklin Heycock; Wiley Scott Russell (1888-)); (d) Ann Eliza Russell (1857-), (married (1878-), Finis Ewing Galbraith (1854-). Children: Zella Mae Galbraith (1880-), who married (1904) Herbert Collie Talley (1879-), and had chidren: Cawl Dean (1905-), Herbert Russell (1907-), and Margaret Moren (1910-), Adah Ewing Galbraith (1883-), S. L. Russell Galbraith (1886-), who married (1913) Sadie Garber (1889-), and had children: James Garber (1914-), Winifred (1916-) and Mary (1919-)); (e) Lizzie Love Russell (1859-), (never married); (f) Samuel Andrew Russell (1861-), (married twice: First, (1889) Hattie Dobbins (1868-1903); Second, (1905) Mary Leola Adair (1883-). Children by first wife: Samuel Andrew Russell II (1890-), who married (1913) Nettie O'Brien (1891-), and had children: Mary Louise (1914-) and Samuel (1916-); Eleanor Ruth Russell (1891-), who married (1916) James Courtney, of Atlanta, Georgia, and had one child, Harriet Agnes (1917-); James Donnell Russell (1893-); Julia Bell Russell (1896-), who married (1918) Herndon Clements Aderhold, and had one child, Herndon Clements Aderhold II (1920-); twins—Annie Rodgers and Margaret Russell (died young); Frank E. Russell (1899-); Hattie D. Russell (1902-). Children by second wife: George Spencer Russell (1906-); Lillian Adair Russell (1909-); Robin Adair Russell (1919-)); (g) Mary Rodgers Russell (1864-), (married (1890) Bratley Russell McBath (1855-). Children: Mary Lucile McBath (1891-), who married (1913-) William Henry Eagle (1887-), and had one child; Hazel McBath (1895-); Bratley Russell McBath II (1901-); Helen Virginia McBath (1904-); (h) Jane Amanda Russell (1867-), (never married); (i) George Donnel Russell (1871-), (married (1894) Kate Watt (1873-). Children: Allie D.

DONALDSON

Russell (1895-), who married (1914) Rollin C. Nichols (1894-), and had one child, Catheryne Teresa (1915-); James M. Russell (1898-); Kathleen Russell (1902-); George Donnell Russell II (1904-); Robert Russell (1906-); Edward Earle Russell (1915).

6 Samuel Andrew Rodgers (1830-1902) married (1863) Sarah Elizabeth Rhea (1843-1893). (see Rhea family). Samuel Andrew Rodgers was born in Knox County, Tennessee. When twenty one years old he went to California in the wake of the "Forty-niners". He graduated from Cumberland University in 1856, and from its Law department in 1858. Practised Law in Knoxville until the courts were closed by the war. In 1878 he was elected, from Loudon, Tennessee, judge of the Third Judicial Circuit Court and served for three successive terms, of eight years each. This is the only office he ever held but he was at one time appointed Attorney General and Reporter for the State, which he declined to accept. He was one of the several men of eastern Tennesse who labored to prevent Tennessee from seceding from the union. When William G. Brownlow was released from Confederate prison he selected Samuel A. Rodgers as his personal friend to accompany him through the lines from Knoxville to Nashville. Judge Oliver P. Temple, in his book, Notable Men of Tennessee, says "Too much credit cannot be given to him for his faithfulness to Mr. Brownlow during all his trials. He exposed his own life to the greatest danger and endured great hardships in serving his friend. Nature has given to the world few as fine men as Judge Samuel A. Rodgers' ". Judge Rodgers had much to do in the establishment of Loudon County. He did much for the promotion of education and the Christian Religion; was an elder in the Presbyterian Church . . . . Had a liberal education, was a close observer and student of men and events, was a farmer and lawyer. Was full of activity and benevolence and the world was better for his having lived in it". (William L. Welcker, in Knoxville Journal and Tribune).

Samuel Andrew Rodgers and Sarah Elizabeth (Rhea) Rodgers had children: (a) Alice Rodgers (died young); (b) California Elizabeth Rodgers (1869-), (married) (1888) Colonel Joseph Marion Greer. Had one child: Rhea Rodgers Greer (1890-), who married (1913) Guy Lycan Hammitt (1887-) of Denver, Colorado); (c) Adaline Mahala Rodgers (1871-1898), (married Captain John Johnston Blair); (d) Samuel Rhea Rodgers (1873-), (Was an attorney at law. Never married); (e) Mary Belle Rodgers

NOTABLE SOUTHERN FAMILIES

(1875-), (married Jasper Porter Stephenson (1871-). No issue); (f) Annie Eliza Rodgers (1877-), (married (1904) Ulrich Ita III (1874-1918). Had one child, Ulrich Ita IV (died young); (g) Arthur Rodgers (1879-) (married (1909) Dean Stuart Penland (1888-), daughter of Judge James R. Penland and Gertrude (Stuart) Penland. Children: Arthur Rodgers II (1912-), James Penland (1914-), Samuel Andrew Rodgers II (1916-) and Jasper Rhea (1919-). Arthur Rodgers lives on the Dodson-Rhea homestead, in Loudon County, Tennessee, which has been in possession of the family since 1825); (h) Minnie Rodgers (died young); (i) John Rhea Rodgers (1885-). (married (1908) George Steele Dewey (1881-), (son of Charles Dewey and Mary Alice (Steele) Dewey, of Goldsboro, North Carolina. George Steele Dewey is a prominent manufacturer of North Carolina). They had children: Elizabeth Rhea (1909-), George Steele Dewey II (1910-), Mary Alice (1913-), Samuel Rodgers (1915-), and Charles Dewey II (1919-).

(7) William Donaldson Rodgers, M. D. (1837-1900) married (1865) Mary Amanda Knox. He was Hospital Steward in the Confederate Army, from 1860 to 1864. Moved to California, in 1875, where he became an eminent physician. He had children: (a) William L. Rodgers, (married (1894) Roberta ———. Children: Donald Rives (1895-) and Helen Singleton (1897-); (b) Julia Rodgers, (died young); (c) Charles Rodgers (died young); (d) Samuel A. Rodgers, (not married); (e) Eva Rodgers (not married).

5 Mary Rodgers, daughter of Joseph Rodgers and Elizabeth (Donaldson) Rodgers, was born in 1796, and married, in 1813 to William Sansbury Gound, and had children: (1) Elizabeth Ritter Gound (1814-), who married M. A. McCullough; (2) James Alexander Gound; (3) Verlinda Rebecca Gound (1819-1894), who married Ezekiel P. Stone, and had one child, Lucretia Jane; (4) Joseph Rodgers Gound; (5) Sarah Jane Gound; (6) Margaret Mahala Gound (1826-1869), who married (1856) Oliver P. Stone, and had children: (a) Hugh Marion Stone; (b) Magnolia Eveline Stone; (c) Charles Lee Stone, (married Mary L. Jett. Children: Mabel Clare, Mary Gladys and Charles Edwin); (d) Lucretia C. Stone; (7) Phylander Davis Gound; (8) Robert Tate Gound; (9) Mary Ann Donaldson Gound, who married Alexander McClelland, and had one child: Callie McClelland, who married ——— Upton; (10) William Edward Gound.

DONALDSON

II Andrew Donaldson

II Andrew Donelson (1768-1823) married Isabella Carmichael, and had children: (1) Mary Donaldson (1797-), who married William Reese; (2) Anna Donaldson (1799-), who married Samuel Hawkins; (3) and (4) Susanna and Elizabeth Donaldson (twins, 1801-). Susanna married Colonel Andrew C. Eaton and Elizabeth married Thomas Snoddy; (5) Margaret Donaldson (1802-), who married Solomon Shipley; (6) Jane Donaldson (1809-), never married; (8) William Donadlson (1813-), who married ——— Whiteside.

III Mary Donaldson

III Mary Donaldson married (1797), in Jefferson County, Tennessee, Thomas Rodgers, who was born (1770) in Washington County, Tennessee. Name of one child known: Thomas Leslie Rodgers, born (1807) in Knox County, Tennessee, who married Elizabeth Pickle, (daughter of Henry Pickle), and had children: (1) Elizabeth Rodgers; (2) Rebecca Rodgers; (3) Catherine Rodgers; (4) William Rodgers; (5) Jonathan Rodgers; (6) Henry Rodgers (killed in Battle of Resasa; (7) Thomas Rodgers II; (8) James Rodgers; (9) George Rodgers; (10) Jacob B. Rodgers (1838-1920), who married (1859) in Roane County, Tennessee, Nancy Ann Magill (1839-1920) daughter of William Magill). Soon after the War Between the States they moved to southern Missouri. Jacob B. Rodgers was a member of Company K, First Tennessee Volunteer Regiment of the Federal Army during the War Between the States. He had children: (a) William Thomas Rodgers, D. D., (1861-), (A prominent minister of the Presbyterian Church. Married (1895) Eula Hunter (1870-). Children: William Hunter Rodgers (1896-); Mary E. Rodgers (1897); Ruth M. Rodgers (1899-); Robert H. Rodgers (1901-); James J. Rodgers (1906-); Elizabeth Rodgers (1908-); (b) Henry A. Rodgers; (c) Frances Elizabeth Rodgers.

IV Ann Donaldson

IV Ann Donaldson (1775-1836) married in Tennessee Alexander Thompson, (1778-1822). Alexander Thompson was the son of James Thompson who came to America about 1774. (James Thompson married (1776), the widow of his cousin, Alfred Carmichael. James Thompson and his wife lived in Virginia, later in Tennessee. It is not known in which state

NOTABLE SOUTHERN FAMILIES

their son, Alexander was born. Alexander grew to manhood in Grainger, now Hamblin, County, Tennessee and later moved to Indiana. From that time the Thompson family has been prominent in the development of that state. Alexander Thompson and Ann (Donaldson) Thompson had children:
1 James Thompson II,
2 Isabella Carmichael Thompson.
3 John S. Thompson,
4 Mary Thompson,
5 Alfred Carmichael Thompson,
6 Janet Thompson,
7 Alexander Thompson II (1817-1825),
8 Celia Donaldson Thompson.

1 James Thompson II (1802-1872) married twice: First, Susan Collier (1802-1850); Second, Phoebe Hicks. Children by first wife: (1) Rebecca Ann Thompson (1826-1882), who married Alexander Breeding, and had children: (a) John Breeding (married Martha Pilford); (b) James Breeding (married Jane Cooper); (c) Effie L. Breeding (married William M. Perry); (d) William Breeding (married Kittie Cutsinger); (e) Mary Breeding; (f) Adelaide Breeding (married James L. Dorsey); (g) Frank Breeding; (2) John Alexander Thompson (1828-1886), who married Mary Cutsinger, and had children: (a) Susan Thompson (married Henry C. Bailey); (b) Samuel C. Thompson (married twice: First: Alice Lewis; Second, Tillie Vanbuskirk); (c) James Edward Thompson (married Frances Wilson); (d) Lily Jefferson Thompson (married Oliver M. Mitchell); (e) William T. Thompson (married Olive Wade); (f) Isaac C. Thompson (married Minnie McDaniel); (3) Isaac Mitchell Thompson (1831-1915), who married (1858) Harriet Pinney (1832-1898), and had children: (a) Laura Estelle Thompson (1859-), (married (1883) Arthur W. McLaughlin. Children: Harry Alfred McLaughlin (1885), who married (1914) Martha Dawson; Edna McLaughlin (1887-), who married (1910) William A. Ambrose, and had children: William A. Ambrose II, Harriet Estelle and Richard Arthur); (b) Jesse Benton Thompson (1861-), (married (1881) William Overstreet (1858-). Had one child, Anette); (c) Alfred Carmichael Thompson IV (1864-1903), (married (1885) Elizabeth Slater. Children: Haskell Alfred and Margaret); (d) Edna Thompson (1867-), (married (1889) Otis Bice (1866-1907). Had one child: Isaac Thompson Bice (1890-), who married Ruth Edelle Pritchard (1895), and had one child, Rose-

DONALDSON

mary); (4) Alfred Carmichael Thompson II (1831-1858); (5) William Hamilton (1833-1912), who married Ann J. Forgarty, and had children: (a) Margaret Thompson (1868-); (b) Florence Thompson (1870-), (married S. R. Mutz); (c) Josephine Thompson (1872-), (married Charles Pruitt); (d) Charles W. Thompson (1875-), (married Claudie Wiley); (e) Genevieve Thompson; (6) Redding B. Thompson (1838-1849); (7) James Irwin Thompson (1841-1876), who married Jane Cutsinger (1842-), and had children: (a) Elizabeth Thompson (1865-), (married Thomas J. Moffet. Children: Jane Moffett who married Oliver Kessing; Ralph Charles Moffett; Mary Louise Moffett who married George Middleton); (b) Minnie Thompson (1867-), (married twice: First, John Maley; Second, Carl F. Payne, M. D., no issue); (c) James Samuel Thompson (1868-1890), (married Lucy Mutz. Had one child, Cornelia who married W. D. Reddish, M. D.; (d) Lewis Jefferson Thompson (1870-1902), (married Ida M. Sherer. Had one child, Margaret (1898); (e) John Alexander Thompson; (f) Stella Thompson; (g) Mary Irwin Thompson (1876-), (married (1902) Samuel Moore (1875-). Had one child, John Thompson Moore (1903)). By second wife, Phoebe Hicks: (8) Mary Emily Thompson (1852-), who married D. R. Malone, M. D., (9) Charles Fremont Thompson; (10) Lydia H. Thompson, who married Daniel Becker.

2 Isabella Carmichael Thompson (1804-1834) married Nathan Wheeler, and had one child, Martha, who married Lee Bradley.

3 John S. Thompson (1806-1845) married Sarah Carvin, and had children: Maria, Harrison, Mary and Alfred Carmichael Thompson III.

4 Mary Thompson (1809-1873) married William Hensley, and had one child, Mary, who married ——— Bickford.

5 Alfred Carmichael Thompson married Maria Carvin, and had children: (1) Edward C. Thompson, who married Mary Pruett, and had children: Maurice, Belle and Bona; (2) Hannah Eliza Thompson, who married Gideon McEwin, and had children: Imogene, Alfred C., Maria and Lilly; (3) John Alexander Thompson.

6 Janet Thompson (1814-1876) married Timothy Thulkeld, and had children: Angie, Mary, William, Otto and Travis.

8 Cecelia Donaldson Thompson (1822-1867) married Darwin M. Sapp, and had one child, Edward.

NOTABLE SOUTHERN FAMILIES

V John Donaldson

V John Donaldson (1778-1859) married (1811) Celia Jordan (1790-1865), and had children:
1 Eliza Porter Donaldson,
2 Maria Donaldson,
3 Celia Donaldson,
4 Catherine Donaldson,
5 Mary Jane Donaldson,
6 William Jordan Donaldson.

1 Eliza Porter Donaldson, (1812-1890) married (1829) Thomas Barton Jarnagin, and had children: (1) Maria Jarnagin (1830-1860), who married Thomas Eckel, and had children: Mollie and Jennie; (2) Martha Ann Jarnagin, died young; (3) Albert Miller Jarnagin; (4) Lavinia Celia Jarnagin (1839-), who married John Leroy Foust, and had children: (a) Eva Lea Foust, (married Augusta C. Bowers. Children: Lawrence Leroy Bowers; Albert Boise Bowers who married Mary Taylor, and had one child, Josephine; Hugh Augustus Bowers who married Winifred Gross, and had one child, Mary Lavinia); (b) Anna Laura Foust; (c) Mary Foust; (d) Wiley Barton Foust; (e) Hugh Jarnagin Foust; (f) Robert Leroy Foust(1879-),(married Edna Farr); (5) Mary Eliza Jarnagin; (6) John Chesley Jarnagin; (7) Hugh Earnest Jarnagin (1847-1907), who married Amelia Fisher, and had children: (a) Nellie Jarnagin; (b) Herbert Jarnagin, married Lucy Lynch. Children: Mary Elizabeth, and Herbert); (8) Laura Amanda Jarnagin.

2 Maria Donaldson (1814-1911) married William Murphy Barton (son of Isaac Barton and Jane(———)Barton), and had children: (1) Catherine Barton; (2) Jesse Barton; (3) David Barton (1838-1912), who married Rebecca Long; (4) Celia Jane Barton; (5) John Isaac Barton; (6) Eliza Barton; (7) Robert Wesley Barton (1850-), who married Phoebe Jane Post, and had children: (a) Jesse Mae Barton, (married Edgar Lee Keener); (b) William David Barton, (married Bessie Glenn Matthews. Had one child, Dorothy); (8) William Joshua Barton(1856-),who married twice: First, Alice Lyle; Second, Laura King. Children by first wife: (a) Lena Barton, (married John G. Kane); (b) Loretta Kate Barton; (c) John Murphy Barton, (married Emma Lee Weiler); (d) and (e) Edith and Ethel Barton (twins); (f) William Joshua Barton II;(g) Mary Alice Barton; (h) Robert David Barton; (i) Lyle Donaldson Barton; (j) James Barton. By second wife: (k) Norman King Barton; (l) Emma Louise Barton.

DONALDSON

3 Celia Donaldson married twice: First, David Wesley Barton; Second, James Craig. Child by first husband: (1) David Wesley Barton II. Children by second husband: (2) Lafayette Craig, who married and had children: Mabel and Roy; (3) Robert Donaldson Craig; (4) Decatur Craig, who married Alice Johnson, and had children: Rollo, Chapman, Oney and Pauline; (5) Joseph Craig; (6) Florence Craig; (7) Mary Craig.

4 Catherine Donaldson (1818-1888) married James T. Carmichael, and had children: (1) John Donaldson Carmichael; (2) James W. Carmichael; (3) George A. Carmichael; (4) Thomas B. Carmichael (1846-), who married Ora Rader, and had children: James, William, Bulah, Stella and Annie; (5) Myra Carmichael (1848), who married John Martin Smith, and had children: Glen, Charles, Catherine, Albert and Roy; (6) Mary Carmichael (1851-), who married Henry Jarnagin, and had children: Kate, Frank, Myra, Minnie and May; (7) Charles H. Carmichael (1857-), who married Merle Kirkpatrick, and had children: George and Charles; (8) Robert M. Carmichael (1860-), who married Laura Goodson, and had children: Robert, George, Jeanette and Mildred.

5 Mary Jane Donaldson (1820-1883) married twice: First, Garvin Leeper Long; Second, Joseph Eckel. Children by first husband: John Robert Long, and Eliza Long who married Elijah Benton Hale, M. D.

6 William Jordan Donaldson (1823-1889) married (1851) Amanda Jane Worley, and had children: (1) John Worley Donaldson (1852-), who married Louise King, and had children: (a) Hugh Donaldson; (b) Leander King Donaldson, (married Camille Ponder); (c) Ollie Kate Donaldson, (married Clinton Dewitt Mater); (d) William John Donaldson (married Anne Frances Stubblefield. Children: Annie and William John Donaldson II); (2) Joseph Eckel Donaldson (1854-1904), who married Mary Elizabeth Lane, and had children: (a) Frank Warren Donaldson; (married Neta Rice. Had one child, Mildred Virginia); (b) William J. Donaldson, (married Emily Craig. Children: Lucile, Mary Elizabeth and Emily); (c) Mamie Lee Donaldson, (married Francis F. Painter, M. D. Children: Francis and Josephine); (d) Robert Lane Donaldson; (e) Adah Beatrice Donaldson, (married Frank Montgomery. Children: Mary, George and Beatrice); (3) Mary Eliza Donaldson; (4) William Gaines Donaldson; (5) Katie Jane Donaldson (1861-), who married (1883) James Alexander Eckel (1856-), and had

NOTABLE SOUTHERN FAMILIES

children: (a) Lucy May Eckel (1884-), (married Henry C. Brandon); (b) Donaldson Kingdon Eckel (1886-); (c) Anna Kate Eckel (1889-), (married Robert B. Holloman); (d) Wayne Alexander Eckel (1892-); (e) Bonnie Swingle Eckel (1897-); (f) James Robert Eckel (1905-); (6) Mildred Donaldson; (7) Charles Donaldson; (8) George Robert Donaldson (1868-), who married Daisy Trent, and had children: George, Jessie, Francis and Richard; (9) Hugh Donaldson;(10) Anna May Donaldson (1874-), who married Harry Dosser, and had one child, Amanda Frances.

VI Rebecca Donaldson

VI Rebecca Donaldson, daughter of William Donaldson and Mary (Sweeny) Donaldson, married Perry Pullen, and lived in Kentucky. They had children: Perry Pullen II, never married, and Mary Pullen who was reared by her aunt, Jane (Donaldson) Ogle.

VII Jane Donaldson

VII Jane Donaldson, daughter of William Donaldson and Mary (Sweeney) Donaldson, married John Ogle, and lived in Kentucky. They had one child who died in infancy.

WORLD WAR RECORD

The Donaldson family, true to its inheritance, nobly responded to its Country's call during the war. The following is a partial list of those who served:

Arthur B. Adams II. Captain in 317th Field Artillery, 81st Division.

Omar Rodgers Anderson.

Edward Barbour.

Lindsley Beal. S. A. T. C., Lafayette, Louisiana.

Julius Trousdale Berry. 2nd Lieutenant in Battery C, 36th Field Artillery, Camp McClellan, Alabama.

Harry S. Berry. Colonel in 115th Field Artillery.

John C. Birch. Camp Hancock, Georgia.

William Landon Bradfield. 1st Lieutenant in 3rd Aviation, Instructor. Center German prison.

Thomas H. Bradford. 1st Lieutenant in 144th Field Artillery, 42nd Division.

Campbell Huxley Brown. Captain, Adjutant to Major, in 3rd Battalion Marine Corps.

Lucius Polk Brown. Captain in Sanitary Corps of the Army.

Dugless Cogdelle. Was one of the Lost Battalion in

DONALDSON

France that had no food or water for several days.

Rhea Cogdelle. On his eighteenth birthday he volunteered for service in the Wireless Department; was promoted, in a few days, to instructor; after going to France he continued in this position until the end of the war. He was so very proficient Marconi took him to South America as soon as he was mustered out of the service.

William F. Cooper. Captain in 165th Depot Brigade, 7th Battalion.

Bradley Currey. Captain, A. P. O. 714, A. E. F., France.

John Dismukes. Captain.

John L. Dismukes. High private. Intelligence Section Headquarters 3rd Battalion, Rainbow Division.

Andrew J. Donelson. Captain in 115th Field Artillery.

Frank Donelson. Captain in Headquarters Development Battalion, Camp Sevier.

Andrew J. Donelson. U. S. A. Training Detachment, S. A. T. C.

Martin Donelson, M. D., in charge of Naval Hospital, Norfolk, Virginia.

John Martin Donelson. Section W. Tennessee Draft Board.

Hammond Curry Dyas, served in the Marine Corps in Belgium and France.

John Branch Donelson. Tank Service, A. E. F.

Harry Smith Dunn. 1st Lieutenant Grenade Instructor Company F, 229th Infantry, A. E. F.

Edward Dunn. S. A. T. C. Vanderbilt University, Nashville, Tennessee.

Joseph Ford. Corporal in 340th Aero Squadron, Field No. 2, Hempstead, Long Island.

William Walton Ford. 1st Lieutenant in 317th Field Artillery, 81st Division.

Lewis E. Ford. 2nd Lieutenant in Air Service, A. E. F.

Eugene C. Ford. Sergeant in Ordnance Department, A. E. F.

William Frost. Cadet C. M. A. Reserve Officers Training Camp, Gulf Port, Mississippi.

Walker Edward Frost. U. S. A. Base Hospital 57, Paris France. He was decorated by the French Minister of War for "extreme devotion to duty in time of peril".

William Franklin. Supply Sergeant, Officers Training Camp, Camp Pike.

Samuel Gordon. Captain, Camp Hancock, Georgia. Recommended for Major when Armistice was signed.

NOTABLE SOUTHERN FAMILIES

T. C. Gordon. Sergeant, Supply Company 49th Field Artillery, Fort Sill.

Rhea Rodgers Greer Hamill. Colorado Volunteers State Service No. 3334.

Wade Hadley. Sanitary Detachment 105 Supply Train. A. E. F.

Charles Hardy. Corporal in 130th Field Artillery.

Andrew J. Hays. 2nd Lieutenant in 113th Machine Gun Battalion Company, C. A. P. O. 749, A. E. F.

Dennis Smith Hays. Corporal in 49th Field Artillery, Battery B, Fort Sill.

Hugh Donelson Hays. Lieutenant in 2nd M. S. Battalion, 1st. Division. Served overseas.

John McLemore Hays. Sergeant, Marines, Paris Island.

Joseph Gregory Hays. 115th Field Artillery.

J. Walker Hays. Field Artilery.

Andrew Jackson. Sergeant in Headquarters 157th Artillery Brigade, 82nd Division.

Albert Marble Jackson. Corporal in Canadian Expeditionary Forces.

A.G.Kean. First-Class Yeoman, Shore duty, New York.

Richard Gordon Kean. Captain in 43rd Company 2nd Battalion 165 D. B.

Harry Kean. Bugler U. S. Albatross.

Charles H. Lake. 2nd Lieutenant in Field Artillery, Camp Zachary Taylor.

Donelson Martin Lake. 1st Lieutenant in 151st Field Artillery, Rainbow Division.

Henry Lake. Captain in Signal Corps Chief Signal, Washington, D. C.

John Marshall Lawrence. Training for Aviation Service, Camp Bowie, Texas.

Frank Littlefield. Sergeant-Major, Gas Defense, Rhode Island.

William Love. 57th Pioneer Infantry.

Paul McKnight. S. A. T. C.

Fitzhugh Murray. S. A. T. C., Baton Rouge, Louisiana.

William Murray. 36th Division.

George W. Polk. 2nd Lieutenant in Air Service, Boston School of Technology.

Harry Polk. 33rd Regiment Engineers, Company D, A. E. F.

Philip Read. Observation Section Aviation, Hempstead, Long Island.

George Read. Commander in Machine Gun Company, Regular Army, 52nd Infantry, A. E. F.

DONALDSON

Hunter Rodgers. Y. M. C. A. Secretary.

Viola Rodgers. Went to France at the commencement of the war and engaged in Hospital work. After America entered the war she and a friend were in charge of a hospital in Paris.

Frank Edmond Russell. S. A. T. C. University of Alabama.

James Donald Russell. Instructon in bayonet practice, was in Engineers Corps at Camp Humphries, near Washington, D. C., and a member of the squad that won the World's highest record in building a pontoon bridge, which they built across the Potomac.

Wiley Scott Russell.

Albert Perrine Smith. Corporal in 115th Filed Artillery.

McGregor Smith. 2nd Lieutenant in Infantry.

John C. Symmes II. Sergeant in Headquarters Department 896th Division, Camp Wadsworth.

Matt N. Thomson. Corporal in Battery E 114th Field Artillery.

Fannie Walton. Red Cross nurse. Went overseas with the Vanderbilt Unit. Served at the Red Cross Base Hospital No. 17, A. E. F.

Priestly Wherry. 55th Field Artillery Brigade, A. E. F.

HARDWICK

William Hardwick was about twenty-seven years old in 1655, according to his deposition made in Westmorland County, Virginia. We may place his birth about 1618. As will be seen below, he died 1668 or 69. He is probably identical with the William Hardige transported into Maryland in 1636, that is, when eighteen years old.

In 1642 William Hardige, Nathaniel Pope et al. were living in St. Mary's Hundred, Maryland. In 1645 William Hardwick and Thomas Sturman, (his father-in-law), being Puritans, were involved in the disturbances of Richard Ingle. In 1650 William Hardwick, John Sturman et al. signed a petition in Maryland. Apparently soon after this, Hardwick and the Sturmans, and probably also Nathaniel Pope, moved to Virginia.

In Northumberland County, Virginia, in 1653, William Hardige received patent for one thousand acres. In 1659 William Hardwick, Gent, sold to Richard Sturman, in Westmoreland County. In 1664 William Hardwick received patent for one hundred acres in Westmoreland County, Virginia.

William Hardwick, who became Lieutenant-Colonel of Militia, married first, Elizabeth, daughter of Thomas Sturman, probably before 1650. She seems to have been the mother of his children. He married second, Margaret, daughter of Colonel Nathaniel Pope, who died in Westmoreland County, in 1660. Colonel Pope's daughter, Anne, married John Washington, ancestor of George Washington. So William Hardwick was great-great uncle by marriage of our first President. Hardwick's second marriage took place in 1659 or before.

William Hardwick, "late of Nominy, Westmoreland County, Virginia, Gent., and now of Bristol, England," made his will October twenty-fourth, 1668, which was probated January eighth, 1669. This will deals with the testator's estate in England and he refers to another of the same date relating to his property in Virginia, which will has not yet been discovered. All the heirs mentioned in the surviving will, seem to be living in England at that time, so far as ascertainable from the will. Possibly there were other heirs in Virginia named in the lost will. The surviving will mentions wife Margaret, who received 150 pounds on condition of fulfilling certain requests mentioned in the other will regarding the estate in Virginia; sister Elizabeth Boyce; Dorothy Cyle and Mary Penyman (no relationship stated); brother Thomas Hardwick; son William Hardwick, who is to continue his schooling in England until he is twenty-one; daughter Elizabeth Wynston. He names brother-in-law Mr. Augustine Hull and Cozen Thomas Youle in his will. Overseers of the present will are Thomas Burges, of Bristol, Chirurgon, and son-in-law Robert Wynston. Witnesses are Frances Bell, James Bell, Thomas Boyce, junior, Fulwood. The executors of the other will undoubtedly lived in Virginia. Of these Cozen Thomas Youle was the son of Captain Thomas Ewell, or Youell, who married Anne Sturman, sister to Hardwick's first wife, hence he is called Cozen (nephew by marriage).

William Hardwick, the first, certainly had two children, namely (1) William Hardwick, the second, (Captain and a member of the House of Burgesses in 1682), and (2) Elizabeth the wife of Robert Wynston. William Hardwick (2), returned to Virginia and married Frances, said to be the daughter of Dr. Thomas Gerrard. Before she married Hardwick she is said to have been the wife of Colonel Thomas Spake, Colonel Valentine Peyton and Captain John Appleton, so her union with Hardwick was her fourth marriage. However, another writer, upon what authority I do not know, while representing the first three marriages of Frances Gerrard as above, gives her Colonel John Washington as her fourth husband. But it is certain that Hardwick was one of her husband's for the reason that said Hardwick's daughter had a brother (half-brother) named Gerrard Peyton (see below).

William Hardige, merchant, of Westmoreland County, received power of attorney June 19, 1677, from Thomas Pope of Bristol, England, made a will September 3, 1684, probated October 20, 1685, in which he mentions plantations on Pope's Creek, Westmoreland County, Virginia, and names "loving friends and dear kinsmen, Mr. William

HARDWICK

Hardridge, Mr. Lawrence Washington and Mr. John Washington, all of Virginia," as guardians of his sons. William Hardridge was one of a jury which on August 25, 1677, found Joseph Hardridge (undoubtedly his kinsman) guilty of rebellion. Apparently Colonel Washington was also involved in this rebellion. William Hardridge was a Burgess at various times from 1682 to 1693 from Westmoreland County. In October, 1692, he is mentioned as living near the mouth of Nominy Creek in Westmoreland County. He seems to have died soon after that date, for John Washington's will, 1697-98, refers to a watch given him by Captain William Hardridge's will (which will has not been discovered). John Washington leaves this watch to Mrs. Elizabeth Hardridge. The only Mrs. Elizabeth Hardridge of whom we know, who might qualify here, is the wife of William Hardwick, son of James, whose relationship to the emigrant William is in doubt. But it is possible that the marriage of William Hardwick (son of James) and Elizabeth (Brown, as we shall see later) had not taken place so early as 1697. If the prefix Mrs. were an error we might suppose that Elizabeth Hartridge, sole heir of Captain William Hardridge, was the recipient of the watch.

Captain William Hardridge had only one child, Elizabeth, born 1678, died February 25, 1722. She is mentioned as sister (half-sister) of Gerrard Peyton in his will of 1687-88 (in which the testator appoints his father-in-law, Mr. William Hardridge, as executor). She is also mentioned in a will of Richard Sturman, 1691, of Westmoreland County Virginia. He was probably her great uncle. She married Colonel Henry Ashton, born July 30, 1671. Colonel Henry Ashton and wife, Elizabeth Hardridge Ashton, had four daughters, namely Frances Elizabeth, Anne and Grace Ashton and their descendants, if any, are the sole descendants of Captain William Hardridge, the emigrant, if Captain William was his only son.

Living contemporaneously with Captain William Hardwick in Westmoreland County, Virginia, we find three others of the name, James, Joseph and George Hardwick. James and Joseph were brothers. George may also have been a brother, though no indication of such relationship has been found. All three may have been sons of William Hardwick the emigrant. The latter will, made in Bristol England, mentions only one son. William was with his father in England at that time. But testator refers to a second will touching property in Virginia and this will, now lost, might have shown relation of these three Hardwicks. They might have been older sons remaining in Virginia. However, no record of any of them earlier than 1670 in Virginia has been found. As will be seen below, James Hardwick was undoubtedly a relative of Captain William Hardwick, for James in his will, 1698, refers to sword and belt given him by Captain Hardwick. This would indicate that Captain William Hardwick having no son bequeathed these manly trappings to his nearest male relation. If James was not the son of William, the emigrant, he may have been the son of the latter's brother, Thomas, mentioned in the will cited above. Beyond this nothing can be said until further evidence is discovered.

George Hardwick married Mary Powell, daughter of John Powell, in 1678, or before. In 1696, he conveyed to John Buller and wife, Sarah, their son, Robert Buller, "for natural affection borne toward them" 100 acres, as an inheritance. Probably Sarah Buller was his daughter, but she is not mentioned in his will dated May 26, 1704. In this will he represents himself as of Cople Parish, planter. He mentions wife Mary; son Robert Hardwick and the latter's son, George Hardwick. If grandson George should die, his estate is to go to the three daughters of William Stewart (no relation shown to testator). Apparently this hope of male offspring depended on his grandson George. Probably this hope failed as no later Hardwicks are found traceable to him. George Hardwick's inventory is dated March 25, 1713.

Joseph Hardwick, as already seen, was involved in the rebellion of 1676. On September 25, 1675, Richard Gotly, of Bristol, England, granted power of attorney to his brother, Peter Gotly, now bound for Virginia, to deal with Joseph Hardwick, late of Westbury in the County of Somerset, England, Sergemaker, but now resident in Virginia or Maryland. This paper was witnessed by Thomas Pope, William Andrews, and John Spencer. Westbury is not far from Bristol and to this region we should probably turn to find the English ancestors of these Hardwicks. The fact that Joseph Hardwick is in 1675 referred to as late of Westbury is a strong indication that he had not yet lived in Virginia and was not therefore a son of William Hardwick, the emigrant. Joseph Hardwick is mentioned by John Carrier of Cople Parish in his will of 1696, as father-in-law (probably for step-father). John Carrier's wife was Elizabeth. In 1698 Joseph Hardwick, of Cople Parish, sold to Elizabeth Currier (sic). Joseph Hardwick, of Nominy, in Parish of Cople, made will June 22, 1698, probated August

HARDWICK

31, 1698. He mentions no wife or children. He mentions kinsman (brother) James Hardwick; cousins (nephews) James Hardwick and Thomas Hardwick; children of William Earle to remain with executor (no relationship stated); refers to land bought of Richard Sturman; other persons mentioned in the will are Sarah Clark, William Sanford, senior, Henrietta Buckley, Richard Sutton, Richard Middleton, Temperance Blanchflower, Benjamin Blanchflower (executor), Colonel William Pierce, and Captain William Bridges.

We now come to JAMES HARDWICK, brother of Joseph. He first appears in a deed in Westmoreland County, of 1670 as James Harditch. He buys of Henry and Sarah Durant land which had once belonged to Richard Sturman. In same year he bought from Thomas Foster. He married Ann Armsley or Armsby, apparently only child of John Armsby (died in Westmoreland County, Virginia, 1659), and wife, Anne. On November 20, 1672, James Hardwick and wife, Ann, sold to Nicholas Spencer, land patented by John Armsby in 1650, whose daughter is wife of James Hardwick at the time of the transaction. All the later Hardwicks of the next and later generations seem to be descended from this James.

JAMES HARDWICK was born about 1647 (he was twentyseven years old in (1674) and died in 1698. His will is dated February 7, 1698, probated March 30, 1698. He mentions wife Ann; sons William, Joseph (who receives the sword left him by Captain William Hardwick); daughters Elizabeth and Lydia Hardwick (Lydia being under fourteen years); wife's daughter Anne (from which we may infer that James Harwick was her second husband); brother Joseph Hardwick; Thomas Hardwick and James Hardwick (no relationship stated but undoubtedly sons of the testator for they receive portion of the estate and are also named as cousins, that is, nephews, in Joseph Hardwick's will; and furthermore as we shall see below Joseph Hardwick in 1708 had brother James; Henry Asbury, John Wright and Benjamin Blanchflower are more executors.

We shall now take up the children of James Hardwick, 1698, leaving WILLIAM, probably the oldest, to the last. No further record has been found of Elizabeth and Thomas. Possibly Lydia, daughter of James Hardwick, married Thomas Walker, whose will dated 1726 in Westmoreland, names wife Lydia, son Hardige Walker, and others. James

NOTABLE SOUTHERN FAMILIES

Hardwick appears on the Westmoreland Order Book for 1708 with wife Elizabeth and with brother Joseph Hardwick. He is undoubtedly the son of James, 1698, and identical with James Hardwick, of Cople Parish, who made will June 12, 1749, probated 1749. In this will he mentions wife Elizabeth, sons Thomas and John Hardwick; son-in-law Elias Davis; daughters Elizabeth Nash, Sarah Summers, and Cyoway (?) Lane. In 1759 Thomas Hardwick, of Cople Parish, and wife Elizabeth, sold to Gerrard Hutts. He was son of the James who died 1749. James Hardige Lane who married Mary Smith on January 12, 1758, in Overwhorten Parish, Stafford County, Virginia, and later appears in Loudon County, Virginia, may be a descendant of the above Hardwick-Lane marriage. In a published work I find mention of a James Lane who about 1834 married Lydia Hardage. She is probably the Cyoway of the above will.

Joseph Hardwick, son of James, 1698, made will December 24, 1726, probated March 29, 1727. He mentions wife Ann; children under 16; "to all my children" (not by name) equally lands at Cople. Wife and nephew James Hardwick are named as executors. So far only two names of Joseph's children have been discovered, viz: Hazel (Haswell) Hardwick and James Hardwick. In 1748 Hazle Hardwick of Stafford County, Virginia, planter, sold to Gerrard Hutt, of Cople Parish, Westmoreland County, land lying in Cople Parish, being part of the land Joseph Hardwick, father of said Hazel, willed to him. No wife signs. In Overwharton Parish, Stafford County, about 1749 Haswell Hardwick married Mary Northcutt. They had children as follows:

Ann Hardwick, born January 4, 1752.
William Hardwick, born September 5, 1753.
Elizabeth Hardwick, born September 8, 1775.
And perhaps others.

In 1753 Hazel Hardwick, of Frederick County, Virginia, patented 407 acres in Frederick County. In same county on May 2, 1763, Hazel Hardwick and wife, Mary, sold the above tract of 407 acres to Andrew Beard and John Tate. The Chester County, South Carolina, census for 1790 shows Hazel Hardwick at the head of a family. Probably he is the same as the above as no record of his in Virginia has been found.

James Hardwick, of Cople Parish, son of Joseph, 1727, on October 25, 1743, sold thirty-five acres of Cople, part

HARDWICK

of land whereon Joseph Hardwick, father of said James, lived. Isabel, wife of James Hardwick, joins in the deed. No further record of the descenants of Joseph, 1727, has been found.

We now take up WILLIAM HARDWICK, probably the oldest son of James Hardwick, 1698. He married Elizabeth Brown, sister of George Brown, whose will dated 1724 in Westmoreland County, refers to his sister Elizabeth, wife of William Hardwick (probably meant for widow). William Hardwick made a will October 31, 1718, probated February 25, 1719. It was witnessed by William Hardwick, Joseph Hardwick, Aaron Hardwick, and Ann Robinson. Of these witnesses Joseph Hardwick was the testator's brother, who died in 1727. But the other two, William and Aaron Hardwick, are not yet placed. Possibly they are older sons of the testator not mentioned in his will. This Aaron Hardwick is probably the Aaron Hardwick, of Cople Parish, who in 1722 bought 100 acres of Henry Asbury.

WILLIAM HARDWICK, 1718-19, mentions wife ELIZABETH, daughters Frances and Dorcas, sons George and James, mentions children under 16; wife Elizabeth and son James are named as executors.

ELIZABETH HARDWICK, widow of the ABOVE WILLIAM, made will August 12, 1734, probated 1734. She mentions grandchildren Bailey Walker, Rachel Walker, Frances Hardwick, nephew (sic) Hannah Hardwick; nephew (sic) Ann, Hannah Ashton (no relationship stated); and son James Hardwick. The nephew Hannah Hardwick has not yet been placed. Apparently one of the daughters of William Hardwick had married a Walker before this date. The grand child Frances Hardwick is probably the daughter of James, see below.

George Hardwick, son of the above William and Elizabeth, in 1724, with Patrick Spence, Thomas Sturman, and Thomas James, took up 1678 acres in Westmoreland County. He died apparently unmarried. He made will June 30, 1732, probated soon afterward. He mentions mother Elizabeth Hardwick, brother James and his son William (under 21). Brother James is appointed executor.

JAMES HARDWICK, son of William, 1718-19, married HENRIETTA GARLAND, daughter of William Garland. He made will June 8, 1737, probated September 27, 1737. In the probate he is called James Hardwick, junior, apparently to distinguish him from his uncle James Hardwick, who outlived him by twelve years, see above. He mentions wife Haney Ritta (sic); sons Aaron, George and WILLIAM HARDWICK; William Garland, junior, "brother of my wife"; daughter Frances, and deceased brother George Hardwick. Henrietta Hardwick and William, land, junior, were executors of will of James Hardwick, junior, in 1737. The father of Henrietta Hardwick was probably William Garland, whose will dated February 21, 1743, in Richmond County, Virginia, mentions son William Garland, daughter Mary and grandson George Hardwick. This George Hardwick was still a minor in 1750, when as heir of James Hardwick, deceased, he chose William Hardwick as guardian (probably his older brother). No further record of George or Frances, children of James Hardwick, 1737, has been found.

However in the records of Jefferson County, Arkansas, is found the will of a Garland Hardwick, who no doubt was the son of the above George. The will, dated December 12, 1850 and probated December 29, 1852, names his wife, Nancy, and grandchildren Garland H. and Margaret R. Dorris, children of deceased daughter, Robinia T. Dorriss, as sole legatees.

We now take up Aaron Hardwick. Aaron, son of James Hardwick, 1737, could not be identical with Aaron Hardwick, who in 1718 witnessed will of William Hardwick, and in 1722 bought land. The reference given below may not all belong to the same Aaron Hardwick. In Westmoreland County in about 1756 Aaron Hardwick is mentioned in connection with the building of a road. About same time Aaron Hardwick sues Thomas Hardwick, which suit was dismissed. About 1760 John Deboc was ordered to pay to Aaron Hardwick 638 pounds of tobacco for his services as witness in case of Deboc vs. Gerrard Hutt. About 1758 William Hardwick was ordered to pay Aaron Hardwick 203 pounds of tobacco for services as witness in case of Hardwick vs. Edmund Bulger. In Prince William County, Virginia, on June 10, 1765, Aaron Hardwick sued George Boland for a small amount.

We now approach this line from a different angel. In Fauquier County, Virginia, on December 12, 1787, license was granted to Cornelius McCarty to marry Sukey Hardwick. The oldest son of this large family was named Aaron Hardridge McCarty, from which fact it seems probable that his maternal grandfather was named Aaron Hardridge (Hardwick). The probability becomes almost

HARDWICK

a certainty when we find that the above Susan Hardwick McCarty had a brother, William Hardwick, who named his oldest son Garland Hardwick, which fact naturally connects him with James Hardwick, 1737, who married Henrietta Garland, see above.

Aside from this brother William, Susan Hardwick McCarty also had brother John Hardwick and sister Elizabeth Hardwick, James Kincheloe was granted license to marry Elizabeth Hardwick in Fauquier County, Virginia, December 7, 1790. They had Brandt, Hardwick, Eleanor Kincheloe, and probably others. The writer has seen a deed (not rcorded apparently) dated December 23, 1816, by which Cornelius McCarty and Susannah, his wife, late Hardridge (sic) of Hardin County, Kentucky, sell to James Kincheloe, of Fauquier County, Virginia, 200 acres in Fauquier County, bought by Margaret Hardridge (mother of the said Susannah McCarty), while a widow, of Thomas Glasscock, which said Margaret Hardridge afterwards married William Turley. The above Margaret Hardridge was born Glasscock and not Orear. She was the daughter of John Glasscock who patented land in present Fauquier County in 1728, and made will in Fauquier County, November 27, 1774, in which will he mentions among others, daughter Margaret Turley. On October 1, 1771, Thomas Glasscock (son of the above John and brother of Margaret) and wife Agnes sold to Margaret Hardwick, 244 acres. It is this transaction that the deed of Cornelius McCarty and his wife Susannah, above mentioned, refers to. In 1774 Thomas Glasscock and wife Agnes sold to William Turley. On March 1, 1815, Sampson Turley, of Fauquier County, sold to James Kincheloe the land which Thomas Glasscock and wife Agnes in 1771 sold to Margart Hardwick. This seems to be the same land referred to in the unrecorded deed of Cornelius and Susannah Hardwick McCarty cited above. We may conclude then that before October 1, 1771, the first husband (Aaron?) Hardwick, of Margaret Glasscock had died and in 1774 or before she had married William Turley, by whom as we know from other sources she had eight children. From this fact we may infer that she was comparatively young when her first husband died. For the reason already given the writer is convinced that her first husband was Aaron Hardwick, son of James, 1737. It also seems certain that Aaron Hardwick was twice married, Margaret Glasscock being the second wife. The reasons are as follows: Susan

NOTABLE SOUTHERN FAMILIES

Hardwick had a brother (half-brother) William Hardwick who was married in 1776. But between 1771 and 1774 Susan's mother Margaret Hardwick married a second time, to Turley, to whom she bore eight children. She was not likely therefore to be the mother of William Hardwick, old enough to marry in 1776. Furthermore confirmatory evidence is found in the fragments of an old letter, which the writer has seen written by the above William Hardwick to Cornelius McCarty and Susan McCarty about 1811. In this letter he calls Susan, his sister, but he also speaks of "your stepfather (William Turley) whom your mother "married'. The pronoun YOUR (twice used) indicates that they had different mothers. He mentions removal of her mother to Goose Creek, near Rector Town. And then "on my return (from where, not shown in existing fragments) I found you, brother John and sister Elizabeth playing in the negro house, which was the first time I ever saw you" (confirms conjecture that he was an older half-brother). "The year 1783 was the last time I ever saw you". He speaks of our "niece Ellen Kincheloe" through whom he had heard of Susan McCarty's whereabouts. He states that he became a Methodist in 1788 and in 1792 he went into the ministry in which he had been laboring for nineteen years. From this statement we placed the date of the letter in 1811. He states that he has been married thirty-five years next June 26 (apparently then in 1776; further confirmed by the fact that their oldest son was born in 1777). "We have five sons and four daughters and have never had a death in our family. Old Sarah, the negro that nursed me, is still with me". "We live near Louisville," (that is Jefferson County, Georgia). He mentions son William P. Hardwick, a surveyor, who is making a trip to Kentucky and who is to carry this letter. He also mentions eldest son Garland Hardwick, near whom they are living. Descendants of this William Hardwick agree that he once lived in Fauquier County, Virginia, and later settled in Jefferson County, Georgia. He married Judith Parker, June 26, 1776. They had five sons and four daughters (see old letter) as follows:

Garland Hardwick (the eldest), born April 8, 1777, in Fauquier County, Virginia, and died April 8, 1837.

William Parker Hardwick 1850. Married Sarah Cheatham.

George W. Hardwick, married first Elizabeth Kennon, second, Nancy Fontaine, and third, Elisabeth Bush.

HARDWICK

John Wesley Hardwick, married Mary Rivers Nallv.
Charles Hardwick.
Huldah Hardwick (married Dawson).
Margaret Hardwick.
Frances Hardwick.
(Names of only three daughters have been handed down, but there was a fourth living in 1811, who probably died soon after).

Garland Hardwick, born April 8, 1777, married, first, Jane Paulett, born July 12, 1783, in Louisa County, Virginia. This marriage took place April 16, 1800. She died August 11, 1807, without issue. He married, second, Dorothy Kennedy, December 22, 1807. She was born January 7, 1785, in Orangeburgh District, South Carolina, and died August 23rd, 1849. They had five sons:
William.
George W.
Benjamin F.
Garland.
Thomas Coke Hardwick.

William Parker (not Park) Hardwick, son of William and Judith Parker Hardwick, married about 1815 Sarah Baker Cheatham. Their son, Thomas William Hardwick, married Mary Elizabeth Davis in 1848 and their son, Robert William Hardwick, was the father of the present Senator Thomas W. Hardwick.

We now return to WILLIAM HARDWICK, son of James Hardwick, 1737, of Westmoreland County, Virginia. About 1752 William Hardwick sued Edmund Bulger. Aaron Hardwick was a witness at this suit. About the same time William Hardwick's attachment against estate of John Story is dismissed. I regard him as identical with William Hardwick who made will on March 23, 1802, in Green County, Georgia, date of Probate April 1, 1803. He mentions heirs of deceased son James Hardwick; sons William Hardwick, George Hardwick, and GARLAND HARDWICK; daughters Martha Jones, Hannah Dawkins, Nancy Daniel, Molly Fitzpatrick, and Peggy Hardwick, granddaughter Cynthia Hardwick Fitzpatrick, daughter of Rene (sic) and Molly Fitzpatrick; sons George and GARLAND HARDWICK are named as executors. Witnesses are P. Park, Susan Park, B. Fitzpatrick. Here again the occurrence of the name Garland seems to connect William with James Hardwick, 1737, of Westmoreland County, Virginia. He seems older than William of

NOTABLE SOUTHERN FAMILIES

Jefferson County, Georgia, and if the name Garland represents any relationship to the above Hardwick-Garland marriage, he could be no other than William, the son of James Hardwick, 1737.

Children of the above William Hardwick, who made will in Green County, Georgia, 1802-1803, and wife Nancy,

(1) James. (Nothing known of descendants).
(2) Martha. (Nothing known of descendants).
(3) Hannah (or Haney).
(4) Nancy. (Nothing known of her descendants).
(5) William.
(6) George.
(7) Garland.
(8) Mollie.
(9) Peggy. (Nothing known of her descendants).

Of the foregoing:

(1) James married and left heirs, but of them the writer knows nothing.

(2) Martha married ———— Jones and is mentioned in her father's will.

(3) Haney (Hannah) Hardwick, (born 1755, died 1837), married, first, ———— Taylor by whom she had one child.

1 Nancy, born 1779.

Her second marriage was to William Dawkins about 1786 or 1787. The children were:

2 Garland Dawkins, born 1788.
3 George Dawkins, born 1790.
4 Daniel Dawkins, born 1793.
5 Reuben Dawkins, born 1795.
6 Patsy Dawkins, born 1798.

Of the above:

Garland Dawkins (1788-1892) married daughter of Captain William Barksdale, Hancock County, Georgia.

Ch. 1 Haney Ann married William Iverson.
 2 Martha Ann, married David Lovejoy, Henry County.
 3 Dewitt Clinton (Jasper County, 1829), married 1854 Fannie Jones, Muscogee County, moved to Jacksonville, Florida.
 4 Garland Dawkins died unmarried.
 5 Virginia.
 6 E. LaFayette Dawkines died in defense of Savannah.

HARDWICK

7 Myrtie, married Dr. S. B. Hopgood, Boaden, Georgia.

DeWitt Clinton Dawkins married Fannie Jones. Ch. 1 Martha L. Ida M., married John H. Howell; 3. Dewitt and Haney Young; 4. Sallie A. and George M. (from Prominent Men of Georgia and Florida).

Reuben Dawkins (1795-1869), married 1. Martha Bird Fitzpatrick (died 1837). Ch. 1. John died unmarried. 2. Walter Scott and Isaac Newton (1833-1866).

Reuben Dawkins (1795-1865), married (2) Elizabeth (Johnson) Hines 1881.

Ch. 1 Sarah Ann Victoria (1839-1885), married John William Pace.

2 Haney Louisiana (1841-1915), married 1. Isaac Pace. (2) Francis A. Boykin.

3 Ann Elizabeth (1844-1869), married 1869 S. A. Garlick.

4 Martha Bird Fitzpatrick (1847-1900), married Edwin A. Houston 1866.

5 William Daniel (1840), married (1) Mary Lou Pollard. (2) Winifred Carter.

John William Pace and Sarah Dawkins.

Ch. 1 Stephen, married Cora Perdue, Carrollton, Georgia. Ch. 1. Alva.

2 Thomas, married. Lives in Texas.
3 Downer, married Sarah Brown, Troy, Alabama.
4 Elizabeth Lou, married Olin Craven.
5 Emmett, married and lives in Texas.
6 Sarah Francis, married Weems Baskins, Carrollton, Georgia.

(3) John, married Annice Petty.

Francis A. Boykin and Haney Dawkins Pace.

1 Frank Marshall, deceased.
2 Marvin, deceased.
3 Cecil, married Corinne Moses, Carrollton, Georgia.

S. A. Garlick and Anne E. Dawkins, deceased.

Edwin A. Houston and Martha Bird Fitzpatrick Dawkins.

1 Elizabeth, married Jere R. Traylor, daughter Martha Elizabeth Taylor.

2 Walter, married Sallie Adair; two children: Adair and Marguerite.

3 Martha Louisiana.

4 Edwin, married Nettie Baxter; two children: Charles and Elizabeth.

NOTABLE SOUTHERN FAMILIES

William Daniel Dawkins and Mary Lou Pollard. (1).
1 Carrie, married Gary Pruett, Hurtsboro, Alabama.
2 Walter, married and lives in Alabama.
3 Marshall, married Miss Evans, Alabama.
Children of William Daniel Dawkins and Winifred Carter:
1 Carter.
2 Reuben.
3 Lollie Belle.
4 Annie Sarah.
(4) Nancy married William (?) Daniels and was mentioned in will of her father. Nothing is known of her descendants.

(5) William Hardwick born March 17, 1760, married Nancy Shipp April 22, 1790, and died March 1, 1828, Hancock County, Georgia. (Nancy Shipp Hardwick, born March 27, 1766, and died February 2, 1854). Their children were:

Betsy, born January 17, 1791, married Allen Roberts November 17, 1809.
Patsy, born March 19, 1792, married David Lewis May 2, 1809.
Frankey, born January 22, 1794, died December 31, 1801.
Polly, born February 11, 1796, married Adam Jones October 16, 1811.
Richard Shipp, born December 7, 1797, married Martha Hamilton April 19, 1825.
Sophie Garland, born March 10, 1800, married Stephen Jones, January 28, 1819, died November 7, 1821.
Eliza Hart, born December 28, 1801.
Nancy Barron, born October 17, 1803, married Eli Mansfield, died April 19, 1852.
James Jefferson, born October 10, 1805, married Milicy Pride January 19, 1826.
William Milerson, born March 19, 1808.
Harriet Washington, born April 30, 1810.

(6) George Hardwick, born ——— 17. Died St. Clair County, Alabama, about June, 1824. Will dated April 16, 1823, recorded July 1, 1824. Married ——— Mary (or Polly) McTyeire. He lived in Jasper County, Georgia, 1809, to about 1818. Moved to St. Clair County, Alabama, about 1818 and died there.
Issue—Children:
1 James, married; had a son, James Hardwick, mentioned in grandfather's will. Son, Pickens Hardwick, at

HARDWICK

Branchville, Ala. Died in St. Clair County, Alabama. Left large family.
2 Daughter, who married Willis Germany. (Name not mentioned in father's will, which mentions son-in-law, Willis Germany.
3 George.
4 William. Was killed in Mississippi.
5 Garland. Died about 1888, aged 84, left number of children, Talledega County, Georgia. Oldest son, Owen Hardwick, Croswell, Alabama. Son B. G. Hardwick, Hartselle, Alabama. (Son, James O. Hardwick, Easonville, Alabama, 1901).
6 Frizzell McTyerie, born July 14, 1806. Represented Cherokee County, Alabama, in Legislature. Died in Cherokee, Alabama. Four or five sons killed C. S. A. Mrs. S. B. Ramey's father). Died November 19, 1869.
7 Robert. Died in Henry or Barbour County, Alabama. Left large family. Colonel McTyerie Hardwick, oldest son. The family lives at Hardwicksburg, Henry County, Alabama.
8 Sidney. Born ————. Married (prior to 1823). Wm. H. Barnhill.
9 Kissiah. Born, July 16, 1800. Died April 16, 1883, at Covington, Georgia. Married, first, October 24, 1816, Cornelius Robinson, Jasper County, Georgia. Married second, January 11, 1838, William Guy Smith. Issue by first marriage, James Hardwick, Caroline, Saline Frances and Sarah Jane. Issue by second marriage, Boykin Smith.
10 Nancy. (Unmarried 1823).
(7) Garland Hardwick. Born in South Carolina (?) about 1770. Married Susan Venable about 1796 and died Benton County, Arkansas, 1847. Their children were:
1 John Wesley. Born August 15, 1797. Married Jane Montgomery September 22, 1818. Died April 4, 1852.
2 George. Born ————, 1800. Married Ellen Andrews and died 1867.
3 Thomas. Married Ann McFarlane.
4 James.
5 Mary. Married Joseph Barnett.
6 Cynthia. Married Rev. Pearson.
7 Joseph Tarply. Born August 3, 1811. Married Rebekah McFarlane and died 1851 or 1852.
8 Charles F. Born ————, 1814. Married Elizabeth Holmes; second, Strong or Stroud.
John Wesley Hardwick. Born August 15, 1797. Mar-

ried Jane Montgomery September 22, 1818, and died April 4, 1852. Their children were:

1 Nancy Caroline Elizabeth. Born October 16, 1819. Died August 27, 1838.
2 William H. Foster June 28, 1838. Died near Decatur, Texas.
3 Celine Augusta. Born June 14, 1822. Married W. Henry Tibbs February 2, 1843. Died September 28, 1888, at Dalton, Georgia.
4 Susan Evaline. Born December 16, 1823. Married J. Milton Holmes November 21, 1849. Died January, 1911, near Decatur, Texas.
5 Hulda Margaret. Born August 12, 1825. Married Robert H. Wallace March 27, 1865. Died near Decatur, Texas.
6 Christopher LaFayette. Born February 14, 1827. Married Isabel Tucker April 3, 1851. Died March 3, 1901, at Cleveland, Tennessee.
7 Martha Eliza. Born October 27, 1829. Married William E. Key December 15, 1852, and died March 10, 1884, near Rodgers, Arkansas.
8 Franklin Eleflet. Born September 27, 1831. Married Sallie B. Barkesdale June 23, 1859. Second, Minnie Kelly July 23, 1878. Died 1912. No Children.
9 Hugh Montgomery. Born September 27, 1833. Married Martha Dean January 5, 1859. Second, Frances P. Grider September 6, 1866. Died August, 1907, in Oklahoma.
11 William Henry Harrison. Born January 29, 1840, and died September 8, 1840.
12 Cynthia Ann Amelia. Born July 30, 1842. Married Lemuel H. Chapman January 27, 1865. Died October 21, 1880, near Cleveland, Tennessee.
13 Mary Virginia Agnes. Born October 31, 1844. Married Andrew M. Rodgers April 28, 1870. Lives in Cleveland, Tennessee.

Literally hundreds of descendants of John W. Hardwick are scattered over the South and West.

(6) Christopher Lafayette Hardwick was born February 14, 1827, at the Cherokee Agency (now Charleston, Tennessee), while his father, John Wesley Hardwick, was acting as Assistant Agent to his grandfather, Colonel Hugh L. Montgomery, who served as Indian Agent to the Cherokees from 1824 to 1838, or until the Indians were moved West. At an early age the above Christopher Lafayette Hardwick moved to Cleveland, Tennessee, where

HARDWICK

later he married Isabel Tucker (daughter of Joseph and Mary Isabel Tucker) on April 3, 1851. He was very active in Church affairs, was one of the founders and most liberal friends of Centenary Female College, President Cleveland Woolen Mill, President Hardwick Stove Works at Cleveland and President of C. L. Hardwick & Son, Bankers at Dalton, Georgia. He Died March 3, 1901.

Children of Christopher Lafayette Hardwick and wife, Isabel Tucker Hardwick, were:

1 Frank Tucker. Born March 23, 1852. Married Carrie Belle McCutcheon March 11, 1880. President C. L. Hardwick Company, Bankers, Dalton, Georgia.

2 Joseph Henry. Born February 23, 1854. Married Cooksey Adella Harris November 16, 1875. President Hardwick Stove Company, Cleveland, Tennessee.

3 John Millard. Born August 14, 1856. Was killed in a railroad accident while on his way to Europe July 2, 1889.

4 James Oscar. Born May 3, 1859. Married Ida Ruff February 12, 1885. Business man at Atlanta, Georgia.

5 George Lee. Born October 13, 1861. Married Fannie McCutcheon January 22, 1885. President Cleveland Woolen Mills, Cleveland, Tennessee.

6 Nora Isabel. Born October 23, 1863. Married John C. Ramsey March 30, 1883. Lives in Cleveland, Tennessee.

7 Maggie Julia. Born May 20, 1866. Married James L. Caldwell January 3, 1888. Died in Chattanooga, Tennessee, September 2, 1897.

8 French Montgomery. Born September 26, 1868, and died May 4, 1869.

9 Houston Lafayette. Born March 29, 1870, and died February 28, 1899.

10 Julius Holmes. Born December 4, 1872. Married Florine Estell Jones October 23, 1895, and died January 19, 1904.

11 Fannie Lucretia. Born September 30, 1875, and died from effects of a burn January 23, 1878.

12 Anna Bell. Born July 16, 1878. Married Reeves Brown October 15, 1903. Lives in Macon, Georgia.

For descendants of above see Howard Family in Vol. 1 Notable Southern Families.

2 George Hardwick. Born 1800. Married Ellen Andrews 1825. Died 1867 in Missouri.

Their children were:
James. Born 1826.
George A. Born 1829.

NOTABLE SOUTHERN FAMILIES

Hillard P. Born 1833.
Fulton E. P. Born 1836.
3 Thomas. Married Ann McFarlane, but of their descendants I know nothing.
4 James. (Nothing is known of him or his descendants).
5 Mary. Married Joseph Barnett.
6 Cynthia. Married Rev. Mr. Pearson.
7 Joseph Tarply. Born August 3, 1811. Married Rebekah McFarlane 1837 and died 1851 or 1852 in Benton County, Arkansas.
Their children were:
Washington. Born 1838.
Thomas B. Born 1840.
Lucy. Born 1843.
Robert. Born 1844.
William. Born 1847.
8 Charles F. Born 1814. Married first Elizabeth Holmes and second Amanda Strong or Stroud.
Children by first wife:
Mary. Born 1837.
Sophronia. Born 1842.
Rachel. Born 1844.
9 Mollie Hardwick married Rene Fitzpatrick February 5, 1798, and died in Jasper County, Georgia.
1 Cynthia Hardwick Fitzpatrick.
2 Nancy Fitzpatrick.
Cynthia Hardwick Fitzpatrick was born ———. Married first John Byrom March 9, 1815, and died December 16, 1882.
Their sons were:
1 William Hardwick Byrom. Born August 21, 1817. Married Susan Maria Gunn (born June 16, 1829), and died August 18, 1873.
2 Seymour Scott Byrom. Born January 15, 1819, and died October 15, 1827.
The children of the above William Hardwick Byrom and Susan Maria Gunn were:
1 John Seymour Byrom.
2 Adella Virginia Byrom.
3 Anne Maud Byrom.
4 William Franklin Byrom.
1 John Seymour Byrom. Born September 3, 1849. Married Mrs. Eoline Butts White (widow of Goodrich White), May 3, 1876.

HARDWICK

Their chldren were:
1 William Hardwick Byrom (unmarried).
2 Seymour Butts Byrom.
(1) Seymour Butts Byrom. Born June 26, 1880. Married Katherine Rogers Clayton January 29, 1901.
1 John Seymour Byrom, Junior. Born 1901.
2 Katherine Eoline Byrom. Born 1903.
(2) Adella Virginia Byrom. Born December 20, 1852. Married James M. DuPree July, 1875.
Their children are:
1 Julia.
2 James.
3 Hattie.
Of the above Julia Dupree married Lacy Boyd and has one son, James Boyd.
2 James Dupree, Junior. Married Ida Clews and has James Dupree third.
3 Hattie Dupree. Married Newman Gallaher and has one daughter, Harriet Gallaher.
(3) Annie Maud Byrom. Born February 20, 1853. Married William H. Clarke December, 1885, and died July 25, 1896.
Their children were:
1 Susie Clarke.
2 Byrom Clarke.
3 William Clarke.
4 Pauline Clarke.
Susie Clarke married James Chapman and has one child, Henry Chapman.
Byrom Clarke married Delphine Marion. Their children are:
1 Louise.
2 Delphine.
3 Marion.
William Clarke is unmarried.
Pauline Clarke married Alver Joiner and has one child, Pauline Joiner.
(4) William Franklin Byrom. Born May 12, 1856.
(5 Julia Brooks Byrom. Born July 23, 1858. Married Dempsy Brown Wimberly October 27, 1875.
Their children are:
1 Mary Wimberly.
2 Brown Wimberly. (Unmarried).
Mary Wimberly married Norwood Robson and has two daughters:

NOTABLE SOUTHERN FAMILIES

  1 Julia Wimberly.
  2 Norwood.
  Cynthia Hardwick Fitzpatrick (widow of John Byrom) was married to Edward Varner July 6, 1823.
  By this marriage there were:
  1 Andrew Jackson Varner. Born 1824. Died unmarried.
  2 Jefferson Monroe Varner. Born 1825 and died unmarried.
  3 Clinton Lafayette Varner. Born 1827.
  4 Mary Josephine Varner. Born 1830 and died young.
  5 John Clark Varner. Born 1832. Married Mary, first, 1884.
  6 Cynthia Amanda Varner. Born 1835 and died unmarried.
  7 Narcissa Josephine Varner. Born 1837 (unmarried).
  Clinton Lafayette Varner. Married ———— and had:
  1 Frank Gunn Varner.
  2 Andrew Jackson Varner.
  3 Julia Varner. Married Chapman.
  4 Paul Varner.
  5 Forrest Lee Varner.
  6 Robert Lee Varner.
  John Clark Varner. Married ———— and had:
  1 Gordon Varner.
  2 Mary Neely Varner.
  3 Valeria Lamar Varner. Married White.
  4 Kenan Varner.
  5 Cynthia Bird Varner. Married Sanders.
  (2) Nancy Fitzpatrick, daughter of Molly Hardwick and Rene Fitzpatrick. Born October 2, 1804. Married John Smith Davenport Byrom March 3, 1818, and died September 3, 1877.
  Their children were:
  1 Henry Crawford Byrom. Born December 15, 1818. Married, first, Miss Lay; second, Julia Harlan and childless. Died December 21, 1849.
  2 William Hardwick Byrom. Born October 2, 1825. Married Julinah Fite 1846 and died August 2, 1853.
  3 Polly Byrom.
  The children of the above William Hardwick Byrom and wife Julinah Fite Byrom were:
  1 John S. D. Byrom, Junior.
  2 Nancy Byrom.
  3 William Henry C. Byrom.

HARDWICK

(1) John S. D. Byrom, Junior. Born 1848. Married, first, Lenora Smith in 1873 and, second, Elizabeth Senter in 1883.

(2) Nancy Byrom. Born 1850. Married O. G. Harris 1873.

(3) William Henry B. (Doc) Byrom. Born November 23, 1852. Married Sudie R. Mayfield 1878.

Their children are:
1 Nancy Byrom. Born June 30, 1881.
2 Julia Byrom. Born September 27, 1883.
3 Alex. Mayfield Byrom. Born November 16, 1885.
4 Ora Byrom. Born November 1, 1887.
5 William Clinton Byrom. Born June 20, 1892.
6 Maud Byrom. Born August 22, 1896.

(9) Peggy, mentioned in William Hardwick's will and unmarried in 1801-1803. She is thought to have later married a Venable.

The tides of emigration seem to have carried the Hardwicks south. The census of 1790 for South Carolina gives the following: In Camden District, Chester County, Hazel Hardrich and Moses Hardridge. In Georgetown District, Prince George Parish, John Hardwick, Aaron Hardwick, and Samuel Hardwick. In Union County, Thomas Hardwick. The descendants of the two William Hardwicks of Georgia are scattered from Georgia to Texas.

The name almost disappears from Westmoreland County, Virginia. On July 11, 1787, Aaron Hardage in this county was granted license to marry Sallie Harrison. In 1819 Aaron Hardwick bought of Richard Straugh. On July 8, 1823, Daniel H. Hardwick was granted license to marry Lucy Smith. The writer is informed that there is only one person now in Westmoreland County of the Hardwick name, and apparently none in Stafford, Prince William, and Fauquier Counties.

HAYWOOD

John Haywood, the founder of the Haywood family in North Carolina, was born in Christ Church Parish, near St. Michael's, in the Island of Barbadoes. He was the son of Sir John Haywood, a younger brother of Sir Henry Haywood, a Knight and magistrate in England and he must have been a man of some note, as Evelyn in his Memoirs speaks of having met him at court, noting his "arrogant manner".

John Haywood settled in 1730 at the mouth of the Conecanarie, in Halifax which was then a part of Edgecomb, North Carolina. He was a man of importance in the settlement and was made treasurer of the northern counties of the Province in 1752. He held this office until his death in 1758.

John Haywood married Mary Lovett. Their seven children were:
(I) William Henry Haywood
(II) Sherwood Haywood
(III) Mary Haywood
(IV) Elizabeth Haywood
(V) Deborah Haywood
(VI) Egbert Haywood
(VII John Haywood, Second.

I WILLIAM HAYWOOD

William Henry Haywood, son of John Haywood, the emigrant and his wife Mary Lovett Haywood, was born about 1735. He was a member of the Committee of safety for the Halifax District, 1775; a member of the Provincial Congress at Halifax in April 1776; also a member of the same body at the same place in November 1776; and was one of the Committee to form the State Constitution and

NOTABLE SOUTHERN FAMILIES

was appointed a member of the Council of State. He lived in Edgecomb County, North Carolina. He married Charity Hare, presumably about 1755. They had ten children:

(1) Jemima Haywood
(2) John Haywood
(3) Ann Haywood
(4) Charity Haywood
(5) Mary Haywood
(6) Sherwood Haywood
(7) Elizabeth Haywood
(8) William Henry Haywood, Second
(9) Stephen Haywood
(10) Elizabeth Haywood

Of the foregoing:

(1) Jemima Haywood, daughter of William Henry Haywood and his wife Charity Hare Haywood, married John Whitfield of Lenoir. She died in 1837. Her children were (a) William Haywood Whitfield (who married twice and left seven children); (b) Constantine Whitfield (who left five children); (c) Sherwood Whitfield (who died unmarried); (d) John Walter Whitfield (who left three children); (e) Jemima Whitfield (who married first ——— Middleton, and second, ——— Williams and left six children); (f) Mary Ruffin Whitfield; (g) Keziah Arabella Whitfield (who left three children); (h) Rachel Daniel Whitfield (who married John Jones and had five children); (i) George Washington Whitfield.

(2) John Haywood, son of Colonel William Henry Haywood and his wife Charity Hare Haywood, was state Treasurer of North Carolina for forty years. He married twice, first, Sarah Leigh, and second Eliza Williams, daughter of John Pugh Williams. He had six children: (a) John Haywood (who died unmarried); (b) George Washington Haywood (who died unmarried); (c) Thomas Burges Haywood (who died unmarried); (d) Dr. Fabius Julius Haywood (who married Martha Whitaker and had four children, Fabius Julius Haywood, second, John Pugh Haywood, Joseph Haywood, and Mary Haywood who married Judge Daniel G. Fowler); (e) Frances Ann Haywood (who died unmarried); (f) Edmund Burke Haywood (who married Lucy Williams and had seven children: Edmund Burke Haywood, second, Alfred Haywood, Dr. Hubert Haywood, Ernest Haywood, Edgar Haywood, John Haywood and Eliza Haywood, who married Preston Bridgers.

HAYWOOD

(3) Ann Haywood, daughter of Colonel William Henry Haywood and wife, Charity Haywood, was born in 1760 and died in 1842. She married Dr. Robert Williams, a surgeon in the Continental Army and had two children: (a) Eliza Williams (who married Reverend John Singleton and had three sons, Colonel George B. Singleton who was killed in battle, Colonel Richard Singleton and Colonel Thomas Singleton); (b) Dr. Robert Williams, second (who married and left children).

(4) Charity Haywood, daughter of Colonel William Henry Haywood and his wife Charity Hare Haywood, married Colonel Lawrence of Alabama, and left three children.

(5) Mary Haywood, daughter of Colonel William Henry Haywood and his wife Charity Hare Haywood, married Ethelred Ruffin and had two children: (a) Sarah Ruffin (who married Dr. Henry Haywood; (b) Henry G. Ruffin (who married ——— Tart and had two sons, Colonel Samuel Ruffin and Colonel Thomas Ruffin (who was killed at the Battle of Hamilton Crossing in Virginia).

(6) Sherwood Haywood, son of Colonel William Henry Haywood and his wife Charity Hare Haywood, was born in 1782. He died in 1829. He married Eleanor Hawkins (who was born 1776, died 1855). They had nine children: (a) Ann Haywood (who married William A. Blount, and had children, Major William A. Blount, second, of Raleigh, and Ann Blount, who married General L. O'Bryan Branch and had Susan O'Bryan Branch, married Robert H. Jones, William A. Branch; and Ann Branch, married Armistead Jones; and Josephine Branch, who married Kerr Craige of Salisbury); (b) Sarah Haywood (who married twice, first John Gray Blount and second Gavin Hogg, leaving no children by either husband); (c) Delia Haywood (who married twice, first General William Williams and second George E. Badger. Her son by her first marriage was Colonel Joseph John Williams of Tallahassee, Florida. By her second marriage she had seven children, namely: Mary Badger, married P. M. Hale, George Badger, second, Major Richard Cogdell Badger, Thomas Badger, Sherwood Badger, Edward Stanley Badger, and Ann Badger, who married twice, first ——— Bryan and second, Colonel Paul Daison); (d) Dr. Rufus Haywood (who died unmarried); (e) Lucy Haywood (who married John S. Bryan and had four children, namely: A daughter who married Bail Manly, a daughter who married Thomas Badger, a daughter who married William H. Young and John S.

Bryan, second,); (f) Francis P. Haywood (who married twice, first Ann Farell and second Mrs. Martha Joyner Austin, daughter of Colonel Andrew Joyner of Halifax; (g) Robert W. Haywood (who married Mary White and left one child, Mary Haywood); (h) Maria T. Haywood (who never married); (i) Dr. Richard B. Haywood (who married Julia Hicks and had eight children, namely: Sherwood Haywood, Graham Haywood, Effie Haywood (who married Colonel Carl A. Woodruff, U. S. A.), Lavinia Haywood, Howard Haywood, Marshall Haywood, Eleanor Haywood and Marian Haywood).

The next child in this list as given by Wheeler's Reminiscence is Elizabeth Haywood (seventh child of William Henry Haywood and his wife Charity Hare Haywood). However the tenth child is also given as Elizabeth Haywood and as married to Governor Edward B. Dudley, there is manifestly an error. I conclude that the error is in the name of this daughter who married Henry Irwin Toole, as Governor Edward B. Dudley is clearly given in the Dudley record as married to Elizabeth Haywood. However the record as given in Wheeler's Reminiscences is:

(7) Elizabeth Haywood, daughter of Colonel William Henry Haywood and his wife Charity Hare Haywood, was born 1759. She died 1832. She married Henry Irwin Toole. First, of Edgecomb, who was born in 1750 and died in 1794. They had three children, (a) Henry Irwin Toole, Second born 1768, died 1816 (who married Ann Blount, daughter of Governor William Blount of Tennessee and left two children, namely Henry Irwin Toole, Third, born 1810, died 1850, married Margaret Telfair and Mary Eliza Toole, born 1812, married Dr. Joseph J. Lawrence of Tarboro, North Carolina); (b) Arabella Toole (who married James West Clarke) and (c) Mary Toole (who married Theophilus Parker, born 1775, died 1849, at Tarboro. They had six children, namely: Reverend John Haywood Parker, born 1815, died 1858, Catherine C. Parker, born 1817, married twice, first John Hargrave and seond Reverend Robert B. Drane; Elizabeth T. Parker, born 1820, Reverend Joseph Blount Cheshire; Mary W. Parker, born 1822, married twice, first Frank Hargrave and married second, Governor Henry T. Clark; Colonel Francis M. Parker, and Arabella C. Parker.

(8) William Henry Haywood, Second, son of Colonel William Henry Haywood and his wife Charity Hare Haywood was born 1770; he died 1857. He married Anne Sheperd and had three children: (1) William Henry Hay-

wood, Third, born 1810. He was United States Senator from North Carolina. He married Jane Graham and had nine children, namely: William Henry Haywood, Fourth, (who was killed in the Battle of the Wilderness); Duncan Cameron Haywood (who was killed at the Battle of Cold Harbor), Edward G. Haywood, Minerva Haywood (who married ——— Baker), Jane Haywood (who married Sion H. Rogers), Ann Haywood (who married Samuel Riggin), Margaret Haywood (who married ——— Cameron), Gertrude Haywood (who married George Trapier), and Elizabeth Haywood who died unmarried); (2) Charity Haywood married Governor Charles Manly and had eight children, namely: Colonel John H. Manly (who married Caroline Henry,) Langdon C. Manly, Cora Manly (who married Colonel George B. Singletary), Helen Manly (who married John Grimes), Julia Manly (who married Colonel ——— McDowell (who was killed in The War Between the States), Sophia Manly (who married ——— Harding), Ida Manly (who married Dr. Joseph Baker of Tarboro), and Basil Manly, Commander of Manly's Battery in the War Between the States, who married Lucy Bryan.

(9) Stephen Haywood, born 1772, died 1824, son of William Henry Haywood and his wife Charity Hare Haywood married twice, first ——— Lane, by whom he had two sons, Dr. John Leigh Haywood and Benjamin Franklin Haywood, and married second, Delia Hawkins by whom he had five children, namely: William Dallas Haywood (who married Mary Cannon), Margaret Craven Haywood (who married George Little); Lucinda Haywood (who married ——— Sasser), Sarah Haywood, and Philemom H. Haywood of the United States Navy.

(10 Elizabeth Haywood is given in Wheeler's Reminiscence, from which most of this data was obtained, as the tenth child of William Henry Haywood, First, and his wife Charity Haywood. As the seventh child is also listed as Elizabeth and is given as married to Henry Irwin Toole, there is manifestly an error. However the record as it appears in Wheeler is: Elizabeth Haywood (tenth child) married Governor Edward B. Dudley. They had six children, namely: Edward B. Dudley, Second, William Henry Dudley (who married ——— Baker), Christopher Dudley, Eliza Ann Dudley (who married ——— Purnell), Jane Dudley (who married ——— Johnson), and Margaret Dudley (who married Colonel McIlhenny).

In an account of the Dudley Family, also in Wheeler,

NOTABLE SOUTHERN FAMILIES

Governor Edward B. Dudley is clearly given as married to Elizabeth Haywood. It is therefore probable that the Elizabeth Haywood who is given as the seventh child and married to Henry Irwin Toole is an error.

II SHERWOOD HAYWOOD

II Sherwood Haywood, son of John Haywood of Conecanarie and his wife Mary Lovatt Haywood, married Hannah Gray and had one son, Adam John Haywood (who married his cousin Sarah Haywood, daughter of Egbert Haywood and his wife Sarah Ware Haywood). They had one daughter, Margaret Haywood (died 1874), who was the wife of Louis D. Henry, born 1788, died 1840, and had one daughter, Virginia Henry (who married Colonel Duncan K. McRea); Caroline Henry (who married Colonel John H. Manly); Augusta Henry who married R. P. Waring); Margaret Henry (who married Edward G. Haywood); Mary Henry (who married Mathew P. Taylor); Malvina Henry (who married Douglass Bell), and Louis D. Henry, second, (who married Virginia Massenburg).

III MARY HAYWOOD

III Mary Haywood, third child of John Haywood of Conecanarie and his wife Mary Lovett Haywood, married the Reverend Thomas Burgess in 1761. Their son, Lovett Burgess, married twice, first, Priscilla Monnie and second, Mrs. Black. By the last marriage he had five children, namely: Mary Burgess (who married ——— Alston, 1824), Elizabeth Burgess (who married ——— Alston of Bedford County, North Carolina 1812), Melissa Burgess (who married General William Williams, whose daughter Melissa Williams married Colonel Joseph John Long, and their daughter Ellen Long married General Junius Daniel who was killed at Chancellorsville), John Burford (who married Martha Alston), and Thomas Burgess (who was a lawyer of Halifax and left no children).

IV ELIZABETH HAYWOOD

IV Elizabeth Haywood, daughter of John Haywood of Conecanarie and his wife Mary Lovett Haywood, married Jesse Hare and died in 1774. She had two children, namely: Ann Hare (who married Isaac Croom; their son Isaac Croom, second, marred Sarah Pierson), and Mary Hare (who married twice, first Richard Croom and second, ——— Hicks).

HAYWOOD

V DEBORAH HAYWOOD

V DEBORAH HAYWOOD, daughter of John Haywood of Conecanarie and his wife Mary Lovett Haywood, married John Hardy, but left no children.

VI EGBERT HAYWOOD

VI. Egbert, the sixth child of John Haywood, of Conecanaire, and his wife Mary Lovett Haywood, married Sarah Ware. He died in 1801. They had five children, namely: (a) Sarah; (b) John; (c) Henry; (d) Mary, and (e) Betsy, or as variously given, Elizabeth.

(a) Sarah married her cousin, Adam John Haywood.

(b) John Haywood, second child and first son of Egbert Haywood and his wife, Sarah Ware, is of especial interest because he became a famous Judge in North Carolina and a great historian. Haywood's History of Tennessee is one of the most important volumes in Tennessee and Southern history. Judge John Haywood is ancestor of the Tennessee family of the name, most of whom reside in West Tennessee.

Judge John Haywood married Martha Edwards and they had, among other children, George W. Haywood (who married Sallie Dabney and whose descendants are in Giles County, Tennessee, one of whom bears the family name Egbert Haywood (who married Susan Cannon Glasgow, and has descendents in Brownsville, Tennessee).

(c) Henry Haywood, a physician, married Sarah Ruffin.

(d) Mary Haywood married a lawyer whose name is given on one page of Wheeler's Reminiscences as Captain Robert Bell and on another Captain William Bell. (As their first son was named William Haywood Bell and as they had no son Robert, it is probable that he was named William Bell). Captain Bell died leaving a large family of small children. Their mother's sister, Betsy or Elizabeth, was married to Colonel William Shepperd. Colonel and Mrs. Shepperd took the orphaned Bells into their family, adopted them and raised them to useful lives. Margaret Bell, the first child, married first ——— Duffie, an eminent lawyer of North Carolina, married second, Dr. ——— Buchanon, of St. Stephens, Alabama, and married third, Adlai Osborne, leaving by him one son, Egbert Osborne, who married Margaret Strudwick, a niece of Colonel Shepperd (daughter of Martha Shepperd, and Major William F. Strudwick, of Hillsboro, North Carolina).

William Haywood Bell entered the United States Army and rose to a Captain's commission. While a second Lieutenant he invented a contrivance for turning heavy ordinance with rapidity. For this invention the Government voted him an appropriation of $25,000, which money he invested in St. Louis real estate. The city grew rapidly and Captain Bell became immensely wealthy. When about to die, shortly after the close of the War Between the States, he willed a large share of his property to the descendants of his "benefactor," Colonel William Shepperd, of Orange County, North Carolina. Henry Haywood Bell became an admiral in the United States Navy. John Bell became a Captain in the United States Navy. Elizabeth J. Bell married Thomas Ashe, grandson of Governor Ashe, and the other daughter, ——— Bell, married Dr. ——— Howell, of West Tennessee.

(e) Betsy Haywood, or Elizabeth as sometimes given, married Colonel William Shepperd. (This couple generously adopted their sister's children and raised them, as noted in foregoing paragraph). Colonel and Mrs. William Shepperd had eight children, namely: (1) Sarah; (2) Betsy;

(3) Susan; (4) Mary; (5) Margaret; (6) William; (7) Egbert; (8) Henry. (1) Sarah married Honorable William B. Grove, of Fayetteville, a member of Congress (1791-1802); they had a son, David, who married Susan Ashe;

(2) Betsy, named for her mother, married Colonel Samuel Ashe, born 1763 and died in 1835. (They had children Betsy Ashe, who married Owen Holmes; Mary Porter Ashe, who married Dr. S. G. Moses, of St. Louis; John B. Ashe, member of Congress from Tennessee, who married his cousin, Eliza Hay, and moved to Texas; William S. Ashe, who married Sarah Ann Green; Thomas Ashe, who married Rosa Hill; Richard Porter Ashe, of San Francisco, who married Lina Loyal; Susan Ashe, who married her cousin, David Grove, and Sarah Ashe who married Judge Samuel Hall, of Georgia. (3) Susan Shepperd married David Hay. (Their child, Eliza Hay, married Honorable J. B. Ashe, as above

noted. (4) Mary Shepperd married Samuel P. Ashe, of Halifax, North Carolina. (5) Margaret Shepperd married Dr. John Rogers. (6, 7, 8) William, Egbert and Henry Shepperd probably died unmarried. Wheeler says that another daughter of this family "married a Mr. Johnston and moved to Tennessee". This may refer to a second marriage of one of the daughters.

VII JOHN HAYWOOD, SECOND

VII John Haywood, second, son of John Haywood of Conecanarie and his wife Mary Lovett, died unmarried.

HOLLIDAY
HALLIDAY

Arms were granted to Walter Halliday in 1470 by Edward IV., and confirmed to his descendant Sir Leonard Halliday who was Lord Mayor of London 1640.

1 Walter Halliday, Master of the Revels to Edward IV., had among others a son, Henry, who married Miss Payne of Paynes Court, and was seated at Minchin Hampton.

2 Their son, William Halliday, married Sarah Bridges, Aunt to Lord Chandas.

3 Their son, Sir Leonard Halliday, married Ann, daughter and heiress of William Dincat. or Dinhold, of Laugham, Suffolk, widow of Henry, Earl of Lancaster.

4 Their son, John, seated at Frome, married Alice, daughter of Alderman Ferravs.

5 Their son, Thomas, settled in Virginia, married the widow of Col. John Hinton.

Vol. II Colonial Families in U. S. by George N. McKenzie, says:

"Thomas Halliday, (son of John of Frome, England), was living in Jamestown in 1660, and had eleven children. But only two are mentioned in the record at Williamsburg, Thomas the ancestor of the Maryland family and John Marshall, ancestor of the Virginia family.

* Thomas Halliday of Jamestown (James City Co.) patented land in Isle of Wight County.

Anthony Halliday of Isle of Wight County, was a son of Thomas of Jamestown, and mentions his brother, Marshall, in his will, "Lands purchased from his in 1717".

The three sons of Thomas Halliday, 1., (son of John of Frome, England), and the first of the name in Virginia, were.

A. Thomas, 2., died 1703, married Miss Trueman, set-

NOTABLE SOUTHERN FAMILIES

tled in Prince George County, Md.

B. Anthony, 2., will dated January 1818, married prior to 1671, the widow of John Brewer, of Isle of Wight County.

C. John Marshall, who settled in Spotsylvania County, Virginia, died in 1742.

The Hallidays gave the land on which old St. John's Church is built. The vestry book is extant in Suffolk now begins in 1749, and the Halliday's from father to son were vestry-men and wardens.

HOLLIDAY

Thomas 2., Thomas 1, of Virginia, (John of England), settled in Prince George County, Maryland, 1703, married Miss Trueman of England. Had sons.

1 James Halliday of Readbourne, Queen Anne Col. Maryland.

2 Col. Leonard Holliday of Brookfield, Prince George County, Maryland. No record.

Hon. James Halliday of Readbourne, born June 18, 1696, died 1747, married May 3, 1720, Mrs. Sarah Covington Lloyd (widow) and had:

1 James Halliday, eminent lawyer and colonial statesman.

2 Henry, born March 9, 1725, died November 11, 1789.

3 Sarah.

4 Talbot, married December 9, 1749, Anna Maria Robins of Peach Blossom, had:

1 Henrietta Maria.
2 Sarah.
3 Anna Maria, born December 9, 1756.
4 James (below).
5 Thomas.
6 Rebecca.
7 Elizabeth.
8 Henry.
9 Margaret.

Prince George County, Maryland, Census, 1776.
James Holliday 35 years, wife Elizabeth 25 years.
William 1 year.
Elizabeth 8 years.
Mary 7 years.

HOLLIDAY

Anthony 2, (Thomas 1, John of England).

Settled in Isle of Wight County, Virginia, married prior to 1671, the widow of John Brewer of same County. An-

HOLLIDAY

thony was Burgess of Isle of Wight in 1690, and other years. Was one of the Justices and according to the records, was a lawyer.

His will is dated 1717, proved January 1718, his children were:

1 Jonas, will dated July 4, 1713-14, died 1717, married Hannah.
2 Joseph, born 1669, (probably the oldest), died about 1712-13, married Charity; had, 1. John, 2. Anthony, 3. Lemuel, mentioned in the will of Jonas, Anthony, Jonas, Sarah and Mary. 4. Brewer had daughters, one Elizabeth.
3 Lemuel, no record.
4 Brewer, no record.
5 Sarah, no record.
6 Mary, no record.
7 Anthony, no record.

Anthony 4 (Joseph 3, Anthony 2, Thomas,) called Anthony II, married Elizabeth Godwin, and their children were:

1 Charity, who married Jonathan Godwin.
2 Mary, who married Jeremiah Godwin.
3 Thomas, who married Mary Brewer.

The children of Thomas Holliday and Mary Brewer were:

1 Elizabeth, who married Josiah Godwin.
2 Brewer, married but no sons.
3 Andrew, left home after quarreling with his father.
4 Captain Joseph, born 1736, died 1814, served in Revolutionary war, married Patience Godwin, had a son, James, who married Anna Gray Godwin.

Joseph Holliday served as Lieutenant in Captain Nathaniel Fox's Company, 6th Virginia Regiment, born in Nansemond County.

Jonas 3, (Anthony 2, Thomas 1, (1st in Virginia.) Was burgess for Norfolk County, is styled as Jonas Halliday Gent. Will dated July 4, 1713-14. Left no children. Mentions his brothers and sisters. Wife Hannah was E. Upon death of his sister-in-law, Charity Halloday, wife of his brother, Joseph, lately deceased, he leaves the property given her to his son, John, at death. Elsewhere in the will, he calls this John and his brother Anthony his Cousins, sons of his brother Joseph, lately deceased.

The first mention of Jonas in Norfolk County, records is in 1705, when as justice he is present at the term of count. He had a patent of land in 1711. Wife, Hannah, maiden name probably Halliday, as in court records she is styled Mrs. Hannah Holliday, Holliday.

Jonas Holliday received 93 acres in Norfolk County, for transporting Robert Sluard and Hannah Holliday into the Colony, April 27, 1711.

Was sheriff of Norfolk County, 1713-14-18.

William Holliday, brother of John Marshall, Thomas and Anthony. St. George's Parish, died December 4, 1744. Will proved May 6, 1746, Ex-sons Charles and Robert, Leg. Wife Anne, sons John, Charles, George and Robert. Daughter, Elizabeth, wife of Thomas Dillard; daughter Ann, wife of John Robinson; grandson of John Robinson; grandson William Holliday, and of Robert; grandson William Holliday, son of John.

(Query).

Could above John be one who married Elizabeth Long and died 1762, and had a son, William, born 1751, who married Catherine Hutton, and had Robert, Thomas, Louise, Harriet and Mary.

Second Generation

Elizabeth 2, daughter of William 1st, (who died 1744), wife of Thomas Dillard. He died October 23, 1774, will proved December 15, 1784, Ex. wife Sarah, son John Dillard and Elisha Desmukes.

My first wife's children, Joseph, John, William, James. Thomas Dillard, Ann Peters, Jane Devall, Lucy, Hannah Dillard, My wife's children, Richard, Fielding and Mary.

NOTE. All page references in following records are to Crozier's Spotsylvania County Reords, unless otherwse stated.

JOHN MARSHALL HOLLODAY, II OF VIRGINIA

Captain John Holloday, II, (Thomas I), Captain of Virginia Rangers of Spotsylvania County, Virginia where he was located in 1702. Lived on East Creek in Southwest part of County where he is buried. Home called Bellefonte, from springs near by. An act of Virginia Assembled ordered court to be held in the home of John Holloday until court house could be completed.

Session was held in Captain John's son's house, John junior, April 7th, 1779. Always called John Holloday Gent. Wife Anne Lewis (or Elizabeth). Find him as witness to many wills and deeds in Spotsylvania County.

He died November 4th, 1742. Will proved at St. Georges

HOLLIDAY

Parish, King William County, December 7th, 1742. Witness John Waller, John Waller, junior and Thomas Cartwright. Ex. sons Joseph and Benjamin and son-in-law Thomas Pulliam.

1 Gives son William 200 acres of land.
2 Gives son John 250 acres of land.
3 Gives son Daniel 200 acres of land.
4 Gives son Joseph 300 acres of land.
5 Gives son Benjamin 300 acres of land.
6 Gives daughter Elizabeth 300 acres of land. (Wife of Pattison Pulliam).
7 Gives daughter Winifred 300 acres of land. (Wife of Thomas Pulliam).
8 Gives daughter Sarah 300 acres of land. (Wife of James Rollins).
9 Gives daughter Susanna 200 acres of land.

October 7th, 1735, John Holloway Gent of Spts. County, to Thomas Pulliam, Plant. of same County, 200 acres in Spts. County.

November 6th, 1739, Thomas Sertain of St. George Parish, Spts. County to John Holloday, senior, of said Parish, 25 pds. curr. and 200 acres, tec.

John Holloday received 400 acres of land. Moved from lower Virginia on Pamusky R. to Spotsylvania County ten miles above N. Wales in 1711. His wife, Elizabeth received 400 acres in 1724 in St. George Parish.

NOTE

Hayden, p. 358.

"Court met at the house of John Holliday, junior, on Wednesday, April 7th, 1779, as John the first (Captain John) was then dead, and John II. who died June 1780 was then John Holliday, senior, the John in question was a son, if not a nephew of John II."

Third Generation

1 William Holliday, III, (John II, Thomas I,) mentioned first in will. Born about 1720. No record but deed dated August 2nd, 1743 (p. 163,) St. George Parsh. "William Holloday and Judey, his wife, to John Holloday, of same Parish, 30 pds. curr. and 200 acres of land in said County, part of patent granted Thomas Sertain May 6th, 1727, and by him conveyed to John Holloday Gent. dec'd father of said William.

Deed p. 149, November 6th, 1739, Thomas Sertain of St.

NOTABLE SOUTHERN FAMILIES

George Parish, Spts. County, to John Holloday, senior, of said Parish and County 25 pds. of curr. and 200 acres, with plantation, said Sertain now lives on, and part of patent granted said Sertain, May 6th, 1727. Wit. Joseph Thomas, Daniel Holloday and Elizabeth Holloday.

Third Generation

2 John Holloday 3, (John 2, Sr. Gent. Thomas 1.) was born about 1728.

His will in Spotsylvania County proved April 8th, 1781. Ex. bond dated November 15th, 1781. Ex. bros. Joseph and Benjamin, wife, Tabitha 2nd wife), sons William and Benjamin, daughters, Lucy, Anna and Elizabeth. Mentions four children of Elizabeth, wife of John Penn, also son John by first wife, Elizabeth Rawlings (Daughter of James Rawlings, who died 1757).

Deed January 16th, 1749

"John Holloday of St. George Parish and Elizabeth, his wife, to Thomas McGee, etc."

Deed August 16th, 1770.

"John Holloday and Elizabeth, his wife, of Spts. County to their son, John Holloday, junior, Deed of gift".

Deed November 21st, 1771.

"John Holloday, senior, and Elizabeth, his wife," and again in 1776, (All children must have been by first wife.)

Then in 1777, December 13th, (p. 336) we find "Tabitha Gatewood, widow, and John Holloday, widower, to William Golson in trust, for use of the Gatewood and Holloday etc.

Tabitha Gatewood, widow of Henry Gatewood, was the daughter of Joseph and Susannah Collins. He died August 1759. Will dated November 1st, 1757.

Henry Gatewood died January 28th, 1777. Sons, Richard, Dudley, Henry, William and Anne, his wife, Peter and Larkin. Daughters, Keziah Sandridge and Dorothy Foster.

Deed (p. 348) September 10th, 1779.

John Hollodday and Tabitha, his wife, of Spts. County, to James Tate, etc. Witness, John Holloday, junior.

Fourth Generation

The children of Elizabeth and Joseph Penn were Phillip, Moses, Thomas, Catherine, Mary and Francis.

HOLLIDAY

"Children of said Joseph, wife Elizabeth Penn. Estate put in trust September 19th, 1763.

John III, or now John junior, appears in deed of 1771, with Mildred, his wife, of Berkley Parish.

John junior, died June 17th, 1784, two months after his father.

Deed June 28th, 1783.

"Benj. Johnson to Mildred Holloday, widow and ex. of John Holloday".

Mildred Holloday, married Abram Simons. See deed p. 482.

Children of John and Mildred Holloday, February 6th, 1786-7, Abram Simons, Guard. to Sally, Benj. and Peggy Holloday, orphans of John Holloday.

1795, John Wood Guard. to Polly Holliday, Vincent Vass Guard. to John Holliday; orphans of John Holloday.

Deed April 1st, 1788, p. 415.

Agatha, Wife of Benj. Weeks.
Elizabeth, wife of John Wood.
Ann (or Nancy) wife of Norcut Slaven.
Sarah, single at the time of deed. Later married Mr. Freeman.

All these in deed went to Wilkes County, Georgia.

Deed February 7th, 1786.

"Owen Thomas Holloday, orphan, son of John Holliday, age 16 years 13th of September last (born 1769), apprentice, etc".

Mildred Holloday, wife of John Holloday, junior, was the widow of Owen Thomas. November 14th, 1768, p. 265, Mildred Thomas, of Spts. County to her two children, James and Agnes, wife of Thomas Merry, etc. Deed of gift, right or title she may have under will of her husband, Owen Thomas, deceased". Witness, O. Thomas, John Holloday, junior.

Deed April 17th, 1772, p. 76.

"John Holloday Guard. to Robert, James and Sally Thomas, orphans of Owen Thomas, with Benj. Holloday and Joseph Holloday".

John Holloday, junior, must have had two wives. If Mildred was still Mildred Thomas in 1768 (time of deed to her children), then Owen Thomas Holloday was her oldest child (born 1769) by John Holloday.

The four daughters who were married at time of deed

NOTABLE SOUTHERN FAMILIES

1788, Agatha, Elizabeth, Ann and Sarah must have been children of first wife. Although no track of her is to be found in deed or County records.

Third Generation

3 Joseph Holloday (third son of John II. senior, Gent. Thomas 1) born 1726. Married Elizabeth Lewis (daughter of Henry Lewis), about 1747-8. He died September 23rd, 1785. (Hayden says July 24th, 1795.
Ex. Bond dated September 1st, 1795. p. 51 Crozier).
Ex. sons Lewis, James Joseph, Benj. Stephen John, William and Thomas.
Daughters. Jemima, Betty and Winifred.
Codicil dated, July 17th, 1795, mentions sons, Stephen, John, Lewis and Thomas, and daughters, Jemima, Betty and Winifred.
Deed July 1st, 1746, Joseph Holloday of Spts. County to Zachary Lewis, of same...........part of lands devised said Joseph by last will and testament of his father, John Holloday, deceased.
Deed October 7th, 1765 ,Joseph Holloday of Sps. County and Elizabeth, his wife, to Benj. Lewis, of said County, etc. part of tract devised said Joseph by his father, John Holloday, deceased.
Joseph Holloday served in the Revolution, Ensign, February 16th, 1776, 2nd, Lieut. September 11th, 1776, 1st, Lieut. March 1st, 1777 Promoted to Captain Continental line, 1780. Was in Battles of Guilford, Camden and Yorktown. Enlisted under Captain Nat. Fox and Col Stubblefield (Crozier p. 234).
Joseph and Elizabeth Lewis Holloday had eleven children.

Fourth Generation

1 John, born September 1749, Spts. County. Died May 21st, 1819. Killed by hogshead of tobacco rolling down hill on him. Served in the Revolutionary War in Captain Thomas Minor's Spts. Troops, 1780. Married Martha Winston. Had son, John.
(Hayden says he moved to Clarke County, Kentucky, in 1795.)
2 Lewis, born 1751, died October 20th, 1820, married, March 15th, 1774, Elizabeth (Lewis) Littlepage, widow of Col. James Littlepage. He died 1769. She was the daughter Zachary Lewis, and was born in 1732. Lewis Holloday was Overseer of the poor in Spts. County, from 1783

HOLLIDAY

to 1788. He served in the Revolutionary War as 2nd Lieut. under Captain Thomas Minor, with his brother, John. Lived at Bellefonte. Had issue:
1 Ann, born April 18th, 1775, died January 26th, 1846, married Hugh Boggs.
2 Waller, born August 17th, 1776, died August 27th, 1863, married September 3rd, 1793, Huldah Fontaine Lewis, daughter of Col. Zachary Lewis and wife, Ann Overton Terrill, married 1771.
3 Major James William, born June 15th, 1753, died 1823, married first 1773, Mary Ann Lewis; married second, Suffler (Sophia). Served in the Revolutionary War as Ensign 1st Con. Reg. of Virginia, February 16th, 1776, 2nd Lieut. 1st Con. Reg. of Virginia, August 10th, 1776, 2nd, Lieut. 1st, Pa. Reg. January 1st, 1777. Issue by first wife:
1 Lewis, born 1775, married, had 1st, James, 2nd, Lewis, 3rd, Polly.
2 William, died at Parkersburg.
3 Mary, born 1780, died 1839, married about 1805, John DeFrees of Rockridge County, had: 1st, James, born November 6th, 1807, died April 3rd, 1883, married Sophia Potter. 2nd, John W., born November 4th, 1890, died March 10th, 1882, married Eliza Ann Lindsay. 3rd, Isabella, born 1810, died 1849, married John Eskew. 4th, William C., born 1812, died 1855, married Kate Campbell.
John and Mary Holloday DeFrees lived in Rockridge County until 1812, when they moved to Ohio, Miami County about two miles south of Piqua. The parents of Mary Holloday DeFrees came out to Ohio to see her, intending to stay if they liked it. They stayed one week, then the old gentleman and his wife started back to Virginia.
4th, Jemia, born Flay 29th, married Isaac Graves of Newberne, North Carolina, later Orange County, Virginia. Had Lewis, Edward and Winifred.
5th, William, barn August 7th, 1756, died June 29th, 1816, married July 31st, 1777, Mildred Jane Lewis,
William, junior, born 1778, Nancy, Sallie, Jemima and James. Moved to Nicholas County, Kentucky about 1800. William, junior, married Margaret Hughes and had eight sons, one William, born 1800. Married Patsy McKim, youngest child, Mary, born 1844. (Hayden places his birth as 1765, August 7th, death April 25th, 1816, married July 31st, 1788, ten years later.)
6th, Winifred, born September 25th, 1758. Baptized Sunday, November 12th, 1758, in New Pamuky Church.

7th, Stephen, born September 8th, 1760, married 1783, Ann Hickman, born Culpepper County, 1754. Moved to Clark County, Kentucky, in 1795. Had issue:
    1st. Elliott, born in Kentucky, 1786, died 1869, married Rachel Johnson. 2nd. Jemima, born 1788, died 1812, married Elizah Harris. 3rd, James, died unmarried. 4th, Joseph, born 1791, married Sarah Woodfolk. 5th, Lewis, born 1793. 6th, Elizabeth, born 1795, died 1833, married John Huston. 7th, Waller, born 1797, married 1843, Sarah A. Dunahoo, widow of Joseph H. Whittington.
    8th, Benjamin, born June 8th, 1763, died in Kentucky, about 1825, married about 1784, Sarah Hampton. Had 1st, Benjamin junior, born June 8th, 1786, died April 1st, 1859, moved to Missouri 1817, married August 16th, 1823, Eliza Basye. 2nd, Mary C., born 1785, died 1859, married Augustus C. Davis. 3rd, Virginia. 4th, Stephen.
    9th, Joseph, junior, born 1765, died ———, married Agnes Holloday, daughter of Benjamin and Susannah Holloday. Son, Joseph III, born 1789, moved to Missouri in 1817 and married Nancy McCune.
    Deed January 26th, 1794, Joseph Holloday of Spts. County and Agnes, his wife, to Robert Hart of same County, 129 acres, part of tract lately belonging to Benjamin Holloday, deceased and alloted to sd. Agnes as her share of her father's land. Wit. Lewis Holloday, Benjamin Holloday and H. C. Boggs.
    10th, Elizabeth, born 1767, died June 15th, 1785.
    11th, Thomas, born 1769. No record.

Third Generation

4 Daniel Holloday 3rd, (son of John 2nd, senior, Thomas 1st.)
    Deed, June 7th, 1743, Daniel Holloday and Agnes, his wife, of St. George Parish, Spts. County, to Thomas Pulliam of same Parish.
    Only record of Daniel, Cozier, p. 6-149-162.
witness to a deed for his father in 1739. Crozier, p. 149.

Third Generation

5 Benjamin Holloday 3rd, (son of John 2nd, senior, Thomas 1st.) Deed p. 176.
    October 4th, 1747, Benjamin Holloday and Susanna, his wife, (first,) of Spts. County, to Zachary Lewis of same, 295½ acres in said County, devised said Benjamin by last will

HOLLIDAY

and testament of his father, John Holloday, deceased, married 2nd, Mary, widow of Isaac Scott.

Will of Benjamin Holloday, p. 42. Berkley Parish, Spts. County, died March 18th, 1785. Witness, Joseph Holloday, junior, Stephen Holloday and William Holloday. Ex. Son-in-Law, Joseph Pulliam. Leg. my wife (Mary) grandson, Benjamin Holloday (son of Joseph) and daughter Susanna Holloday, daughter Agnes Holloday, married Joseph Holloday, junior, Martha Holloday, daughter Mary Holloday, married Austin Sandridge, daughter Nancy Holloday, married John Rawlings, daughter Elizabeth Holloday, married Joseph Pulliam.

"November 19th, 1778, Benjamin Holloday and Mary, his wife," Sons, Joseph and Benjamin, not mentioned in will.

Children by first wife: 1st, Elizabeth, wife of Joseph Pulliam. 2nd, Joseph, born 1747, died 1783, married 1780, Mrs. Fannie Johnson, had, 1st, Benjamin, born 1781. 2nd, Fanny, born 1783. 3rd, Susanna. 4th, Agnes, born 1750, died 1792, married Joseph Holliday, junior. 5th, Sarah, born 1752, died 1800. 6th, Mary, born 1756. 7th, Martha, born 1757. 8th, Benjamin, born 1758.

By second wife. 9th, Mary, born 1760, died 1830, married Austin Sandridge. 10th, Nancy, born 1762, died 1800, married John Rawlings.

Fifth Generation

Children of Nancy Holloday and John Rawlings: 1st, Thomas Rawlings, born April 1st, 1784. 2nd, Mary Rawlings, born April 13th, 1785. 3rd, Benjamin Holloday Rawlings, born August 29th, 1786. 4th, Levi Rawlings, born February 29th, 1788. 5th, John Rawlings, born December 22nd, 1789. 6th, Robert Rawlings, born June 2nd, 1794. 8th, Oliver Rawlings born 1796. (Lt. Gov of Mo.)

"Levi Rawlings, I learn from old letters and understand from elsewhere, was the only son of the children who remained in Virginia. John and Nancy Rawlings, the parents, also went to Kentucky about 1800, later to Missouri, where John died in 1820. John Rawlings married for second wife, Jane Bush Emery (or Embree) in Kentucky and Gen. John Aaron Rawlings was a grandson of this marriege".

Levi Rawlins married Eliza Hansbrough, May 29th, 1817, and he died October 29th, 1824. Their children were: 1st,

Mary Ann, born March 9th, 1818, married William Parker. 2nd, Frances Virginia, born November 14th, 1819, married Charles Hume 3rd, Nancy Holloday, born May 18th, 1822, married George Waugh, 4th, Sarah Ellen, born June 7th, 1823, unmarried, died 1905.

Among the children of Charles Hume and Frances Virginia Rawlins was Frank Hume, born July 21st, 1843, who married Emma Phillips Norris, and among their children is Alice, wife of Rev. Thomas Worthington Cooke.

Rev. Thomas W. Cooke and Mrs. Alice Hume Cooke have, 1st, Alice, 2nd, Margaret, 3rd, Thomas, junior.

Third Generation

6 Elizabeth 3rd, (daughter of John 2nd, senior, Thomas 1st.) Married Patterson Pulliam. He died prior to April 6th, 1758, as on that date John Holloday and Joseph Hawkins act as Adm. for Patterson Pulliam, deceased. (p. 60).

Son, Joseph, mentioned in deeds. Son Patterson appears in deeds of 1760-61, etc., after the father's death.

Third Generation

7 Winifred, 3rd, daughter of John 2nd, senior, Thomas 1st. Wife of Thomas Pulliam. Will of Thomas Pulliam, p. 17.

"St. George Parish, died April 17th, 1758, proved June 6th, 1758. Witness Joseph Holloday and Benjamin Holoday. Ex. sons, James and Thomas Pulliam. Leg. sons, James, Thomas and Benjamin, daughters, Winifred, Susanna, Elizabeth, Agnes, Mary, Anna, wife of David Sandridge, Sarah, wife of Christopher Dickin".

Third Generation

8 Sarah 3rd, (daughter of John 2nd, senior, Thomas 1st.) Wife of James Rawlings.

Will, p. 41.

James Rawlings, died November 15th, 1781. Ex. Bond dated April 15th, 1785. Witness. Lewis Holloday, Rawlings Pulliam and Sarah Pulliam. Ex. wife, Sarah Rawlings. Sons, Thomas, Joseph, James and John. Daughters, Mary Gaines, Agnes Gaines and Rebecca.

9 Susanna 3rd, daughter of John 2nd, senior, Thomas 1st.) Unmarried in 1742. No record.

HOLLIDAY

Holliday, James, Ensign in Captain Stubblefield's Company. Spts. Militia.
From Crozier's Spts. County Records, p. 523.

Holloday, James. Captain John F. Mercer's Company No. 1, as it stood February 1st, 1778.
From Saffell's "Soldiers in the Revolution from Virginia," p. 292.

Holloday, James, pr. W. D. 72, 1: W. D. 78, 1: W. D. 293, 1: W. D. 307, 4. (Which means "Photographs of payrolls of Virginia Continental Line, referred to by folder. There are 353 folders.)
From "Virginia Soldiers in the Revolution" Supplement, p. 152.

Holloday, James, pr. Penn. Continental Line. Drew pension in 1833, in Ohio County, Virginia.
From Virginia pension rolls, U. S. War Dept. Pension Rolls, 1835, Vol. 2, p. 180.

Holloday, Joseph (Va.) Ensign 6th, Virginia, 16th, Febtal Army (Page 179.) Order book 129-1832, Spts. County, Virginia, Court Chapter leading, "Revolutionary Prisoners".
From Crozier's Spts. County Records, p. 534.

Holloday, Joseph (Va.) Ensign 6th, Virginia, 16th, February 1776, 2nd, Lieut. 11th, September 1776, 1st, Lieut. March 1777, registered 23rd July 1777, Captain Virginia Militia, 1780-1781.
From Heitman's "Officers of the Revolution" p. 296.

Holloday, Joseph, Ensign, February 16th, 1776.
From Staffell's "Soldiers in the Revolution" from Virginia, p. 289.

Holloday, Joseph, (Lieut.) H. D. 1835-6. (Which means House of delegates.)

Holloday, Joseph, War 4,43,207 (Which means) "A Collection of ms. volumes bearing on the military establishment of the state during and after the Revolution".
From "Revolutionary Soldiers of Virginia" p. 222.

HOLLINGSWORTH

James Hollingsworth came from Winchester, Virginia, about 1786, and settled in the Meeting Street section of Edgefield County, South Carolina. He left one brother in Virginia, another went to North Carolina, a third went to Ohio, a fourth to Kentucky and one to Mississippi.

James Hollingsworth was born ———, died September 12, 1821, in Edgefield County.

Agnes Evans (wife) born ———, died in 1812.

Children

(1) John, born in Virginia 1773, died in Florida in 1841.

(2) Alexander, born in 1775. Two sons, James and Alexander.

(3) James, born 1778. One son, James.

(4) Lucy, born in 1780, married ——— Miller, daughter Ginsey Miller.

(5) Sarah, born 1782, married James Carson.

(6) Mary, born 1776, married in 1808, James Harrison (born June 6, 1781, died 18—, a son of James and Susannah Harrison of Virginia.

(7) Daughter (name illegible in the will, but seems to be Lotty or Letty, married Enoch Walton. Son, Enoch Walton.

John the eldest child, married Beersheba Oliphant, third daughter of John and Nancy (Fraser) Oliphant (born 1786). Their children were:

(1) William F. Hollingsworth, born 1809, died October 23, 1831.

(2) John Hampton Hollingsworth, born February 15, 1811, died July 31, 1887.

(3 Eliza A. Hollingsworth, born September 3, 1813, died September 19, 1903.

(4) Emily D. Hollingsworth, born May 20, 1816, died June 26, 1900.
(5) Diomede F. Hollingsworth, born June 25, 1819, died February 25, 1857.
(6) Mansfield E. Hollingsworth, born August 2, 1821, died October 23, 1853.
William, the eldest son, married but left no heirs.
John Hampton Hollingsworth (son of John H. and Beersheba Oliphant) was married twice.
(1) Elizabeth Richardson, on November 15, 1853. (2) Lucinda Brunson, born 1838; married December 23, 1858; died May 16, 1883.

Issue—By First Wife
(1) Elizabeth Richardson Hollingsworth was born August 24, 1855; married January 15, 1880 to William Hayne Folk; issue: one daughter, Julia Folk, born September 8, 1895. Col. Folk died May 16, 1898.

By Second Wife
(1) Diomede, born 1895; died 1862.
(2) Lucretia Helen, born 1861; died 1865.
(3) John Hampton, born 1864; died 1865.
(4) Daniel Brunson, born July 14, 1868 (still living).

Daniel Brunson Hollingsworth married October 19, 1889, Sallie Strothers, born April 25, 1871; their children are:
(1) John Hampton, born April 24, 1892 (unmarried).
(2) Anna Ball Strother, born February 24, 1894, married Wad. D. Allen, June 1915, and has one son, Horde, junior, March 7, 1916.
(3) Elizabeth Folk, born February 23, 1896, married William S. Anderson and has one daughter, Elizabeth, born November 7, 1920.
(4) Diomede Franklyn, born July 12, 1898 (unmarried).
(5) William Strother, born February 18, 1900 (unmarried).

Eliza Ann Hollingsworth, third child of John Hollingsworth and his wife, Beersheba Oliphant, married Alexander Walker, December 15, 1831, and had six children, viz:
(1) Virginia, married Mr. Harmon.
(2) Caroline, married (1) Mr. Freeman, (2) Mr. Williams and has children by both marriages.
(3) John H. (died without issue).
(4 Alexander Spann, died in Louisiana but left daughters.
(5) Milton Scott (died without issue).

HOLLINGSWORTH

(6) Emma E., died unmarried.
(7) Herbert W., living but unmarried.

Emily D. Hollingsworth, the fourth child of John Hollingsworth and wife, Beersheba Oliphant, married Tzra G. Talbert and had children: (1) Cornelia, (2) John, (3) Ezra. Ezra only had children. They live now in Edgefield County.

Diomede Franklin, fifth child of John Hollingsworth and his wife, married Eliza Griffin and had one son who died in childhood.

Mansfield Emilius, sixth child of John Hollingsworth and his wife, Beersheba Oliphant, married Margaret Gomillian, May 10, 1843; their children:

(1) Margaret Cornelia, born August 26, 1846, died March 13, 1906. She was twice married, first to Robert D. Brunson (born December 11, 1841; died October 1, 1870); second to Artemas Lowe Brunson (born January 28, 1846 and left two children by each marriage.

(1) Susan Brunson, born February 2, 1869; married J. Walter Hill (no issue).

(2) Cornelia, born June 6, 1870; married Wade S. Cothran and has a son, James S. Cothran, born October 20, 1895 (unmarried), and a daughter, Margaret Cornelia, born December 25, 1900, married March 15, 1921 to Julian D. Holstein, junior.

(3) Cleora, born January 17, 1881, married Wallace C. Tompkins, November 25, 1908; has no children.

(4) Artemas Lowe, junior, born October 28, 1886; married Virginia L. Thomason, August 9, 1917. They have two children, Artemas Lowe (third) and Idalia Walker Brunson.

(2) Mansfield E. Hollingsworth, junior, second child of Mansfield and Margaret (Gomillian) Hollingsworth, married Jane Holcomb and has eight children: (I do not know their ages). They are: Jane (married Manton McCutcheon and has four daughters); Thomas Thompson (married but no children); Margaret (married William Addy; Septima (married Roy Gillerland); William Grover Mansfield, junior, and Laurence are unmarried; Cornelia married Mr. Creech.

HOUSTON

The Houston who is the most famous in American annals is General Sam Houston who achieved the distinction of being Governor of awo states, Tennessee and Texas, and President of Texas when that state was an independent republic. It is believed that all the Houstons of the Southern States are more or less connected with the family which produced Governor Sam Houston.

The family is of Scotch-Irish origin, like so many of those which have ben written of in this series.

In 1835 John Houston emigrated from the North of Ireland to America settling first in Pennsylvania and from thence removed to Virginia. He was accompanied by his mother (who is recorded as being a widow, Mrs. John Houston, showing that John Houston's father was also John Houston) and his wife who was before her marriage, Margaret Cunningham. One child of John Houston and his wife Margaret Cunningham Houston, James Houston, was left in Ireland and died there. They had six other children all of whom married. Their descendants are in the entire Southern territory.

The widow Houston who accompanied her son John Houston to America in 1735 was born about 1650. She lived to be 97 and died in Rockbridge County, Virginia, and was buried not far distant from thepresent New Providence Church cemetery, Rockbridge County, Virginia.

In the name of the father of the emigrant John Houston, there appears to be divergence of opinion. On page 426, "Ninth Scotch-Irish Congress", the name is given as Samuel Houston, with the following additional data regarding his ancestry:

"Hugh Huston came from Wighanshire, Scotland, to Ireland: there he married Sarah Houston of County of Antrim (Ireland) family of Houstons: their son Samuel married Margaret McClung and their son, John,c ame to America early in the Eighteenth Century: remained for a time in Pennsylvania, then prior to 1750, removed to the 'Borden Grant', Virginia".

NOTABLE SOUTHERN FAMILIES

The above record is taken from the family chart given by Archibald Wood Houston, Toledo, Ohio, 1895, a descendant from John Houston the emigrant, through his fourth child, John Houston who married Sarah Todd. Mr. Houston is also a descendant of the Rev. James Waddell—the Blind Preacher of Augusta County, Virginia, and it would appear that he would have at his command the best authority.

John Houston, the emigrant, from whom the lines given in this article diverge, was born in Ireland in 1689-90. He died in Rockbridge County, Virginia, in 1754 and is buried there beside his wife and mother.

As the family record states that they remained in Pennsylvania until their three eldest children were married, they must have left Pennsylvania for Virginia not earler than 1744 when their second daughter and third child, Ester, would have been about twenty years old. The three children referred to are: Robert (who married Margaret Davidson), Isabella (who married a Henderson) and Esther (who married John Montgomery).

Seven Children of the Emigrant John Houston

The children of John Houston and Margaret Cunningham Houston were:
- I Robert Houston.
- II Isabella Houston.
- III Esther Houston.
- IV John Houston, Third.
- V Samuel Houston.
- VI Matthew Houston.
- VII James Houston.

I. ROBERT HOUSTON

Robert Houston, son of John Houston the emigrant and his wife Margaret Cunningham Houston, who was born about 1720 in Ireland, married Margaret Davidson, daughter of Samuel and Ann Dunlap Davidson. The children of Robert Houston and his wife were:
- (1) John Houston.
- (2) Samuel Houston.
- (3) Bettie Houston.
- (4) Margaret Houston.
- (5) Esther Houston.
- (6) Mary Houston.

Chalkley's "Chronicles of Augusta County, Virginia," gives the will of a Robert Houston dated September 11, 1760, in which the wife's name appears as Mary and his

HOUSTON

children as follows: Son John (infant) 95 acres on Collier Creek: son, James (infant) 200 acres adjoining place testator lives on: son, Samuel (infant) plantation testator lives on, 307 acres: daughter, Elizabeth—5 shillings, already provided for: daughters Ann, Esther, Margaret, Mary. Wife Mary, son John and brother Samuel Huston, Executors. Witnesses: Daniel Lyle, Moses Trimble, Sam'l McCroskey. Will proved 19 May 1761 by Lyle and Trimble. Executors qualify with Daniel Lyle, John Huston as sureties..

Also Chalkely gives the will of Robert Davidson, dated January 10, 1751, in which mention is made of wife, Ann, son John and daughter Mary Houston.

While the Houston Genealogy by Rev. S. R. Houston gives the name of Robert Houston's wife as Margaret Davidson, daughter of Samuel Davidson and Ann Dunlap, the records above indicate that her name was Mary Davidson and that she was a daughter of Robert and not Samuel Davidson.

Of the foregoing (1) John Houston, son of Robert Houston and his wife married March 16, 1769 Ann Logan. They lived and died in Colliertown. Note the land will John in Robert Houston's will above was on Collier Creek.

(2) Samuel Houston, son of Robert Houston and Margaret Davidson Houston married Elizabeth Paxton. They had nine children: Paxton Houston, Robert Houston, James Houston, John Houston, Samuel Houston (General), William Houston, Isabell Houston, Mary Houston and Elizabeth Houston.

Of the eight brothers and sisters of the famous General Samuel Houston: Paxton Houston, died young; Robert Houston died unmarried; James Houston settled in Nashville and left a family; John Houston, called Major John Houston lived in Memphis and left a family; William Houston married Miss Ball, of Kentucky, and had three children, a daughter Mary Houston and two sons, Eugene Houston and Williams Houston, Second; Isbella Houston died young; Mary Houston married twice, first Colonel Matthew Wallace and second his kinsman General William Wallace, leaving one son by the first marriage; Eliza Houston married ——— Moore and lived in Texas.

Samuel Houston became the most famous member of the family and one of the famous men of American. In 1793 at the time of his birth, the family was residing in Rockbridge County, Virginia. The father of the sturdy family of nine died when the little Sam was thirteen—that is in 1806. There were six sons and three daughters. The widow Elizabeth Paxton Houston and her group of children undertook the arduous journey from Virginia to what is now Tennessee.

Various historians have speculated her reasons for this move which had results of such importance to her famous son of Samuel and to the two great States which claim him as hero and almost patron saint.

However at that time a wave of emigration to the new country had set in and already many of the widow's kinspeople were in the new country and doubtless urging her to follow. There were better opportunities also apparently in the "new country" for her sons and daughters. Her husband's kinsman, ——— Houston had married Alice Armstrong and the Armstrongs and that branch of the Houstons were already in Tennessee. Her husband's uncle, Matthew Houston, had married Martha Lyle and was already a resident of Tennessee. Her husband's aunt, Esther Houston had married John Montgomeri and they were in Tennessee. Also Elizabeth Paxton Houston's own kinsman, Joseph Paxton had married into the Lyle family and was living in Tennessee.

Arriving in Tennessee the nine children are said to have developed amazingly. Sam picked up an intimate acquaintance with the Indians and very soon practically left the ways of civilization for the Indian camps. He learned their language and to the end of his life conversed fluently with members of many tribes. He wore their dress and followed their customs. His influence and authority among them continued until his death.

His fame and political career are not the subject of this article. It is enough to say he was elected Governor of Tennessee, resigned the office at the height of his popularity and power, and went to Texas, fought to make it free became its first President in the days of the Republic and later its Governor when Texas entered the Union.

In 1829 while he was Governor of Tennessee he married Eliza Allen of an old and aristocratic family. The marriage was most unhappy and as a result of it Governor Houston resigned his exalted office and went to Texas where he became identified with that state. May 9, 1840 he married for his second wife Margaret Moffett Lea in Marion, Alabama, Eliza Allen Houston having secured a divorce by authority of the Tennessee legislature.

HOUSTON

General Sam Houston, by his second marriage had eight children:
(1) Samuel Houston, Third.
(2) Nannie E. Houston.
(3) Margaret Lea Houston, daughter of General Sam
(4) Mary W. Houston.
(5 Nettie Power Houston.
(6) Andrew Jackson Houston.
(7) Temple Houston.
(8) William Roger Houston.

Of the foregoing:

(1) Samuel Houston, Third, eldest son of General Sam Houston and Margaret Moffett Lea Houston, married Anderson and had two children: Maggie Belle Houston and Henry Howard Houston.

(2) Nannie E. Houston, daughter of General Sam Houston and Margaret Moffett Lea Houston, married J. C. S. Morrow and had six children: Maggie Morrow, Mary Morrow, Jennie Morrow, Preston Morrow, Temple Morrow and Elizabeth Morrow.

(3) Margaret Lea Houston, adughter of General Sam Houston and Margare t Moffett Lea Houston, married Weston L. Williams and had five children: Houston Williams, Madge Williams, Franklin W. Williams, James Royston Williams and Marian L. Williams.

(4) Mary W. Houston, daughter of General Sam Houston and Margaret Moffett Lea Houston, married ———— Morrow and had three children: John H. Marrow, Maud Morrow and Jesse Morrow.

(5) Nettie Power Houston, daughter of General Sam Houston and Margaret Moffett Lea Houston, married W. L. Bringhurst and had two children: Sam Houston Bringhurst and Nettie Bringhurst.

(6) Andrew Jackson Houston, son of General Sam Houston and Margaret Moffett Lea Houston, married twice, first Carrie Parnell and second Bettie Goode and had three children: Ariadne Houston, Marguerite Houston and Josephine Houston.

(7) Temple Houston, son of General Sam Houston and Margaret Moffett Lea Houston, married Laura Cross and had three children, among them being Temple Houston, Second, and Samuel Houston, Fourth.

(8) William Rogers Houston, son of General Sam Houston and Margaret Moffett Lea Houston, never married.

Five of the eight children of General Houston survive

NOTABLE SOUTHERN FAMILIES

(1921), and they are Mrs. Nannie E. Houston Morrow, Mrs. Mary W. Houston Morrow, Mrs. Nettie Houston Bringhurst, Colonel Andrew Jackson Houston and William Rogers Houston.

(3) Bettie Houston, third child of Robert and Margaret Davidson Houston, married John McClung, and had six children: John McClung, Second, Jane McClung, Samuel McClung, Margaret McClung, James McClung and Mary McClung.

(4) Margaret Houston, fourth child of Robert Houston and Margaret Davidson Houston, married James Hopkins and had two children: John Hopkins and James Hopkins, Second.

(5) Esther Houston, sometimes called Nannie, fifth child of Robert Houston and Margaret Davidson Houston married James McKee and had four children, Nancy McKee, Robert McKee, John McKee and William McKee.

(6) Mary Houston, sixth child of Robert Houston and Margaret Davidson Houston, married John Lechter and had nine children: John Letcher, Second; Hannah Letcher, Sallie Letcher, Ann Letcher, William Houston Letcher, Isaac Letcher, Mary (Polly) Letcher, James Letcher and Giles Letcher.

II ISABELLA HOUSTON

Isabella Houston, daughter of the emigrant John Houston and his wife Margaret Cunningham Houston was born about 1722. Accounts conflict as to her marriage, but it is believed that she married first John or George Henderson, and married second William Gillespie and that her children were:

(1) William Henderson.
(2) Jane Henderson.
(3) Susan Henderson.
(4) Ann Gillespie.
(5) Pollie Gillespie.
(6) Betsy Gillespie.
(7) James Gillespie.
(8) John Gillespie.
(9) Robert Gillespie.
(10) Nancy Gillespie.

III. ESTHER HOUSTON

Esther Houston, daughter of John Houston the emigrant and his wife Margaret Cunningham Houston was born

HOUSTON

about 1724. She married John Montgomery and settled in Augusta County, Virginia. She had twelve children:
1. John Montgomery, Second.
2. Mollie Montgomery.
3. Ann Montgomery.
4. James Montgomery.
5. Dorcas Montgomery.
6. Jane Montgomery.
7. Robert Montgomery.
8. Esther Montgomery.
9. Alexander Montgomery.
10. Isabella Montgomery.
11. ——————
12. ——————

Of the foregoing Dorcas married John Lowry and settled in Rockbridge County, Virginia. She had five children, John Montgomery Lowry, David Lowry, Robert Edmonson Lowry, James Lowry and William Lowry. Robert Edmondson Lowry married Elizabeth Moore and settled in Washington County, Virginia, They had six children: William Moore Lowry, John Montgomery Lowry, James Moore Lowry, Dorcas Lowry, Samuel Moore Lowry and Elizabeth Moore Lowry. William Moore Lowry settled in Greeneville, East Tennessee and subsequently moved to Atlanta, Georgia. He married Julia Easton, a descendant of the Deaderick family. See that family in Notable Southern Families Volume I. They had nine children. (1) John Easton Lowry, (2) Robert James Lowry, (who married Emma Celestia Markham), (3) Fannie Talbot Lowry (who married ——— Porter and has two children, Lowry Porter who married Annie May Crass and has Margaret Crass, and Julia Lowry Potter who married E. Bates Block) (6) Mary Hazeltine Lowry, (7) Julia Margaret Lowry, (8) Alice May Lowry, and (9) Lelia Prentice Lowry.

IV. JOHN HOUSTON, THE THIRD

John Houston the fourth child of John Houston the emigrant, was born in Ireland in 1726. He married Sarah Todd. They had nine children:
(1) James Houston.
(2) John Houston, Fourth.
(3) Samuel Houston (Rev.)
(4) William Houston.
(5) Robert Houston.
(6) Matthew Houston.
(7) Alice Houston.

NOTABLE SOUTHERN FAMILIES

(8) Margaret Houston.
(9) Esther Houston.

The descendants of this John Houston, fourth child of John Houston, the emigrant, have been identified very closely with Tennessee history since the days of the ill-fated state of Franklin whose constitution Rev. Samuel Houston, third son of above John, assisted in framing. Rev. Samuel Rutherford, son of Rev. Samuel Houston, was the compiler of "Biographical Accounts of the Houston Family accompanied by a Genealogical Table", published in Cincinnati 1882.

Three daughters of John Houston and Sarah Todd married in Tennessee and their descendants have played a prominent part in the church history of the of the state. Alice Houston, seventh child of John and Sarah (Todd) Houston married William Stephenson of Jonesboro, Tenoessee. Their third child, Elizabeth Stephenson, married her first cousin, John McEwen, and through the marriage of their fifth child, Elizabeth McEwen who married William T. Mason, is descended the Mason family of Memphis, Tennesse. Carrington Mason, second son of William T. Mason and Elizabeth (McEwen) Mason, married Maria Boddie and to them were born seven children: Elleston, Carrington, Lunsford Yandell, Yandell, Maria B., Alfred D., and Elizabeth McEwen Mason. Lunsford Y. Mason, third child above, married Sarah Sale: their elder son, Lunsford Y. Mason, junior, graduated from Annapolis and is now in the U. S. Navy. They have another son also: William Cornelius Mason. Maria B. Mason above, married ——— Stanford of U. S. Navy and has two children: Eliza Stanford Sackett and Carrington Stanford. Alfred D. Mason, sixth child above, married Mary E. Walker and has two children: Alfred D. Mason, junior, and Carrington Mason. Elizabeth McEwen Mason last child of Carrington Mason and Maria (Boddie) Mason, married Dr. Henry Lloyd and has three children: Henry Lloyd, junior, Carrington Lloyd and Elizabeth Lloyd.

Margaret Houston, eighth child of John Houston and Sarah Todd married Alexander McEwen who died at Jonesboro, Tennessee, and at advanced age she married Rev. Samuel Doak, senior, the venerated Founder of Higher Education in the State of Tennessee. Margart Houston by her first marriage had five children: John McEwen. Ebenezer McEwen, Alexander McEwen, Robert Houston McEwen and Sarah McEwen. Robert Houston McEwen,

HOUSTON

fourth child, married Henrietta Kennedy and became a pillar in the Presbyterian Church in Nashville, Tennessee. Through the marriage of their fifth child, to Judge John T. Jones of Helena, Arkansas, was descended thet two eminent physicians of Memphis, Dr. Kennedy and Dr. Heber Jones, and their brothers, Thomas Jones, late of Memphis, and Paul Jones, Attorney of New York City.

V. SAMUEL HOUSTON

Samuel Houston, fifth child of John Houston the emigrant and his wife Margaret Cunningham Houston, was born in Ireland about 1728 and came to America with his parents in 1735. He died 1797 at the age of sixty-nine years in Blount or Knox County, Tennessee. He married Elizabeth McCrosky, daughter of John McCrosky and his wife Elizabeth of Augusta County, Virginia. Their children were:

(1) John Houston.
(2) James Houston.
(3) Robert Houston.
(4) Margaret Houston.
(5) William Houston.
(6) Mathew Houston.
(7) Elizabeth Houston (by second ? wife).

Robert Houston, third son of Samuel Houston and his wife, Elizabeth (McCrosky) Houston, was born in Rockbridge Couny, Virginia, 1760. About the year 1792 Robert Houston removed from Washington County, Virginia, to Tennessee where he lived till his death in 1835. His farm was about eight miles South-east of Knoxville, on the south side of the French Broad River. At about the same time another Robert Houston came to Knox County from Abbeville District, South Carolina, and singularly enough the death of the latter Robert Houston occurred April 2, 1834—thus but a few months difference in the decease of the two. The above facts have led to a considerable confusion by historians as to the county offices held by each. It is certain that Robert of Abbeville was the Territorial Secretary and that he for a time was Sheriff of Knox County, but it seems likely that Robert Houston of Rockbridge County, Virginia, also held office of Sheriff of Knox and 1810-1814 that of Clerk of the Circuit Court of Blount County.

Robert Houston of Rockbridge County, Virginia, son of Samuel Houston and wife, Elizabeth McCrosky Houston, married twice: first Elizabeth Lochart (or Lochard) granddaughter of Col. David Campbell who established Campbell's station near Knoxville in pioneer days; second wife was Martha Blackburn, daughter of Lieut. William Blackburn who fell at the Battle of King's Mountain, October 1780, and whose widow Elizabeth (Black) Blackburn, with her brother Joseph Black and John Blackburn administered upon her deceased husband's estate, 1780-1796, as the records of Washington County, Virginia, show. It is said that Martha Blackburn was a niece of the distinguished Presbyterian Divine, Rev. Gideon Blackburn; since a complete list of the children of Robert Blackburn, father of Rev. Gideon Blackburn, has not been found this statement can not be verified fully. Elizabeth Lochard and Martha Blackburn were devoted friends before the death of the first. Elizabeth (Lochard) Houston) died young, leaving but four small children to survive her—four having died previously.

The children of Robert Houston and his first wife, Elizabeth Lochard Houston, were as follows:
1 Elizabeth Houston.
2 William L. Houston.
3 Samuel Houston.
4 James Houston.
5 Mathew Houston.
6 John Houston.
7. Robert Houston.
8 Mary Houston.

But three of the foregoing left descendants: William L. Houston married Rebecca Woodward and to them were born the following children: Robert, Cicero and Richard. Mathew Houston (No. 5) above married Jane McCrosky a third cousin, and the family removed to Iowa. Robert Houston, No. 7 above, married Dorthea Cresswell: heir eldest daughter married Robert Pickens of Blount County where their descendants live.

Robert Blackburn and Martha Blackburn, his second wife were married October 17, 1809. To them were born five children, as follows:
9 George Blackburn Houston.
10 Joseph Erasmus Houston.
11 Lochard E. Houston.
12 Samuel Moore Houston.
13 Elizabeth L. Houston.

9 Of the foregoing children, George Blackburn Houston married Lamanda Monday: their descendants live near Cottonwood, Kansas.

HOUSTON

10 Joseph E. Houston, No. 10 above, came in 1834 to Madisonville, Tennessee, where during his long and eventful life he held nearly every public office in the County. April 2, 1834, he married Eliza McDonald Clark Haire, daughter of Monroe County's second Sheriff, James A. Haire and his wife, Mary Brown McDonald Haire, of York District, South Carolina. To Joseph E. Houston and his wife, Eliza Mc. C. Haire Houston were born:
1 Captain Robt. E. Houston.
2 Mary Caroline Houston.
3 Martha Eliza Houston.
4 James Haire Houston.
5 Josephine Elliot Houston.
6 Lizzie Alice Houston.
7 Blanche McDonald Houston.

Of the foregoing, Capt. Robert Houston, C. S. A on the staff of Gen. J. C. Vaughn, married Miss Mary Weaver of Columbus, Mississippi But one child survived him: J. E. Houston of Aberdeen, Mississippi, who married first, Miss Willie Cox. Shortly afterwards she died leaving one daughter who is now Mrs. Lawrence Tucker of Holly Springs, Mississippi. J. E. Houston married second, Fannie G. Carlisle: they have the following children: Fannie May, Joseph E., Blanchard Weaver Houston, Birt C. Houston, Mary Weaver Houston. Captain Robt. E. Houston had no children by his second wife, Mrs. Helia Stoddard.

Mary C. Houston, second daughter of Joseph E. Houston and his wife Eliza Mc. C. Haire Houston, married Samuel Matlock Browder and to them were born three daughters: (a) Blanche McKinney Browder who married Chas. Frederick Lattimore and has the following children: Mary Ella Lattimore who married King Walker and has two children, King Benson Walker and Frances Lattimore Walker. Margaret Houston Browder, who married Mr. Heffington and has three children: Chas. A. Heffington, Nancy Heffington, Blanche B. Heffington. Samuel Browder Lattimore who married Ruth Gail McPeek: and lastly, Chas Frederick Lattimore, junior. (b) Elizabeth Alice Browder, second daughter of Samuel and Mary C. (Houston) Browder, married David Erskin Lowry and they have three children: Frank H., Mary Emeline, and Addie Blanch Lowry. (c) Ellen Browder, third daughter, married Ulysses Milligan and has two children: Elizabeth and Ulysses, junior.

11 Judge Lockhart E. Houston, third son of Robert Houston by his second wife, Martha Blackburn, removed

when a young man to Aberdeen, Mississippi, where he pursued his beloved profession—the Law, and where he served as Circuit Judge, later helping to frame the Constitution of that state after the War Between the States. He married Miss Sue Maury Parrish. See "Early Settlers of Northern Alabama" by Saunders. To Judge Houston and his wife, Sue Maury Parrish, were born the following:
1 Mamie Houston.
2 Robert P. Houston.
3 Lizzie Houston.
4 Loch'd Houston.
5 David Winston Houston.
6 Joseph. S. Houston.
7 A daughter who died young.
8 Sue Maury Houston.

1 Mamie Houston, above, married Benjamin Gillespie of Aberdeen, Mississippi: their only daughter, Jessie married first, Howard Ward of Memphis, and later Acker Rogers of Aberdeen, Mississippi.

2 Robert Parrish Houston married a Miss Honey: four children were born to them: Robert P. Houston, junior; Newton Houston died unmarried; D. Winston Houston, junior, who married Beatrice Jenkins. They have two children: Winston Houston, junior, and a daughter, ———. The fourth child of Robert Parrish Houston and his wife, Miss Honey, is Mary Sue Houston who married ——— Franklin of Aberdeen, Mississippi.

3 Lizzie Houston married Frank Johnson of Madisonville, Tennessee, and they have two children: Elizabeth Johnson and Locke Johnson, now a student at Vanderbilt University.

4 Dr. Loch'd Houston died unmarried.

5 David Winston Houston, fifth child of Judge Loch'd Houston is a distinguished lawyer in Mississippi and is being urged for the nomination of Governor of that state. He married Pinkie Sykes of Aberdeen, Mississippi, and they have only one daughter, India Sykes Houston, who was recently married to Hiram Cassedy Holden, son of Judge Holden of Jackson, Mississippi.

6 Joseph S. Houston resides in St. Louis. He has never married.

7 A twin sister of Joseph S. She died young.

8 Sue Maury Houston, who resides in Aberdeen, Mississippi.

12 Samuel Moore Houston, fourth son of Robert

HOUSTON

Houston by his second wife, Martha Blackburn, settled in St. Louis about 1867. He married Mary P. Hendon, eldest daughter of Dr. William P. Hendon of Newbern, Alabama. They had among other children the following: William S. Houston of Chichasaw County, Mississippi, who married Miss Mary Foorsche, of Oklahoma. To them have been born children: Samuel and Mary Houston. Mary Houston, second child of Samuel Moore Houston: Jessie Houston, another daughter married a lawyer of St Louis, ——— Walker; Hannah Houston; Albert Houston.

13 Elizabeth L. Houston, fifth child of Robert Houston by his second wife, Martha Blackburn, married J. W. Norwood of Jackson, Tennessee. Thy had the following children: John Norwood, Samuel Norwood, Sallie Norwood who married Mr. Johnson of Loudon, Tennessee, a 'yer; Robert Loch'd Norwood who married in Kentucky and resides there.

Martha Eliza Huston, third child of Joseph E. Houston of Madisonville, Tennessee (No. 10) above, married Thomas Elisha Moore of Cocke County, Tennessee. To them were born six sons and three daughters, namely: William Thomas Moore of Cleveland, Tennessee, who married Jennie Willis; Janie R. Moore and Elizabeth Moore d d unmarried; Joe McDonald Moore, who married Bessie Clark and who with their six children: Thomas E., Edward, Paul, William Glenn, J. Don and Martha Mae Moore reside in the West; Paul Andrew Moore of Knoxville, married Stella Haun and has one daughter, Freda Haun Moore; Robert Locke Moore of Morristown, Tennessee, who married Tessie Courtney and to whom have been born four daughters: Allyn, Edna Lynn, Mattie Roe, and Elizabeth Moore; Lyle Stickley Moore of Newport, Tennessee, who married Madge Mims and who have two children: Lyle and Myra Lucia Moore; Hal Moore of Cleveland, Tennessee, who married Margaret Hardwick, and to whom two daughters have been born: Margaret Hardwick Moore, deceased, and Martha Francis Moore. Margaret Eliza Moore, youngest daughter of Martha Eliza (Houston) Moore and her husband, Thomas E. Moore, resides with her widowed mother in Cleveland, Tennessee.

Josephine Elliot Houston, sixth child of Joseph E. Houston of Madisonville, Tennessee, married September 13, 1880, Vastine Stickley, son of Vastine Stickley of Lee County, Virginia and his wife, Elizabeth Duff, granddaughter of Robin Duff and Mary Powell (Dickenson) Duff of Russell County. To Vastine Stickley and his wife, Josephine E. (Houston) Stickley have been born three sons and three daughters, namely: (1) Elizabeth Duff Stickley who married Thomas M. Hines of the Virginia Marshall-Keith family. Thomas M. Hines died March 17, 1920 leaving his widow and their five children: Maxwell A., Robert S., Elizabeth H., Josephine E., and Thomas Keith Hines. (2) The second child of Vastine Stickley and his wife, Josephine E. (Houston) Stickley is Robert Houston Stickley, attorney of Memphis. He married Nancy E. Jones, daughter of John M. Jones of Sweetwater, Tennessee. (3) Eliza McDonald Stickley, third child of Vastine and and Josephine (Houston) Stickley married Dr. Robert C. Kimbrough of Monroe County. They have one son, Robert Cook Kimbrough, junior. (4) Dr. Jseph E. Houston Stickley of Madisonville, married Edith Rhoerer of Kentucky and has one daughter, Antoinette Houston Stickley (5) Mary McDonald Stickley married Thomas Frederick Wildsmith of Birmingham and they have three sons: Vastine, Thomas Frederick, junior, and Edward Taylor Wildsmith. (6) Vastine Stickley, third son of Vastine and Josephine (Houston) Stickley now a student in College of Pharmacy at Louisville. Blanche McDonald Houston, seventh child of Joseph E. Houston of Madisonville, Tennessee, married her cousin. Hon. Robert Crompton McCroskey of Garfield, Washington. To them have been borne three sons and three daughters, namely: Eliza Priscilla McCroskey, Robert Crompton McCroskey, junior, Houston McDonald McCroskey, Gladys McCrosky, Blanche McCroskey and Earl McCroskey. Of these children, Eliza died in infancy; Robert Compton McCroskey, junior, is married and lives in Garfield: he has a son Robert McCroskey. Houston McCroskey lives in Garfield also, and has a daughter, Jeanette. Gladys McCroskey married a banker of Spokane, Mr. Kimbrough, and has two daughters. Blanche McCroskey is married and lives in Garfield, as dies Earl McCroskey, who is also married.

James Haire Houston, fourth child of Joseph E. Houston of Madisonville and Lizzie Alice Houston, sixth child of the same, died shortly after maturity unmarried.

VI. MATTHEW HOUSTON

Matthew Houston, son of John Houston the emigrant and his wife, Margaret Cunningham Houston, was born about 1730.

He married Martha Lyle, daughter of Mathew Lyle.

HOUSTON

Martha Lyle was born about 1740.

Matthew Houston and Martha Lyle Houston moved in 1790 from Virginia to Tennessee, settling first on the French Broad River in Blount County and later on Nine Mile Creek. They had seven children:
(1) John Houston.
(2) Samuel Houston.
(3) James Houston.
(4) Matthew Houston, Second.
(5) Robert Houston.
(6) Esther Houston.
(7) Margaret Houston.

A large family comes through these seven children. Their descendants are in Tennessee, Alabama, Mississippi and Texas in hundreds.

John Houston the first child married Rachel Balch and had eight children: Samuel Houston married Nancy Gillespie and had ten children; James Houston married Phoebe McClung and had five children; Matthew Houston, Second, married Margaret Cloyd and had two children; Robert Houston died unmarried; Esther Houston married her cousin Major James Houston and had four children; Margaret Houston married Captain James Gillespie and had ten children.

James Houston the third son in the foregoing group, married Phoebe McClung and had five children, namely: Robert, Matthew, McClung, Hettie and Ann. Of these; Matthew Houston married Mary Gillespie and had among other children Martha Gillespie Houston who married John Elder and had among other children, Leander M. Elder and Eva Grace Elder.

Leander M. Elder married Mary Saffarvaus and had six children, namely: Blanche Louise Elder (who married Thomas H. Urmston and has Thomas H. Urmston, Second), Irene Houston Elder (who married Chester Watkins and has Elizabeth Watkins, Charlotte Watkins and Chester Watkins, Second), George Saffarvaus Elder (who married Hazel Garrison and has Oliver Lawrence Garrison Elder and Mary Elder), Elizabeth Elder (who married Halsey B. Leavitt and has Halsey B. Leavitt, Second, and Martha Elder Leavitt), Mary Grace Elder (who married Henry Berry and has one son, Dan Berry); and Martha Elder (who married James T. Monahan and died without issue).

Eva Grace Elder married Forrest Ferguson of St. Louis.

From Matthew Houston and his wife Martha Lyle

Houston comes also the family of which Mrs. S. C. Peeples, of Chattanooga, and her brother, Mr. John Russell Pitner are members.

VII. JAMES HOUSTON

James Houston, son of John Houston the emigrant and his wife Margaret Cunningham Houston was born in Ireland sometime previous to 1735 as in that year his parents emigrated to America and left him behind. He died in Ireland.

Though last in this list, it is said that he was the eldest son; in that case he was born about 1715. He died in young manhood, unmarried.

A Houston, probably closely related to the family called the "Sam Houston Family" because it produced that famous character, married Alice Armstrong. The two families Armstrong and Houston, came from the north of Ireland in the same year, (1735) and settled near each other in Pennsylvania. Alice Armstrong was a daughter of the emigrant Robert Armstrong and John Houston was the emigrant Houston. Since his sons' marriages are accounted for in the family record, herein given the Houston whom Alice Armstrong married may have been his brother, (tradition says he had two brothers who came to America with him) or more probably a nephew. A further point of connection in addition to the name, location and date of emigration is the fact that Alice Armstrong's brother, Robert Armstrong, married Margaret Cunningham and John Houston's wife was also Margaret Cunningham.

────── Houston married Alice Armstrong in Abbeville District, South Carolina, where they remained for a short time, later moving to Tennessee. (A large family was born to them. Among their children was Robert Armstrong Houston, born in Abbeville District, South Carolina, in 1765, died in Tennessee April 2, 1834. He was appointed by Secretary of War John C. Calhoun (his mother's kinsman) United States Commissioner to the Indians. This was for the Indian Treaty of 1819. Robert Armstrong Houston married Margaret Davis and had four daughters and at least two sons, Alice Houston, Amelia Houston, Malinda Houston and Rutelia Houston, James Houston and Horace Houston.

Alice Houston, daughter of Robert Houston and Margaret Houston, married James McMillan and had Robert Houston McMillan (who married twice and had by his first wife

HOUSTON

(Martha Isbell) two children Alice McMillan who is not married and James Benjamin McMillan who married Cynthia Cunningham and had William Cunningham McMillan, Alice McMillan, Rutelia Isbell McMillan, Mary McMillan and Kitty B. McMillan; and had by his second wife (Missouri Isbell) tow children, Robert Houston McMillan, Second, who married Sarah Grey and left Robert Houston McMillan, Third, died young, Allen Gray McMillan and Catherine McMillan, and Fannie McMillan (who married J. F. Winkle and left Robert McMillan Winkle and J F. Winkle; Alice McMillan (who married Major Gaines McMillan as his second wife and had no children); and James White McMillan (who married Laura Hendrick and had Julia Hardin McMillan, Amelia Alice McMillan, Annie L. McMillan, Mary Lurina McMillan, William Hendrick McMillan, Nannie Missouri McMillan, James White McMillan, Second; Luke Hampton McMillan, Laura Houston McMillan, Frances Louise McMillan and Frank Alexander McMillan.)

Amelia Houston, daughter of Robert Houston and Margaret Davis Houston, married her cousin, Drury Paine Armstrong in 1823. Their children were Robert Houston Armstrong (who married Louise Franklin and had three children, Robert Franklin Armstrong who married twice, first Celia Houston and second Annie Wetzel and has no children, Elizabeth Armstrong who married James P. McMillan and had Robert Armstrong McMillan, died young, James P. McMillan and had Robert Armstrong McMillan and Laura McMillin who married Thomas H. Wagner and has Mary Elizabeth Wagner and Annie McMillan Wagner, and Adelia Armstrong who married J. Edward Lutz and has Louise Lutz who married Dr. Victor Holloway, and Edwin Lutz, who married Eleanor Atkin); Marcellus Murat Armstrong, called Whack (who married Elizabeth C. McGee and had Drury Paine Armstrong, died unmarried, Joseph McGee Armstrong married Mary L. Hampton, Leonidas Bruce Armstrong, Second, married first Pauline Fearn and married second Margaret Bradford, and Amelia Armstrong who married J. A. Bankston); Leonidas Bruce Armstrong, First, (who died unmarried); and Adelia Armstrong (who married William Calvert Hill and had George Armstrong Hill married Georgia Ann Wallis and has children and Amelia Hill who married Clement C. Douglas and has children).

Malinda Houston, daughter of Robert Houston and

NOTABLE SOUTHERN FAMILIES

Margaret Davis Houston married Robert McNutt.

Rutelia Houston, fourth daughter of Robert Houston and Margaret Davis Houston married James Isbell and had Margaret Isbell (who married Major James Hardie and had no children); Fannie Isbell (who married William Boynton); Houston Isbell (who died unmarried); Thomas Livingston Isbell (who married Mattie J. Norris and had Rutelia Houston Armstrong who married W. H. Lane and has one child, Rutelia Isbell Lane); and Alice Isbell (who married her cousin William Park Armstrong, and had William Park Armstrong, Second, married Rebeka Purvis and has Rebekah Purvis Armstrong, Wiliam Park Armstrong, Third, George Purvis Armstrong, Ann Elizabeth Armstrong and Jane Crozier Armstrong; Houston C. Armstrong married Mina Lamar and has Houston Church-Carey Armstrong); Margaret Hardie Armstrong married Ainslie Power Ardagh and has Margaret Ardagh, Ainslee Power Ardagh, Second, Alice Ardagh, Kathleen Ardagh and Edith Ardagh, and Annie Elizabeth Armstrong married Thomas Stoo Johnson and has no children).

James Houston the eldest son of Robert Houston and his wife Margaret Davis Houston married ―――――.

Horace Houston, the second son of Robert Houston and Margaret Davis Houston married in Blount County, Tennessee a ―――――― Howard.

GEORGE HOUSTON, EMIGRANT

George Houston married a Miss Ware about 1760. He came from Ireland to Pennsylvania thence to Mecklenburg County, North Carolina, along with the Jacks, Rosses, Wilsons and others. This couple, George Houston and wife had at least four sons, Thomas, William, Samuel and George Ware. Of these four sons, nothing is known of the two first named.

Samuel Houston married Mary Kirk in Mecklenburg County, North Carolina, 1795. Their children were John, Margaret, George Ware, Nancy, Abner, Mary Melissa, Jane Eliza, Samuel Allison, William Wilson and Seth. John was last heard of in Arkansas; Margaret married Joseph Wallace and lived in North Carolina. Nancy married W. A. Brown, lived in Tennessee and moved to Texas; Abner married and lived in Texas; Mary Melissa married John McCann and lived in Tennessee, afterwards moved to Texas; Jane Eliza married William Naill and lived in Tennessee

HOUSTON

then in Texas; Samuel Allison, William Wilson, and Sarah died young.

George Ware Houston went to Georgia as early as 1820, and finally settled in Harris County where he lived until his death in 1886. He was four times married, first, to Miss Sarah Blackmon. She died leaving one son, James, who died young. Second, he married Amy Bean, daughter of Alexander and Isabella (Youngblood) Bean. She lived only a short time leaving one son, Edwin, who married Martha Bird Fitzpatrick Dawkins, daughter of Reuben and Elizabeth Johnston Dawkins. They had four children, Elizabeth Ware (deceased married Jere R. Traylor, one daughter, Martha Traylor; Walter Reuben married Sallie Adair, had two children, Adair and Marguerite; Martha Lou; Edwin (deceased), married Antoniette Baker and left two children, Charles and Elizabeth. George Ware Houston married third, Nancy Oliver Ward, daughter of Thomas and Edna (Poole) Ward. She died leaving six children: Martha Caroline (died young); Samuel Oliver died unmarried; Mary Edna married W. E. Palmer and died leaving four children: Lee May, George Houston, Ralph Alexander and Edith; Sarah Frances married Theodore Dwight Power and has one son, Samuel Houston; Thomas Ward and Georgia Lee died unmarried. George Ware Houston married fourth, Mrs. Mary Wright Moore, no children. Of these Mrs. T. D. Power, S. H. Power, Miss Martha Lou Houston, and Miss Martha Taylor live in Columbus, Georgia.

George Ware Houston, son of George and ——— (Ware) Houston married Jane Kirk in Mecklenburg County, North Carolina, and had eleven children: James Amzie, Margaret, Harris, Wilson C., Frank, George W. Thomas D., William Lee, Eliza, Robert Allison and B. K Thomas married Hester Crockett and had, Archie, Alma Lena, Lee, Hester, Lidia, Thomas and James. Archie married Belle Gray and had Thomas D., Alma and Mary Lee. Lee married Nannie Lou Moore and had Hester Josephine, and Thomas. Alma married Oscar Alexander Nearly all of these last named live in Mississippi. Some of the descendants of George Ware and Jane (Kirk Houston live in Mecklenburg County, North Carolina. One descendant, Samuel Frank Houston, lives in Selma, Ala bama. He married Miss Pearl Whitman and they had two children, Samuel Frank and Margaret.

Mary Kirk and Jane Kirk were daughters of John and Sarah (Steele) Kirk of North Carolina.

JOHNSTON

The Johnstons are often referred to as the "Gentle Johnstons," and in a Border ballad, entitled "The Lads of Wamphray," we find the Galliard after stealing Sim Critchton's 'wisdom dun', calling an invitation:
'Now Simmy, Simmy of the side,
Come out and see a Johnston ride,
Here's the bonniest horse in a 'Nith side,
And a gentle Johnston aboon his 'hide'.

The family honors include the Marquisate of Annandale; the Earldoms of Annandale, Hartfell and Bath; the Viscounts of Annandale; the Baronies of Lochwood, Lochben, Moffatdale, Evandale, Bath and Derrvent, and the Baronetcies of Caskieben, Elphinstone, Westerhall, Hackness and Gilford.

A Scottish border antiquary (A. 85) was of opinion that the original Johnstons like Bruce, Baliel, Gordon and Jardine, came from France with William I. He identified him with the Seigneur de Joinville, mentioned by the old chronicler Guillamme de Tailleur, as assisting at the battle of Hastings, and the name appears again half-Saxonized into Janvil, on the roll of Battle Abbey.

Sir William Wallace is said to have been brought up in the family of a Johnston, and the assertion is quite credible as his home was in Lenark, just North of Annandale.

In Scotland it was allowable for each knight to wear the same design on his shield as his chief; some change in color or line being necessary, of course, to distinguish one from another. The first lords of Anonandale were the Bruces, whose arms were silver, with a red saltire (diagononal cross) and a gold chief band across the upper section; and while serving as vassals of the Bruces the Johnstons wore for their arms a silver shield with a black

199

saltire and red chief. After the Bruces came the Randolphs, whose arms consisted of three red cushions on the silver field; and in order to show their allegiance to their new masters, the Johnstons put three gold cushions on the red chief of their shields. When the Johnstons were raised to the peerage their arms were confirmed in the above design, which is officially described Argent, a saltire sable, on a chief gules, three cushions.

The crest of the clan is a winged spur, or "flying spur", as Sir Walter Scott calls it. There is a legend explaining the way in which the crest was awarded, which recites that while John Baliol was King of Scotland, Edward, King of England, tried to make him acknowledge Scotland to be tributary to England, and Robert Bruce, then Earl of Carrick, bitterly opposed the scheme. Edward, upon hearing of Bruce's opposition, laid a plot to seize him, and was only prevented from doing so by Baliol's sending the chief of the Johnstons to Bruce with a warning. Baliol did not wish to write to Bruce for fear the message should be intercepted by the followers of Edward, so he sent a spur to which was tied a bird's wing. Bruce took the hint and saved himself by flight, and when he became King he conferred the crest of the winged spur upon the messenger.

When Sir James Johnston was Lord Warden of West Marches his motto was "alight thieves all"; but when the chief of the clan was raised to the peerage the motto was changed to 'Nunquam non paratus' (Never unready). This motto was particularly appropriate, as it is said that when the chief used to muster his clan for battle it was the custom for him to ask: "Men of Annandale, are ye ready?" and the answer was invariably, "Aye, ready".

The Clan badge is red hawthorn. The Seat of the Johnston clan, is Locherby, near center of district of Annandale-Castle of Lochwood, situated at that place.

Though their origin is Scotch, some of the Johnstons went to Iriland, County of Antrim, at the time so many Scotchmen emigrated here as has been often noted 'n this series. The tradition that the emigrant to Ireland, or possibly one of his immediate successors married an "Irish lady" is scarcely borne out by the records of the people, for it was their boast that for two hundred years the Scotch Nation of Ireland" as they liked to call themselves never "intermarried" with the Irish. Of course, the Johnston, who is said to have married the Irish lady may have been the exception which proved the rule. This would seem

JOHNSTON

indeed to be indicated by the birth near Dublin of the seven Johnstons, who emigrated to America.

After living in Ireland a length of time not now known, the Johnstons like hundreds of their Scotch Irish neighbors decided to emigrate to the new land of America. In 1768 the four Johnston brothers, John, William, Francis and Joseph who were all born near Dublin and presumably their three sisters, Margaret, Nancy and Jean, all set sail for America. They landed in Philadelphia and settled for a short time in Pennsylvania, when following the tide of emigration, they moved to Virginia and from thence to South Carolina and Tennessee.

While this article primarily concerns the Tennessee Johnstons, a brief reference to the North Carolina group is not amiss. Governor Johnston and his family of that state are all from the same stock, and it is believed that the extinct Marquisite of Annandale should be vested in the North Carolina branch. Alabama Johnstons are from the North Carolina family, the late Governor Joseph Forney Johnston being of North Carolina extraction.

There were three Governors of North Carolina of the family and name. All were emigrants from Scotland and all were born in or near Dundee. They were: Governor Gabriel Johnston, Governor John Johnston, and the latter's son, Governor Samuel Johnston. Samuel Johnston was born near Dundee, Scotland, in 1733 and this date shows the approximate date of his father's and uncle's birth to be about 1700, or a little earlier. Gabriel Johnston was Governor of the Province of North Carolina in 1734 and was followed in 1736 by his brother, John Johnston. Governor John Johnston's emigration evidently took place between the date of his son's birth in Dundee in 1733 and this appointment to the Governorship in 1736. No approximate date of Governor Gabriel Johnston's emigration can be given.

Samuel Johnston, born in Dundee, Scotland, in 1733, emigrated with his father, John Johnston, say 1734. He held almost every possible office in the Province and State and in 1787 was elected Governor of that State.

Governor Johnston's wife was Helen Scrymsour. Governor Samuel Johnston's wife was Penelope Eden, only daughter of Governor Eden.

In America in the Revolution there were many Johnstons and in the War Between the States there were four Generals in the Confederate Army all supposedly kinsmen and all of the names spelled with a "t". Brigadier General

NOTABLE SOUTHERN FAMILIES

George D. Johnston, Lieutenant General Albert Sidney Johnston, Lieutnant General Joseph Eggleston Johnston and Brigadier General Robert D. Johnston. Of the most famous are General Albert Sidney Johnston, who gave his life for the South at Shiloh, April 6, 1862, and General Joseph E. Johnston whose brilliant career throughout the War is also well known.

The Tennessee family of Johnston comes from the line of the four brothers who were born near Dublin, Ireland, in the middle of the Eighteenth Century. These four brothers, John Johnston, Joseph Johnston, Francis Johnston and William Johnston had three sisters, Margaret Johnson, Nancy Johnston and Jean Johnston. Margaret married a Mr. Shaw, Nancy a Mr. Henderson and Jean a' Mr. Jones.

It is the belief of the family that they sprang from the Annandale Johnstons, and that one of the family went over into Ireland during the perscution and married an Irish lady.

John Johnston, the eldest child of the foregoing group was born near Dublin, Ireland, in 1735. His half brother, Joseph Johnston, was born near Dublin February 28, 1745, the births of the other five brothers and sisters have not been given.

The family of four brothers emigrated from Ireland to Pennsylvania about the year 1768. Two years later they went to Virginia and there made settlements in 1770. John Johnston settled in Rockbridge County, Virginia, married and raised a family.

The seven brothers and sisters who came from Dublin to America about the year 1768 will be token up in the following order:
    I. John Johnston.
    II. Joseph Johnston.
    III. Francis Johnston.
    IV. William Johnston.
    V. Margaret Johnston.
    VI. Nancy Johnston.
    VII. Jean Johnston.

I. JOHN JOHNSTON

John Johnston, eldest of the group of brothers who emigrated to America from Ireland about the year 1768, was the only son of his mother and was a half brother to Joseph Johnston, Francis Johnston, William Johnston, Margaret Johnston, Nancy Johnston, and Jean Johnston.

JOHNSTON

He was born near Dublin about 1735 and emigrated to America about 1768. They moved to Virginia about 1770 and from there to Washington County, Tennessee, about the year 1800. He died there about 1806. He had married and had a family. Some of his children remained in Virginia, but his son Samuel Johnston accompanied him to Tennessee and after his father's death moved to Blount County.

Samuel Johnston married Nancy Shaw and died in 1846. He left ten children:

(1) John Johnston, Second.
(2) Samuel McMillan Johnston.
(3) Esther Johnston.
(4) Margaret Johnston.
(5) William Johnston.
(6) Josiah Johnston.
(7) Francis Johnston.
(8) James Harvey Johnston.
(9) Anna Johnston.
(10) Hamilton Johnston.

(1) John Johnston the eldest son of Samuel Johnston and Nancy Shaw Johnston married Keziah Rowan in 1815.

(2) Samuel McMillan Johnston, son of Samuel Johnston and Nancy Shaw Johnston, married his cousin, Margaret Johnston, daughter of Joseph Johnston, about 1817. Their children were: Nancy A. (who married Z. Edwards and had Samuel Edwards, William Edwards and Sarah Edwards, all of whom died without issue and Margaret Edwards who married W. H. Lowry and had four children); James Harvey Johnson (who married Jane Caldwell in 1845 and had six children); Ebenezer E. Johnson (who married Armina Montgomery in 1846 and had four children); Lucinda Jane Johnston (who married O. H. P. Caldwell in December 1843 and had five children, James A. Caldwell who married Elizabeth Gillespie and has Percy A. Caldwell, Rhobie Caldwell married Fred Smallman and Elsie Caldwell married Roland Olmstead; Alice Caldwell; Mary Caldwell; Samuel Caldwell; and Sarah Caldwell); Jefferson LaFayette Johnston (who married Bettie Blair in 1858 and had one child and, after her death married Bettie McGhee and had five children. Among their children are: Hugh M. Johnston, who married Lillie Shipp and has

two daughters, Lynn Russell Johnston and Elizabeth Johnson, Samuel Hugh Hardin, who married Lillie Shipp and has Thomas H. Johnston, whose wife was Nona G. McDermott. They have Hugh Samuel Johnston and Louise Johnston.

Ester Johnston (who married Peter Hardin and left one son, Samuel M. Hardin, who mtrried Lillie Shipp and has no children); Margaret Johnston (who married J. F. McGill and died in 1910, having had eight children, five of whom are living).

(3) Esther Johnston, daughter of Samuel Johnston and Nancy Shaw Johnston married Josiah Rowan in 1819. They had several children, one of whom was Colonel John A. Rowan who commanded 62 Tennessee Confederate Regiment.

(4) Margaret Johnston, daughter of Samuel Johnston and Nancy Shaw Johnston married her cousin, Samuel Johnston, son of Joseph Johnston in 1818.

(5) William Johnston, son of Samuel Johnston and Nancy Shaw Johnston, married Nancy Finley in 1820.

(6) Josiah Johnston, son of Samuel Johnston and Nancy Shaw Johnston married Clarissa Prater about 1828.

(7) Francis Johnston, son of Samuel Johnston and Nancy Shaw Johnston married Jane Ferguson in 1838.

(8) James Harvey Johnston, son of Samuel Johnston and Nancy Shaw Johnston, married Nancy Walker in 1835.

(9) Anna Johnston, daughter of Samuel Johnston and Nancy Johnston, never married.

(10) Hamilton Johnston, son of Samuel Johnston and Nancy Shaw Johnston, married Isabella Auneau in 1835.

II. JOSEPH JOHNSTON

Joseph Johnston, who was born in or near, Dublin, Ireland, February 28, 1745 and emigrated to America in about the year 1767, settled with his brothers in Virginia in 1770. He served in the Revolution and was a Sergeant in Captain Joseph Spencer's Company.

In July 1778, Joseph Johnston and his brother Francis Johnston made a trip to Charleston, South Carolina, and were so delighted with the country that Joseph Johnston decided to remain there. He married Margaret Graham, of Graham's Ford, in 1781.

Margaret Graham had emigrated from Ireland in 1770 with her brother, Robert Graham. They had settled in Southwestern Virginia near Wytheville, according to Dr. J. T. Graham, of Wytheville. The ten sons and daughters of Joseph and Margaret Graham Johnston were born in York

JOHNSTON

District, South Carolina. They lived on the Paden River near the "Old National Ford".

About the Year 1816, Joseph and Margaret Graham Johnston and their entire family moved to Tennessee, Blount County, and he later bought ten farms in Monroe and Roane Counties, Tennessee, leaving one farm to each of his ten children.

He died August 15, 1825, on the farm where he lived for several years, one and a half miles south of Blair's Ferry, now near Loudon where his grandson, James Harrison Johnston now lives. Joseph and Margaret Graham Johnston are buried at the Old Brick Church where they lived in Blount County.

From a memorandum book kept by Joseph Johnston, beginning February 16th, 1770, we find that he came to Virginia from Pennsylvania. Other items in the book show that he had business transactions with Francis Johnston, who must have been a brother.

He kept accounts with the Exchange Bank of Georgetown, Mechanics Bank of Baltimore, and a Virginia Bank in 1773. In July 1778, he and Francis Johnston made a trip to Charleston, South Carolina, and an account of the expenses of both on that trip was kept. He has accounts also with John Johnston and James Johnston, presumably brothers. He has entries of notes on Bank of Tennessee, payable at Nashville, and the State Bank of North Carolina, Wilmington, North Carolina.

Another entry in the book reads: "Received from Robert Graham on a note, 13 pounds and 12 shillings. Received from John Johnston, on Francis Johnston's account, six pounds and six shillings, April the 10th, 1797, and 260 feet of board. December ye 10th, 1779; this is the bargain between Francis Johnston and Joseph Johnston, viz., that Joseph Johnston bought ye half of a steel and vessels for 300 pounds".

After Joseph Johnston removed to South Carolina he accumulated a fortune, and when his children were all grown, he moved to Blount County, Tennessee, and afterwards to Roane, which is now Loudon County.

He bought ten plantations in that section of the country known as "Sweetewater Valley", between Blount County, and Chattanooga. He gave a plantation to each one of his children and furnished it with stock and negroes; but he set most of his own negroes free after he moved to Tennessee, and sent them back to Liberia. One negro who was liberated, was very young at the time, and started, with his mother, to Liberia, but when they embarked at Savannah, Georgia, he turned back with one or two others, preferring rather to bear the ills he already had than to fly to those he knew not of. His mother, after she arrived in Africa, wrote to her mistress several times, and occasionally sent presents of coffee and other products of the country, in exchange for tobacco and presents sent them from this county. They were not satisfied in Liberia and wished to return. In Joseph Johnston's will it will be found that he gave to each of his children a body servant or maid, with the proviso that they should be taught to read and and be set free at the age of thirty. In his will he also ordered that his books of divinity should be divided amongst his sons and daughters, but that his other books should be divided amongst his sons only. Evidently believing that it was not necessary for women to know anything except religion. Joseph Johnston served as courier in he Continental forces, during the Revolutionary war, and, for many years, the family possessed the note book, kept by him, with remarks upon the campaign from Newport, Rhode Island, to Charleston, South Carolina.

He, his ancestors and most of his descendants have been Scotch-Irish Presbyterians, of the strictest faith, and have been noted for their integrity of character and solid qualities, although a trifle austere. They acknowledge but one right and one wrong, and recognize no circuitous routes between the two.

The children of Joseph Johnston and Margaret Graham Johnston were:

(1) James Johnston.
(2) Josiah Johnston, born 1785.
(3) Frances Johnston.
(4) Samuel Johnston.
(5) Joseph Johnston, Second.
(6) Robert Johnston.
(7) Ebenezer Johnston.
(8) William Johnston.
(9) Margaret Johnston.
(10) Jean Johnston.

(1) James Johnston married Rachel Martin. Their children were: Joseph Johnston, William Johnston, Ebenezer Johnston, Francis Johnston, Polly Johnston, Michael Johnston and Martha Johnston.

(2) Josiah Johnston married Esther Walker, of Penn-

JOHNSTON

sylvania. Their children were: Joseph Johnston, Walker Johnston, James Johnston, Francis Johnston, William Johnston, Emmett Johnston and Nancy Ann Johnston (who married Dr. Ford).

Of the foregoing:

Joseph Johnston married Caroline Hair and had seven children, namely: James Johnston, Inez Johnston, Hester Johnston, Alice Johnston, Caroline Johnston, Francis Johnston and Joseph Johnston. James Johnston married Lucy Callaway. She died soon after their marriage. He lives at the old Johnston place near Madisonville, Tennessee. Inez Johnston married Captain H. H. Taylor of Knoxville and left two children, Caroline Taylor and Alfred Taylor. Hester Johnston married —— Reed, of Lexington, Kentucky and had two sons, one of whom died in infancy, the other, Joseph J. Reed married Felicia Murray of Anderson, South Carolina and lives in Knoxville. Alice Johnston died young. Caroline Johnston married Luke Callaway, and had two children, Lucy Callaway who died young and Thomas Calloway who married Rhoda King Shields and lives in Knoxville. Francis Johnston married Elizabeth Houston and has two children, Elizabeth Johnston and Locke Johnston.

Joseph Johnston ——.

Walker Johnston never married.

James Miller Johnston, married Sarah Tucker who was the daughter of John Tucker and Mary (Polly) Haigler of Lenoir County, North Carolina, who had moved from North Carolina to Tennessee in 1838 and settled at Tucker's Springs in Bradley County, seven miles south of Cleveland, Tennessee.

The children of James Johnston and Sarah Tucker, were John Tucker Johnston, Ida Johnston, Josiah Emmett Johnston, Esther May Johnston, James Francis Johnston, Samuel Marshall Johnston and William Thomas Johnston.

John Tucker Johnston married Mary Tipton of Cleveland, they had three children, James Johnston who died young; Willie Johnston, "Bunnie" (as she was affectionately called) who died at the age of twenty-two in Hahnemann hospital in Philadelphia upon returning to The States after a visit in Jamaica; and Clyde Johnston, who married C. L. Hardwick and lived in Cleveland.

Ida Johnston married John A. Steed of Cleveland; their oldest child, Mary Johnston Steed married W. C. Nevin of Sewickley, Pennsylvania, and had three children: Sarah

NOTABLE SOUTHERN FAMILIES

Amelia Nevin, Esther Johnston Nevin (died in infancy) and William Cunningham Nevin, Sadie Steed married Walter Wilson of Cleveland, Tennessee; they have two children: Sarah Gordon Wilson and William Steed Wilson. Campbell Steed died young. Gertrude Steed married John Blackwood of Osceola, Arkansas, Francis Graham Steed.

Josiah Emmett Johnston married Ruth Frances Nuckolls of Galax, Virginia, they have one child, Mary Ruth Johnston, who married Dr. Carl Thomas Spec, of Morristown, Tennessee.

Esther May Johnston married first, James H. Bible of Cleveland, they had one son who died in infancy; she married second, John G. Brown of Blackfoot, Idaho, and has no children.

James Francis Johnston married Bessie Key of Chattanooga, they had two children, a daughter, Mary Frances Johnston, who died young and a son, Summerfield Key Johnston.

Samuel Marshall Johnston married Ophelia Knox of Charleston, Tennessee, they have one daughter, Elizabeth Johnston and one son, James Miller Johnston.

William Thomas Johnston married Gertrude Morgan, who died in 1906, they had three children, Morgan Johnston, Rhoda Inman Johnston and William Thomas Johnston.

Francis Johnston never married.

William Johnston married Belle McCarty and lived near Charleston, Tennessee. They had three children, namely: Mary Johnston, Nannie Johnston and Betty Johnston. Mary Johnston married Elijah Brown of Atlanta, and has two children, William Brown and Esther Brown. Nannie Johnston married J. E. Craig and had two children, Frank Craig and J. E. Craig, junior. They lived in Gainesville, Georgia. Betty Johnston married ——— Mozier. She lives with her mother, Mrs. William Johnston in Calhoun, Tennessee. William Johnston was a surgeon in the Confederate Army and was killed in the Battle of Vicksburg while attending wounded soldiers.

Emmett Johnston married Caroline Tucker (See Howard Family) and had six children, namely: Eugene Johnston, Francis Johnston, and French Johnston. Eugene Johnston died in 1915. Mary Johnston married M. L. Beard and had three children, Frankie Beard, May Beard and French Beard. Joseph Johnston married Ella Wehunt

JOHNSTON

and had one child, Caroline Johnston. French Johnston died in 1907.

Nancy Ann Johnston married Dr. Ford. They had three children, J. D. Ford, William Ford and Francis Ford, all of whom are married and live in Texas.

(3) Francis Johnston married Katie Duncan. Their children were: Joseph Johnston, George Johnston, and two daughters, all of whom moved to Iowa in 1855.

(4) Samuel Johnston married his cousin, Margaret Johnston. Their children were: Francis Johnston, John Johnston, Ebenezer Johnston, Joseph Johnston and Margaret Johnston.

(5) Joseph Johnston, the Second, married Hester Henderson. Their children were: John Johnston, Francis Johnston, Margaret Johnston, Cynthia Johnston and another daughter.

(6) Robert Johnston died unmarried.

(7) Ebenezer Johnston, seventh child of Joseph Johnston and Margaret Graham Johnston was born August 30, 1800. He married August 5th, 1830, Hannah Hughes Huff.

Ebenezer and his bachelor brother, Robert, inherited the plantation where their parents died, and continued to dwell there until their death; Robert in July 1863, and Ebenezer in September 1867; the wife of Ebenezer also died at the same place, in September 1878, and the three are buried in the old burying ground there. Their homestead has descended to James H. Johnston, third son of Ebenezer, who is at present living with his family in the house originally built by Joseph Johnston.

Robert Johnston served as Colonel and Ebenezer Johnston as Captain of the State militia for many years, having received their commissions from Governor Carroll.

All the sons of and the two sons-in-law of Ebenezer served in the Confederate army, except William McEwen Johnston, who was too young—his next older brother, Jerome Von Albade having entered the service at the age of seventeen. He was shot through the leg at the battle of "Big Block" near Vicksburg, Mississippi, and made a prisoner. His older brother, John Yates Johnston, Captain of Company F, 62nd Tennessee Volunteers, was captured at the same time and was a prisoner on Johnston's Island, Ohio, for twenty-two months. After the war was closed Joseph Marshall Johnston went to New York and was for many years a partner in the firm of R. T. Wilson & Company, bankers. He afterwards settled in Macon,

Georgia. He was one of the largest planters in the State and president of the American National Bank. John Yates Johnston was a capitalist of Knoxville, Tennessee, James H. Johnston, as previously mentioned, is living at the homestead in Tennessee; Jerome Von Albade Johnston is largely interested in developing the mineral resources of Southwestern Virginia.

William McEwen Johnston, the youngest son, after leaving Washington College, in Lexington, Virginia, in 1870, went to New York City, where he was a member of the firm of R. T. Wilson & Company, Bankers for many years. After his marriage he removed to Macon, Georgia, where he now lives, not being actively engaged in any business.

The children of Ebenezer Johnston and Hannah Hughes Huff Johnston were: Melissa Clementine Johnston, born May 9th,1831; Robert Franklin Johnston, born December 8th, 1832; Mary Jean Johnston, born October 9th, 1834; Joseph Marshall Johnston, born May 21st, 1837; John Yates Johnston, born October 20th, 1839; James Harrison Johnston, born January 22nd, 1842; Jerome Von Albade Johnston, born February 4th, 1845; Milton Graham Johnston, born November 14th, 1847; William McEwen Johnston, born July 20, 1850; and Hannah Elizabeth Johnston, born October 17, 1857.

Melissa Clementine Johnston married Richard Thornton Wilson. She lived in New York and lived to be nearly eighty. They had five children, the oldest daughter Mary Wilson married Ogden Goelet. Their children were was frequently compared to that of Queen of Denmark, who married every child to a crown. The Wilsons married the American equivalent—wealth. The eldest daughter, Mary Wilson Married Ogden Goelet. Their children were: May Goelet, who is Duchess of Roxburghe and Robert Goelet. Orme Wilson married Caroline Astor and has two sons. Richard Thornton Wilson, and Marshall Orme Wilson. Junior Leila Belle Wilson, the second daughter, married Michael Henry Herbert, then an attache of the British Embassy at Washington. At the time of his death he was Sir Michael Herbert and British Ambassador at Washington. Lady Herbert has two sons. Richard Thornton Wilson, Junior, the second son of Mr. Richard Thornton Wilson and Melissa Clementine Johnston Wilson married Marian Mason of Boston and has two children. Grace Wilson, the youngest daughter married Cornelius Vanderbilt, Brigadier General of the United States Army

JOHNSTON

Army and has two children, Cornelius Vanderbilt, Third, who was also in the United States Army and Grace Vanderbilt. Cornelius Vanderbilt, third married Rachel Littleton. Robert Franklin Johnston died young. Mary Jean Johnston married Simeon D. Reynolds. She had no children.

Joseph Marshall Johnston married Martha Fannin Hueguenin and had two children, Martha Johnston, who married William de Lacey Kountze, and had two children, Martha and Helen; and Richard W. Johnston, who married Isabelle Thomas and left daughters, Isabelle and Pamella. Richard W. Johnston died December 28, 1808. 28, 1808.

John Yates Johnston married Sue Ayers and had three children, a son who died in infancy, and two daughters: Janie Johnston, who married Hepburn Saunders and Sue Johnston,, who married David C. Chapman.

James Harrison Johnston is living on the old Johnston place near Loudon. He married Mary Ann Kline and had four children: Mamie Johnston who died unmarried, Sallie Johnston (who married John C. Griffiss, junior, and has John C. Griffiss, Third and James Johnston Griffiss). Albert Sidney Johnston who is unmarried and Elizabeth Johnston(who married Hugh McClung Thomas, and has Lucy Thomas and Charlie McClung Thomas).

Jerome Von Albade Johnston is unmarried and lives in Macon.

William McEwen Johnston married Llewellyn Reese and has two children, Viola Johnston who married Kingman Moore and William McEwen Johnston, junior.

Hannah Elizabeth Johnston married Almstead Mason Cooke and has no children.

(8) William Johnston married Ann Maclyn. Their children were: John Johnston, Campbell Johnston and Robert Johnston.

(9) Margaret Johnston married her cousin, Samuel McMillan Johnston. Their children were: Nancy Ann Johnston (who married Z. Edwards), James Harvey Johnston, Ebenezer E. Johnston, Lucinda Jane Johnston, Jefferson Lafayette Johnston, Margaret Johnston, Esther I. Johnston and had two sons who died in infancy. (See descendants of Samuel McMillan Johnston).

(10) Jean Johnston married David Walker. They had ten children, among others, William Walker, Francis Walker and Eliza Walker.

NOTABLE SOUTHERN FAMILIES

(s) William Johnston, son of Joseph Johnston and Margaret Graham Johnston, who was born 1800 and died 1864, aged sixty-four, married Anne McClyn, born 1805, died 1869. They had six children, namely: Robert Alexander Johnston, Adaline Johnston, Francis Carlyle Johnston, Jackson Graham Johnston, William Campbell Johnston, and Columbus McCivin Johnston.

Of the foregoing:

Robert Alexander Johnston, first child of William Johnston and Margaret Graham Johnston, married three times and had children by his first and second marriages. He married first, Vuity Turner and they had eight children, namely: Ann Johnston, Hester Johnston, Susan Johnston, William Johnston, Frank Johnston, Columbus Johnston, Belle Johnston, Nancy Johnston. Robert Alexander Johnston, married second, Mrs. Lucy Jane Bean and they had seven children, namely: Lyle Johnston, Ida Johnston, Lula Johnston, Charlie Johnston, Mollie Johnston, Oscar Johnston and Ora Johnston. Robert Alexander Johnston married, third, Tabitha A. Goodner and they had no children. Of the children of Robert Alexander Johnston by his first wife: Susan Johnston, married Henry Berger and had nine children, namely: Mary Berger, Lucy Berger, Nannie Berger, Clara Berger, Oscar Berger, George Berger, Fred Berger, and Frank Berger; William Johnston married Ellen Pair and had four children, namely: Eugenia Johnston, Samuel Johnston, Arthur Johnston and Horace Johnston. Frank Johnston married Minerva Wolf and had six children, namely: Stella Johnston, James Johnston, Margaret Johnston, Ollie Johnston, Johnny Johnston and Abbey Johnston; Columbus Johnston married Lelia Wolf and had two children, namely: Carl Johnston, and Burta Johnston. Belle Johnston married Sim Harris and had seven children, namely: Ida Harris, Robert Harris, Eula Harris, Hentie Harris, Mary Harris and Jessie Harris; Nancy Johnston married James Everhart, and had five children, namely: Clarence Everhart, Unity Everhart, Ruth Everhart, Robert Everhart, and Willie Everhart. Of the children of Robert Alexander Johnston by his second wife: Lyle Johnston married Eugenia Hawk and had two children, namely: Maurice Johnston and Eugene Johnston; Ida Johnston married Champ Ramsey, and had ten children, namely: Ora Ramsey, John Ramsey, Lillian Ramsey, Nannie Ramsey, Thomas Ramsey, McKinley Ramsey, George Ramsey, Perry Ramsey, Robert Ramsey, and Mary Ramsey; Charles

JOHNSTON

Johnston married Sarepta Sims, and had four children, namely: Cate Johnston, Willie Johnston, Myrtle Johnston, and Victor Johnson, Mollie Johnston married William Nathanbarger and had two children Clay Nathanbarger and Ora Nathanbarger; Oscar Johnston married Burta Martin and had three children, namely: Robert Johnston, Lyle Johnston and Oscar Johnston, junior; Ora Johnston married Samuel Bean, junior, and had no children.

Adeline Johnston, second child of William Johnston and Margaret Graham Johnston married A. W. Ford.

Francis Carlyle Johnston, third child of William Johnston and Margaret Graham Johnston, was born December 22, 1829. He married Mary Katherine MacPhearson, born February 10, 1837, died October 30, 1851. They had five children, namely: William Jackson Johnston, John MacPhearson Johnston, Robert Samuel Johnston, Charles Franklin Johnston, and Frances Henry Johnston. Of these, William Jackson Johnston married Harriet Hunter and had five children, namely: Frederick Johnston, Margaret Johnston, Arthur Johnston, Augusta Johnston and Robert Johnston. Robert Samuel Johnston, married three times and had children by each marriage. He married first, Elizabeth Karr and had three children, namely: Mary Johnston, John Johnston and Robert Johnston; he married second, Nannie Westmoreland and had one child, namely: Francis Jeffie Johnston; he married third, Martha Ann Williams and had one child, namely: Ruth Emily Johnston. Charles Franklin Johnston married Nannie Stanfield and had one child, namely: Lula Johnston. Frances Henry Johnston married Emma Smalling and had four children, namely: Clint Johnston, Charlie Johnston and Clarence Johnston.

Jackson Graham Johnston, fourth child of William Johnston and Margaret Graham Johnston married Nancy Ann Francisco.

William Campbell Johnston, fifth child of William Johnston and Margaret Graham Johnston married Nancy A. Prater. They had twelve children, namely: James Johnston, Samuel A. Johnston, Thomas N. Johnston, Sarah A. Johnston, Francis C. Johnston, George G. Johnston, Alice Johnston, Carrie Lea Johnston, J. W. Johnston, Addie Johnston, Minnie V. Johnston, and Martha Johnston. Of these, James H. Johnston married Fannie Julian and had seven children, namely: Warren Johnston (who married ——— an l had four children) Clifford Johnston (who married ———) Wheeler Johnston (who married Nora Jones and had three children), Myrtle Johnston; Mack Johnston (who married Claude Johnston and had one child), and Julia Johnston. Sarah A. Johnston married Anderson Barger and had twelve children, namely: John Barger, William Barger (who married —— and had one child), James Barger, Thomas Barger, Blucher Barger, Mollie Barger, (who married —— Francisco and had one child), Leona Barger (who married Joseph Seaborn), Ida Barger (who married —— Steele and has one child), Jessie Barger, Bertie Barger, Sallie Barger, and Addie Barger; Francis Johnston married Jennie Smalling and had four children, namely: Mae Johnston (who married John A. Lee and has one child), Benjamin Johnston (who married Minnie Rinehart and has three children), Thomas Lee Johnston (who married Lucy Davis and has one child), and Pearl Johnston. Alice Johnston married James Helm and had eight children, namely: John Helm (who married Margaret Allison and had three children), Byron Helm, Lucy Helm (who married —— Johnston and had one child), Fred Helm, Minnie Helm, Addie Helm, Mary Helm, and Douglas Helm. Carrie Johnston married Horace Luttrell and had three children, namely: Hugh Luttrell, Carl Luttrell, and Bernice Luttrell; J. W. Johnston, married Nannie Butts and had four children, namely: Willie Johnston, Fae Johnston, Addie Johnston, Mae Johnston and Ray Johnston.

Addie Johnston married John Brenizer and had two children, namely: Morris Brenizer and Edison Brenizer, Minnie V. Johnston married Andrew Moore and had three children, namely: Earl Moore, Mack Moore and Cecil Moore. Martha Adie Johnston married William Smalling and had one child, Ira Smalling.

KELTON

The Keltons are an ancient family in Scotland. Many references are given to them in Scottish history. There the name is pronounced with the accent on the second syllable. The land on which the new city of Edinburgh is built is said to belong to the Kelton heirs. Mary Kelton married John Glasselle, of the family who accompanied Mary, Queen of Scots from Poictiers, on her return to her native land. The Keltons early began to emigrate to America, the first emigrant of that name reaching South Carolina between 1640 and 1645. Like many other Scots, the Keltons aided in colonizing Ireland. Some of these later came to America with the Ulster immigration. One of them, James Kelton came from Ireland to Chester County, Pennsylvania, about 1735 and was the great-grandfather of General John Cunnigham Kelton the soldier and author of a treatise on military affairs. They came here in great numbers for the Census of 1790 gives twenty-one heads of families of this name in Massachusetts, four for Rhode Island, one for Pennsylvania, two for North Carolina, and one for South Carolina. Dr. Claude Kelton, who served six years in the Hospital Corps of the U. S. Army, says that the records at Washington show that the U. S. Army has had Kelton recruits from nearly every state in the Union. Also that the name has not been missing from the record a single year since 1776.

WILLIAM AND ELIZABETH KELTON

William Kelton was born September 26, 1753. His wife Elizabeth was born March 8, 1754. As to whether William Kelton came direct from Edinburgh, or was the son of the emigrant from that place, has not been ascertained; but that he and his wife Elizabeth were in North Carolina, with a large family and numerous slaves, is given in the Census of 1780. Of William Kelton's Revolutionary record, nothing definite is known, but that he was of Revolutionary timber a few scattered facts attest. He was Scotch-Presbyterian, He is traditionally known to have been concerned with the Mecklinburg Declaration of Independence and belongs to the region where it was framed. His name does not appear on the list of signers, probably because of his youth. He does appear as a member of the Militia of Morgan District in the period immediately following the Revolution.

By way of Smith County, Tennessee, where he had resided for a short time, William Kelton came to Rutherford County, Tennessee, and in 1801 purchased a large tract of land known as "Black Fox Camp". Black Fox was an Indian chief who formerly hunted and encamped at the magnificent spring not far from the present site of Murfreesboro. The story is that Black Fox was pursued to this place, and rather than be caught by the soldiers, sprang into the water and disappeared from sight. The soldiers believed him to be lost, but by an underground channel, he came to surface again at Murfree's Spring, two and one-half miles below. This Black Fox camp has often been mentioned in the history of Tennessee, its unusually large spring being a land mark. The expedition of General Robertson, in 1792, sent one if its scouts over the old trail from Nashville to Chattanooga, who reported that he "had been as far as Black Fox Camp, where he had seen the signs of a numerous army of Indians. Again in 1794, Major Orr's Expedition against the Creek and Cherokees of the Lower Town, "marched to Black Fox's camp and remained there for the night". The deed to this tract of land says that it was granted by the State of North Carolina to Thomas Harris, and that the said Thomas Harris of Mecklenburg County, North Carolina, conveys to William Kelton of Smith County, Tennessee, in 1801, the Black Fox Camp, a tract of 619 acres for six hundred dollars. The witnesses were: L. Sullivan and Alexander Sloan. It is of interest to know that this deed was acknowledged before Andrew Jackson, at that time one of the judges of the "Supreme Court of Law and Equity". William Kelton purchassed my other tracts of land, owning finaly many thousand acres in this and other parts of Tennessee.

Rutherford County, formerly included in Davidson and Williamson Counties, was organized by an act of the General Assembly at Knoxville, October 25, 1803. The first court met at the home of Thomas Rucker, January 3, 1804.

KELTON

Of this court, William Kelton was one of the first grandjurymen. Murfreesboro was founded in 1811, but it was not until 1813 that elections were ordered to be held at Murfreesboro instead of Black Fox Camp, showing that much of the county business has been transacted at the latter place.

A family story of the four sons of William going into the woods to hew logs for the first Presbyterian Church is sustained by the record of their mother, Elizabeth, being a charter member of the congregation. There is now on the original site a neat new brick building.

Here, then, on a plantation of several thousand acres around this spring, from which the town of Murfreesboro is now supplied with water, William and Elizabeth Kelton established their large familiy. William Kelton died in 1813. A chart now on file shows the division among his heirs of the original holdings. This division was made October 10, 1816. Samuel Bigany, Moses Bellak and Sam Barber being the trustees. This names the heirs as Archibald Sloan and wife Agnes, John Sloan and wife Mary, Robert Kelton, Samuel B. Kelton, Elizabeth Kelton, senior, James Kelton, Elizabeth Kelton, junior, William, Alexander Larkey and wife Margaret, these being the widow and eight children. David, another child, died quite young, and was not living at this time.

I. MARY KELTON

Mary Kelton, daughter of William and Elizabeth Kelton was born August, 1774. She married William Sloan.

II. ROBERT KELTON

Robert Kelton, oldest son of William and Elizabeth Kelton was born May 6, 1776. He married while still in Mecklenburg County, North Carolina, Rachel Jetton. This name has been variously spelled Jeton, Gieton and Jelton, the latter spelling is used in the first Census of North Carolina (1790). He died in Rutherford County, Tennessee, in 1826, intestate, and his brother William was appointed administrator. His wife Rachel survived him a number of years, certainly until 1844, as deeds signed by her at that date are on record at Murfreesboro. Robert Kelton, probably lived on the southwest corner of the Black Fox Camp plan-

tation, as that had been set aside for him in the division his father's estate. Their children were:
A. William Pleasant, 1800.
B. Jackson, 1802.
C. Samuel, 1805.
D. Emily, 1808.
E. Mary, 1810.
F. Robert, 1812.
G. George and David, 1814.
H. Margaret, 1816.
I. James H., 1818.

Of these children:

A William Pleasant, son of Robert and Rachel Jetton Kelton, was born in Mecklinburg County, Salisbury District, North Carolina, on January 11, 1800, being the only one of the children who was born before they came to Tennessee. He was married in 1819 to Lucinda White, who was born in South Carolina in 1802. They left Rutherford County and settled in Gibson County, Tennessee, some time in the thirties. William Pleasant Kelton became sheriff of Gibson County and at one time knew every man in that county. He reared a large family and accumulated a large fortune. He died in 1886. His wife, Lucinda, died in 1875. Their children were:

1 Thomas White Kelton, of whose family a complete account will be given below
2 Lavinia, married Abraham Penn.
3 Julia, married James Hill.
4 William, married Hester Rucker.
5 Elizabeth, married Jasper Hardy, and lives in Denver with her daughter Mrs. Inez Hoover, who has one daughter Margaret.
6 Joseph, never married.
7 Frank, married Sarah Hardy. They had a daughter, Elizabeth, who married Mr. Finis White of Missouri. They had also one or two sons.
8 Samuel, married Harriet Britton.
9 Mary, married F. P. Hill.

1 Thomas White Kelton, the oldest child of William Pleasant and Lucinda White Kelton, was born August, 28, 1821. He married Catherine Margaret Guthrie, daughter of John and Minerva Wear Guthrie. John Guthrie came first from Glasgow to Richmond, Virginia, thence to Tennessee, where he met Minerva, daughter of Colonel Samuel Wear, a full account of whose services can be found in the history of

KELTON

the Wear family. Catherine Margaret Guthrie was born in Greene County, Tennessee, June 11, 1830, and died in Van Buren, Arkansas, December 24, 1918. Thomas White Kelton was educated at the old Bradley Academy, Murfreesboro, and at the Louisville Medical College. Tht marriage took place at Vernon, Hickman County, Tennessee, on March 12, 1848. After a short residence at Eaton Tennessee, and at Jacksonport, Arkansas, the family removed with their slaves to Mount Vernon, Missouri, where Dr. Kelton practised his profession for many years. He died there October 28, 1883. Their children were: (a) Eudora; (b) William Pleasant; (c) Thomas White, junior; (d) Lucie Belle; (e) Richard Lee; (f) Martha Guthrie; (g) Charles George; (h) Harry Clay; (i) Granger Latta; (j) Ona; (k) Thaddeus White. Of these:

(a) Eudora was born April 13, 1849 in Eaton Tennessee She was married in 1872 to Dr. M. L. Gaither. They had no children. Her death occured in Aurora, Missouri, January 26, 1905.

(b) William Pleasant Kelton was born in Eaton Tennessee, November 18, 1851. He died in Mount Vernon, Missouri, December 11, 1862.

(c) Thomas White, junior, was born September 1, 1853, in old Jacksonport, Arkansas. He died in Oklahoma, October 16, 1891, unmarried.

(d) Lucile Belle Kelton was born October 10, 1858, married Martin Franklin House Smeltzer on April 25, 1877. He was born May 26, 1853, in Middletown, in the famous and beautiful Maryland valley of that name. His family were Swiss Lutherans and were among the early emigrants to this country. They live in Van Buren, Arkansas, where Mr. Smeltzer established a fruit ranch. Their children are: (1) Homer Cecil Smeltzer, born August 28, 1878, a fruit grower of Sapulpa, Oklahoma, who married in Van Buren, Arkansas, Nov. 1, 1905, Myra Orrick born in Ft. Worth, Texas, April 26, 1885, and has two children: Marion, born May 18, 1912 and Franklin, born May 23, 1915. (2) Catherine, born July 27, 1882, unmarried, (3) Edna, born August 22, 1887, married April 3, 1905, Earl Ward, who was born in Van Buren, June 23, 1884, and has three children, Smeltzer, born February 14, 1906, Virginia, born July 1908, and Catherine born August 31, 1910; (4) Dora Smeltzer was born October 21, 1890, and was married April 25, 1911, to William Reynolds, who was born October 5, 1884, in Ft. Smith, Arkansas. James R. Reynolds, great-grandfather of Will Reynolds was one of the defenders of Fort McHenry in Chesepeak Bay, when the British tried to take it (1814). Francis Scott Key was on board the British ship negotiating for an exchange of prisoners and looking out on the defense of Fort McHenry was inspired to write the "Star Spangled Banner". The Reynolds came to America with Lord Baltimore.

(e) Richard Lee Kelton was born in Mount Vernon, Missouri, October 18, 1860, married in Palmyra, Missouri, in 1894, Jesse Lee. They have no children. He has lived in Van Buren Arkansas, for many years, and is a student of literature and art.

(f) Martha Guthrie Kelton, born July 8, in Mount Vernon, Missouri. She married in 1883 to George Arthur McCanse, a banker of Mount Vernon, who was born November 24th, 1860. He is of an old Scotch-Irish Presbyterian family of Rhea County, Tennessee, who early emigrated to Mount Vernon and were its most prominent and public spirited citizen. Their children are:

(1) William Keith, born May 10, 1885, marred June 1909 in Jefferson City, Missouri, Estelle Wagner, who was born April 17, 1887, and has three children, William Keith, Junior born September 21, 1910, died March 29, 1913 Marjorie, born in Springfield, Missouri, August 7, 1912, and George Arthur born in Dallas, Texas, January 15, 1915; (2) Francis Marie McCanse, born December 6, 1887, and died unmarried November 22, 1920; (3) Catherine Bernice McCanse, born December 25, 1889, married in Springfield, Missouri, November 16, 1910, Henderson Percy Mayberry and has the following children: Martha Emma, born in Quincy, Illinois, February 6, 1913, died April 21, 1913, Mary Jane, born in Kansas City, Missouri, November 3, 1916, Thomas Henderson born September 6, 1921; (4) Caroline Margaret McCanse, born May 22, 1893, married December 23, 1917, Leslie Roseberry Millsap, who served in the World War; (5) Chauncey Arthur McCanse, born August 27, 1895, served in the World War, and unmarried; (6) Martha Lois McCanse, born June 30, 1895, unmarried.

(g) Charles George Kelton was born February 23, 1867, died August 9, 1868.

(h) Harry Clay Kelton was born March 23, 1868, died July 19, 1916. He married Hattie Ferguson on July 15, 1899

KELTON

at Norman, Oklahomas. They had one son, William Paul, who was born October 22, 1902 and is now a medical student in the University of Oklahoma.

(i) Granger Latta Kelton born Sept. 16, 1870. During the Spanish American War he volunteered and served in the 17th Battery Field Artillery, George F. Gatting, Captain A. C. and was transferred to Hospital Corps.

(J) Ona Kelton was born September 13, 1872 died May 4, 1874.

(k) Thaddeus White, youngest son of Thomas White Kelton born Jan.,4, 1875, married Nora Whitmore, by whom he had a son Harold Lee, born May 24, 1899 and who volunteered for service in the Navy during the World War. Dr. Thaddeus Kelton married December 24, 1920, Mrs Lillian Anderson (Miss Runyon) a granddaughter of the first American Ambassador to Germany, Theodore Runyon of New Jersey.

B. Jackson, son of Robert and Rachel Jetton Kelton was born in 1802.

C. Samuel, son of Robert and Rachel Jetton Kelton was born near Fox Camp Rutherford County, Tennessee He married twice. His first wife was Margaret C. White to whom he was married June 17, 1829. They had four children, Minerva, Bradshaw, Isabella, and Martha. His wife died February 16, 1838. He married a second time to Margaret Shepherd, February 18, 1839 and had three children, Mary Ann, Rachel and Samuel T. His second wife died December 16, 1889 and he died April 9, 1891, aged 86 years, one month and 26 days. His children were:

1 Minerva Kelton, oldest child of Samuel and Margaret White Kelton, was born August 22, 1830. She was married January 30, 1849 to Calvin C. Lowe, who served in the Confederate Army in the War Between the States. To this union were born eight children: Samuel, Elizabeth, Sarah, Wesley, Martha, Margaret and Calvin, junior. Minerva Kelton Lowe died April 14, 1863.

2 Bradshaw Kelton was born January 1833 and died August 11, 1842.

3 Isabella Kelton was born December 11, 1834, and married September 5, 1854, Jackson Prater, who had served in the Mexican War. They had ten children: Thomas, Robert, Minerva, Charley, James, Mattie, Alice, Hattie, Ernest and Rachel. This family removed to the State of Texas,

where Isabella Kelton Prater died and her children married and reared families.

4 Martha Kelton was born September 12, 1837, and was married on September 14th, to Walter Lowe and had four children: Margaret, Calvin, William and James. Martha Kelton Lowe is still living, having reached the advanced age of 84 years.

5 Mary Ann Kelton, daughter of Samuel Kelton and his second wife, Margaret Shepherd, was born July 24, 1845 and married December 20, 1860, to Samuel Fox, who served as a Confederate soldier. They had three children, Bettie, Maggie and Samuel T. There are now eleven grandchildren and thirty-four great grandchildren.

6 Rachel Kelton was born October 4, 1846 and was married January 20, 1869 to James Y. Lowe, a soldier in the Southern Army in the War Between the States. They had two children: Sammie S. Lowe and William Lowe.

7 Samuel T. Kelton was born July 15, 1850 and was married to Mary F. Lowe, February 5, 1871 and had one child, William S. Kelton.

There are many descendants of Samuel Kelton living in different states. Their number would be in the hundreds if it had been possible to get records of all of them. Three sons-in-laws were soldiers in the War Between the States, and one, Jack Parter, served in the Mexican War. He also had two great grandsons, Kirk Lowe and Elam Kelton to serve in the World War. He has three children now living, Martha Kelton Lowe, aged 84 years, Mary Ann Kelton, aged 76 years and Samuel T. Kelton, aged 72 years.

There is a record of a William Kelton, who was made a prisoner in the War Between the States, and while in prison in Erie County, Ohio, made a will, which was probated in Rutherford County, October 4, 1864, in which he mentions wife Nancy and his son, Andrew. It is not known just what relationship he bore to the first William Kelton.

D. Emily, daughter of Robert and Rachel Jetton Kelton, was born near Murfreesboro, Tennessee, February 3, 1808. She died September 7, 1884. She married William Clark who was born in North Carolina Oct. 28, 1807. He died October 23, 1880. Their children were:

1 Rachel.
2 James A., born September 13, 1837.
3 Robert Newton.
4 Sarah E.
5 William G.

KELTON

6 John Thomas.
7 Margaret Jane
8 Mary E.
9 Melissa Tennessee.
10 Susan Cassie.

Of these children:
1 Rachel Clark was born August 9, 1835, and married in 1857, Moses Woodfin, who was born March 8, 1829 and died January 30, 1908. Their children were: White Woodfin, who was an elder in the Presbyterian Church, and Moses Woodfin, junior, who was an elder in the Cumberland Presbyterian Church.
2 James A.
3 Robert Newton was born August 24, 1839. He was in the 45th Regiment of Tennessee Infantry, and was killed at the battle of Missionary Ridge in 1863.
4 Sarah E. was born September 22, 1841 and died December 22, 1883.
5 William G. was born February 6, 1844 and was in the same Regiment as his brother Newton, and was killed in the same battle.
6 James Thomas born February 3, 1846 and died August 4, 1860.
7 Margaret Jane, born August 1, 1849, died November 1, 1913.
8 Mary E. Clark was born March 11, 1851 and married at Liberty Gap, by the Reverend Miller on September 5, 1840 Henry L. Woodfin, born December 5, 1840. Their children are: (a) John T. Woodfin, born December 13, 1867, married in 1895 Beulah Jacobs and had Rice Woodfin, born October 10, 1897 at Christiana; Mary Clark Woodfin, born August 19, 1900 at Murfreesboro; John, junior, born August 23, 1903 at Murfreesboro; James Collins born December 26, 1909, at Murfreesboro; (b) Cicero N born August 27, 1871, married December 1893, Lida G. Sims, and had one child Eva Fletcher born January 9, 1901 at Christaina, Tennessee. They now reside in Nashville, where Cicero N. Woodfin is an insurance man; (c) Lizzie L., born November 9, 1874 and married Andrew Miller, who was born in September 1874. Their children are: Evelyn, born November 1905; Tracy, born October 1908; (d) Susan E., born December 8, 1876, and married May 21, 1896, Charlies B. Marlin. Their children are: Hugh Robert, born August 31, 1897; Welburn, born August 24, 1900; Roy Benton, born March 10, 1906; Charles, junior, born June 1, 1909; (e) William

Moses, born December 28, 1878, a Presbyterian minister in Pittsburgh, Pennsylvania; (f) Eva S., born March 13, 1884 and married December 25, 1914, James Miller and they had one child, James Woodfin Miller, born January 29, 1916.

9 Melissa Tennessee was born February 22, 1855 and married Harvey Arnold who was born in 1837.

10 Susan Cassie was born June 5, 1859, married 1881 Buck Arnald, and died in 1917.

E. Mary, daughter of Robert and Rachel Jetton Kelton, married Robert Brothers.

F. Robert Kelton, the second, son of Robert and Rachel, was born in 1812. About 1838 he married Sarah Clark and had Mary Jane, born in 1839; Elizabeh born in 1841, and Eliza, born in 1844. Robert's wife died in 1858. He married Nancy Clark, by whom he had Reuben Grady Kelton, who was born April 21, 1860. The daughter Elizabeth, born 1841, married Harvey Clark in 1859, who was born in December 1839, and they had the following children: (a) Sarah Frances, born May 9, 1860, died February 16, 1913. She married Mr. Beavers, who died December 16, 1912; (b) William Riley, born October 3, 1868; (c) Eliza Green, born September 1, 1871; (d) Charley H., born July 1, 1874; (e) Molly, born August 8, 1877. Reuben Grady Kelton born 1860, married Maggie Clark in 1886. He is now a substantial farmer of Rutherford County, Tennessee, and has several children: (a) Robert James, born September 14, 1887, who married Beulah Taylor in December, 1914; (b) William B., born October 2, 1889, who served in the World War; (c) Charles C., born October 25, 1891, who also served overseas and died of pneumonia in France; (d) Frank E., born December 1893, married Lela Earles in 1916; (e) Nancy A., born March 9, 1895; (f) Reuben Grady, junior, born October 2, 1897, married Alice Thomas in December 1920.

G. George and David, twins of Robert and Rachel Kelton, were born in 1814. George married Sallie Clark. David married and went to Arkansas, but we have no record of his family. It is known, however, that he lived to a good old age.

H. Margaret, daughter of Robert and Rachel Jetton Kelton, was born in 1816. She married William Stevenson. Their children were: John, who married a Miss Adock; Robert, Newton, Sis and Tobe, who married Miss Summers.

I. James H. Kelton, youngest son of Robert and Rachel Jetton Kelton, was born October 21, 1818. He married

KELTON

Martha Jane Yardley, who was born June 15, 1824, daughter of Captain Thomas Yardley, who was in Jackson's Army at the Battle of New Orleans. James H. Kelton was in the army that took the Indians from Tennessee to the Indian Territory. He and his wife had seven children, namely:
1. John Thomas.
2. Sarah Elizabeth.
3. Alice Jane.
4. Mary Louise.
5. William James.
6. Margaret Tennessee.
7. Mattie J.

Of the foregoing:

John Thomas was born July 1, 1841, is now nearly eighty He served in the War Between the States as a member of Company E, 23rd Tennessee Infantry, C. S. A., under Captain W. S. Lowe. He married Amanda E. Prater. Their children are: (a) Mollie, who was born March 3, 1866 and died August 20, 1866; (b) William T., born August 10, 1867 and married Mrs. Amanda Stammer, December 18, 1870; (d) Octa, born December 31, 1871, died October 8, 1874; (e) Etta Atrice, born March 31, 1875 and is unmarried; (f) Charles Ephraim Kelton was born July 31, 1877, was married December 11, 1911 to Lula Ridley, who was born September 3, 1884. Their children are: Samuel Weakley Kelton, born January 7, 1913; John Knox Kelton, born April 24, 1914; Robert Ridley and William Thomas were twins born March 5, 1917, William died April 1, 1917; Sarah Elizabeth was born April 29, 1920. (g) Elizabeth Kelton was born July 12, 1884. She married December 3, 1907, Samuel Pearson and lives in Murfreesboro. Their children are: James Franklin, born November 1, 1908, Minnie Jane, who was born June 12, 1909; Willie Lewis, born March 17, 1913.

2 Sarah Elizabeth, daughter of James H. and Martha Jane Kelton, was born March 15, 1845. She married Mr. Prater, by whom she had children as follows: (1) Ida, born September 25, 1867, married the Reverend C. A. McNabb, a Baptist preacher, and had one son, S. B. McNabb; (b) W. F. Prater, born May 10, 1869; (c) Janie Prater, married S. E. Pearson; (d) Edward Prater; (e) Celia Prater.

3 Alice Jane, daughter of James and Martha Jane Kelton, was born July 26, 1847. She married William

Mankin, junior. They had one child, Lily, born January 25, 1870, who married July 18, 1887, G. F. Prater, and had three sons, William Gregg, married Molly Todd and had three small children; Leslie married a young lady from Ohio. He was second Sergeant of his company in the World War. G. F. Prater, junior, was born February 8, 1894, married Helen Herrell on December 17, 1919.

4 Mary Louisa, daughter of James and Martha Jane Kelton, was born May 20, 1849.

5 William James Kelton, son of James H. and Martha Jane Kelton, was born August 19, 1853. He married November 20, 1895 Mollie Frizzel, born 1872. He is a substantial farmer and lives on or near the old Black Fox Camp plantation. Their children are: (1) Lorenzo, born March 3, 1897. He served in the World War. (b) Lulu Lee, born June 25, 1899, died July 10, 1900. (c) Bernice Pauline, born August 25, 1901. (d) Mary Aileen, born May 23, 1904. (e) William Royce born December 3, 1905(died March 30, 1917).

6 Margarett Tennessee Kelton, daughter of James and Martha Jane Kelton, was born June 19, 1855. She married T. L. Webb, whose family were among those who first settled Rutherford County. He was born in 1849. They live in sight of their old place. Their children are: (a) Lelia Agnes, born December 29, 1874, died in infancy. (b) James Robert, born January 28, 1877, married Kate Johnston and has Kirk, Hall and Smith. (c) Mattie Myrtle Webb was born February 26, 1879 and married Burriel Johnston; children are Rolley, Thomas Webb, junior, Marguerite, Lyla Bell, B. F., Elizabeth and Jo. (d) Joseph William was born September 13, 1881 and married Lillian Wallace. No issue. (e) Bessie Lee Webb was born December 31, 1883, married Clayton Bowen. Their children were: Orman, J. T., Elizabeth and Christine. (f) Newton Thomas Webb was born November 8, 1886, and married Frances Buchanan, daughter of Ex-Governor J. P. Buchanan.

7 Mattie J. Kelton, daughter of James H. and Martha Jane Kelton, was born October 6, 1865.

III. AGNES KELTON

Agnes Kelton, daughter of William and Elizabeth Kelton was born January 20, 1776. She married Archibald Sloan.

IV. WILLIAM KELTON

William Kelton, second, son of William and Elizabeth

KELTON

Kelton, was born July 12, 1718. He died October 23, 1866. His wife's name was Minerva. He had several children. Little is known of his life. Some time before the War Between the States, he left Rutherford County, Tennessee, and settled in the more mountainous county of Warren. There, during the War, Mr. John Thomas Kelton, a private in the Confederate service, found himself in front of a large brick residence, the owner of which, on hearing the name of Kelton, introduced himself, and it was established that he was William, the great uncle of the soldier. The old man asked the young private into his house and pointed out an oil painting with the remark that it was the work of a son. This son, we think, became a resident of Philadelphia and had a son who lives in New York City. The Tennessee relatives recall Robert, William and Wilson as the names of his sons, the last probably being the grandfather of Miss Winifred Kelton, a teacher of Satanta, Kansas.

V. DAVID KELTON

David Kelton, son of William and Elizabeth Kelton, was born December 15, 1783. He died young.

VI. ELIZABETH KELTON

Elizabeth Kelton, daughter of William and Elizabeth Kelton was born December 7, 1785.

VII. JAMES KELTON

James Kelton, son of William and Elizabeth Kelton was born in 1788, and married Elizabeth White, who was born in 1790, of a Presbyterian family of South Carolina and a kinswoman of the Lucinda White who married William Pleasant Kelton. They lived in Rutherford County and had the following children:
A. Margaret, born in 1818, married G. G. Peay.
B. Martha, born 1820, married William Vaughn.
C. William, born 1822, died in 1844 or 1846.
D. Matilda, born 1824, married Jenkins McCaul.
E. Mary, born 1826, married William Henry.
F. Thomas Eggleton, born 1829 and married Sarah E. Dunn, who was born in 1826. He died in 1880. Their children were: 1, Elizabeth, born 1848, married Andrew McClendon. They live in Williamson County, Texas. 2 James T. Kelton, born 1850, married (1) Hattie White Bostick and had by her one daughter, Edna, who married Mr.

de Jarnette and lives in Atlanta, Georgia, and has two sons, William who lives in Jacksonville, Florida, and Dr. Claude M., lives in Kentucky, is married and has five children. (3) William Ramsey, of Bastrop County, Texas, born August 14, 1851, married Amanda Comer, who was born in Tennessee in 1858, and has: (a) Lillian Belle Kelton, born December 4, 1876, married Claude Thomas Wynn, who died in 1921, and has five children: Claudine Elizabeth, born February 28, 1900, Doris Amanda, born July 11, 1902, Thomas Kelton, born June 27, 1904, Lillian Belle, born October 2, 1906, and William Ramsey, born October 5, 1913; (b) John Samuel married Susanna Hickerson. 4 Harvey, born 1863, is unmarried and lives in Texas. (5) John Samuel, born in 1865 married Mary Comer of Tennessee. (6) Helen Grafton Kelton, born January 29, 1872 at Vervilla, Tennessee, married D. B. Spillar on December 23, 1894. They live in Austin Texas and have the following children: (a) Homer Kelton born March 24, 1893; (b) Beulah Roseland, born June 23, 1894; (c) Willis Robinson, born May 31, 1897; (d) Thomas Bascom, born April 1, 1901; (e) Olive Elizabeth, born March 13, 1903; (f) Kelley Wilson, born March 10, 1906; (g) John Harvey, born May 10, 1907; (h) Howard Willard, born September 25, 1910.

G. Nancy, daughter of James and Elizabeth Kelton, was born in 1831, and married G. G. Peay after the death of her sister, Margaret.

H. Elizabeth, daughter of James and Elizabeth Kelton was born in 1833 and married Colonel James Goode.

I. Paulina, born in 1835 and married Samuel Briggs.

J. Sarah, daughter of James and Elizabeth Kelton was born in 1837, and married Samuel Burgess and had children: Sammie, who married Charles E. Rhodes; Matilda who married a McCaul; Thomas and James.

K. Justine was born in 1839 and married Dr. Dill.

L. Amanda, daughter of James and Elizabeth Kelton was born in 1841, and married John Frost.

M. James Peay Kelton, son of James and Elizabeth Kelton was born in 1844 and died in 1910. His parents died when he was three years old, and his uncle, James Peay raised him. He was married December 8, 1868 in Tennessee to Nettie Carnes, who was born in 1848, the daughter of William and Elizabeth Carnes. Their children are: 1 Leslie Eugene Kelton, a physician of Corsicana, Texas, who married Emma Gray and had Leslie Eugene, junior, Philip, David and Elizabeth; 2 Herschell, who died in infancy. 3

KELTON

Alva Lee Kelton, who is connected with a wholesale drug company and lives in Dallas, Texas. He married Lula Rice of Frost, Texas, and has two daughters, Mona Ruth, born January 1, 1901, and Nettie Rebecca, born August 24, 1902. These girls are students at Williamsburg, Virginia, in William and Mary College. 4 Walter, a physician, unmarried, lives in Seattle, Washington. 5 Horace Almanezer, married Edith Bennett of Greenville, Texas, in 1903. They live in San Antonio, where he is in the real estate business. Their children are: Edward Carnes, born in 1912; Harry Bennett, born January, 1916; Mary Anette, born Janu ry 1, 1921; 6 William White Kelton, married Stella Ricketts. They live in San Antonio. Their children are: William White, junior, born in 1913, Hugh Ricketts born 1914, Katherine, born 1915. 7 Myrte Kelton married David W. Lowe and lives in Roswell, New Mexico. They have no children. 8 Lillie Kelton married Charles E. Erickson of Seattle, Washington, and has one child, Elizabeth, born 1921.

VIII. SAMUEL KELTON

Samuel Kelton, son of William and Elizabeth Kelton, was born in 1791 and married Elizabeth Manley in 1815. All her family were massacred by the Indians, while she was away from home. Afterwards she was reared by James Montgomery. They have five children:
A. Mary.
B. Elizabeth.
C. Jane.
D. William.
E. James Leander.
Of the foregoing:
A. Mary Kelton married Anderson Ott and had a son, Captain William Ott of the Confederate Army. He died in 1919.
B. Elizabeth married William Clark. They went to Texas about 1850.
C. Jane Kelton, after the early death of her sister Mary, became the second wife of Anderson Ott and had: Robert, Deleska, Erskine, Rosa, Laura and Callie.
D. William Kelton married Ann Rowland, 1848 and went to Mississippi. Their oldest son, born about 1850 was named Granville.
E. James Leander, born about 1824, married Eugenia

NOTABLE SOUTHERN FAMILIES

McKnight, daughter of Major David McKnight, December 10, 1844. They had six children: Mary, Sarah, Janie, Samuel T., Adolphus A., and James E.

1 Mary, born in 1846, married W. L. Lewis in 1863. They had no children.

2 Sarah, who was born in 1850 and married Michael Lawrence, had one child Elizabeth, and died in 1873.

3 Janie Lived until maturity and died unmarried.

4 Samuel T. was born in 1847, married about 1877, Martha Lawrence, who died in 1914. He died in 1915. Their children were: George, James, Henry, William, Clyde, Rebecca, Mary and Lola.

5 Adolphus A., who was born in 1852, was married three times. He married (1) in 1869, Mary Barker and had one child (a) Dr. James C., who was born July 4, 1870 and married December 19, 1894 Elizabeth Harris. They live at Lascassas, Tennessee, and have the following children: Marcella, born October 10, 1895, married Clyde Jennings in 1914 and has one child, Clyde Stacy, junior; Mary, Ruth, Katherine, Richard A., born December 17, 1900 and married Betsy Nix on August 10, 1921. Mary Barker Kelton died in 1872. Adolphus A., married (2) Sallie A. Barker, sister to Mary, and had by her three children: (a) William, died in infancy; (b) Florence, born in 1874, married W. A. Jordan in 1891. They had eight boys and one girl and live at Centertown, Tennessee. (c) Lillie J. married Prof. Homer Knox in 1901. She died in a few months without issue. Sarah Barker Kelton died in 1878, and in 1900 Adolphus A. was married to (3) Mattie F. Crockett who is now living. They had three girls and one boy: (a) Nettie, born in 1881, married G. C. Smotherman in 1905. They had two boys, Fred and Cecil and live in Murfreesboro. (b) Bessie, born in 1884, married E. L. Crockett in 1904 and had William, Edwin, James and Elizabeth. They live near Murfreesboro; (c) Mattie Lou, was born 1893 and married O. B. Pemberton in 1909 and has: Neal, Clarence, Allen and Lorena. They live in Rossville, Georgia; (d) Robert H. who was born in 1886, married Nannie McGrew in 1920 and lives in Murfreesboro, Tennessee. He served for two years on the battlefields of France.

6 James E., lived until maturity and died unmarried.

7 Janie, died young.

IX. MARGARET KELTON

Margaret Kelton, daughter of William and Elizabeth Kelton married Alexander Lackey.

MAGILL

In the year 1907 there issued from Magill Publishing Company, of Richmond, Virginia, "The Magill Family Record," the author being Robert M. Magill, of Maryville, Tennessee. It is, as told on the explanatory page, "The complete record of descendants of James Magill, a native of Virginia, Revolutionary soldier, and pioneer in the settlement of Tennessee".

Since the paternal family of the writer has more than once "crossed hands" with members of the Magill family at the marriage altar and because of ability to add a few leaves to the Magill Family Record, the writer has compiled the following sketch.

Origin of the Magill Family

The name Robert is legion among the Magill families of America. The first Robert, so far as is known, was "ye Sir Robert Magill of the Isle of Mull," off the coast of Scotland, who, April 19, 1651, was knighted by Charles II for "heroic action" in assisting the said Charles to effect his escape from the Army of the Covenanters. According to tradition Robert Magill hid the King in the forests of Scotland and provided him with wine and bread during his exile. Thus a jug and a loaf of bread are said to have formed a part of the escutcheon of some of the early families of Magills.

Besides being created Viscount of Oxingford, Robert Makgill received a large estate in Tullycairn, Ireland. Here he established a family seat—and from there came his descendants to America. Prior to the Revolutionary War, families of Makgills had been planted in Connecticut, Pennsylvania and Virginia. These families were closely related, and were possibly descended from Charles, a son of Sir Robert, since the name Charles seems to have been a favorite one in all branches of the different families.

NOTABLE SOUTHERN FAMILIES

When coming to America the Makgills dropped the "k" and picked up a "c". The Revolutionary and pioneer families spelled the name McGill, and this spelling is adhered to by many families today. The present "Magill" was a natural corruption.

The Pennsylvania McGills

The first two emigrants are believed to have been brothers, Charles and William, who emigrated to Pennsylvania probably to that part now lying within the Maryland boundary.

Charles McGill a Lieutenant in the Colonial Militia from "ye Susquehank" from 1742 until 1748.

In 1765 Charles McGill settled in Cumberland County, Pennsylvania. This is the same year in which another Charles is said to have come from Ireland and settled in Connecticut. Whether the latter Charles first settled in in Pennsylvania and later in Connecticut can only be conjectured. The Cumberland County family is thought to have been founded by the first Charles, Lieutenant of Militia.

Charles' wife was probably named Sarah, and the following were his children:

James McGill, who married first Elizabeth Johnson, 1764, and married second Esther Black, 1766.

John McGill, who married Mary Winston, 1765.

Sarah McGill, who married George Ely, 1765.

Robert McGill, who married Sarah Dunlay, 1765.

Another theory which cannot be overlooked is that William McGill, brother of Charles McGill (Lieutenant), who emigrated from Pennsylvania to Virginia about 1742, only mentions children, William McGill, John McGill and Elizabeth McGill, in his will and probably had other children in Pennsylvania. Alexander Hamilton, South Carolina Revolutionary hero and statesman, married Jane McGill in Rockingham County, Virginia, and emigrated to South Carolina about 1765. She was probably a granddaughter of William McGill, the emigrant, and possibly born in Pennsylvania.

The Pennsylvania family was not large at any time prior to the Revolution, and it could easily have been descended from William McGill, the emigrant. In this case it is not probable that Charles McGill, the brother, left any issue.

However, it is evident that the Cumberland County

MAGILL

family had Charles McGill as a progenitor, whether son of Charles or son of William.

Charles, probably a brother of James and John (whose marriages are recorded), resided in Cumberland County in 1865, Charles, probably a son, and Hugh resided in the same township. John, William and the Widow McGill in 1781 were living in Bucks County, Pennsylvania. John was a Revolutionary soldier.

WILLIAM McGILL THE FIRST
Of Rockingham County, Virginia.

William McGill, presumably a grandson of Sir Robert Makgill, of Tulycaim, Ireland, and either brother or father of Lieutenant Charles McGill, of the Provincial Militia of Pennsylvania, settled in Rockingham County, Virginia, while it was yet a part of Augusta County, about the time that so many of the Scotch-Irish families from the Cumberland Valley of Pennsylvania were filling up the Borden and other grants on the Virginia frontier.

William McGill died in Virginia in 1749. He left a widow, Margaret, a second wife, formerly the "Widow Gass" (Glass), by whom he had no children. The children by the first wife as mentioned in his will were John, James, William and Elizabeth.

The Magill record states that the name of John McGill has been found attached to a demand for the militia companies of Augusta County, Virginia, 1776, "That all religious denominations be given equal liberties without preference of pre-eminence".

In his will William leaves John "a mare and ye brown cote (coat)"; William inherits his father's "white cote" and "half of the household plenishings," and shares with James an equal division of the lands. He is requested to spend the winter on the plantation, retaining there, with his own cattle, the stock of his step-mother and sister, Elizabeth.

Whether because of some domestic disagreement or because possessed of independent means or independence of disposition, when the will was probated the widow, Margaret Gass McGill, appeared in court and refused to accept any legacy whatever from the estate.

Other McGill Emigrants—John, Arthur and Charles, Grandsons of Sir Robert McGill.

Near the year 1766 the above mentioned brothers emigrated from County Down, Ireland. Charles and Arthur

NOTABLE SOUTHERN FAMILIES

are both said to have located in Middletown, Connecticut. John, a lawyer of some note prior to the Revolution, settled near Winchester, Virginia. He was a pronounced Royalist. Little else is known concerning him except that he was the father of Colonel Charles McGill, of the Patriot Army, from whom are descended many distinguished Virginia and other Southern families.

Families Who Trace Descent From the Connecticut Emigrants

Through correspondence with the Honorable Henry L. Messieur, at that time Assistant Collector of Ports at St. Johns, Nova Scotia, it was learned that the family to which his mother belonged and which has many representatives, not only in Canada, but in many of our Western states, was descended from one McGill, who married Elisabeth Denny and resided in New Haven, Connecticut. Elisabeth Denny outlived her husband, dying in 1806. The Denny family is an old and well-known Colonial family, claiming as forbear Sir Anthony Denny, the personal medical attendant of Henry VIII. The Dennys seem also to have claimed favor with Charles II, since the Canadian family possess a cup with the Denny "arms" engraved upon it, presented to Charles Denny by this monarch.

A daughter of Elizabeth Denny McGill, Sarah by name, married a Bermuda merchant, John Dunscomb by name, and removed to Newfoundland. Sarah took with her her youngest brother, evidently an orphan, named William. This Willam founded the Canadian family of Magills.

There is a tradition in the family of the Reverend Mathew Magill, who married Lucinda Merwyn in Parish Church, Ireland, and emigrated to America in 1827, that the Magill family had for several generations been famed for its wanderlust. It is quite probable that some of the early McGills returned to Ireland (perhaps certain estates were involved, as was often the case) and in after years the children again emigrated to America.

It would seem from family names and certain coincidences that this family must have originally belonged to one of the Connecticut families.

The Reverend Mathew Magill first located in Ontario, but later removed to Illinois. Here his wife died in 1883. He returned to Ireland, where he subsequently remarried. Three sons, however, remained in the United States. Henry married and located in Kentucky; Arthur resided in Oakland, California, and Robert in Pasadenia, California, a few years ago.

COLONEL CHARLES MAGILL
Virginia Patriot and Statesman

Charles Magill, educated to his father's profession, the law, notwithstanding his father's Royalist sympathies, before he was twenty-one entered the Patriotic Army. He spent the memorable winter at Valley Forge with General Washington and was wounded in one of the early battles. He gradually rose in rank and when General Lincoln took over the Southern Division he was made a member of General Washington's staff.

Incensed because his eldest son, Charles, had entered the Patriot Army, John Magill disinherited him, leaving the family estate and moneys to his second son Arthur (or Archibald).

Colonel Charles Magill began the practice of law in Winchester. He purchased twenty-five thousand acres of land lying within five miles of Winchester. On a slight eminence he built a commodious brick mansion renowned for its hospitalty among old Virginians. The grounds were laid off by landscape gardeners and are said to have contained many rare and beautiful shrubs and flowers. Colonel Charles was a large slave owner and negro "patches" and quarters were also much in evidence. Because of the great stretch of fertile grazing fields or meadows the estate was called "Meadow Lands".

Colonel Charles Magill was twice married. His first wife was a Miss Dangerfield; by her he had no issue.

The second wife, Mary Buckner, bore him eleven children, as follows:

1 John Magill, who inherited Meadow Lands and in whose family it was retained until after the War Between the States, married a Miss Glass, of Frederick County.

2 Alfred Magill, who was a professor in the University of Virginia, married a daughter of Judge Henry St. George Tucker.

3 Henry Magill, a physician,, of Leesburg, married a daughter of the Honorable Temple Mason, of Temple Hall, Virginia.

4 Augustine Magill, who was a lawyer in Louisiana, married a Miss Weeks.

5 Buckner Magill, a surgeon in the United States Army, died unmarried.
6 Elisabeth Magill, who married Colonel Smith, of the United States Army.
7 Anne Magill, who married General Turner Fauntleroy.
8 Mary Magill, who married Robert Lee Randolph.
10 Frances Magill, who married Alfred Thurston, of Washington, District of Columbia.

WILLIAM MAGILL
Tennessee Pioneer, Born 1749.

Since all roads lead to Rome—in these articles the Tennessee trail—we have at last reached the patriarch of the first Tennessee family of McGill, or Magill, as some of them were soon to become known. This was William Magill, son of William Magill, of Rockingham County, Virginia.

William Magill was twenty-four years of age at the time of his father's death in 1749, and some thirty-four years had elapsed when we find him in Tennessee in the year 1783.

The author of the Magill Family Record states "That in his old age William accompanied his son, James to Tennesse, and that James cared for him during his declining years". William Magill was sixty years of age at the time of the migration, and he lived to be ninety-two.

He accompanied not only one son, but six sons, one daughter and a wife. It is supposed he had a second wife, named Jean.

It is thought that most, if not all, of his children were born in Virginia. During the years 1777-78-79 Jean resided in Bedford County, Pennsylvania, but had disappeared from the township in which she lived in the year 1785. A probable theory is that William McGill married Jean in Pennsylvania, and that she returned there while her husband and his sons were serving in the Revolution.

Mention has been made in a previous article of the North Carolina families who settled around old "Timber Ridge Church" in Greene County. William McGill and his family were among the charter members of this church. Almost all of the families in this vicinity were Scotch-Irish who originally settled in the Cumberland Valley, but who had branches in Augusta County, Virginia, and in North Carolina. Some of the families came direct from Pennsyl-

MAGILL

vania and a number from the township in which Jean McGill resided during the Revolution. It is possible that the family of William Magill emigrated with the Pennsylvania colony.

The William McGill, senior, plantation lay on what is now known, as it was then, as Meadow Creek, and contained three hundred acres; he owned other tracts of land in the county. James lived on two hundred acres nearby. The oldest, perhaps, of the sons lived on what is known as "Pigeon Creek". He married either in Pennsylvania or Virginia, and did not long survive his father. He was a widower at the time of his death, and left ten children, five of whom were married daughters.

Another son, who married in Greene County, died just about the time the author of the Magill Record terms "the breaking up" of the Magill family in Tennessee—that is, the breaking up of the "James Magill family" in 1829 or possibly a little later. With the exception of these two brothers and their families, probably the youngest of the children of William Magill, the other Magills had long since migrated to other counties and other states. Two of the sons of William, senior, moved to Wayne County. The daughter, Elizabeth, married John Walker.

JAMES MAGILL
Virginia Patriot and Tennessee Pioneer.

James McGill, son of William, and grandson of William, of Rockingham County, Virginia, was born in 1756, in Augusta County, Virginia. He served in the Revolution in the Twelfth Virginia Regiment.

He emigrated with his father's family to North Carolina, now Greene County, Tennessee, about 1783. He married twice his wives belonging to neighboring families. By his first wife, Elizabeth Evans, he had a daughter, Margaret, and a son, William. James McGill married a second time, Mary McMeans; the issue of this marriage was nine sons and one daughter. In 1839, James Magill moved to Monroe County, Tennessee. A year later, 1840, he died at his home, three miles west of Madisonville. The widow of James Magill, Mary McMeans Magill, after her husband's death, made her home with her daughter, Mrs. Nathan Anderson, in Ringgold, Georgia, where her death took place December 4, 1845.

The following data is taken from the Magill Family Record:

"Margaret, daughter of James Magill and Betsy Evans, married Adam Wilson and emigrated to Indiana about 1832. William, son of James Magill and Betsy Evans, married in Tennessee, Sarah Henry; he emigrated to Hopewell, Indiana. Here his wife died and he married again Nancy Henderson. Thomas, eldest son of James Magill and Mary McMeans, married in Greene County, Tennessee, Mary Hall; he, too, emigrated to Indiana.

"James, John and Harvey died unmarried.

"Nathaniel, married in Greene County, Jane Rankin, and removed to Madisonville, Tennessee.

"Samuel Wallace McGill, married in Greene County, Margaret Wilson Rankin, widow of David Rankin, and removed to Madisonville, Tennessee.

"Hugh Marshall Magill, married Eliza McSpadden in Monroe County, and emigrated to Catoosa County, Georgia.

"Isaac Newton Magill, married in Greene County, Tennessee, Hannah Evans, and removed to Kentucky.

"Susan Matilda McGill, married Nathan Anderson in Greene County, and removed to Ringgold, Georgia.

"Robert Magill married Fannie Lowry".

They had a son, Aurelius Newton Magill, who married Jane Louise Wilson.

Their children were:
1 William Leonidas Magill.
2 Robert Edward Magill.
3 James Alexander Magill.

William Leonidas Magill married, first, Mary Gaines, and had four children, Alexander Magill, William Magill, Bessie Magill and Sadie Magill; William Leonidas Magill married for his second wife, Frances Bachman.

Robert Edward Magill married Elizabeth Lynn, of Bowling Greene, Kentucky, and had two children, Elizabeth Lynn Magill and Cornelia Magill, who married Robert McClennon Whittet and has one child, Robert McClennon Whittett, junior.

James Alexander Magill married Alice Patton and died without issue.

The descendants of James Magill are intimately associated with three historic churches: "Timber Ridge," Greene County, one of the pioneer churches whose congregation settled in its neighborhood while Tennesse was yet a part of North Carolina; Hopewell Presbyterian Church."

near Franklin, Indiana, where the fifth generation,—descendants of William Magill and Sarah Henry still worship. And the "Old Stone Church" at Chickamauga, Georgia, founded about 1848.

Robert McCorckle Magill, son of Robert Magill and Fanny Lowery and author of "The Magill Family Record," in his reminiscence, says: "His father, Robert Magill, son of James Magill, moved from Monroe County to North Georgia and settled on East Chattanooga Creek in 1837. The Indians had not yet been removed to their Western Reservation. In a little valley to the east of the house where the Indians had kept the leaves burned off each winter and called 'The Flat Woods' it was not an uncommon sight to see from six to ten deer grazing".

Perhaps no other family in Tennessee has by marriage allied itself with so many of the most prominent and old pineer stock of the state as has the Magill family.

Early Magill Marriages in Rockingham County, Virginia

James Magill, junior, married Jane Fulton May 28, 1781.
Esther Magill married Alexander Gilmer September 24, 1728.
Samuel Magill married Martha Shannon November 4, 1782.
Margaret Magill married Robert Henry March 28, 1872.

MONTGOMERY

Tradition in several branches of the family says the Montgomerys (the name means "Mount Gomer" or Mountain Dwellers) were driven on account of religious persecution from Scotland early in the 1700's, to the north of Ireland. There, James, founder of this particular branch and son of ——————————— Montgomery and wife, Miss Cunningham was born. Tradition also is very strong that
The supposition that he came first to Pennsylvania (perhaps with his parents) and later to Augusta County(Virginia, before finally settling in old Pendleton District, South Carolina in 1849, has much to support it. Certain it is that many of the name along with other Scotch-Irish settlers took that route. The name is found most frequently in the early history of Pennsylvania.

James Montgomery, born about 1740, was married twice. First to Elizabeth McConnell, by whom he had three sons. After her death in old Pendleton District, South Carolina, he married Susannah Strange, who bore him six (some say seven) children.

Living almost on the line between South Carolina and Georgia, he elected to join the Burke County, (Ga), Militia and fought with that company during at least a part of the Revolution as a Second Lieutenant. He was commissioned November 8th, 1777, by John Adams Neisler, Esq. Proof of this is found in "Commission Book B", Page 276, at Capitol, Atlanta, Georgia.

In 1786, he applied for and received a land grant in Franklin County, Georgia and evidently moved there soon afterwards.

In old documents concerning the Talasee Colony and published in Mr. Wilson's History of Jackson County ,Georgia", frequent mention is made of him. An account of a skirmish with the Indians in which he is seriously wounded is given. Dr. G. G. Smith's History of Georgia and Her People" also records this incident. Mention is also made of the fact that he built the first house in the County and that "Cabin Creek" derived its name therefrom.

He died in Jackson County, (which only a few years before had been formed from Franklin) on January 1st, 1808 and was buried on the old home place, now owned by a Mr. Twitty. His wife, Susannah Strange Montgomery, died October 8th, 1804.

Children by first wife, Elizabeth McConnell were I. John (said to have died a British prisoner at Battle of Waxhaws).

II. Hugh born January 8th, 1767, married Margaret Barclay, (born February 8th, 1768), November 1788, died January 22nd, 1852. She died, July 28th, 1848.

III. James McConnell, born May 19th, 1770, married Nancy Farlow, (born October 7th, 1781. November 14th, 1797). Both died 1842.

Children by the second wife, Susannah Strang (she died October 8th, 1804) were:

IV. John (?).

V. Jeanette, born 1780, married Jos. N. McCain, (born 1777).

VI. Virginia, born 1781, married James Appleby, June 1, 1806. She died 1875.

VII. William, born July 11th, 1783, married (1st, Katherine Boyle, March 31, 1807), (2nd Mrs. Adelia Turner, October 12th, 1854), died December 4th, 1877.

VIII. Margaret or Susie, born 1785, married Thomas Niblack.

IX. Eleanor, born 1787, married Henry Cunningham.

X. Sarah A., born 1789, married Nathaniel Venable, he died 1832, she died 1864.

II. HUGH MONTGOMERY

II. Col. Hugh L. Montgomery (second son of James and his first wife, Elizabeth McConnell) was born in South Carolina, January 8th, 1767, and married, November 1788, Margaret Barclay, (daughter of John and Agnes).

His name appears first in the Georgia records, when in 1786 he was employed to survey the line "between Franklin County and the Indians". This line has always been known as the Hawkins line from the fact that Col. Benj. Hawkins, the United States Indian Agent, authorized the survey of the Government. The original plats made by

MONTGOMERY

Hugh Montgomery and bearing his signature are on file and are almost daily consulted, being recognized as authority in line disputes, etc.

The story of this survey has been recalled by an older member of the family just as told to him when a boy, by Uncle Dave, one of the slaves once owned by Col. Montgomery and who accompanied the surveying party. It seems the Cherokees had agreed for the usual trinkets, blankets, straps, ponies, etc., to give over all the land that the surveyors could run off in a given length of time. Beginning at Savannah River they traveled west to the Oconee, thence south so many miles. After while the Indians began to lag back and only with much persuasion accompanied by more trinkets could the white party persuade them to move on. After a few hours of travel though, the Indian leader stuck his tomahawk in a large oak tree saying, "Indians go no further" hence the origin of 'Cherokee Corner" of today.

Col. Montgomery represented Jackson County in the state legislature for the years 1807-08-09-10 and 1811. In the state senate he served in 1812, '13, '14, '15, '16, '17, '18, '23, '24 and 1825. Being a Scotchman, he was an ardent Presbyterian and with Ex-Governor McMinn of Tennessee, he became interested in mission work among the Cherokee Indians of North Georgia and really financed the sending of the first missionaries to them. Upon the death of Ex-Governor McMinn, he was nominated on March 3rd, 1825 by President Monroe to be Indian Agent of the Cherokee Purchase, his appointment being confirmed by the senate a few days later. He entered upon his duties shortly thereafter, making his headquarters at or near Calhoun, Tennessee and served until the Indians were moved West in 1838. His salary was $1500.00 a year (quite large for those days) and upon retirement was also given a tract of 3,000 acres in Chattooga County, Georgia. There, surrounded by several members of his large family, he lived until January 22nd, 1852. He was buried at Alpine (same county) by the side of his wife who died July 25th, 1848. She was born February 8th, 1768.

His will recorded in Chattooga County has been lost along with other records, though minutes of the Inferior Court state that it was offered for probate by three witnesses, John Montgomery, John Wyatt and William Smith on February 2nd, 1852.

His children were:

243

1st, Agnes, 2nd, Barclay, 3rd, Mary, 4th, Cynthia, 5th, James, 6th, Elizabeth, 7th, Jane, 8th, Christopher, 9th, William, 10th, Madison, 11th, Eliza Ann.

(1) Agnes born February 7th, 1790, married Joseph Thomas Cunningham June 25th, 1807 and died December 8th, 1862.
The children were:
1 Hugh Montgomery Cunningham, unmarried.
2 Margaret Cunningham, married ————Liddell. Their daughter, (A) Betty married Mr. Boswell. Their children, (a) John, married Hallie Boswell (two children) (b) Frank, married Mrs. M. C. Jinks (no children), (c) Agnes, married ————————————, (d) Margaret unmarried.
3 Jane Cunningham, married John Cunningham, (son of Ansel). No children.
4 Cynthia Cunningham, married ————Storey.
5 Amanda Cunningham, married Dr. John Nesbit. They had one daughter, Addie Nesbit who married James Henry and has a daughter Mary Henry who married————.
6 Andrew Cunningham, married Jane Veneable. Their children: (a) Margaret, married J. A. Storey. Their children: (a) A. G. Storey, married Nellie Toole. Their children are: Barckley Augustus Storey, Margaret Virginia Storey. (B) Agnes Elizabeth, married John Winbourne. Their daughter, (a) Agnes Elizabeth, married D. M. Remson. Their children: Andrew Cunningham Remson, Caroline King Remson, John Winbourne Remson, Agnes Elizabeth Remson and David Murry Remson. (c) Robert Joseph (living) unmarried, (d) John Reid, died unmarried. (e) Fanny Forrester, married W. E. Storey. (f) Jean Veneable, married Otis Cook.
7 Columbus Golden Cunnigham, married Fredonia Cameron. Their children: (a) Joseph Thomas, married, ——————, (b) Sarah Agnes, married ——— Leveret, (c) Adeline, married McDonald. (d) Hugh Montgomery, married ——— McDonald.
8 Joseph Cunningham, married Martha R. Mclellan. Their children: (a) Amanda Storey, married, (b) John Reid, married Ann Eliza Turner, (c) Martha Roby, married Rufus Turner.

(2) Barclay, born January 31st, 1792, married Miss Chandler.

(3) Mary, born March 16th, 1794, married Samuel

MONTGOMERY

Knox (uncle of her sister Elizabeth's husband) October 5th, 1809.
Their children:
 1 Dr. James Croll Knox, born March 28, 1812, married first, Mary Jane Bowie, second, Mary Elizabeth Barnett and third, Mrs. Margaret Johnston Rice.
 2 Cynthia L. Knox, born May 24, 1813, married Judge T. J. Davis and died November 19, 1861.
 3 Hugh Montgomery Knox, born December 12, 1814, married Harriet Lamar (daughter of Gen. John Lamar).
 4 John Barclay Knox, born February 5, 1816, married Agnes Boyle in 1840.
 5 William W. Knox, born July 7, 1819, married Mary Bowie, Decmber 23, 1843.
 6 Margaret Ann Knox, born September 30, 1820, married Samuel McWhorter.
 7 Christopher C. Knox, born April 19, 1822, married first Miss Clark, and second Julia A. Strickland in 1865.
 8 D. L. Knox, born August 25, 1824, died in infancy.
 9 Samuel M. Knox, born May 31, 1826, died without issue.
 10 Mary J. Knox, born November 7, 1827, married John Mackey and died January 7, 1846.
 11 Elizabeth E. Knox, born August 6, 1829, died February 16th, 1882, unmarried.
 12 Thomas J. Knox, born February 21, 1831, married first, Maggie Bannar, second, Ann Montgomery and third, Jane Maddox.
 13 Eliza Agnes Knox, born July 14, 1832, married Dr. R. Y. Rudicil in 1857 and died January, 1897.
 14 Evelyn Knox, died unmarried.
 (4) Cynthia, born April 5, 1796, married Robert Broyles April 10, 1817 and died 1835.
 (5) James, born March 20, 1798, married first, Ann Cunnigham March 28, 1820, (daughter of Ansel, a Revolutionary soldier) and second, Sarah Orr.
 (6) Elizabeth, born April 20, 1800, married David L. Knox 1820 and died February 7, 1859.
Their children were:
 1 Cynthia Ann Knox, married James Parks, had several children all of whom died young.
 2 James Montgomery Knox, born July 11, 1822, married Nancy Camp in 1848, no children.

NOTABLE SOUTHERN FAMILIES

3 Hugh Crawford Knox, never married.
4 Samuel Knox, married Mary E. Grills, and died 1887.
5 Christopher C. Knox, born February 21, 1827, married Melita Jane Weir February 21, 1850, and died April 11, 1899.
7 Mary Jane, married Eleazer Freeman and died 1884
(7) William Knox, born September 10, 1828, married Tennessee Smith, March 14, 1861.
Their children were:
(A) Elizabeth M., married George Nixon.
(B) John C., married Annie Laura Johnston.
(C) Ernest Lee, married Josephine Isabella Wheeler.
(D) William Luckie, died unmarried.
(E) Walter Smith Knox, married Annie Carmack.
(F) Henry Thomas.
(G) James Montgomery, died in infancy.
(H) Pearl Ophelia, married Samuel Johnston.
(I) David Knox.
8 Joseph Scott Knox, born November 1829, married Mary Elizabeth Carlock, October 9, 1860, and died March 23, 1886.
9 Margaret Knox, born April 15, 1830, married Henry Rice 1857, and died November 23, 1876, no children.
10 Thomas Jefferson Knox, born January 10, 1833, married Martha A Morrison August 29, 1859, and died——.
Their children were:
(A) Hattie E., married James McKamy (her cousin).
(B) Robert Lee, married Belle Featherstone.
(C) Ebon Thomas, married Florence Wheeler.
(D) Oscar A., married Harrie Hardwick (distant cousin).
Their children were:
(A) Adella, married Joseph Jarnigan.
(B) Irene, married James F. Corn.
(E) Mary Leonia, married Frank Harle.
(F) Hugh Montgomery, married Agnes Gaut.
11 Juliet E. Knox, born May 23, 1834, married William H. McKamy November 2, 1854, and died ——————.
Their children were:
(A) David Knox, married Laura S. Wailes.
(B) James, married Hettie Knox (above mentioned).
(C) William H., junior, died unmarried.

MONTGOMERY

(D) Annie, died unmarried.
(E) Thomas J., unmarried.
(F) Joseph A., died unmarried.
(G) Minnie J., married D. G. McLean.

12 Nancy Agnes Knox, born 1836, died unmarried.

13 Caroline Elizabeth Knox, born December 28, 1838, married Alexander C. Robeson November 9, 1859.

Their children were:

(A) William Henry Knox Robeson, married India Ferguson, and had Edith Maxwell Robeson, died unmarried; Gertrude Robeson; India Robeson, married George Featherstone; and Louise Robeson died in infancy.

(B) Katherine Elizabeth Robeson married Edgar V. Carter and has Roberson Carter; Edgar V. Carter, junior, Frank Carter and Katherine Carter.

(C) A. C., junior, died in infancy.

14 Henry Harrison Knox, born July 16, 1840, married Jennie Vaughn. H. H. Knox died June 18, 1910. Jennie Vaughn Knox was born December 31, 1845 and died October 3, 1905.

Their children were:

(A) Emma Sue Knox who married George Madison Smartt and had Henry Knox Smartt (who married Mrs. Elizabeth Collier Meade); Cora Vaughn Smartt (who married James Ferguson Finlay and has Elizabeth Smartt Finlay and James Ferguson Finlay, junior); Harold Robert Smartt (who married Virginia Hill and has Harold Robert Smartt, junior); George Madison Smartt; Emma Sue Smartt (who married Richard Gwyn Brock and has Richard Gwin Brock, junior); James Polk Smartt; and Foley Vaughn Smartt.

(B) Cora Knox, died young.
(C) Foley Vaughn Knox.

(7) Jane, born August 1, 1802, married John Wesley Hardwick, September 22, 1818, and died in Dalton, Georgia, March 28, 1879. Was buried in Cleveland Tennessee.

For list of her descendants see Hardwick Family.

(8) Christopher C., born December 12, 1804, died 1824 in Athens, Georgia, while attending the University of Georgia.

(9) William, born December 20, 1807, married 1st, Ann Jones, 2nd, Ann Moore.

(10) Madison, born March 29, 1810, married Narcissa Hemphill. Lived and practised medicine in Chattooga County, Georgia.

NOTABLE SOUTHERN FAMILIES

Among his children were:
1 Ann R. C., born 1838.
2 Hugh, born 1840.
3 James, born 1842.
4 William, born 1844.
5 Margaret, born 1846.
6 Sarah, born 1849.

(11) Eliza Ann, born December 13, 1812, and married Dr. George R. Grant of Memphis, Tennessee.

III. JAMES McCONNELL MONTGOMERY

III. James McConnell (third son of James Montgomery and first wife, Elizabeth McConnell), was born in South Carolina, May 19, 1770, and moved with his father's family to Jackson County, Georgia. Here in 1806 to 1807 he served as Sheriff. Was also judge of the Inferior Court in 1829. About this year he moved to DeKalb County, and settled at Montgomery's Ferry (now DeFoors). He died October 6, 1842. James M. C. Montgomery served in the War of 1812 as a wagonmaster in Floyd's Brigade, Georgia Militia. His services began October 31, 1813. He also served with rank of special commissiary in said organization from October 13, 1813 to March 1, 1814 (Record from War Department). He married in Hancock County, Georgia, Nancy Farlow, who was born in Maryland, October 7, 1781. She died July 27, 1842.

Their children were:
(1) Adecia F., born April 4, 1799, married Samuel Pruitt, junior, 1st, in 1816, and Wyatt 2nd.
(3) Lucinda Mc., born October 28, 1800, married D. J. Connally, 1821.
(3) Amelia S., born April 19, 1802, married Joseph D. Shumate, 1819.
(4) Sophronia P., born October 24, 1803, married John Franklin, 1819.
(5) Ulysses Mc., born December 15, 1805, married Elizabeth Humber, 1826.
(6) Telemachus F., born January 14, 1808, married Emily Felder, 1st, and Mary Turner, 2nd.
7 Rhadamanthus J., born November 29, 1811, married Harriet Bogle, 1835.
(8) James Floyd, born September 10, 1813, married Elizabeth Young, 1837.
(9) Newman G., born August 8, 1815, died in infancy.

MONTGOMERY

(10) William F., born December 16, 1816, died November 2, 1833.
(11) Joseph T., born May 23, 1819, married Julia Cameron, 1842.
(12) Rhoda Narcissa, born March 22, 1822, married Alfred B. Brown, 1st, and Henry Dean, 2nd.
(13) Hugh B. Thorpe, born April 17, 1824, married Mary Broughton, 1849.
Of the above, Rhadamanthus and Telemachus were Presbyterian ministers.
Joseph and Hugh Thorpe were teachers, and founded the Lagrange Female College.
Ulysses and James Floyd were planters.
The above Floyd Montgomery was born in Jackson County Georgia, September 10, 1813, married Elizabeth Ann Young (daughter of Samuel Young), January 12, 1837, and died in DeKalb County, Georgia, June 8, 1847. She was born in Abbeville, South Carolina, August 1, 1816, and died October 1900.
Children were:
1 Emma M., born October 13, 1837, married C. P. Haynes May 17, 1855, and died January 23, 1913. Had three children.
2 William Rhadamanthus, born February 15, 1839, married 1st, Emma Northcutt May 17, 1866, and 2nd, Anna Towers September 12, 1895. He died in Marietta, Georgia, November 30, 1906.
3 Nancy Jane, born December 17, 1841, and died June 11, 1855.
4 Joseph S., born December 26th, 1843 and died at Harne, Texas. Left two children.
5 Henry T., born December 20th, 1846, married 1st, Mary Linder. His second marriage was to Willie Wallis, September 4, 1907.
Children of William Rhadamanthus Montgomery and 1st wife, Emma Northcutt were:
(A) Jessie Lee, born June 24, 1867, married James T. Anderson, February 6, 1895. They have five children.
(B) James Harrold, born November 23, 1868, and died July 18, 1870.
(C) Lilly Asenah, born October 31, 1872, died November 1874.
(D) Mary Emma, born March 14, 1874.
(F) Julia Pearl, born July 6, 1877, and died July 31, 1879.

(G) George Floyd, born May 14, 1879, married Susie May Wallace November 27, 1900.
(H) Nellie May, born November 8, 1880, and died August 13, 1881.
(I) William R., junior, born September 10, 1882, and died September 2, 1886.
(J) Annie Elizabeth, born October 1, 1883, married Harry Du Pree, January 8, 1902.

IV. Jeannette Montgomery, (the oldest child of James Montgomery and his second wife, Susannah Strange, was born 1780, married Joseph N. McCain, and had several children, among whom were:

(1) James Montgomery McCain, born 1805, married Louisa Wood (?). They had at least one child.
(A Joseph, born 1837.
(2) Joseph H. McCain, born 1820, married Susan ————, and had children, among whom was:
(A) Elizabeth, born 1884.

The above mentioned Jeanette Montgomery after her marriage to Joseph N. McCain, of North Carolina, seems to have lived several years in that state—her children having been been born there—before moving to Chattooga County, Georgia, where she is thought to have died.

V Virginia Montgomery, (the second child of James Montgomery and his second wife, Susannah Strange), was born 1781, married James Appleby, June 1, 1805, and died 1875. He was born 1779, and died 1866.

Their children were:

(1) William, born June 16, 1806.
(2) John, born May 24, 1808, married Virginia Key, October 14, 1830.
(3) Casandria, born August 1, 1810, married Thomas Cheatham, October 18, 1827.
(4) Evelyn, born December 7, 1812, married Bishop Thomas T. Scott, November 25, 1830.
(5) James M., born June 2, 1815, married Elizabeth Horton, Septmber 3, 1836.
(6) Hugh C., born June 21, 1818, married Eliza Davis, October 15, 1840.
(7) William D., born March 2, 1821, married Mary E. Williamson, December 29, 1841.

Many of the descendants of the above Virginia Montgomery Appeby live in and around Jackson County, Georgia.

MONTGOMERY

VI. William Montgomery, (the third child of James Montgomery and his second wife, Susannah Strange, was born n South Carolina, July 11, 1783, lived in Gwinnett, County, Georgia, then moved to Vann's Valley near Rome, Georgia, where he died Dcember 14, 1877. He was twice married, 1st to Catherine Boyle, March 31, 1807. She was born December 23, 1786, and died December 16, 1851. After her death he married Mrs. Adelia Turner, October 12, 1854.

Children by first wife:

(1) Mildred Boyle, born February 13, 1808, never married, died December 29, 1890.

(2) John, born January 23, 1810, married Mary Galiton Stewart, and died November 3, 1891.

(3) Polly (or Mary), born April 17, 1812, married —— McNeese (no children), and died July 23.

(4) Hugh, born February 22, 1814, married Caroline Orr, and died April 11, 1887.

(5) Cynthia Ann, born July 27, 1818, married W. C. Orr, and died August 31, 1889.

(6) Rebecca Caroline, born May 23, 1816, married Wm. Cunningham, and died March 8, 1875.

(7) James Madison, born June 22, 1820, never married, and died October 26, 1891.

(8) Wm. Martin, born April 27, 1822, never married, and died September 4, 1845.

(9) Jane Amanda, born April 25, 1824, married Thomas Mayfield, and died July 23, 1867.

(10) Katherine Narcissa, born June 5, 1826, never married, and died November 23, 1846.

(11) Christopher Styles, born September 12, 1828, victim of War on November 21, 1864.

(12) George Cicero, born August 13, 1830, victim of War on November 1, 1863.

(John's daughter married Thomas Knox).

VII. Margaret Montgomery, (the third child of James Montgomery and his second wife, Susannah Strange, was born 1785, married Thomas Niblack.

Their children were:
(1) William.
(2) Samuel.
(3) Hugh, married Miss Howard.
(4) Augustus.

NOTABLE SOUTHERN FAMILIES

(5) Virginia, married ——— Epperson.
(6) Caroline, married Hartsford Howard.
(7) Amelia, married Benj. Lampkins.

Margaret Montgomery Niblack and all her family except her son Hugh, moved to Texas.

Descendants of this Hugh lived in and around Jackson County, Georgia.

VIII. Eleanor Montgomery, (the fifth child of James Montgomery and his second wife, Susannah Strange, was born 1787, married Henry Cunningham.

They had several children, among whom was Isabelle who married Robert Veneable.

Agnes Veneable, daughter of above, married her cousin, Andrew Cunningham.

Mr. A. G. Storey, of Talladega, Alabama, is a grandson of Andrew and Agnes Cunningham.

IX. Sarah Montgomery, (the sixth child of James Montgomery and his second wife, Susannah Strange, was born in Georgia, 1789, married Nathaniel Veneable.

Their children were:
(1) Buford.
(2) Elizabeth.
(3) Cynthia.
(4) Martha.
(5) Anna.
(6) Pleasant.
(7) John.
(8) James.
(9) William Richard, married Sarah Cornelia Hoyt.
(10) Sarah.
(11) Jane.

Children of William Veneable and wife Sarah Cornelia Hoyt are:

1 William Hoyt, married Sallie Miller, and died September 1, 1905.
2 Sarah Mariah, died March 1857.
3 Samuel Hoyt, (unmarried).
4 Walter Louis, (unmarried).
5 Arthur Orr, married Blanche Beverly Cooke.
6 Charles, married Sarah Adair, (died July 11, 1890).
7 James Darius, died 1865.
8 Clarence Darius, married Mattie Ragon.
9 Lelia Ella, married Dr. James Nims Ellis, and died 1920.
10 Elizabeth Richard, married Frank Tucker Mason.

RHEA

The Rhea family descends from the Campbells of Scotland. The Campbell family was of Norman and Celtic descent, and "of large possessions, and being allied to the royal family did much to secure the people of that country from relapsing into the barbarious independence of their ancestors". (Scott's History of Scotland).

From the time of Archibald Campbell, Fourth Earl of Argyll, who embraced protestanism, the House of Argyll was the bulwark of protestantism in Scotland.

Archibald Campbell, Ninth Earl of Argyll, in taking the test oath, under Charles the Second, added the phrase, "so far as consistent with the protestant faith," for this he was tried for treason and condemned to be executed. The sentence was suspended by royal orders.

On the accession of James the Second, a Roman Catholic, Argyll took a leading part in fomenting the rebellion in favor of the protestant, Duke of Monmouth. When Monmouth sailed to England the Duke endeavored to raise an army but the Scotch were not ripe for rebellion and he succeeded in levying only a small body of men, one of whom was his cousin, Matthew Campbell.

After two or three skirmishes most of these followers deserted the standard of the Earl of Argyll, but he, and the faithful few remaining, undertook to make their way into England to join the Duke of Monmouth, but were surrounded and taken prisoners. Argyll was executed, in June 1865, without trial, under the old sentence. His cousin, Matthew Campbell, was tried and condemned to life imprisonment, and was confined on the Isle of Man. From thence he escaped, fled into Ireland, and assumed the name of Reah, (variously spelled Reagh, Reahgh, Rea, Ray and finally established into Rhea) and by this act became the founder of the family of Rhea, in Ireland. (Some of the descendants in Nova Scotia use the spelling Reah).

After locating in Ireland, true to his Presbyterian blood, he took a prominent part in the siege of Londonderry.

John Rhea, in his memoirs of the Rhea family, says it is not known whether the wife of Matthew Campbell Rhea was married to him in Scotland, before his imprisonment, or whether he married a wife in Ireland, but he had three sons. The names of two are unknown, but a third, Matthew Rhea II, married a wife, whose name is unknown, and had four sons:

I Samuel Rhea,
II William Rhea,
III Isaac Rhea,
IV MATTHEW RHEA III,

By his second wife, Elizabeth McLain, he had five children:

V Abraham Rhea, died without issue,
VI James Rhea, died without issue,
VII Margery Rhea,
VIII Agnes Rhea,
IX JOSEPH RHEA.

I SAMUEL RHEA

I Samuel Rhea, born in Ireland, came early to America and settled at Port Pin, near New Castle, Delaware. Wife's name unknown. They had one son, name unknown, who married a wife, name unknown, and had a son and daughter. This son was a surgeon on one of the largest armed ships of the American Navy during the Revolutionary War. This ship sailed on a cruise and was no more heard of. The daughter married twice: First ——— O'Hara; Second, ——— Frazier. They lived near New Castle, Delaware. She had children by her second husband.

II WILLIAM RHEA

II William Rhea, born in Ireland, came early to America and settled in Chester County, Pennsylvania. He married a wife, name unknown, and had three children: (1) James Rhea; (2) Mary Rhea, who married John Brown and lived near Wilmington, Delaware; (3) Elizabeth Rhea, who married James McCorkle, and lived in Washington, D. C. They had several daughters and two sons: (a) James

RHEA

McCorkle; (b) William McCorkle, who lived in Pennsylvania and was editor of a newspaper

III ISAAC RHEA

III Isaac Rhea came early to America and lived in Pennsylvania. He married a wife named ——— Peoples and had a daughter, name unknown.

IV MATTHEW RHEA III

IV Matthew Rhea III lived and died in Kinnically, near St. Johnston, Ireland. He had a son named William Rhea II, who married Elizabeth Lockhart. William Rhea was born and married in Ireland. After the birth of his children he moved, with his family to America (1785) and located in Washington County, Virginia, where he lived until his death. He had children: (1) Matthew Rhea IV, who married Margaret Breden, (sister of Frances, Elizabeth and Nancy Breden, who married, respectively, Joseph, William and Samuel Rhea) and had children: (a) Elizabeth Rhea; (b) William Rhea; (c) Margaret Rhea; (d) Robert Bruce Rhea (1814-1888) (married twice: First, Sarah Ann White, no issue; Second, Sarah Sells. Children: Margaret Rebecca Rhea, (1876-) who married Robert Earhart Rhea (son of Joseph Rhea and Elizabeth Ann (Earheart) Rhea). Children under Robert Earheart Rhea: John Matthew Rhea, (1878-) who married Elizabeth Payne Gresham, and had children: Eleanor Elizabeth and John Matthew Rhea II; William Rankin Rhea, (1880-) who married Mary Zeta Slack, and had children: Robert Bruce and Julia Holston); (e) Sallie Rhea; (f) Jane Rhea, (married Alexander Doggett, and had chldren: Catherine, James, and William); (2) Jennie Rhea; (3) Joseph Rhea; (4) William Rhea; (5) Sarah Rhea; (6) Elizabeth Rhea; (7) ROBERT RHEA, (1784-1841) (was born in Ireland and came to America with his father (1785) and located in Washington County, Virginia. Later he moved to Sullivan County, Tennessee. where he lived until his death). He married twice: First, Elizabeth Rhea (daughter of Rev. Joseph Rhea and Elizabeth (McIlwaine) Rhea); Second, Jane Scott (daughter of John Scott, a colonel in the Revolutionary War). By his first wife he had four children, given in full under Elizabeth Rhea. By the second wife he had children: (a) Mary Rhea, (1827-1882) who married James J. Snapp, and had children: Robert L. Snapp; Mary J. Snapp; James B. Snapp; Sarah E. Snapp; Margaret V.

NOTABLE SOUTHERN FAMILIES

Snapp, (1857) (who married Robert Snapp, and had children: Mary E. Snapp, who married Charles R. Bright, and had children: Virginia and William; Myrtle Snapp: James Snapp; Mattie L. Snapp, who married Joseph Booher, and had children: Belle and Everett; Margarett Snapp; Landon Snapp); Loueja Snapp; Laura Snapp; William Snapp; (b) Jane Rhea, who married ——— Smith; (c) Margaret Rhea, who married Audley Anderson (son of Edward B. Anderson and Eleanor (Rhea) Anderson). Children under Edward B. Anderson.

Note: William F. Rhea, member of congress from 9th Virginia District, is a grandson of William Rhea and Elizabeth (Lockhart) Rhea.

VII MARGERY RHEA

VII Margery Rhea married ——— McCrabb, lived and died in Ireland. Names of children unknown excepting one son, John McCrabb, who married his cousin, Elizabeth Latta, and came to America (1783) and located in Wilmington, Delaware. After the birth of his children he moved to the Holston Country, Tennessee, and located on a farm where he and his wife lived until their death. William, his eldest son (names of other children unknown) lived on the paternal farm.

VIII AGNES RHEA

VIII Agnes Rhea married William Latta, of Costitan, near St. Johnston, Ireland. She had childrn, names unknown excepting Elizabeth Latta and Joseph Latta. Joseph Latta came to America, married and lived near Brandywine, Pennsylvania.

IX JOSEPH RHEA

IX Joseph Rhea, (1715-1777), son of Matthew Rhea II and his second wife, Elizabeth (McClain) Rhea, was born in Parish Laughlin, Ireland, died in Piney Creek, Maryland. He married (1752) Elizabeth McIlwaine (1732-1793) (daughter of John McIlwaine and Margaret (Scott) McIlwaine, of Tifannan, near Londonderry, Ireland. A will executed in 1773 by her father, John McIlwaine, shows tha he possessed a large property in money, lands and leases). They had children:
I   JOHN RHEA,
II   MATTHEW RHEA IV,
III   MARGARET RHEA,

RHEA

IV WILLIAM RHEA,
V JOSEPH RHEA,
VI ELIZABETH RHEA,
VII SAMUEL RHEA,
VIII JAMES RHEA.

Joseph Rhea graduated at the University of Glasgow, Scotland, with honor and distinction, in 1742; was a minister of the Presbyterian Church and had charge of a church at Fahan, Ireland, at the time he resigned to go to America.

Rev. Joseph Rhea with his wife and children, John, Matthew, Margaret, William, Joseph, Elizabeth, (Samuel and James were born later in America), sailed from Ireland and landed in America, at Philadelphia, in 1769.

He commenced preaching in Piney Creek, Maryland, in 1772. In 1775 he went to the Holston Country, Tennessee, to locate land, and there purchased about two thousand acres of land. In 1776 he joined as Chaplain, the troops under Col. Christian, and in this capacity campaigned into Virginia and Tennessee.

There is much in Draper's Mss. (Historical Society, Madison, Wisconsin), about Christian's Cherokee Company.

The following is cited from an orderly book, once the property of Capt. Joseph Martin:

"Six Mile Camp, Oct 5, 1776.
"Parole William Burge.
General Orders:
"Mr. Ray will preach on the Augusta Line at one o'clock, and Mr. Cummins on the Fincastle Line. All others who choose to attend may do it.

"The church will be at the time to give warning, the men to attend with their arms by companies, and to observe as much decency and regularity as the ground will admit of."

In their capaciy as chaplains, at this time, Rev. Rhea and Rev. Cummins were the first ministers to preach in the territory that is now Tennessee.

Rev. Joseph Rhea died in Piney Creek, Maryland, in 1777.

In the following year, 1778, his family moved, by wagons, to the land in Sullivan County, Tennessee, which he had purchased and which is still in possession of his descendants.

Rev. Joseph Rhea became the founder of a large family

NOTABLE SOUTHERN FAMILIES

which resides, principally, in Tennessee and Virginia. His descendants are more numerous than those of the other emigres of the Rhea family.

I JOHN RHEA

1 John Rhea, first child of Rev. Joseph Rhea and Elizabeth (McIlwaine) Rhea, was born in 1753 in Ireland, and died in 1839 in Sullivan County, Tennessee. He graduated at Princeton in 1789. He and his father were noted as Latin and Greek scholars, and while John was in Gen. Washington's army they corresponded in Latin. A letter from the father, dated April 19, 1777, ends thus: "Benignus esto illi qui hostili tibi."

John Rhea assisted in the organization of the state of Tennessee, and the writing of its constitution, and was chosen the first representative from Sullivan County to the legislature. When Tennessee was divided into three Congressional Districts John Rhea, in 1803, was elected to Congress from the First District, where he served with distinction. In 1815 he accepted an appointment from the President, James Madison, as a commissioner to treat with the Choctaw Indians, but in 1817 was returned to Congress where he continued to serve until 1823 when he retired to private life.

He was a Jeffersonian democrat and a friend of Andrew Jackson.

Rhea County, Rheatown and Rhea Springs, Tennessee, were named in his honor.

He died, unmarried, and left a very large estate in lands, much of which had been Government grants for special services rendered. (Ramsey's History of Tennessee, Porter's History, Historic Sullivan).

II MATTHEW RHEA IV

II Matthew Rhea IV (1755-1816), (son of Rev. Joseph Rhea and Elizabeth (McIlwaine) Rhea) married (1778) Jane Preston (a sister of Robert Preston who married III Margaret Rhea). They had children:
    1 Joseph Mathew Rhea,
    2 Robert Preston Rhea,
    3 Margaret Rhea,
    4 Matthew Rhea V.

1 Joseph Matthew Rhea (1789-1860), married (1806) Catherine Myers (daughter of Charles Myers and Annie

RHEA

(Case) Myers). According to tradition they had eleven children, names of six known: (1) Emma Rhea; (2) Edmund Rhea; (3) Jane Rhea; (4) Eleanor Rhea; (5) Margaret Rhea; (6) Walter Preston Rhea (1831-1897), who married Sarah Jane Pile. They moved from Tennessee to Arkansas, in 1866. They had children: (a) Laura Ella Rhea (1856-), (married R. A. Robbins. Children: Maude Ethel, Lillian, Bernice Preston, Sarah, Neill Rhea, Pauline Elizabeth and Alfred Gerald); (b) David Charles Rhea (1858-), (married M. Ripetoe); (c) Joseph Matthew Rhea (1860-), (married Alice Powell. Children: Preston, David, Samuel and Virginia Lee); (d) Margaret Lillias Rhea (1862-), (married A. W. Ellis. Children: Eula Maude and Maggie Lee); (e) Edmund George Rhea; (f) Elizabeth Eleanor Rhea (1868-), (married E. N. Keiger); (g) Robert Preston Rhea; (h) Kittie Rhea; (i) Oscar Lee Rhea (1876-), (married Jennie Rand. Children: Orion, Lucile and Walter Preston; (j) Holmes Gans Rhea (1878-), (married Ethel Waters. Children: Lelia, Hugh and Edmund).

2 Robert Preston Rhea (1791-1872), married (1868) Nancy Davidson. Children: (1) Jane Rhea, who married Dr. Rivers; (2) Josiah Davidson Rhea; (3) Sarah Rhea, who married ——— Jackson; (4) John Preston Rhea, who married Matilda Longacre; (5) Matthew Rhea VI. who married Sallie Rhea, no issue; (6) Robert Campbell Rhea M. D. (1837-1911), who married Margaret Caroline McQueen, and had children: (a) Samuel Robert Rhea (1868-), (married Nellie Hendrickson. Children: Caroline, Robert Randolph and Margaret); (b) Mary Elizabeth Rhea (1869-), (married Dr. Joseph Shoun Donnelly. Children: Irene, Harrison Rhea and Margaret Edith); (c) Nancy Martitia Rhea (1871-), (married Dr. Charles Meigs Dulaney. Children: Charles Meigs Dulaney II, Robert Nathan, William Davis, Mary Elizabeth, John Jay, Laura and James Rhea); (d) Margaret Bell Rhea (1873-); (e) Josiah Davidson Rhea; (f) Frances Preston Rhea; (g) John Wayne Rhea; (h) Charles Caldwell Rhea; (i) Edwin Bruce Rhea; (j) Eleanor Campbell Rhea (1885-), (married William C. Wright. Child: Charles McQueen); (k) Beulah Carolyn Rhea (1890); (7) Margaret Rhea, never married.

3 Margaret Rhea married ——— Fickle and had one son, Robert P. Fickle.

4 Matthew Rhea V (1795-1870), married (1818) Mary Looney, of Middle Tennessee. Matthew Rhea V was born

NOTABLE SOUTHERN FAMILIES

near Bluff City, Sullivan County, Tennessee. Moved to West Tennessee about 1836. Was President of the Female Institute of Somerville. He was a man of great learning and took an especial interest in history. Assisted by his cousin, Matthew Campbell Rhea, he made the first map of the state of Tennessee. He was a man of great learning during the War Between the States. He had children: (1) Margaret Rhea (1820-1880), who married twice: First, Nicholas Long; Second, James Dysart Rhea, (son of William Rhea and Elizabeth (Breden) Rhea). By her first husband she had one child, Nicholas M. Long II (1849-), (married E. Shirley Wilson. Nicholas M. Long II is an eminent minister of the Presbyterian Church and lives in Memphis, Tennessee. He has children: Richard, Margaret Rhea, Shirley W. (1888-), Walter Preston (1889-), Phelps W. (1891-), Frances M. (1893-) and Emma Law). By her second husband she had one child, Matthew Belmont Rhea; (2) Elizabeth Rhea (1822-1892), who married John Rhea (son of William Rhea and Elizabeth (Breden) Rhea). Children under John Rhea; (3) Ellen Preston Rhea; (4) Sarah Lucinda Rhea, no issue; (5) John William Rhea (1828-), who married Italia G. Porter, and had children: William, Annie, Lillian and Pearl; (6) Abram Rhea (1830-1942), who married Emma Cross, and had children: (a) Matthew D. Rhea; (b) William Rhea; (c) Jennie Lou Rhea (1874-), (married George T. Webb. Children: Abram Rhea and Virginia); (d) Richard Cary Rhea (1877-), (married Mrs. Mattie L. Anderson. Children: Louise and Richard Cary Rhea II); (e) Frank P. Rhea; (f) Nell C. Rhea (1881-), (married E. L. Steward); (g) Elizabeth Rhea (1883-), (married G. L. Rhodes, and had one child, Albert H.); (h) Ruby F. Rhea; (7) Mathew Rhea VI, died without issue; (8) Mary Annis Rhea; (9) Samuel Doak Rhea; (10) Jennett Preston Rhea; (11) Walter Preston Rhea (1841-1880), who married Jennie Edmondson, (daughter of William C. Edmondson and Susie E. (Rhea) Edmondson and had children: (a) Hugh Preston Rhea (1871-1901), (married Louise Brown, and had one child, Hugh Preston Rhea II); (b) William Edmondson Rhea; (c) Susie Bowen Rhea (1875-), (married Thomas Buford. Children: John Edmondson, Clara May and Thomas Edmondson); (d) Mamie Looney Rhea (1877-), (married Lunsford Y. Williamson, and had one child, Jean Rhea); (e) Walter Preston Rhea II (1879-), (married Mazie Sale. Children: Walter Preston Rhea III and Henry Sale Rhea); (12 Ellen Preston Rhea

RHEA

(1844-), who married Hudson Cary, and had children: (a) Miles Fairfax Cary; (b) Marion Cary; (c) Rhea Preston Carey (1871-), (married Charlie Ewing); (d) Eleanor Marion Cary (1884-), (married Samuel Earnest Ragland. Children: Eleanor Marion, Margaret Elizabeth and Fairfax Cary); (e) Hudson Fairfax Cary; (13) Frances Bell Rhea (1848-), who married James T. Rhea (son of James Dysart Rhea and Elizabeth (Carter) Rhea). Children under T. Rhea.

III Margaret Rhea

III Margaret Rhea (1757-1822), (daughter of Rev Joseph Rhea and Elizabeth (McIlwaine) Rhea). Lived in Washington County, Virginia. She married Robert Preston (1750-1833) (son of John Preston and Eleanor (Fairman) Preston). They had one child, John Preston II.

John Preston II (1781-1864), married (1802) Margaret Brown Preston, (daughter of Col. William Preston and Susanna (Smith) Preston) and had children:

1 Thomas Preston, has no living descendants,
2 Henry Preston,
3 William Alfred Preston,
4 John Preston III, no issue,
5 James T. Preston,
6 Robert Fairman Preston,
7 Frank Preston,
8 Susan Rhea Preston,
9 Margaret Rhea Preston.
10 Eleanor Fairman Preston,
11 Elizabeth Preston, never married,
12 Walter E. Preston, no issue,
13 Jane Preston,
14 Joseph Preston, never married.

2 Henry Preston (1826-1905), married Ann Carter, and had children: (1) Mary Coles Preston; (2) Margaret Brown Preston; (3) Elizabeth M. Preston; (4) Ellen Preston, who married ——— Bailey; (5) Cary Preston; (6) Jane Preston; (7) Isaetta Preston; (8) Eugenia Preston; (9) Henry Preston II, who married Nell Carson; (10) Percy Preston.

3 William Alfred Preston (-1864), who married twice: First, ——— Wylie, no issue; Second, Elizabeth Radford, his cousin, who had one child, William Alfred Preston II.

5 James T. Preston (1824-1883), who married (1850) Frances Rhea, (daughter of VIII James Rhea and Elizabeth (Snapp) Rhea) and had children: (1) John Preston IV,

(1851-), who married Annie Lewis White, (daughter of John Preston White and Annie Stuart (Lewis) White). John Preston is a physician and Superintendent of State Insane Asylum at Austin, Texas. They have children: (a) Walter White Preston (1880-), (married Annie Marie Frederick Bonhan. Children: Walter Bonhan, John Courtney, and twins—Frederick Lewis and Frances); (b) John Lewis Preston, M. D. (1883-), (married Leonora McKellar. One child: John Lewis Preston II); (c) James Rhea Preston (1885-);(d) Fannie Rhea Preston (1890-); (e) Robert White Preston (1892-); (f) Annie Lewis Preston (1898-); (g) Margaret Lynn Preston (1904); (2) James Rhea Preston (1853-), who married Elizabeth Vaughan, and had children: Elizabeth McIlwaine, Frances Rhea and James Rhea; (3) Walter Eugene Preston; (4) Robert Fairman Preston (1857-), who married Elizabeth McDonald Preston, and had children: Arthur Cummings, Mildred, Lucy, Eleanor Fairman, Fannie and a twin, died unnamed, and Robert Fairman Preston II; (5) Fannie Rhea Preston; (6) Frances McIlwaine Preston.

6 Robert Fairman Preston (1805-1889), who married Sarah Marshall. Dr. Robert Fairman Preston was an eminent physician of Philadelphia. In 1884 he retired to his ancestral estate in Virginia, where he lived until his death. He had children: (1) Mary Marshall Preston; (2) Elizabeth Preston, who married Dr. Ezra N. Sheffey, and had children: (a) Robert Preston Sheffey, (married and had children: Robert Preston Sheffey II and Margaret Sheffey); (b) Charles Marshall Sheffey, (married Carrie Winston); (c) Sarah Sheffey, (married ———— Biddle); (d) Henry Sheffey, (married Faith Fulkerson).

7 Frank Preston (1820-1891), who married twice: First, Virginia Moffet; Second, Mattie Fulton. Children by first wife: Robert, Frances and John. Child by second wife: Mary.

8 Susan Rhea Preston (-1828), who married (1825) Joseph Campbell Rhea, (son of IV William Rhea and Elizabeth (Bredden) Rhea). Children under Joseph Campbell Rhea.

9 Margaret Rhea Preston, who married (1825) James Lowry White, of Abingdan, Virginia. Children: (1) Elizabeth Wilson White (1827-1902), who married David C. Cummings, and had children: (a) James White Cummings, M. D. (1855), (married twice: First Elizabeth Madison Preston, no issue; Second, Fannie Clark, and had children:

Frances, Mary Campbell and Eliza Preston); (b) Robert P. Cummings (1858-), (married Susie Kellar. One child, Arthur Cummings); (c) David C. Cummings II; (2) Margaret Rhea White (1828-), who married Gen. W. Y. C. Humes, and had children: James Lowry and Newton; (3) Jane Conn White, married John Gordon Ogden; (4) John Preston White (1832-1904), who married Annie Stuart Lewis, his cousin, (daughter of John B. Lewis and his second wife, Mrs. Caroline Smith, nee Thompson). He lived at Abingdon, Virginia, later Austin, Texas. He had children: (a) James Lewis White (1857-), (married Ellen Douglas Clark. Children: Annie Preston White (1880-), who married Dr. George Gilbert Crawford, and had children: Ellen Clark, Annie Preston, James Jamison and Jean Maxwell; Colin Clarke White (1884-), who married Ethel Halloran, and had one child, Phyllis); (b) Annie Lewis White (1861-), (married Dr. John Preston, (son of James T. Preston and Frances (Rhea) Preston) Children under Dr. John Preston); (c) Milton White; (d) Mary Magdalene White (1867-), (married Benjamin Mills Crenshaw. Children: Benjamin Mills Crenshaw II and Margaret White Crenshaw); (e) Walter Lewis White; (f) Montgomery Lewis White (1871-1916), (married Mary Bell Nelson. One child, Lewis Nelson White); (g) Bessie Lelia White (1883-); (5) James Lowry White I; no issue; (6) William Young Conn White, M. D. (1835-1904), who married Elizabeth Campbell Carter, and had children: (a) Stuart White (1870-), (married Emily West); (b) Pauline Campbell White (1871-), married Thomas Hill Mason); (7) Ellen Sheffey White (1836-1912), who married Dr. Edward Campbell, and had children: (a) Daniel Trigg Campbell; (b) Edward Donald Campbell; (c) Margaret Preston Campbell (1863-), (married Col. Laurens W. Youmans. Children: McDonald Campbell, Margaret Preston and Lucile, who married Walter Haines); (d) Bessie Cummings Campbell (1866-) (married Henry Ramsey Lenoir, Children: Ellen White Lenoir (1890-); Virginia Ballard Lenoir (1894-) who married Wyall H. Stover; Edward Campbell Lenoir (1896-)); (e) Susie Trigg Campbell (1868-), (married Edwin Elisha Hundley. Children: Elizabeth Estes (1895-), Campbell (1896-), Margaret Preston (1898-) and Frances Edmunds (1902-)); (f) William White Campbell (1869-), (married Hallie McCracken. One child, Mary Ellen); (g) Josephine Trigg Campbell; (h) James White Campbell; (i) Frank Campbell (1871-), married Sallie Jonett. Children: Jonett,

NOTABLE SOUTHERN FAMILIES

Ellen Frances and Malcolm); (j) Preston White Campbell (1874-), (married Louise Howard. Children: Preston White and Edward Malcolm); (k) Malcolm Campbell, M. D. (1875-), (married Charlotte Luella Brader); (8) Susan Preston White (1838-1908), who married Abram Byrd Twig, (1872-), (married Robert R. Campbell); (b) Margaret Preston Trigg.

10 Eleanor Fairman Preston (-1887), who married (1835) Judge James Sheffey. Children: (1) Margaret Sheffey (1836-1869), who married Col. William E. Peters, and had children: James White Sheffey and William Edgar; (2) John Preston Sheffey (1837-), who married Josephine Spiller, and had children: (a) Margaret Peters Sheffey (1865-), (married Percy C. March); (b) Eleanor Fairman Sheffey (1866-), (married B. F. Buchanan. Children: John Preston Buchanan, who married and had children: Eleanor Fairman and John Preston Buchanan II; Josephine Spiller Buchanan; Campbell Buchanan; Virginia Buchanan; Frank Buchanan; Nellie Buchanan; David Buchanan); (c) Susie Montgomery Sheffey (1867-), (married Dr. E. M. Oopenhaver. Children: Preston and Elizabeth Marcellus); (d) Josephine Spiller Sheffey; (e) James White Sheffey (1871-), (married Lucy Lee Carlock. Children Lucy Lee, Caroline, James White Sheffey II, Josephine Spiller White, Eleanor Fairman and Harold Carlock); (f) Miriam Sheffey; (g) John Preston Sheffey II (1876-), (married Virginia Harrington. Children: Margaret and Virginia); (3) Jane Sheffey; (4) Elizabeth Sheffey (1842-1875), who married Maj. James A. G. Pendleton, and had one child, James Sheffey Pendleton, (1874-) who married Margaret Fudge, and had children: Albert G., Elizabeth and Granville F.; (5) Ellen White Sheffey (1843-1904), who married Joseph Brainard Rhea, (son of Rev. Samuel Rhea and his second wife, Martha (Lynn) Rhea). Children under Joseph Brainard Rhea; (6) Mary Sheffey (1844-1906), who married Col. William E. Peters, (whose first wife had been her sister, Margaret), and had one child: Don Preston Peters (1887-), who married Rhetta Ghangh, and had children: Mary Peters and Don Preston Peters II; (7) Martha Sheffey (1849-1899), who married Robert J. Preston, M. D., and had children: (a) Eleanor Fairman Preston (1876-), (married Dr. J. T. Watkins. Children: James Thomas Watkins II, Robert Sheffey, William and Sherman); (b) Robert Sheffey Preston (1885-), (married

RHEA

Alice Reed); (8) Virginia Sheffey (1850-), who married H. B. Haller.

13 Jane Preston, who married twice: First, James B. Craighead; Second, ―――― Marshall, no issue. Children by first husband: David, John, Jennie, James, Preston and Thomas.

IV WILLIAM RHEA

IV William Rhea, (1761-1836), (son of Rev. Joseph Rhea and Elizabeth (McIlwaine) Rhea). He was married (1795) to Elizabeth Breden (1766-1835), who was born in Ireland and died in Tennessee. They lived on the old farm on Beaver Creek, Sullivan County, Tennessee, and had children:
1 Margaret Breden Rhea,
2 Elizabeth Rhea,
3 Joseph Campbell Rhea,
4 James Dysart Rhea,
5 William R. Rhea,
6 Frances Rhea,
7 John Rhea II.

1 Margaret Breden Rhea (1798-1864), married (1828) Samuel Wood Netherland, and had children: (1) Elizabeth Rhea Netherland (1830-1896), who married William Phillip Brewer, and had children: (a) Margaret Duffield Brewer (1852-), (married Rev. James Chalmers Cowan. Children: William McLamin Cowan (1876-), Robert L. Cowan (1880-), who married Bessie Brown; Fred C. Cowan (1882-), who married Grace Brisbo; Sidney K. Cowan (1884-); Hugh Brewer Cowan (1886-)); (b) Eva Neil Brewer (1854-), (married Henry H. Newman); (c) Samuel Netherland Brewer; (d) John Alf Brewer (1859-), married Willie Sue Hoge. Children: Bessie (1884-), who married John Alf Muse, and had children: Eliza B., James Arthur, Mary Mintola and John Alf Muse II; Mary Eva Brewer (1885-), who married Herbert C. Marcy, and had children: John Arban and Herbert C. Marcy II; Horen Hoge Brewer (1885-), who married Jamie Bachman; William Phillip Brewer; A. Thelma Brewer; (e) Benjamin Willis Brewer; (f) James King Brewer (1864-), (married Mary Olive Carlock. Children: James Carlock (1896-1918), Catherine T. N. Louise and Douglas C.; (g) Hattie Adelaide Brewer (1864-), (twins of James King Brewer), (married Dr. Joseph S. Bachman. Children: Harry W., Phillip M., Joseph S. Bachman II, and Elizabeth); (h) Nicholas Vance Brewer;

NOTABLE SOUTHERN FAMILIES

(2) Harriet Samuel Woods Netherland, who married John G. King (brother of James King), and had children: (a) Lynn King (1857-), (married Joseph W. Owen. Children: Hattie King (1890-) and Rively King (1892-)); (b) Hattie Goodson King (1858-), (married Hugh W. Taylor); (c) Ella Watkins King (1860-), (married Dr. Frank Maxwell Children: Evelyn King Maxwell (1891-), (who married E. Harris; Annie Maxwell (1893-)); (d) Samuel Lee King (1863-), (married Annie Phipps. Children: Samuel Lee King II, John G. King and Charles Logan King).

2 Elizabeth Rhea (1798-1856), married Reyburn Buchanan, and had children: (1) Elizabeth Buchanan (1828-1900), who married James King II, (brother of John G. King, who married Harriet Samuel Woods Netherland), and had children: (a) James King III; (b) William Ryburn King; (c) Micajah Watkins King, (married Robert Hartzell Gray. Children: William Micajah, James King, John Buchanan, Campbell Watkins, Elizabeth and Robert Hartzell Gray II); (d) Margaret Elizabeth King; (e) John Buchanan King, (married Louise Barrett); (2) William Buchanan, who married Addie Hill, and had chldren: (a) John Hill Buchanan; (b) Elizabeth Rhea Buchanan; (c) Nellie Scott Buchanan, (married John B. McCord); (d) Margaret Shannon Buchanan, (married Sturm Carson. One child, Clifton); (e) William Harvey Buchanan; (3) John Buchanan, who married Mattie Cross, and had children: Ryburn DeBarry, William Lane, Edward King, Sarah Elizabeth, Annie Green, Fannie Linn and John Matthew.

3 Joseph Campbell Rhea (1800-1853), married twice: First, Susan Rhea Preston (-1828) (daughter of Robert Preston and Margaret (Rhea) Preston); Married second, (1836) Catherine Reynolds (-1857). Joseph Campbell Rhea lived in Sullivan County, Tennessee, until 1841 when he moved to Giles County, Tennessee, where resided until his death. He assisted his cousin, Matthew Rhea, in making the first map of Tennessee. He was colonel in the Tennessee Militia. By his first wife he had children: (1) Margaret Rhea, who married Dr. Ezra N. Sheffey (whose second wife was Elizabeth Preston, daughter of Robert Fairman Preston and Sarah (Marshall) Preston), and had children: William, Elizabeth and John Preston; (2) Susan E. Rhea (1828-1860), who married William Campbell Edmondson, and had children: (a) John Preston Edmonson, (no living descendants); (b) Jennie Edmonson (1851-1919), (married Walter Preston Rhea, son of Matthew Rhea II and Mary

RHEA

(Looney) Rhea. Children under Walter Preston Rhea); (c) Louise Smyth Edmonson, (married William Abram Rhea, a cousin. No issue); (3) William Rhea, never married. Joseph Rhea by his second wife, Catherine Reynolds, had children: (4) James David Rhea (1838-1882), who married Bettie Buford (daughter of Hon. Thomas Buford of Giles County, Tennessee), and had children: (a) James Buford Rhea; (b) Clifford Rhea (1866-), (married Delia Donovan. Children: Margaret (1898-), Clifford Campbell (1900-), David (1901-), Mamie Louise (1902-), Annie Delia (1905-), Joseph (1908-) and Edward Buford (1910-)); (c) Annie Rhea (1868-), (married William Presley Dabney. One child, William Rhea Dabney (1892-)); (d) James David Rhea II (1870-), (married Sadie Gardner. Children: James David Rhea III, William Gardner Rhea and Joseph Campbell Rhea. James David Rhea III, a medical student Vanderbilt University, is the only first year man to receive Founders Medal for Oratory); (e) Frank Buford Rhea; (f) Bessie Buford Rhea; (g) Joseph Campbell Rhea (1877-), (married Addie Martha Booth. Child: Buford Booth Rhea. Joseph Campbell Rhea graduated in Law at Harvard University, his son Buford, is now a student at Leland Stanford University); (h) Louise Buford Rhea (1880-), (married Harry H. Chandler. Children: Bettie Buford (1905-) and Annie Rhea (1913-)); (i) Mary Sumpter Rhea, (who died young); (5) Mary A. Rhea (1840-), who married (1857) Dr. James A. Sumpter (-1885), and had children: (a) Edward Randolph Sumpter, M. D., (1858-1917), (married (1885) Minnie Wade. Children: James A. Sumpter II (1888-), who married Berta Porter, and had one child: James A. Sumpter III (1916-); Ella Sumpter (1890-), who married Wyker, and had one child, William Wyker II (1913-); Mary Sumpter (1829-); Edward Randolph Sumpter II (1898-)); (b) Bulah Sumpter (1863-), (married (1887) Edgar Anderson (-1911). Children: James Sumpter (1893-) and Mary Frances (1903)); (c) William D. Sumpter, M. D., (1872-), (married (1902) Tommie Wrenn, (daughter of Thomas Wrenn, of Nashville. Children: Clara (1903-), Tom (1906-) and Mary Rhea (1910-). Dr. Sumpter is an eminent surgeon and member of the board of the Protestant Hospital at Nashville, Tennessee); (d) Joseph Rhea Sumpter (1874-1913), (married twice: First, Julia Flounoy (-1900); Second, L. May Hayes. No issue); (6) Ellen Rhea (1846-), who married (1871) Oscar Abernathy, and had children: (a) Katherine Abernathy (1872-), (married Will Farmer. One child, Katherine (1913-)); (b) Mary Abernathy (1874-), (married Bayless Froman); (c) Nellie Abernathy (1878-), (married D. Landis); (d) Oscar Abernathy II (1881-), (married Annie Adams); (7) William Samuel Rhea (1849-1894), who married (1876) Ida Eudora Osborne, and had children: (a) Caleb Osborne Rhea, M. D. (1877-), (married Margaret Donelson. Children: Caleb Osborne Rhea II (1912-) and Samuel Donaldson Rhea (1916-)); (b) Erma Valena Rhea (1879-), (married George Reed. Children: Ida Catherine (1902-) and Erma Rhea (1912-)); (c) Edward Sumpter Rhea (1882-), (married Hannah Smith. Children: Robert (1908-), Alice Cordelia, (died young), Helen Pearl (1912-) and David Osborne (1914-)); (d) William Samuel Rhea II (1885-), (married Hattie Miller. One child, William Samuel Rhea III (1912-)); (e) David Rankin Rhea (1886-), (married Vernon Porter. One Child, Robert Porter Rhea (1914-)); (f) Alwyn Porter Rhea, died young; (g) Alice Catherine Rhea, (died young).

4 James Dysart Rhea (1802-1886), married twice: First, (1831) Elizabeth Carter; Second, (1858) Margaret Long, nee Rhea. Children by first wife: (1) Matilda Wendel Rhea, died without issue; (2) William Rhea, never married; (3) Elizabeth Rhea (1836-), who married Beverly Norvell, and had children: Maude, Maggie Lou, Adah, Mary, Clara, Frank and Wade; (4) Alfred Rhea, never married; (5) Margaret Rhea (1840-1912), who married (1863) Byron Giggs McDowell, and children: (a) James Rhea McDowell, (died without issue); (b) Irene McDowell; (c) Albert Sidney McDowell, (1870-), (married Inez Carter. One child, Marjorie Carter); (d) Elizabeth McDowell (1868-), (married James B. Lyons. One child, McDowell (1895-)); (e) Mary Eva McDowell (1875-), (married William S. Stuart. One child, Ellen Irene); (f) Margaret Rhea McDowell (1880-), (married William Ferguson. Children: Margaret and Robert); (6) John H. Rhea, never married; (7) Sarah F. Rhea; (8) James T. Rhea (1847-1914,) who married Frances Bell Rhea, (daughter of Matthew Rhea and Mary (Looney) Rhea), and had children: (a) James Rhea, (died young); (b) Alfred Long Rhea, (married Mary Wauchope. Children: James Taylor Rhea II, Katherine Wauchope, Mary Frances and Ellen Preston); (c) Mary Ellen Rhea, (married Dr. John Kerr Crawford. Children: Mary Frances, Louise Edmonson, Eleanor, James Taylor, Mary Rhea and John Kerr Crawford II); (d) James Dysart Rhea

RHEA

II, (married Jesse Hearn. One child, Jessie Hearn); (e) Howard Matthew Rhea, (married Wilhelmina Litterer. One child, Elizabeth Weaver); (9) Mary Ellen Rhea (1849-1882), who married Edward Anderson McClellan, and had children: (a) Samuel David McClellan (1880-), (married Mary Effie Sugle. Children: William Edward McClellan (1895-), who married Clara Isabella Sims, and had one child, Mary Evelyn); (b) James Nicholas McClellan (1872-1912), (married Almira Levenia Benham. Children: Bertha Elizabeth McClellan (1894-), who married Thomas Hubbard, and had children: James DeVerne and Burnidene; Howard Plemey McClellan (1895-), who married Sarah Burton, and had children: Madge Lorain and Mildred Bettie; Lora Irene McClellan (1898-), who married Avery Morton Sheldon; (c) John Looney McClellan (1874-), (married Myrtle Benner); (d) Margaret Elizabeth McClellan (1877), married William Edward Cogswell. Children: John McMcClellan, Levert DeVere, Morton Edward and Alice Rhea); (e) Abraham Rhea McClellan (1879-), (married Georgia Desgranger. Children: J. Wallace, Walter Rhea and Hugh); (f) Edward Anderson McClellan (1882-), (married Grace Edric Helms. One child, Ralph Edward); (10) Susan Elizabeth Rhea (1853-1905); James Dysart Rhea by his second wife had one child, Matthew Belmont Rhea, died young.

5 William R. Rhea (1804-1861), married (1833) Mary Ann Moseley Rockhold, (sister of Ruth Rockhold who married John N. Rhea), and had children: (1) Harriet Netherland Rhea (1834-1880), who married Dr. John W. Sehorn. Children: (a) Charles Lee Sehorn (1863-), (married Rella Amos. Children: Howard Rhea (1891-), Charles Lee Sehorn II, died young, and Thomas Lund (1903-)); (b) John Sehorn, (married Sue Addie Susong); (2) Elizabeth Breden Rhea; (3) Frances Ruth Rhea (1838-1904), who married Oscar Marville Lewis, M. D. Children: (a) William Dulaney Lewis; (b) Mary Cecelia Lewis (1866-), married John M. Lyon. Children: Rhea B. Lyon (1885-), who married A. Maney, and had children: Cathline, Fowler, James and John,; John P. Lyon (1887-), Jessie Lewis Lyon (1889-), who married R. Burton, and had children: Lamar and Marie; Earnest J. Lyon (1892-); A. Ruth Lyon (1896-), who married W. McNew, and had one child, B. Ruth); (c) Harriet Elizabeth Lewis (1867-), (married D. Riley Proffitt.

Children: Eilene, Vivian, Ruth and Harriett); (d) Ida Lee Lewis, not married; (e) Oscar Rhea Lewis (1872-),

NOTABLE SOUTHERN FAMILIES

(married Margaret W. Ray. Children: Dora, Elizabeth, Ralph, Margaret, Joe Lee, Oliver and John Rhea); (f) Dora Lynn Lewis (1874-1902), (married George W. Anglon); (g) George Gertrude Lewis (1877-), (married Samuel Clayton Riddle. Children: Phyllis Cecelia, Oscar Lewis and Frances Margaret); (h) Charles Grant Lewis; (4) William Rockhold Rhea (1840-1903), married twice: First, Sue Netherland; Second, Margaret R. Carr, no issue. By his first wife he had one child: May Rhea, who married Dr. Robert Lee Gallaher; (5) George Duffield Rhea, who married Mrs. Lottie Jane Rhea, nee Ross, widow of his brother James Campbell Rhea). No issue; (6) Joseph Cunningham Rhea; (7) John Adolphus Rhea (1848-1903), who married Lora Abernathy, (see Donaldson Family), and had children: (a) William Abernathy Rhea (1882-1913), (married Daisy Vaughn Hasson. No issue); (b) Mary Rhea; (c) John Rhea; (c) John Rhea); (8) Charles Rhea (1853-1890), who married Emma Sarah Robertson, and had one child: Hattie Mabel Rhea (1883-), (who married Claude Bennett. Children: Rhea Worth and Sarah Bess); (9) James Campbell Rhea (1855-1912), who married Lottie Jane Ross, and had children: (a) George Sehorn Rhea (1882-), (married twice: First, Alma Petty; Second, Emma Jones. Children by first wife: James Clarence, Charles William and George Hunter. By second wife, one child, Eldridge); (b) William Rockhold Rhea II (1887-), (married Elva Blalack. Children: Roger Jackson, Rita Aline and Elizabeth Lloyd); (c) Charles Lyon Rhea (1889-), (married Willie Kate Blalack).

6 Frances Rhea (1808-1854), married Montgomery Irvin, and had children: (1) Elizabeth Irvin; (2) William Rhea Irvin (1875-), who married Josephine Earley, and had children: James and Mary; (3) Maggie Irvin (1844-), who married Capt. George W. Allen, and had children: Annie Mary, Cora, Willie V. and Lillie, (4) Mary R. Irvin (1840-), who married William Abram Rhea, (son of John Rhea and Elizabeth (Rhea) Rhea). Children under William Abram Rhea; (5) Sarah Irvin (1849-), who married Samuel Wood Rhea, (son of John Nancy Rhea and Mary (Rockhold) Rhea). Children under Samuel Wood Rhea.

7 John Rhea (1811-1862), married (1840) Elizabeth Rhea, (daughter of Matthew Rhea V and Mary (Looney) Rhea), and had children: (1) Mary Elizabeth Rhea, never married; (2) William Abram Rhea (1844-1869), married twice: First, Mary R. Irwin; Second Louise Edmondson. Children by first wife: (a) Elizabeth Rhea (1870-), (mar-

RHEA

ried Thomas Delany Cobb. Children: Mollie Rhea and Delaney); (b) Allie Rhea; (c) Fannie Rhea (1874-), (married Samuel Taylor. Children: Matthew Edmund (1899-), Rhea Venable, Mary Louise, Lois, Jennie and Samuel Chunn); (d) Harriet Rhea (1876-), (married Arthur P. Winfrey. Children: Mattie Sweeney, Elizabeth, John Allen, Montgomery Rhea, Arthur Peter, Harriet and William Rhea); (e) John Montgomery Rhea; (f) William Rhea; (g) Jennie Edmondson Rhea (1883-), (married Rev. Herman A. Butts); (3) Matthew Robert Rhea (1846-1902), married Addie Tucker, and had children: (a) Thomas Tucker Rhea (1871-), (married Sue Mae Thomson); (b) John William Rhea; (c) Lula May Rhea (1876-1912), (married Dr. George M. Shaw. One child, Lucy Adelaide); (d) Edward Frances Rhea (1878-), (married Adele Herbert. One child, Frances Adele); (4) James Samuel Rhea (1849-1898), married Fannie Trotter, and had children: (a) Benjamin Edward Rhea; (b) Matthew Rhea; (c) James Wilson Rhea (1883-), (married Mary Lou Cross. Children: Frances Elizabeth, Marion Overton, Sarah Bell, James Samuel and William Cross); (d) John Edmondson Rhea, (married Fannie Watkins. Children: Addie Frances and Thomas Watkins); (e) Sarah Bell Rhea, (married Sidney A. Baynes); (f) William Abraham Rhea; (g) Hudson Cary Rhea; (h) Mary Elizabeth Rhea; (i) Robert Henry Rhea; (5) Margaret Ellen Rhea, never married; (6) Sarah Frances Rhea (1853-), (married Henry Harrison Lewis, and had children: (a) Bessie May Lewis (1876-), (married Thomas A. Jayroe. Children: Thomas A. Jayroe II, Frances L., Henry Lewis, Jack C., Robert Rhea, Frank C., and Henry Lewis); (b) John Hampden Lewis (1878-), (married Lula May Morris. Children: Fannie Lou, William H. and Bessie); (c) Maggie Lou Lewis (1881-), (married Arthur Fleming. Children: W. Arthur, D. Henry, Gilly M. and M. Frances); (d) James Rhea Lewis (1883-), (married Rosa Reviere. Children: James Rhea Lewis II, Carolea, John Montgomery and Henry H.); (e) Wiltshire M. Lewis (1885-), (married Margaret Maclin. Children: Robert Spencer and Henry Harrison); (f) Gilly M. Lewis; (g) Matthew H. Lewis (1891-), (married Mrs. Louise Haynes Moorer); (h) Gilly C. Lewis; (7) John Rufus Wells Rhea (1855-1917), married twice: First, Tillie Lockett; Second, Eleanor Lockett, (sister of Tillie Lockett). Children by first wife: (a) John Lockett Rhea; (b) Frank Lee Rhea (1886-), (married Mary Teall. Children: John, Patricia, and twins—

NOTABLE SOUTHERN FAMILIES

Gerald and Geraldine); (c) Walter H. Rhea; (d) Oscar P. Rhea; (e) Lizzie Sue Rhea (1894-), (married Egbert Smith. One child: Egbert Franklin); (f) Annie Rhea (1897-); (8) Walter Rhea; (9) Lucinda Harriet Rhea.

V JOSEPH RHEA II

V Joseph Rhea II (1762-1825), son of Rev. Joseph Rhea and Elizabeth (McIlwaine) Rhea. He married (1789) at Abingdon, Virginia, Frances Breden (1764-1850). "Joseph Rhea and wife, Frances, reared their family in a house which he erected, in 1800, on Back Creek, Sullivan County, three-fourths of a mile from where his father located on Beaver Creek. Most of the building was of logs, ceiled insde and weather-boarded outside. At this time (1915) the house is in fine condition". ((extract from letter of William Lynn Rhea). Joseph Rhea II had children:
1 Elizabeth Rhea,
2 Margaret Rhea,
3 John Rhea, died in infancy,
4 Samuel Rhea,
5 Ellen Rhea,
6 Fannie Rhea,
7 Nancy Rhea,
8 Robert J. Rhea.
9 Sarah Rhea.

1 Elizabeth Rhea (1789-1853), married twice: First, (1812) Audley Anderson, (brother of Isaac Anderson who married her sister, Margaret); Second, Nicholas Fain. Children by first husband: (1) Fannie Rhea Anderson (1812-1856), who married 1830) William King McAlister, and had children: (a) John Audley McAlister, (died young); (b) Harry Hill McAlister (1833-1893), (married Maggie Shapard. Children: Frances Rhea McAlster (1806-), who married Morgan William Brown IV, and had children: Morgan William Brown VII (1894-), who married Minnie Bell, and had children: Morgan William Brown III, died in infancy, and Morgan William Brawn IX; Marjorie McAlister Brown (1895-), who married John Marshall Ewing, and had one child, John Marshall Ewing II; Harry Hill McAlister II (1864-), who married Maude Davidson, and had children: Maud McAllister (1888-), who married twice: First, ———— Franklin; Second, ———— Ebbert; Harry Hill McAlister III (1890-); Margery McAlister (1892-), who married Mark W. Libbart, and had children: Mark W Libbert I and Margery; Iro Burns McAlister, who married

RHEA

—— Cox; James Aiken McAlister II (1868-), who married twice: First, M. R. ——; Second, Elizabeth Fry. By first wife he had one child, James Aiken McAlister III; Rachael Carter McAlister (-1911), who married Robert Lee Burch, and had children: Robert Lee Burch II and Hill McAlister Burch); (c) Margaret E. McAlister (-1919), (married James Erwin. Children: James Erwin II; William McAlister Erwin, (1857-), who married Annie May Jolly; Charles Bosley Erwin (1859-); Joseph Gibson Erwin (1861-), who married Clara Davidson, and had children: Joseph Gibson Erwin II, Robert Davidson Erwin and James Erwin III; (d) Elizabeth Anderson McAlister (-1919), (married Robert Biddle. Children: Eliza McAlister Biddle (1875-), who married J. Whiteford Russell; William Kink Biddle (1876-), who married Netta Russell, and had one child, Mary Elizabeth); (e) Frances Aiken McAlister (1840-) (married John F. Wheless. Children: John Wheless (-1891) and Percy Wheless; (f) Sarah Lucky McAlister, (died young); (g) James Aiken McAlister; (h) Marion McAlister (-1890), (married William Summerfield Sawrie. Children: William G. Sawrie (-1906), who married Mamie Bang; Frances McAlister Sawrie, who married J. Eaton Webb, and had children: Marion (1894-) and Frances (1899); Margaret Sawrie, who married John T. Henderson, and had children: Marion McAlister Henderson (1894-), who married Edwin Craig, and had children: Maron Henderson Craig, and Margaret Craig; Margaret Henderson, (1896-), who married William T. Hutcheson, and had one child, William T. Hutcheson II; Ideela Sawrie, who married Sheffield Clark, and had children: Margaret McAlister and Sheffield Clark II; Henry Sperry Sawrie, who married Florence Johnson, and had one child, Florence; Herbert Sawrie, who married Bessie Beach, and had children: Bessie Beach and Earnest William); (i) Samuel McAlister; (j) William K. McAlister II (1850-), (married Laura Brown Dortch. Attorney at law. Served on the bench of the Supreme Court of Tennessee. Receiver for the Tennessee Central Railroad Company. He had children: Medora McAlister (1873-), who married George F. Blackie, and had one child, William McAlister Blackie; Harry Hill McAlister (1875-), who married Louise Jackson, daughter of Judge Harold E. Jackson, and had children: Mary Jackson, Louise Jackson, and Laura; Samuel Dysart McAlister (1868-), who married Evelyn Krumbhaar); (k) Florence McAlister; (l) John Walter McAlister; (m) Lady Louisa

NOTABLE SOUTHERN FAMILIES

DeSaulles McAlister (1856-), (married Lewis Randolph Donelson. (see Donaldson family). Children: Lewis Randolph Donelson II (1881-), Elsie Donelson (1883-), Jennie Donelson and Andrew Jackson Donelson); (2) Rebecca Anderson (1814-1863), who married William B. Gammon, (brother of Abram Gammon who married her sister, Nancy Anderson), and had children: (a) George Gammon, (married Barsheba Rutledge. Children: Robert and Rebecca); (b) Audley Anderson Gammon (1834-1905), (married Mary John Farris. Children: William Farris Gammon (1860-), who married twice: First, Minnie Hicks; Second, Ida Lee Baumgardner); Eliza Rebecca Gammon; Samuel Rhea Gammon (1865-), married twice: First, Willie Brown Humphreys; Second, Clara Gennet Moore. "He is the Honored Rev. Samuel Rhea Gammon of Lavras, Brazil, one of the highly esteemed missionaries of the Southern Presbyterian Church"; Nannie Spence Gammon (1867-) married Charles Edward Gammon; Minnie Gammon (1869), married Dr. Charles K. Kernan); (c) Nancy Gammon; (d) Sallie J. Gammon; (e) Elizabeth Gammon; (f) William D. Gammon, (married Aurelia Shields, daughter of Judge J. K. Shields); (g) Frances Gammon, (married Robert Allen); (h) Abram Looney Gammon; (i) Martha Ellen Gammon, (married twice: First, Richard McGhee; Second, John W. Spence); (3) Eliza Rhea Anderson (1816-1892), who married Gen. Richard Gammon Fain (stepbrother), and had children: (a) Hiram Fain (1834-1869), (married Bettie Lyons. Children: Mattie Matilda Fain, who married Joseph Sevier Vance, and had children: James Foster Vance, Charles Rutledge Vance (1885-), who married Lula Burt Warrick, and had children: Ethel and Joseph LaFayette; Elizabeth Lyons Vance (1887-), who married William S. Pierce and had one child, William Vance Pierce; Samuel Fain Vance (1893-); David Lyon Fain (1865-); Samuel Kemp Fain; Annie Hiram Fain); (b) Elizabeth Fain; (c) Sarah G. Fain (1838-1912), (married Colonel Samuel N. Fain, a distant relative. Children: Samuel, Sallie, Eliza Amelia, Mattie, Frances, Bessie, John and Lida); (d) Nicholas Fain (1840-1899), (married Annie Kingsbury. Children: Mary, Richard and Catherine); (e) Samuel Audley Fain; (f) Isaac Anderson Fain (1844-1917), (married Mattie Jones. Children: Lillie Bell, who married John Bonnett, and had one daughter; Richard, Jessie and Olive); (g) G. Powell (1846-1914), married Sallie E. Fain. Chidren: William Rhea, Robert Rogan, Samuel, Nellie Foster, and twins—

RHEA

Richard and Hiram Rathbone, and Julia); (h) Frances Fain (1848-1914), (married Amos Lee Smith. Children: Richard Fain and Lee Jackson); (i) John Fain; (j) Richard Gammon Fain II (1851-), (married Julia Brace. One child: Leonhard Brace Fain (1885-), who married ———, and had one child, Mary Helen); (k) Nancy Anderson Fain (1854-1876); (1) Ellen Rhea Fain; (m) Eliza Ruth Fain; (4) Nancy Anderson (1818-), who married Abraham Gammon. Elizabeth Rhea by her second husband, Nicholas Fain, had children: (5) Hiram Fain, who married Bettie Lyons and had two children: Ernest, Lucia, Molly and Sallie; (6) Lizzie Fain, who married Rutledge Powell, and had a son who married ——— and had a daughter who married Walter Lyons.

2 Margaret Rhea (1791-1883), married (1816) Col. Isaac Campbell Anderson (brother of Audley Anderson who married her sister, Elizabeth). "This family was born and reared in a house in Scott County, Virginia, which was formerly used as a block house and fort against the Indians. It was bought by Joseph Anderson, father of Isaac Anderson" (Seldon Nelson, Knoxville Sentinel, 1908). Margaret Rhea had children: (1) Rebecca Maxwell Anderson (1818-1893), who married Joseph Newland, and had children: (a) Martha Newland (1836-1911), (married William A. Dooley. children, Currell; Ruth; Charles; James Isaac Andes, and had children: J. Earnest (1890-), Mary Lynn (1891-)) and George Andes (1894-); Rebecca Dooley (1862-1916), who married J. Wright Hoss, and had children: Margaret, J. Wright Hoss II, Stanton M. and Dooley; Joseph March Dooley (1864-1906), who married Bell Thoma, and had children: Maude, who married Leb Harding, Martin and Joseph Dooley II; Nellie Dooley (1872-), who married John R. Snow, and had children: Nellie Martha and Joseph); (b) Martha Jane Newland (1838-1914), (married Charles Robertson Vance. Children: James Isaac Vance (1862-), who married Mary Currell, and had children Currell; Currell; Ruth; Charles; James Isaac Vance II. James Isaac Vance is a minister of the Presbyterian Church. He is pastor of Grace Church at Nashville, Tennessee; Joseph Anderson Vance (1864-), who married Mary Forman, and had children: Dorothy, Mary and Joseph Anderson II. Joseph Anderson Vance is a prominent evangelist of the Presbyterian Church; Charles Robertson Vance II; Margaret Jane Vance; Rebecca Malinda Vance (1874-), who married Charles L. Hendrick, and had chil-

dren: Margaret and Mary); (c) Eliza Barbara Newland (1840-1912), (married William Powell Duff. Children: Joseph Newland Duff (1869-), who married Nettie Delila Young, and had children: Lelia Rhea .(1891-), who married Clifford E. Maze; William Vastine (1893-), who married Blanch Irene Hunt; Ralph Tyler (1900-); Carrie Anita; Powell Rhea Duff (1870-), who married May Richmond Youny, and had children: Edith Viola, Rebecca Elizabeth and Paul Eugene; James Emmett Duff (1872-1911), who married twice: First, Mary Ellen Asten; Second, Virginia Rush. Children by the first wife: Vera Eugenia (1896-) and Robert William (1897-); By the second wife: James Emmett Duff II, Guy Rush. Cecil Harold and Joseph Davidson; William Forest Duff (1875-), who married Cora Wood, and had children: William Wood, James Fred, Robert Rhea and Mary Lyde; Robert Cecil Duff (1877-), who married Martha Thompkins, and had children: Barbara and Charlotte Mace; Rebecca Elizabeth Duff; Guy Duff (1880-), who married Stella Shepherd, and had children: Willis Powell and Lucile; Mace Duff (1883-), who married Dr. William S. Gray, and had children: Joseph William and Robert Cecil); (d) Isaac Anderson Newland (1842-), (married twice: First, Martha Lewis; Second, Nannie Vance. Children by first wife: Joseph Henry Newland (1867-), who married Nannie Elizabeth Hensley, and had children: Ernest Wolsey (minister of Presbyterian Church), Joseph Mitchell (1893-), Mattie Anderson (1894-), Clarence Frances (1897-), James Lacy (1899-), Charles Logan, William Isaac, Annie Lee and Kate; Hugh Mitchell Newland (1870-), who married three times: First, Lynn Stewart; Second, Nastings Perry; Third, Laura Carter Sandidge. Children by first wife: Emmett (1893-), Joseph Anderson (1895-), Maxie Jayne (1896-), who married Joseph Dorton Cox, Samuel Rhea (1898-), Hugh Lynn, Vernon Ross, Mabel Angeline and Robert Rhea. By second wife one child, William Perry. By third wife one child, James Dobyns; Mamie Newland (1874-), who married . W. Houser; Carey Newland (1876-), who married J. A. Jayne, and had one child, Sarah Francis; Maxwell Newland (1889-)); (e) Ellen Anderson Newland (1844-), (married James P. Doggett. Minister of Presbyterian Church. Children: Lida Beatrice Doggett (1873-) who married Nicholas Peter Ernest. Children under Nicholas Peter Earnest; Rebecca Hall Doggett (1875-); Fan Lin Doggett (1877-), who married Walter Reeve Earnest, and had children: Walter Reeve Eearnest II,

RHEA

Robert Doggett and Martha Beatrice; Joseph Newlad Doggett (1879-), who married Cora Leftwich; Margaret Eleanor Doggett (1885-), who married Samuel Rhea Earnest, brother of Nicholas Peter Earnest. (Children under Samuel Rhea Earnest)); (f) Joseph Mitchell Newland (1847-), (married Judith Lesley. Children:)Rebecca Newland (1876-), who married Rev. R. H. Taylor, and had children: Joseph Harold, Mary Newland, Ruth Lesley and Hubert Vance; Allie Newland; Lesley Newland; Joseph Newland); (g) Fannie Anderson Newland (1849-), (married Elkanah Dulaney Pence. Children: Martha Ellen (1886-) and Joseph James (1888-)); (h) Samuel Anderson Newland (1852-), (married Helen Brown. Children: Margaret Rebecca Newland (1887-), who married Albert Pendleton Henderson, and had one child, Albert Pendleton Henderson II; Joseph Newland (1888-); Mary Eleanor Newland (1890-); Stella Rhea Newland (1892-); Vance Newland (1896-); Helen Brown Newland (1899-); Nathan Newland (1902-)); (i) Robert Rhea Newland (1860-), (married Elizabeth Wolford. Children: Lyndsay Wolford Newland, M. D. (1887-), who married Agatha Gregg; Lydia Rebecca Newland; Grace Newland (1892-); Lois Salome Newland (1897-)); (2) Joseph Rhea Anderson (1819-1888), who married Malinda Williams King. Joseph Rhea Anderson was a banker and merchant of Bristol, Tennessee, in fact the founder of Bristol. He had children: (a) James King Anderson; (b) Sarah Ann Anderson; (c) John Campbell Anderson (1850-1913), (married twice: First, Annie Anderson; Second, Fannie Williamson. Children by first wife: Audley King (1878-), Joseph Rhea, Alice Melinda, Florence Alexander and John Campbell. By second wife: Margaret Williamson, John Campbell, Thomas Parrish and Robert Banks); (d) Margaret Micajah Anderson (1857-), (married John Henderson Caldwell. Children: Margaret Melinda Caldwell; John Henderson Caldwell II (1882-), who married Genevieve Rice, and had children: Margaret Rice and Genevieve; Joseph Anderson Caldwell (1884-), who married Isabella Hawley, and had children: Joseph Anderson and John Henderson; George Aiken Caldwell (1887-), who married Harriet Parish; Walter McFarland Caldwell; Mable Caldwell (1893-); Almedia Brooks Caldwell (1896-)); (e) Isaac Samuel Andersn (1854-), a minister of the Presbyterian Church, (married Ollie Gibson. One child: Nancy Melinda (1894-), who married John Frank Kincaid, and had one child,, John Frank Kincaid II); (f) Joseph King Anderson; (3) John Anderson; (4) Audley Anderson (1822-1894), married twice: First Cornelia Alexander; Second, Mrs. Jane Preston Vance, nee Rhea, his cousin. Children by first wife: (a) Annie Anderson, (married John Campbell Anderson, son of Joseph Rhea Anderson and Melinda (King) Anderson. Children under John Campbell Anderson); (b) Alice Anderson, (married Rev. A. S. Newman); (c) John P. Anderson, a minister of the Presbyterian Church, (married Roxie McCoslan); (d) Audley S. Anderson; (e) Alexander Anderson (1856-), (married Elizabeth Rhea, daughter of Theoderic Bland Rhea and Frances Elizabeth (Rhea) Rhea. One child: Audley Rhea Anderson (1881-), who married Bertha Eleanor Short, and had one child, Audley Rhea Anderson II); (f) Campbell Anderson; (5) Dr. Samuel Anderson; (6) Fannie Anderson (1824-1874), married James Hughes, and had children: (a) James Hughes II; (b) Margaret Hughes (-1893), (married John Mongle. One child, Josephine); (c) Mollie Hughes (married Thomas Mongle, a brother of John Mongle. Children: Margaret and Fannie Rhea); (7) Eliza Anderson (1826-1890). who married David Carr, and had children: (a) Aaron B. Carr, (married Mrs. Angie Dodd. Children: Edith, Laura and David); (b) Margaret R. Carr, (married twice: First, William Rockhold Rhea, (son of William R. Rhea and Mary Ann Mosley (Rockhold) Rhea), no issue. Second, John Mitchell Fain, (son of John H. Fain and Fannie Anderson (Rhea) Fain). Children under John Mitchell Fain); (c) James W. Carr (-1886), married Woodie Johnson. Children: James and Alda); (d) William Carr; (e) Joseph Carr; (f) Jennie Carr, (married ―――― Baldwin, and had children: William Lusbrooke and Margaret Rhea); (g) Lucky Carr; (8) Sarah Anderson (1827-1906), married Henry S. Kane, and had children: (a) Margaret Kane (1856-), (married James M. Barker. Children: Lucile (1880-), Sarah (1885-), James M. Barker II (1888-), Henry Neville (1892-), and Margaret Kane (1894-)); (b) Hannah Kane; (c) Henry S. Kane II (1860-), (married Francis A. Koiner. Children: Henry S. Kane III (1885-); Patrick Lee Kane (1887-); Letcher Kane (1888-), who married Pearl Potter; Estelle Kane (1893-); Elisha Kent Kane (1895-), who married Eula MacGaven; Jane Kane (1897-); Katherine Kane (1899-); Julian Kane (1815-));(d)I. Patrick Kane; (e) Robert Rhea Kane (1868-1901), (married Josephine Edmonds. Children: Robert Rhea Kane II (1894-) Esther

RHEA

Kane (1895-) and Sarah Kane (1898-)); (9) Caroline Anderson; (10) Mary Anderson (1830-1877), who married Jesse R. Earnest, and had children: (a) Mattie Earnest, (married George F. Robertson. Children: Paul D. Earnest, Lynn, Jesse, Robert, Carl William and George Oliphant); (b) William A. Earnest, (married Florence Donelly. Children: Jesse, Robert, Carl King, Joseph, William, Charles and Samuel Rhea); (c) Isaac Earnest, (married Minnie Mirt. One child, Charles); (d) Walter R. Earnest; (11) Isaac Campbell Anderson (1832-), who married Nannie Stewart; (12) Jane Anderson (1833-), who married William Stewart, and had one child, Linn Stewart, who married Hugh Mitchell Newland, (son of Isaac Anderson Newland and Martha (Lewis) Newland). Children under Hugh Mitchell Newland.

4 Samuel Rhea (1795-1863), married twice: First, (1826) Ann M. Rutledge (daughter of Gen. John Rutledge); Second, (1832) Martha Lynn (1810-1878). Child by first wife: (1) Samuel Audley Rhea (1827-1865), who married twice: First, Martha Ann Harris. No issue; Second, (1859) Sarah Jane Foster. Samuel Audley Rhea was a minister of the Presbyterian Church, and a missionary to Persia where he died, and was buried at Mount Seir. (A Tennesseean in Persia, by Marsh). He had children: (a) Robert Leighton Rhea; (b) Annie Dwight Rhea (1861-), (married Samuel G. Wilson, a missionary to Persia. Children: Samuel Rhea, Mary Agnes, Rose Dulless, Esther, Andrew, Annie Rhea and Robert Leighton); (c) Foster Audley Rhea; (d) Sophia Perkins Rhea (-1907), (married Rev. William Dullness. Children: Mabel Rutledge, Dorothy, Edith, Foster Rhea and Winslow); Samuel Rhea by his second wife had children: (2) John Lynn Rhea (1832-1910), never married. He and his brother, William Lynn Rhea, engaged in the mercantile business in Knoxville, Tennessee, in which they prospered and were noted for their honesty and integrity. After the death of John, in 1910, William sold out the business and retired. They with their sister Ellen had a home in Knoxville, where they were members of the Presbyterian Church and were active in the religious life of the city. John and William devoted a great deal of time and study to collecting a history of the Rhea family, and have the most complete record of it's members and early history in existence at this time (1921); (3) Fannie Anderson Rhea (1834-1903), who married John H. Fain, and had children: (a) Samuel Rhea Fain; (b) Martha Ellen Fain (-1901), (married Robert N.

NOTABLE SOUTHERN FAMILIES

Dosser. Children: Fannie Rhea, Margaret Cowan, Mary Nell and Robert N. Dosser II; (c) John Mitchell Fain, (married twice: First, Laura Gertrude Worley; Second, Margaret R. Carr, widow of William Rockhold Rhea. Children by first wife: Worley, James Rhea, Martha Ellen and John Mitchell Fain II); (d) James Rhea Fain, (married Lillian Mae Linkheart. One child, Margery Cowan Fain); (e) Mary Lynn Fain (-1894), (married Samuel D. Stuart. One child, Samuel); (4) Mary Martha Rhea (1836-1894), who married Benjamin Franklin Earnest, and had children: (a) Samuel Rhea Earnest (1869-), (married Margaret Eleanor Doggett, (sister of Lida Doggett who married his brother Nicholas Peter Earnest). One child, Eleanor Elizabeth); (b) Nicholas Peter Earnest (1871-), (married Lida Doggett. Children: Mary Eleanor, James Doggett, Joseph Rhea, Benjamin Foster, Charles Edward and Katherne Louise); (c) Eleanor Lynn Earnest, (never married); (5) Joseph Brainerd Rhea (1838-1902), who married Ellen White Sheffey (daughter of Judge James White Sheffey and Ellen Fairman (Preston) Sheffey), and had children: (a) James White Sheffey Rhea (1869-1918), never married. (Was a prominent educator); (b) Eleanor Lynn Rhea (1871-), married twice: First, William H. Adams; Second, Sturn W. Carson, no issue. Children by first husband: Charles Linwood (1896-) and Brainerd Rhea (1898-); (c) Margaret Preston Rhea (1886-) (married Henry Boyd Stanley. Children: Ellen Sheffey, Pauline Hull and Henry Boyd Stanley II); (d) Virginia Sheffey Rhea, (died in infancy); (6) James Alexander Rhea (1840-1871), no issue; (8) Robert Morrison Rhea (1842-1903), who married Bella W. Cowan, (daughter of James Cowan and Lucinda (Dickinson) Cowan), and had children: (a) Mamie Rhea, (died young); (b) Charles McClung Rhea (-1903); (c) Lucy Foster Rhea; (d) Martha Lynn Rhea, (married Fayette VanDeventer. Children: Christopher, Robert Rhea, Latitia and Isabella); (8) Margaret Elizabeth Rhea (1848-), who married Rev. Perez D. Cowan, (brother of Bella Cowan who married her brother, Robert Morrison Rhea), and had children: (a) Margaret McClung Cowan, (died young); (b) Eleanor Rhea Cowan, (married Allen Davies); (c) James Dickerson Cowan, (married Elsie Bailey. One child, James Dickinson Cowan II); (9) Eliza Eleanor Rhea (1844-1914), never married; (10) William Lynn Rhea (1846-), never married; (11) Charles Stoddard Rhea, died in infancy.

5 Eleanor Rhea (1797-1865), married (1848) Edward

B. Anderson and had children: (1) William R. Anderson (1821), who married Louise Smith, and had children: (a) Bettie Anderson; (b) William S. Anderson, (married Ella Spurgeon. Children: George, Joseph, Rhea and Paul); (c) Edward B. Anderson, (married Fannie Waskey. Children: Clarence, Lynn and Glenn); (d) Ellen Anderson; (e) Margaret Anderson; (f) Robert Anderson; (g) Ollie Anderson; (h) Joseph Anderson; (i) Mary Anderson; (2) Joseph Anderson (1824-); (3) Audley Anderson (1826-), who married Margaret Rhea, (daughter of Major Rhea and Jane (Scott) Rhea), and had children: Joseph and Robert; (4) Fannie Anderson; (5) Margaret E. Anderson (1832-); (6) Robert R. Anderson (1834-), who married Winnie Boy, and children: (a) Amanda B. Anderson, (married Joseph Neal. Children: Kate and Rhea); (b) Alexander Anderson, (married Mary Smith. Children: Hal and Ethel); (c) Ellen Anderson; (d) Samuel R. Anderson, (married Melissa Blevins. Children: Samuel, Sallie and Robert); (e) James Anderson; (f) Fannie May Anderson; (g) Frank B. Anderson; (7) Samuel R. Anderson, (a twin of Robert R. Anderson born 1834); (8) Sarah Anderson.

6 Fannie Rhea (1799-1850), married (1825) Jonathan Bachman, and had children: (1) Joseph R. Bachman; (2) Ann Peoples Bachman (1827-1901), who married three times: First Joshua Phipps; Second, Rev C. Waterbury; Third, ——— Lyons. By her first husband she had one child: Joshua McKinney Phipps (1853-), who married Mary McKinney, and had children: (a) Annie Phipps (1884-), (married Samuel Lee King. Children: Samul Lee King II, J. Phipps, John G. and Charles Logan); (b) Charles McKinney Phipps (1877-), (married Annie Sevier Morrison. Children: Mary McKinney, and Margeret Sevier); (c) Kenneth Logan Phipps; (d) James Gaines Phipps (1881-), (married Mabel Sevier Morrison. Children: Kenneth Logan and James Gaines Phipps II); (e) Mary Phipps; (f) Joshua McKinney Phipps II; (g) Fannie Phipps (1889-), (married Arthur S. Cosler. One child: Arthur S. Cosler); (3) Frances Bachman; (4) Elizabeth Bachman; (5) Nathan Bachman (1832-1914), an eminent evangelist of the Presbyterian Church, who married Sarah Jane Cunningham, and had one child: Sarah Jane Bachman, who married John Charles Moore, and had children: John Charles Moore II, Nathan, Lawrence and Robert; (6) Samuel Rhea Bachman; (7) Mary Jane Bachman; (8) Jonathan Waverly Bachman D. D., (1837-). Has been a

minister of the First Presbyterian Church at Chattanooga, Tennessee, since 1873, and is lovingly referred to as "The Bishop of Chattanooga". He married Evalina Dulaney, and had children: (a) Frances Taylor Bachman, (married William L. Magill); (b) Mary Bachman (-1897), (married Charles C. Anderson. Children: John Waverly Anderson (1890-), who married Dorothy Morgan, and had one child: Dorothy Dulaney Anderson; William Dulaney Anderson (1892-); Mary Margaret Anderson (1895-), who married Charles Shelby Coffey and has two children); (c) Annie Rhea Bachman, (married Rev. Charles R. Hyde. One child: John Bachman Hyde (1890-), who married Willia Foster and has one child, Rose); (d) William Bachman; (e) Margaret Walker Bachman (-1899), (married James L. Caldwell); (f) Nathan Lynn Bachman, (married Pearl Duke. One child, Martha Dulaney Bachman. Nathan Lynn Bachman is an attorney-at-law and is a member of the Supreme Court of Tennessee); (g) Evalina Dulaney Bachman, (married Charles Edward Buck); (h and i) Alfred Jackson and Robert Rhea Bachman, (twins); (j) Carrie VanDyke Bachman; (9) John Lynn Bachman (1842-1918). A minister of the Presbyterian Church; founder and President of Sweetwater College, at Sweetwater, Tennessee. He married Fannie Rogan, and had children: (a) James Rogan Bachman (1874-), (married Elizabeth Eubanks); (b) Annie Lynn Bachman (1876-), (married Dr. William A. McClain. Children: William A. McClain II, Fannie, Lynn and Annie); (c) Byres Bachman; (d) Bessie Bachman (1881-), (married James R. Patton. One child, James H.; (e) John W. Bachman; (f) Lillie Bell Bachman (1886-. (married James M. Harris. Children: James M. Harris II. and Fannie); (g) Fannie Rhea Bachman; (10) Robert Lucky Bachman (1844-), (married May Rose. Children: Robert, Elsie, who married Fred Clymer and has one child, Rose, and Kirk).

7 Nancy Rhea (1801-1839), married John Lynn, (brother of Martha Lynn who married Samuel Rhea). She had children: (1) Frances Lynn; (2) Martha Lynn (1827-1887), who married John Lampson, and had children: (a) William Royal Lampson (1860-); (married Amanda Hopkins Parker); (b) John Lynn Lampson; (c) Nannie Rhea Lampson; (d) Eleanor W. Lampson (1864-), (married Elbridge James Baxter. Children: Martha (1894-) and Eleanor Lynn (1897-)); (3) Ellen Lynn; (4) John Lynn: (5) Joseph Lynn; (6) Mary Ann Lynn (1835-1871).

RHEA

(married Dr. Joseph Walker. Children: (a) Fannie Rogan Walker, (married Earnest Powell. Children: Hugh, Ella, and Sallie); (b) Hugo Kelso Walker, (A minister of the Presbyterian Church. Married Lizzie Moore. Children: William Moore, Hugh Wiles, Allie Rhea who married F. E. Prior, Elizabeth, Mary Linn, Ruth, Joseph, Margaret Eleanor and Jennie); (c) James Rhea Lynn Walker (A minister of the Presbyterian Church. Married twice: First, Venable Holt; Second, Mrs. ————. By first wife he had one child: Catherine); (d) Thomas Frances Walker; (e) Joseph Rogers Walker; (f) Jonnie Walker; (7) James Lynn (1837-), who married Sallie Rogan, and had children: (a) Samuel Edward Lynn; (b) Carrie Lynn; (c) Rev John Lynn; (d) Fleming Lynn; (e) Mary Lynn; (f) Nannie Lynn; (g) Perry Lynn; (8) Samuel Alexander Lynn (1839-), who married Ophelia Rogan, and had children: William, James, Annie Bell, John Rogan and Adah.

8 Robert P. Rhea (1803-1881), married Sarah J. Preston and had children: (1) Jane Preston Rhea; (2) Frances Elizabeth Rhea (1832-1870), who married Theoderic Bland Rhea (son of VIII James Rhea and Elizabeth (Snapp) Rhea. Children under Theodoric Bland Rhea); (3) Joseph Rhea III (1830-1909), who married Eliza Ann Earhart, and had children: (a) Robert Earhart Rhea (1869-) (married Margaret Rebecca Rhea, daughter of Robert Bruce Rhea and Sarah (Sells) Rhea, and had children: Eleanor and twins Margaret, and Helen Bruce); (b) Alexander Preston Rhea (1871-); (c) Joseph Anderson Rhea (1873-); (d) Lady Sarah Rhea (1874-); (e) Margaret Davis Rhea (1876-), (married Chester Bullard. Children: Willie Margaret and Joe Rhea); (f) John Rhea (1878-); (4) Margaret Preston Rhea (1835-1913), who married John Taylor Earhart, and had children: (a) George Jackson Earhart; (b) Charles Balfour Earhart (1864-), (married Etta Emma Powell. Children: John Powell Earhart, who married Viola Sanders, and had one child, Charles Sanders; Samuel Pierce Earhart (1887-), who married Eveleen B. Mauk, and had children: Margaret Cathleen and Etta Elizabeth; Robert Rhea Earhart; Charles Balfour Earhart II; Margaret Earhart (1893-); Violet Etta Earhart (1898-); Nellie Roller Earhart; Ralph Preston Earhart); (c) Robert Rhea Earhart; (d) Sarah Ella Earhart (1866-), (married William Edgar Carter. Children: Joseph, Hubert and Carrie); (e) Joseph Preston Earhart (1869-), (married Sarah Ann Boy. Chil-

NOTABLE SOUTHERN FAMILIES

dren: John Sidney, Mary Lillian and Phillip Boy); (f) Margaret Jane Earhart (1872-), (married Thomas J Fain. Children: William, Ruth, Thomas J. Fain II, Florence and Margaret Preston): (g) John Henry Earhart (1874-), (married Frances Susan Fleenor. Children: Claren Wade, Hazel Etta, Charles Henry, William Hurman and twin Martha Evalin, and John Howard); (5) Robert James Rhea.

9 Sarah Rhea (1806-1862), married (1831) Judge Seth J. W. Lucky, and had children: (1) Frances A. Lucky; (2) Sarah Jane Lucky (1834-1884), who married William Kirkpatrick Moore, and had children: (a) Allie Rhea Moore (1859); (b) Lizzie Moyers Moore (1861-), (married Hugh Kelso Walker. Children: William Moore (1885-), Hugh Kelso (1887-), married Fannie Carpenter, Allie Rhea (1891-) married Ford Prior, Elizabeth Sterling (1893-), Mary Lynn (1895-), Jane Smith (1897-), Ruth Rankin (1899-), Joseph R. and Margaret Eleanor); (c) John Lucky Moore (1866-1897); (d) Rhea Moffett Moore (1870-1895); (e) Nell Williams Moore (1873-); (f) William Kirkpatrick Moore II (1876-); (3) Ellen Lucky (1836-), who married Jesse Hamilton Gaut, and had children: (a) Sarah Lucky Gaut (1868-1902), (married James G. DeArmond. Children: Cornelius Hamilton and Margaret Eleanor); (b) John Watson Lucky; (c) Jesse Rhea Lucky; (d) Agnes Moore Lucky (1875-) (married Hugh Montgomery Knox. Children: Agnes Moore and Thomas Jefferson); (e) Luella Erwin Moore (1875-), (married Thomas Oscar Marshall. Children: Orlando Gaut and Agnes Lucky); (f) Cornelius Lucky (1877-), (married Willa Cleveland. One child, Cornelius Lucky); (4) Sophia Lucky; (5) Joseph Lucky; (6) Cornelius Eugenia Lucky (1841-), who married Julia Sims. One child: Mary who married H. J. Kelso, M. D.; (7) Martha McAlister Lucky (1843-), who married John E. Williams. Children: (a) Edmund Lucky Williams; (b) Annie E. Williams, (married D. O. Milander); (c) Cornelius L. Williams, married Georgia Burgette); (d) Bessie Williams, (married William Dempster. One child. Elizabeth Ann); (e) Agnes Williams; (8) Agnes Mitchell Lucky (1845-1903), who married Dr. Joseph R. Walker, and had children: Cornelius L., Seth L., Margaret Kelso, Jesse G., Mary Gaines married George Webster, and Bell Moore; (9) Elizabeth Dysart Lucky (1847-), who married George W. Hamilton, and had children: Jennie Moore, Bessie, Seth, George W., Cornelius, Henry and Jane Rhea.

RHEA

VI ELIZABETH RHEA

VI Elizabeth Rhea (1767-1821), daughter of Rev. Joseph Rhea and Elizabeth (McIlwaine) Rhea, married Major Robert Rhea (1784-1841). Major Robert Rhea and Elizabeth Rhea were born in Ireland, the former, presumably near St. Johnstone, the latter at Fahan, near Londonderry. He came to America, with his parents, in 1785, she, with her parents, in 1769. They were married and lived until their deaths in Sullivan County, Tennessee. She had children:
1 Sarah Rhea,
2 Joseph R. Rhea,
3 John Rhea,
4 Elizabeth M. Rhea.

1 Sarah Rhea (-1849), married (1826) George Woodson Gaines, (Notable Southern Families, Vol. I), and had children: (1) John Rhea Gaines (1827-1911), who married three times: First, Sarah Rice; Second, Elizabeth Blair; Third, Harriet Amanda Craig. Until the last three years of his life John Rhea Gaines lived on his farm in Monroe County, Tennessee. He was distinguished for sterling honor and loyalty. By his first wife he had children: (a) Frances Henry Gaines (1852-), a minister of the Presbyterian Church and President of Agnes Scott Institute, which he established. (He married Mary Louise Lewis. One child: Lewis McFarland Gaines, M. D. (1878-), who married Ethel Alexander, and had children: Mary Eloise, Alexander Pendleton and Virginia Ethel); (b) William Strother Gaines, M. D. (1854-), (married Laura Brown. Children: Sue Brown Gaines (1878-), who married Edward F. Betz, and had children: Dorothy and William Edward; Sallie Rice Gaines (1880-), who married Reese B. Brown; Mable Josephine Gaines; Hattie Pendleton Gaines (1884-), who married Thomas W. Secrest, and had one child, William Gaines; Minnie Laura Gaines (1887-), who married Howard Shubert; William Rhea Gaines (1891-); Frank P. Gaines (1892-)). John Rhea Gaines had children by his second wife: (c) Mary Gaines (1861-1902), (married William L. Magill. Children: Bessie Wilson (1885-), Sadie Gaines (1886-), Edward Alexander (1890-), and William L. Magill II (1899-)). John Rhea Gaines had children by his third wife: (d) Annie Rhea Gaines (1880-), (married Charles Leonidas Clark. Children: James William, John Craig, Charles Palmer and Mary Clark); (e) Susie Rice Gaines

NOTABLE SOUTHERN FAMILIES

(1883-), (married Frank Knox Hutcheson. Children: John Gaines, Frank Hutcheson II, Susan Craig and Charles Strother); (f) Frances Louisa Gaines (1888-), (married Jack Cotton Oates. Children: Jack Cotton II and Catherine Craig); (2) Robert J. Gaines (1829-1890), who married Sarah Cook, and had children: George W. Gaines, M. D. John A. Gaines, M. D., and Allie Gaines; (3) William Gaines (1834-1854); (4) August Pendleton Gaines (1831-1902), who married Dorcas Henderson. They lived on their farm near Sweetwater, Tennessee, and were noted for their hospitality. He had children: (a) Mollie Gaines; (b) Sadie Gaines; (c) Carrie Gaines (1862-), (married Hugh Mack Willson. Children: James Gaines (1893-), Dorcas Henderson (1895-), Mintie N. (1897-) and Sadie Gaines (1899-)); (5) Elizabeth McCuin Gaines (1837-1873), who married Frank Bogart, M. D. (1827-1887), and had chidren: (a) Walter Gaines Bogart, M. D. (1858-), (married Lorella J. Magill. Walter Gaines Bogart was a professor in Chattanooga Medical College and owns Highland Sanitarium, which he established, at Chattanooga, Tennessee. He had children: Elizabeth Gaines Bogart (1886-), who married Tolcott Crosby Olney; Frank Magill Bogart (1888-), who married Pauline Stauffer); (b) Thomas C. Bogart; (c) John Newton Bogart; (d) Anna Bogart; (e) Frank Bogart II; (f) William Moore Bogart, M. D. (1867-), (married Keturah Montgomery Thompson. He served on the Chattanooga Local Draft Board during the World War. He had children: Franklin Blevins Bogart, M. D. (1894-), who married Alice Harloff; Martha Josephine Bogart (1898); Anna Mary Bogart (1901-)); (6) Sarah Gaines (1840-1904), who married John W. Johnston (1871-1915), (married Pearl Snapp. Children: Ellen Elizabeth and Clifford Snapp); (c) Ella Johnston; (d) Annie Johnston (1874), married Frank C. McKenzie. Children: John Lee, Harry Gaines, Frank Blair, William Yancy, Sarah Louise, Mary-Ella, Margaret Elvira and Donald Penland); (e) John Johnson (1876-), married Julia Forkner. Children: James Rhea, Bessie Lee, Mary Melvina and Lula Frances); (f) Robert Johnston; (g) Walter Johnston; (h) Mary Johnston.

2 Joseph R. Rhea, married (1830) Emaline M. Alexander. They lived in London County, Tennessee, until 1855, when they moved to Collin County, Texas, where they prospered in business. They built mills which gave the name, Rhea's Mills, to the town in which they lived. He had children: (1) Robert P. Rhea (1831-1915); (2) William

RHEA

Alexander Rhea (1833-1906), who married twice: First, Ella Foote; Second, Mrs. Florence Parkins, no issue. Children by first wife: (a) Jean Foot (1872-), (married Clifton Emerson. Children: Ella Emerson (1895-), who married Robert Fitzhugh Newsome, and had one child, Robert Fitzhugh Newsome II; James Frederick Emerson; Clifton Alexander Emerson); (b) William Alexander Rhea II, M. D. (1874-), (married Mary Herndon. Children: Lawrence Herndon (1897-), and Alexander Foote (1899-)); (c) Lawrence Joseph Rhea, M. D. (1878-); (d) Mary Elliott Rhea (1880-), (married Lewis Lindemuth); (e) John Edwin Rhea (1883-), (married Ida Dowell. Children: John Edwin Rhea II and Mary Ida); (3) John W. Rhea (1835-1862) married Veronica Slaughter Mayes and had children: (a) Joseph E. Rhea (1858-1917), (married Florence Bass); (b) John W. Rhea II (1861-), (married Winfield Ledbetter. Children: Olivia, John W. Rhea III, Veronica and Winfield); (4) James C. Rhea (1837-), who married Mary A. Gossett, and had children: (a) Lula May Rhea; (b) William Joseph Rhea (1877-), (married Elizabeth Groves. One child, William Joseph Rhea II); (c) Hattie Emma Rhea; (d) John Alexander Rhea; (e) Robert Lee Rhea, M. D. (1882-), (married Margaret Buckholz. One child, Robert Lee Rhea II); (f) James Long Rhea; (5) Mary Elizabeth Rhea (1840-1913), who married William Miller, and had children: (a) Rhea Miller (1874-), (married May McKamey. Children: Truman, Willam Frederick and Sarah Elizabeth); (b) Mary Emma Miller; (c) Joseph W. Miller; (d) Stella Ella Miller; (e) Lula Alexander Miller (1882-), (married J. Fred Smith. Children: Rhea Marsh and J. Fred Smith II.

3 John Rhea (1810-1863), married (1839) Elizabeth Dodson. John Rhea was born in Sullivan County, Tennessee, moved to Roane, later Loudon, County, Tennessee. He had children: (1) Alexander Dodson Rhea (1841-1917), who married Mary Frances Hatchett, and had children: (a) John Rhea; (b) Sam Rhea; (c) Robert Rhea (1865-), (married Maude Love. One child, John Love Rhea (1881-) (d) Adaline Rhea (1866-1909), (married Lee E. Burgess. Children: Addie Lee Burgess (1891-), who married Joseph A. Rudnick; Rhea Burgess (1897-)); (e) Joseph Rhea (1871-), (married Anna B. Peeples. One child, Frances Ann (1906); (f) Elizabeth Rhea; (g) Louise Rhea (1877-1911), (married Lillan Lester Davis); (h) Frances Rodgers Rhea (1879-), (married Mrs. Annie Wright Maxey); (i) Cleaves Rhea (1882-), (married Mae B. Lowdon. Children:

NOTABLE SOUTHERN FAMILIES

Mary Alice and Helen Louise); (j) Alexander Dodson Rhea II (1885-), (married Annie L. Boesch. Children: Elizabeth and Alexander Dodson Rhea III;) (2) Sarah Elizabeth Rhea (1843-1893), who married Samuel Andrew Rodgers (see Donaldson Family), and had children: (a) Alice Rodgers; (b) California Elizabeth Rodgers (1869-), (married Joseph Marion Greer. One child; Rhea Rodgers Greer (1890-), who married Guy Lycon Hammitt; (c) Adaline Mahala Rodgers, (married John Johnston Blair); (d) Samuel Rhea Rodgers; (e) Mary Belle Rodgers, Married Jasper Porter Stephenson); (f) Annie Eliza Rodgers, (married Ulrich Ita III. One child, Ulrich Ita IV); (g) Arthur Rodgers (1879-), (married Dean Stuart Penland. Children: Arthur Rodgers II, James Penland, Samuel Andrew Rodgers II and Jasper Rhea Rodgers); (h) John Rhea Rodgers (1885-), (married George Steele Dewey. Children. Elizabeth Rhea, George Steele Dewey II, Mary Alice, Samuel Rodgers and Charles.

4 Elizabeth M. Rhea (1807-1853), married (1831) Joseph Anderson, and had children: (1) Robert Anderson (1832-1895), who married Emily Huff, and had children: (a) Elizabeth Anderson; (b) Adah Anderson; (c) Rhea Huff Anderson; (d) Emily Jane Anderson; (1871-), married Oscar Everett Mahoney. Children: Robert Rhea (1894-), Martha Emily (1896-), and Oscar Everett Mahoney II (1899-); (2) Sarah G. Anderson; (3) Isabella J. Anderson; (4) Elizabeth M. Anderson (1840-1881), who married James Huff, and had children: (a) Elizabeth K. Huff (1868-), (married Dr. Jump); (b) William E. Huff (1872-), (married Lucy Gallaher. Children: James Gallaher (1898-) and Hugh McCroskey (1901-)); (c) James Anderson Huff (1875-), (married Mabel Wilson. Children: James Anderson Huff II, F. Elizabeth, Woods Wilson, Mabel Claire, Margaret Ann and Isabel Rhea); (d) Mamie Huff (1877-), married James C. Miller; (6) Samuel Anderson (1845- Huff); (5) John A. Anderson, (1842-1868), who married Isabella Hotchkiss, and had one child: Lou Addie, who married James C. Mller; (6) Samuel Anderson (1845- 1900), who married Margaret Huff, and had children: (a) Emma Anderson (1868-), (married Samuel O. Henly. Children: Margaret, Janie, Lena Reese, Marshall Franklin, Frances Adaline and Maude Teressa); (b) Joseph Marshall Anderson; (8) Rachel A. Anderson (1848-1911), who married J. Ebb Crowder, and had children: (a) John A. Crowder (1869-), (married Bettie Eldridge. One child:

RHEA

John Eldridge); Crowder); Elizabeth Jane Crowder (1871-), (married William H. Boggs. Children: Annis Irene (1891-) and Lloyd Watson (1897-)); (c) Addie Amelia Crowder; (d) Maggie Sue Crowder (1877-1901), (married A. B. Smith. Children: Robert Reagan (1898-) and Raymond Crowder (1901-)); (e) Samuel Rhea Crowder (1879-), (married Dorothy Shaw. Children: Dorothy Helen, Winfield Rhea, Joe Anderson and Rachel Elizabeth); (f) Willie Anette Crowder (1882-), (married Charles Kirby. Children: Hugh Herbert, Paul Jennings, Clarence Birchfield and Oliver Jay); (g) Rachel Adah Crowder; (h) Nellie Hugh Crowder; (9) Amanda Anderson (1851-1907), who married John Taylor Lowery, and had children: (a) Mary Emma Lowery (1872-), (married Edgar Evans); (b) Hugh Fain Lowery (1874-), married Laura Bell Click); (c) Elizabeth Lowery (1876-); (d) Ella Lowery; (e) Maggie Lowery (1883-); (f) Rhea Evans Lowery (1889-); (g) Robert Lowery (1895-).

VII SAMUEL RHEA

VII Samuel Rhea (1769-1843), son of Rev. Joseph Rhea and Elizabeth (McIlwaine) Rhea, was born and died in America. He married Nancy Breden (-1856), sister of Elizabeth and Frances Breden who married his brothers, William and Joseph Rhea. He had children:

1 John Nancy Rhea,
2 Fannie B. Rhea,
3 Margaret Rhea,
4 Joseph S. Rhea,
5 Jane Rhea,
6 Ellen Rhea,
7 Elizabeth Rhea.

1 John Nancy Rhea (-1876), married Ruth M. Rockhold (-1872), (a sister of Mary Rockhold who married William Rhea), and had children: (1) Elizabeth Crawford Rhea, who married Samuel Patton Spurgeon, and had children: (a) Alice Ann Spurgeon, (married William Henry Fain. Children: Rachel, Thomas, Margaret E., Lilla Linn, Carrie Ruth who married S. T. Moser, and Samuel Patton Spurgeon); (b) Olivia James Spurgeon; (2) Samuel Wood Rhea (1841-), who married Sarah Irvin (daughter of Montgomery Irvin and Frances (Rhea) Irvin), and had children: (a) John Irvin Rhea (1869-), (married Retta Slagle. Children: Alpha Josephine, John Irvin Rhea II,

Sarah Harriet, and Tom Rye); (b) Fannie Ruth Rhea (1870-), (married John J. Hicks. One child, Velma E.); (c) Myrabel Rhea (1872-), (married Daniel A. Witcher. Children: Mary Irvin, James Rhea and John Daniel); (d) Jennie Dysart Rhea (1874-), (married James I. A. Hughes. Children: James Rhea, Samuel Dysart and Allen Campbell); (e) Mary Margaret Rhea (1877-), (married Charles L. Cooper. Children: Perry Carson, Sallie Lavine, Carl Lee and Ardline); (f) Sarah Alice Rhea(1880-); (g) Elizabeth Breden Rhea (1883-), (married Henry A. Glover); (h) Flavia Converse Rhea (1885-), (married J. Monroe Broyles. Children: Sallie Kate, Nannie Bess, Lillian Ruth and Irvin Lewis); (i) Samuel Wood Rhea II (1889-), (married twice: First, Minola Lindenwood; Second, Margaret Harr. Children by second wife: Glena Leota and Kenneth D.) (3) John M. Rhea, a minister of the Presbyterian Church, married Elizabeth Smith, and had children: Carrie, May, Cora Lee, John W., William Plummer, Joseph C., Maggie, Pearl and John L.;(4)Harriet Rhea, who married Rev. L. M. Cartwright, and had children: Rhea, Laura, Joseph W., Fannie, Robert, Lizzie and Bettie; (5)Mary Rhea who married W. R. Smith, and had children: Mary (-1891) and Lydia; (6) Joseph Rhea (-1906), who married Addie Smith, and had children: Elizabeth, John, Ezra and Mary; (7) Maggie Rhea (-1906), who married W. R. Hull, and had children: John H. and Minnie L.

3 Margaret Rhea, married Wendell Sturm, and had children: (1) Nancy Strum, who married Fulton Hall; (2) Fannie Strum, who married ———— Cartwright; (3) Kate Strum, who married Samuel Hall.

4 Joseph S. Rhea, D. D. S., married Saraphina S. Williams, and had children: (1) Nannie A. Rhea; (2) Archie W. Rhea, M. D., who married Mary Smith, and had children: (a) Lucia Rhea, (married Charles Mims. Children: Myrtle, Madge, Carl, Myra, Mary, Edward and Drew); (b) Archie W. Rhea II, (married Mary Smith); (3) Rhoda J. Rhea, who married Capt. John Pierce, and had children: Nola, John, Ethel, Rhea, Henry and Rhoda; (4) Samuel W. Rhea, D. D. S., (1850-), who married Ella D. Carter and had children: Joseph Carter, James Wendell and Janie.

5 Jane Rhea, married John F. Preston (son of Rev. Rhea Preston), and had children: (1) Nannie Preston (-1906), who married John C. Summers, and had children: John Fairman P. who married Mary Elder, and had children: Von Moltke and Mary Elder; Lewis Alivia; Robert J.; Jennie

RHEA

Pinkney who married George T. Mitchell; Nannie A. Fannie Rhea; Sunshine Andrew; Von Moltke and John Carlisle; (2) Robert J.Preston, M. D., (-1906) who married Martha Sheffey, and had children: Eleanor Fairman, and Robert J. Preston II; (3) Sarah Ellen Preston, who married David Flournoy Bailey, and had children: Jane Rhea, Julia Flournoy, Nannie Louise, Martha Preston, Robert P. and Daniel Ella; (4) James Brainerd Preston, who married Hattie B. Tinsley, and had one chlid, Seaton Tinsley; (5) Samuel R. Preston, who married Ida Sulphen, and had children: John Fairman, Samuel Rhea, Mary Florence, James Brainerd, Robert James and Ida Sutphen; (6) Jennie Fairman Preston who married Thomas James Newman.

6 Ellen Rhea, married Washington Montgomery, and had one child, Nannie who married ——— Jones.

7 Elizabeth Rhea (-1876), married Thomas Crawford, and had children: John R. Crawford, M. D., who married Mary Bachman; Seraphine Crawford, who married Rev. William Crawford; Joseph R. Crawford, who married Cornelia Rogan; Samuel H. Crawford, who married Fannie Bachman; Nannie Crawford, who married James Darr

VIII JAMES RHEA

VIII James Rhea (1774-1885), son of Rev. Joseph Rhea and Elizabeth (McIlwaine) Rhea, married (1815) Elizabeth Snapp, (1833-1857), who married Rev. Alexander Blair, (2)

1 Margaret Rhea,
2 John Quintas Rhea,
3 James Rhea II,
4 Elizabeth Rhea,
5 Frances Rhea,
6 Samuel Rhea,
8 Theoderic Bland Rhea.

1 Margaret Rhea (1815-1898), married (1832) John Pemberton Snapp, and had children: (1) Elizabeth Rhea Snapp, (18331857), who married Rev. Alexander Blair, (2) Florence Diana Snapp (1835-1908), who married Paul Williams, and had children: Frederick Williams; Rebecca V. Williams who married ——— McNight; Elsie Williams; Florence Williams who married ——— Peak; Elizabeth Williams; (3) Vivolune M. Snapp (1839-), who married twice: First, Rev. Alexander Adams Blair; Second, ——— Brazelton. She had a daugther who married B. A. Williams; (4) Cynthia Lodoville Snapp (1844-1917), who married

Wendell Daniels Snapp, and had children: (a) Abram Lawrence Snapp (1870-), (married Flora C. Martin. Children: Tennie, John Wendell, Hawkins Sevier, Elmer E., and Elizabeth Rachel); (b) John Pemberton Snapp II (1872-), (married Julia Adah Shields. Children: Lecta Pemberton and Ivan Shields); (c) Hawkins Wendell Snapp (1874-), (married Laura Bayle); (d) Rhea McIlwaine Snapp (1880-), (married Dora Rowe. Children: Onell Rhea, Lester Wiseman, Alta Junetta and Janeva Florena); (5) John Raymond Snapp; (6) Tulen Velosso Snapp (1846-), (married Isaac Earnest); (7) Cicero DeForest Snapp.

2 John: Quintas Rhea (1818-1883), married twice First, (1843) Cynthia Williams; Second, Cornelia Catherine Williams, sister of first wife. Children by first wife: (1) Margaret Francis Rhea; (2) William Fort Rhea; (3) James Rhea; (4) John Rhea, who married ———, and had children: Joseph and Ivy; (5) Elizabeth Rhea. By second wife he had one child: (6) Annie Copeland Rhea, who married Thomas Humes Williams II, and had children: Copeland Rhea and Thomas Humes Williams III.

3 James Rhea II (1820-1891), married (1847) Louisa Smith, and had children: (1) Wright Smith Rhea (1848-1917), who married Jennie Rice, and had children: Walter Preston, Grover C., Wright Smith Rhea II and Alexander; (2) James Rhea III (1850-1917), who married Eugene Cochran, and had children: Willa (1890-) and Elizabeth (1899-); (3) Alexander Smith Rhea (1852-), who married Sallie Virginia Harris; (4) Bryant Whitfield Rhea (1854-), who married Sadie Roseberry, and had children: Raymond, Ruby, Wilber and Lesley; (5) Priscilla Ada Rhea (1856-1920), who married Dr. J. G. Ivey; (6) Florence Rhea (1859-1893), who married John C. Locke, and had children: Charles L. and David Rhea; (7) David M. Rhea (1870-), who married Margaret Haston, and had one child, Flora; (8) Robert Lee Rhea (1872-1909); (9) Thomas B. Rhea (1873), who married May Legg, and had one child, Robert L.

5 Frances Rhea (1826-1888), married James T. Preston, son of John Preston and Margaret Brown (Preston) Preston. Children under James T. Preston.

6 Samuel Rhea (1829-1902), married (1857) Lucy J. Williams (sister of Cynthia and Cornelia Williams), and had children: (1) James Copeland Rhea (1862-1889), who married Anna Louisa Owens, and had one child, James Copeland Rhea II; (2) Samuel Williams Rhea (1864-), who

RHEA

married Dora Welsh, and had one child, Frances; (3) Thomas Humes Rhea, who married Mrs. Latham, and had one child, Thomas Humes II; (4) Mary Lucy Rhea, who married Jacob W. Denny, and had children: Lucy who married Charles Worley, Maxie who married Wilbur Hanner, and Mary who married Scott Patton. (These sisters had a triple wedding); (5) Annie Elizabeth Rhea, who married William T. Enser; (6) Kate Rhea, who married John H. Anderson, and had children: George Rhea and Lucy; (7) Hal Henry Rhea: (8) Fannie McIlwaine Rhea.

7 Theodora Bland Rhea (1833-1868) married (1856) Frances Elizabeth Rhea (daughter of Robert P. Rhea and Sarah G. (Preston) Rhea, and had children: (1) Elizabeth Dysart Rhea (1857-), who married Alexander Anderson (son of Audley Anderson and Cornelia (Alexander) Anderson), and had one child: Audley Rhea Anderson II; (2) Robert Preston Rhea (1859-), who married Nannie Bell Gillespie, and had children: Joseph Earhart Rhea (1882-), who married Jeannette McNabb; Frank Bland Rhea (1884-), who married Nell Hill, and had one child, Sara Carolyn; Lillian Burts (1889-); Robert Preston Rhea II (1894-); (3) James Theoderic Rhea (1860-), who married Caroline Lea Riggs and had children: Clarence Ward (1890-), William Edwin (1894-), and James Theoderic Rhea II (1902-); (4) Sarah Gilleland Rhea (1862-), who married Frank Milton Adams, and had children: Frank Milton Adams II, (1888), who married Jessie Lee French; Leta Rhea Adams (1894-); Yancey Dailey Adams (1899-); (5) Fannie Rhea (1863-1864).

As a family the Rheas have followed principally the pursuits of ministers, lawyerr, doctors, farmers and merchants. There were several of the family who were stockholders and assisted in organizing the East Tennessee and Virginia Railroad (now the Southern).

Seldon Nelson, in his series of articles on the Rhea family says: "The descendants (of Rev Joseph Rhea) have occupied nearly every position in life . . . . The ministry seems to have been the chief calling in the professional line, but there have been some merchant princes among them . . . . There have been very few politicians among the descendants, and very few who have held office"

The family has always responded to the country's call in time of war. There were three who served in the Revolutionary War: Rev. Joseph Rhea as Chaplain, and his sons John and Matthew Rhea, as officers. At least four of the

NOTABLE SOUTHERN FAMILIES

Rhea family were in the War of 1812, of two were captured, Three served, and one died, in the Mexican War. About eighty members of the family served in the War Between the States, all but two being in the Confederate Army. Of these, two died from their wounds; five were killed in battle; and were made prisoners, or captured. Many were on staffs of officers or commanded companies, regiments or battalions. At least fourteen of the family served in the Spanish-American War. One entered the World War, during its first year, as a surgeon with the Canadian Contingent. More than sixty, most of whom were officers, served at the front and at least one was killed and several were wounded or gassed.

The following is partial list of those who have served:

WAR RECORD

Revolutionary War

Rev. Joseph Rhea. Chaplain with Colonel Christain's Cherokee Company.

I John Rhea, son of Rev. Joseph Rhea and Elizabeth (McIlwaine) Rhea, Ensign in the Fifth Virginia Regiment of Continentals. Took part in the battles of King's Mountain and Brandywine.

II Matthew Rhea, son of Rev. Joseph Rhea and Elizabeth (McIlwaine) Rhea. He served with distinction, as Major, in the Fifth Virginia Regiment of Continentals and took part in the battles of King's Mountain and Brandywine.

War of 1812

Joseph Matthew Rhea, son of Matthew Rhea and Jane (Preston) Rhea. Orderly sergeant. Was in Canada as a private secretary to an officer.

Robert Preston Rhea, son of Matthew Rhea and Jane (Preston) Rhea. Served under General Scott. Was captured by the British near Canadian Border and taken to Quebec, cast into prison, and put in irons.

Robert Rhea, son of William Rhea and Elizabeth (Lockhart) Rhea. Major in Allison's Regiment East Tennessee Militia.

Mexican War

Audley Anderson, son of Edward B. Anderson and Eleanor (Rhea) Anderson. Served under Colonel George R. McClellan. Was also in War Between the States.

RHEA

Dr. Samuel R. Anderson, son of Colonel Isaac Campbell Anderson and Margaret (Rhea) Anderson. Lieutenant in Shaver's Company, Colonel McClellan Commander. Was in two battles. Captured many prisoners and did not lose a man.

William Rhea, son of Joseph Campbell Rhea and Susan Rhea (Preston) Rhea. Graduated at West Point. Was First Lieutenant in United States Army. Died of measles at Monterey, Mexico, while in service, and was buried there.

War Between the States

Federal Army:

John A. Anderson, son of Joseph Anderson and Elizabeth (Rhea) Anderson. Served in First Tennessee Infantry. Died of hardships and exposure.

Alexander Dodson Rhea, son of John Rhea and Elizabeth (Dodson) Rhea. Enlisted as a private in First Tennessee Infantry. Promoted, in turn, to Lieutenant and Captain in First Tennessee Infantry, and later, Major in Eleventh Tennessee Cavalry.

Confederate Army:

Audley, Robert R., Samuel R. and William R. Anderson, sons of Edward B. Anderson and Eleanor (Rhea) Anderson: Audley Anderson (who had previously served in the Mexican War) served in Fourth Tennessee Cavalry: Was wounded seven times in Battle of Chattanooga (September 1863) and died of his wounds. Robert R. Anderson was in Company G. Sixtieth Tennessee Cavalry. Samuel R. Anderson served, first, in Third Tennessee Infantry; later transferred to Sixty-Third Tennessee Infantry. William R. Anderson was an enrolling officer and belonged to the Reserve Corps.

William and John Buchanan, sons of Ryburn Buchanan and Elizabeth (Rhea) Buchanan: William Buchanan served in Sixty-third Tennessee Infantry, and John Buchanan in the Western Army.

Samuel, Jonathan Waverly, John Lynn and Robert Luckey Bachman, sons of Jonathan Bachman and Fannie (Rhea) Bachman: Samuel Bachman enlisted in a Hawkins County, Tennessee, Company. Died of Fever at Cumberland Gap in early part of the war. Jonathan Waverly Bachman first enlisted to serve under General Cooke, in Virginia; later served as Lieutenant, Captain, and Chaplain in Sixtieth Tennessee Cavalry. John Lynn Bachman served in Thirty-seventh Virginia Infantry, Stonewall Jackson Division.

NOTABLE SOUTHERN FAMILIES

Robert Lucky Bachman served in Company G. Sixteenth Tennessee Cavalry.

Joseph R. and Samuel H Crawford, sons of Thomas Crawford and Elizabeth (Rhea) Crawford: Joseph R. Crawford was third sergeant, Company G. Nineteenth Tennessee Infantry, and, later, Captain of Company G., Sixteenth Tennessee Cavalry. Samuel H. Crawford served in Company F., Sixty-third Tennessee Infantry.

Robert P. Fickle, son of ―――― Fickle and Margaret (Rhea) Fickle. Was First Lieutenant of Reserve Corps.

Nicholas, Samuel R., Isaac and Powell Fain, sons of General Richard Fain and Eliza (Anderson) Fain. Nicholas, Samuel., and Isaac Fain served in Sixty-third Tennessee Infantry, and Powell Fain in Sixtieth Tennessee Cavalry.

William D. and Abraham L. Gammon, sons of William Gammon and Rebecca (Anderson) Gammon. William D. Gammon was First Lieutenant, Company C., Nineteenth Tennessee Infantry. Abraham L. Gammon was in Reserve Corps and served in latter part of war.

Samuel R. Gammon, son of Captain Abraham L. Gammon and Nancy (Anderson) Gammon. Captain of Hawkins County Company, Tennessee.

William Rhea Irvin, son of Montgomery Irvin and Frances (Rhea) Irvin.

Cornelius E. Lucky, son of Judge Seth J. W. Lucky and Sarah (Rhea) Lucky. Served in Company K., Sixtieth Tennessee Infantry.

Samuel Alexander Lynn, son of John Lynn and Nancy (Rhea) Lynn.

Harry Hill McAlister, son of William King McAlister and Fannie Rhea (Anderson) McAlister. Commissary Department of Confederate States Army.

Isaac Anderson Newland, son of Joseph Newland and Rebecca (Anderson) Newland. Second Corporal, Company B., Fourth Tennessee Battalion. Was captured at Woodbury.

Thomas and James T. Preston, sons of Colonel John Preston and Margaret Brown (Preston) Preston: Thomas Preston was killed in Battle of Shiloh. James T. Preston served in Militia of Virginia.

Robert J. Preston, son of John F. Preston and Jane (Rhea) Preston. Officer in a Virginia Regiment.

John H. and James T. Rhea, sons of James B. Rhea and Elizabeth (Carter) Rhea: John H. Rhea First Corporal, Company G., Nineteenth Tennessee Infantry. Wounded at

RHEA

Chickamauga (1863) and died from his wounds. James T. Rhea was in Tennessee Reserve Corps.

Matthew, John Preston and Robert Campbell Rhea, sons of Robert Preston Rhea and Nancy (Davidson) Rhea. Matthew Rhea served in Company F., Sixty-third Tennessee Infantry. John Preston Rhea was a sergeant in Reserve Corps.

William R. and John A. Rhea, sons of William Rhea and Mary (Rockhold) Rhea. William R. Rhea served in Company G., Nineteenth Tennessee Infantry. Lost a leg at Battle of Resacca, Georgia. John A. Rhea served in Tennessee Reserve Corps.

Samuel Wood Rhea, son of John Nancy Rhea and Ruth M. (Rockhold) Rhea. Served in Company F., Sixty-third Tennessee Infantry.

William Abram and Matthew Rhea, sons of John Rhea and Elizabeth (Rhea) Rhea. William Abram Rhea served in the Fifth Tennessee Cavalry, Company H. Matthew Rhea served in Company G., Fifth Tennessee Regiment.

Walter Preston Rhea, son of Joseph Matthew Rhea and Catherine (Myers) Rhea, served as First Lieutenant in Company F., Sixty-third Tennessee Infantry.

Matthew Rhea VI, Abram Rhea and Walter Preston Rhea, sons of Matthew Rhea V and Mary (Looney) Rhea: Matthew Rhea VI was First Lieutenant, Company A., of a Tennessee Regiment. Was carrying the sword which had belonged to his grandfather, Matthew Rhea IV, when captured, at Belmont, Missouri. This he refused to surrender and was killed. Abram Rhea served in Company B., Thirteenth Tennessee Infantry. Walter Preston Rhea was Captain, Fourth Tennessee Cavalry.

James C., John W. and William Alexander Rhea, sons of Joseph Rhea and Emaline M. (Alexander) Rhea. All were in Company D., Sixth Texas Cavalry. William A., Captain; John W., Orderly Sergeant. All were wounded in Battle of Corinth. John W. was taken prisoner and carried to a Federal Hospital where he died of his wounds.

Robert Bruce Rhea, son of Matthew Rhea and Margaret (Breeden) Rhea, was in Reserve Corps.

Joseph and Robert James, son of Robert P. Rhea and Sarah G. (Preston) Rhea: Both served in Company G., Nineteenth Tennessee Infantry. Robert James Rhea was wounded, in battle, near Atlanta, Georgia, and died from his wounds.

John Lynn, Joseph Brainerd, James Alexander, Robert

Morrison and William Lynn Rhea, sons of Samuel and Martha (Lynn) Rhea: John Lynn Rhea served in Company G., Nineteenth Tennessee Cavalry. James Alexander Rhea was First Lieutenant, Company G., Nineteenth Tennessee Infantry; later, Sixtieth Tennessee Regiment; was elected Major and, afterwards, Lieutenant Colonel. Was wounded and captured by Federals and recaptured by his own men. Robert Morrison Rhea was Orderly Sergeant in Company F, Sixty-third Tennessee Infantry. William Lynn Rhea was in Reserve Corps of Tennessee.

James David Rhea, son of Joseph Campbell Rhea and Catherine (Reynolds) Rhea, was Captain, Company G., Third Tennessee Regiment. "Captain James David Rhea was captured at Fort Donaldson, and carried prisoner to Camp Chase from which he escaped". (Confederate Veteran, Feb. 1914).

John Preston Sheffey, son of Judge James White Sheffey and Eleanor Fairman (Preston) Sheffey, was Captain of a Virginia Company.

James Lowry White II, Dr. William Young Conn White and Preston John White, sons of James Lowry White and Margaret Rhea (Preston) White: James Lowry White II was Captain of Company K, Thirty-seventh Virginia Infantry, in Stonewall Jackson's Brigade. Dr. William Young Conn White was Captain in Company B, Thirty-seventh Infantry, Virginia.

Spanish American

William Buchanan II, son of William Buchanan and Addie (Hill) Buchanan, was Sergeant, Company I, Sixth U. S. Volunteers, Immunes.

James R. Fain, son of John H. Fain and Fannie A. (Rhea) Fain, was Second Lieutenant of Engineers, Volunteers, U. S. Regiment.

Samuel Edward Lynn, son of James Lynn and Sarah (Rogan) Lynn, was First Lieutenant, Company F, Third Tennessee Infantry.

Perry Lynn, son of James Lynn and Sarah (Rogan) Lynn, was Sergeant, Company K, Third Tennessee Volunteers, Infantry.

Samuel Dysart McAlister, son of Judge William K. McAlister II and Laura Brown (Dortch) McAlister, was First Lieutenant, Company G, Fourth Tennessee Infantry.

William A. Rhea son of John A. Rhea and Lora (Abernathy) Rhea, served in Third Tennessee Infantry.

RHEA

Francis Rodgers Rhea, son of Alexander Dodson Rhea and Mattie (Hatchet) Rhea, was Corporal, Company L, Second Texas Volunteer Infantry. While encamped, in Florida, he suffered a severe attack of typhoid fever.

Samuel Rhea Rodgers, son of Judge Samuel Andrew Rodgers and Sarah Elizabeth (Rhea Rodgers. Was Second Lieutenant, Company B, Fourth Tennessee Infantry. Served in Cuba.

WORLD WAR

Aviation

Robert Lee Burch II, son of Robert Lee Burch and Rachel C. (McAlister) Burch. Student in Marine Aviation Corps. When volunteered was under twenty years of age.

Earnest Dooley, son of I. Earnest Dooley and Mary (Andes) Dooely. Lieutenant. Served overseas.

Marshall Franklin Henly, son of Samel O. Henly and (Anderson Henly. Student in Samp.

McDowell Lyon, son of J. B. Lyon and Lizzie (McDowell) Lyon. Served as instructor in Aviation.

Robert Rhea Mahoney, son of Oscar E. Mahoney and Emma (Anderson) Mahoney. Student at Camp Sarfley, which was an aerial gunnery school.

Nathan Bachman Preston, son of Samuel Rhea Preston and Ida (Sutphen) Preston. Clerical of Aviation Corps. Served Overseas.

Medicals

William Anderson, son of Charles Anderson and Mary (Bachman) Anderson.

James Sumpter Anderson, son of Edgar Anderson and Beulah (Sumpter) Anderson. Was at Camp Gordon in hospital work and was returned to Vanderbilt University to finish his medical corse.

Malcom Campbell, M. D., son of Dr. Edward M. Campbell and Ellen Sheffey (White) Campbell. Captain. First served for one year on the Local Draft Board in New York City; later was in active service at Camp Syracuse. During the influenza epidemic the Government took over Crouse-Irving Hospital, in Syracuse, and he was put at the head of it, until transferred to Fort Ethan Allen where he was discharged from service.

Lindsley Newland, M. D., son of Robert Rhea Newland and Bettie (Wolford) Newland. Served overseas in Ambulance Corps, Rainbow Divison.

NOTABLE SOUTHERN FAMILIES

Don Preston, M. D., son of Colonel William Peters and Margaret (Sheffey) Peters. Served overseas.

John Preston IV, M. D., son of James T. Preston and Frances (Rhea) Preston. Was in Volunteer Medical Service Corps, in Texas.

Robert Sheffey, M. D., son Dr. Robert J. Preston and Martha (Sheffey) Preston.

Lawrence Rhea, M. D., son of William A. Rhea and Ella (Foot) Rhea. Offered his services to the British Government at the commencement of the World War. He was attached to the McGill Medical Staff as Lietenant, and sailed for France with the Second Canadian Contingent, in 1915. Pending the completion of the Canadian General Hospital, No. 3, at Boulogne, he was stationed in London as purchasing agent for equipment, and, on its completion, he assumed charge if its pathological work. He was promoted to Major, in 1916. His health failing, from over work., he was sent to England for complete rest but did not recuperate sufficiently to resume active duty and was invalided to Canada in 1918. Major Rhea received many honors while in England and France. He was a member of he committee pppointed by the British Government to inspect all Military hospitals in France. And was selected to personally conduct the Queen of England on her inspection of hispitals.

Edward Randolph Sumpter, son of Edward Randolph Sumpter and Minnie (Wade) Sumpter. Served overseas in Ambulence Corps No 55. Was on the Loraine Sector, bringing wounded from the front, when his amublance was blawn up and he escaped with slight wounds.

Navys

Charles Linwood Adams, son of W. H. Adams and Eleanor Lynn (Rhea) Adams.

William King Biddle son of Robert Biddle and Elizabeth A. (McAlister) Biddle. Lieutenant Commander of Inspecton office U. S. Navy Yard, Boston.

Lloyd William Boggs, son of William H. Boggs and Eliza Jane (Crowder) Boggs. Machinist First Class.

Henry Hamilton, son of George Hamilton and Bettie Dycart (Lucky) Hamilton.

Edward Alexander Magill, son of William L. Magil and Mary (Gaines) Magill. Entered Naval service December, 1917; was commissioned Ensign, April 1918, and sent to Annapolis for further training, from there was ordered to U. S. S. South Dakota, a battleship doing convoy duty,

where he remained until the Armistice was signed.
Army:
Brainerd Adams, son of W. H. Adams and Eleanor (Rhea) Adams.
John Waverly Anderson, son of Charles Anderson and Mary (Bachman) Anderson. Second Lieutenant in Regular Army.
Paul Fain Anderson, son of William S. Anderson and Ella (Spurgeon) Anderson. Served overseas.
Joseph S. Bachman II, son of Dr. Joseph S. Bachman and Hattie A. (Brewer) Bachman. Died in Camp of Influenza.
William Lasbrooke Baldwin, son of ——— Baldwin and Jennie (Carr) Baldwin. In Engineering Corps.
Horen Hoge Brewer, son of John Alf Brewer and Willie Sue (Hoge) Brewer. Sergeant First Class. In Quartermasters Department, at Camp Gordon, Georgia.
William Phillip Brewer II, son of John Alf Brewer and Willie Sue (Hoge) Brewer. Served overseas, Company A, 356th Infantry, 89th Division.
James Carlock Brewer son of James King Brewer and Olive (Carlock) Brewer. Lieutenant. Was killed in Battle of Bellau Woods. Received two Citations for bravery.
Morgan William Brown VII, son of Morgan William Brown VI, and Fannie R. (McAlister) Brown. Volunteered.
Hill McAlister Burch, son of Robert Lee Burch and Rachel C. (McAlister) Burch. Was in S. A. T. C.
John Jonett Campbell, son of Frank Campbell and Sallie Jonett. Mechanical Department. Camp Mabry.
Clifton Carson, son of Sturm W. Carson and Margaret (Buchanan) Carson. Sergeant First Class. Served in Company E, 302 Stevedore Infantry.
Hugh Brewer Cowan, son of Rev. James Chalmers Cowan and Margaret D. (Brewer) Cowan. Served overseas.
Benjamin Mills Crenshaw II, son of Benjamin Mills Crenshaw and Mary Magadelene (White) Crenshaw. Captain. Served in France; was wounded and gassed. He remained in the Army after the Armistice was signed.
William Rhea Dabney, son of William Presley Dabney and Annie (Rhea) Dabney. Captain.
Robert N. Dosser II, son of Robert N. Dosser and Martha E. (Fain) Dosser.
Foster Rhea Dulles, son of William Dulles and Sophia (Rhea) Dulles.
James Doggett Earnest, son of Nicholas P. Earnest and Lida (Doggett) Earnest. Student in Camp.

NOTABLE SOUTHERN FAMILIES

Carl, Joseph and William Earnest, sons of William A. Earnest and Florence (Donnelly) Earnest. All served overseas, and were in several battles.

Joseph Gibson Erwin, son of James Erwin and Margaretta (McAlister) Erwin. Corporal in Battery D, 115th Field Artillery. Served overseas.

Robert Davidson Erwin, son of James Erwin and Margaretts (McAlister) Erwin. Home guard; too young to go to France, was seventeen years of age.

Robert Rogan and Richard Fain, sons of G. Powell and Sallie E. (Fain) Fain.

Worley W. Fain, son of John Mitchell Fain and Gertrude (Worley) Fain. First Lieutenant in Virginia Coast Artillery.

James Rhea Fain, son of John Mitchell Fain and Gertrude (Worley) Fain. Lieutenant. Was sent by the Government to teach in a Military School in South Carolina.

Samuel Rhea Gammon, son of William F. Gammon, of Bristol, Tennessee. Lieutenant.

Joseph Dooley Hoss, son of Wright Hoss and Rebecca (Dooley) Hoss. Served overseas.

John Hyde, son of Rev. Charles R. Hyde and Annie Rhea (Bachman) Hyde.

Samuel Lee King II, son of Samuel Lee King and Annie (Phipps) King. Second Lieutenant. After going overseas was loaned to Great Brittain; was assigned to Twenty-first London Rifles. Was in battle.

Edward Campbell Lenoir, son of Henry Ramsey Lenoir and Bessie (Campbell) Lenoir. Sergeant in 105th Trench Mortar Battery, a unit of the Thirtieth Division (Old Hicory Division). Served in France. His unit was sent to the front with another division where they were used as shock troops when not using their trench mortars. Was at the front when the Armistice was signed; was sent into Luxemburg as part of the Army of Occupation. After arriving in France he was offered an opportunity of going into an Officers Training School but preferred going to the front.

David Rhea Locke, son of John C. Locke and Florence (Rhea) Locke.

Robert Anderson Lowery, son of John Taylor Lowery and Amanda (Anderson) Lowery. Corporal in Battery A, Thirty-sixth Division of 133rd Field Artillery. Served overseas. While enroute to France his transport had a battle with submarines.

RHEA

John Charles Moore II, son of John Charles Moore and Sarah J. (Bachman) Moore. In Radio Service.

Nathan T. Moore, son of John Charles Moore and Sarah J. (Bachman) Moore. In Artillery.

Oscar E. Mahoney II, son of Oscar E. Mahoney and Emily Jane (Anderson) Mahoney. Was in S. A. T. C.

Harry Hill McAlister III, son of Harry Hill McAlister II and Maude (Davidson) McAlisaer. Sergeant in Q. M. C. Camp Dix.

Iro Burns McAlister son of Harry Hill McAlister II and Maude (Davidson) McAlister. Sergeant in 107th Supply Train. Served overseas. Was on the ill fated Tuscania when it went down off the north coast of Ireland.

Vance Newland, son of Samuel A. Newland and Helen (Brown) Newland. Served overseas.

Joseph James Pence, son of Elkana Pence and Fanny A. (Newland) Pence.

Robert White Preston, son of Dr. John Preston IV and Annie Lewis (White) Preston. Served in Quartermasters Department, Camp McArthur, Texas.

Seaton Tinsley Preston, son of James B. Preston and Hattie B. (Tinsley)) Preston. Lieutenant. Served overseas.

James Dysart Rhea, son of James T. Rhea and Frances Bell (Rhea) Rhea. Captain. Served overseas in the Renting, Requisition and Claims branch of the Supply Department.

Lawrence Herndon Rhea, son of William Alexander Rhea II and Mary (Herndon) Rhea. Second Lieutenant in Coast Artillery. Was under orders to sail when Armistice was signed.

Paul D. Robertson, son of Rev. George E. Robertson and Mattie (Earnest) Robertson. Served overseas.

Raymond, Wilber and Lesley Rhea, sons of Bryant W. Rhea and Sadie (Roseberry) Rhea.

McDonald Campbell Youmans, son of Lawrence W. Youmans and Margaret P. (Campbell) Youmans. Entered as private, his Second Lieutenant commission reached him just as the Armistice was signed.

Note. To William Lynn and Mary Rhea Sumpter, the compiler of this article is indebted for the early data given here, and for other generous assistance.

SHELBY

The first Shelby in America, said to have come from Glammorganshire, in Wales, was "Evan Dhu Shelby married Catherine Davies". This couple came to America about 1730 and settled in Prince George County (afterwards Frederick County, Maryland), near Hagerstown, in what is now Washington County, Maryland, had the following children:

I Maj. Moses Shelby, born in Wales, 1718, died Mecklenburg County, North Carolina; married Isabel ―――――, born in Maryland, died after 1780.

II Brig.-Gen Evan Shelby, born Wales, 1720, died King's Meadow, December 4, 1794; married first, Letitia Coxe, daughter of David Coxe of Maryland, born Maryland 1723, died September 6, 1777, and is buried at Charlottesville, Virginia; married second, Mrs. Isabella Elliott, widow of James Elliott, in the state of Franklin (now Washington County, Tennessee).

III Thomas Shelby, born about 1725, died Mecklenburg County, North Carolina, about 1776; married ―――――.

IV Eleanor Shelby married John Polk in North Carolina, born Carlisle, Pennsylvania, about 1740, died Tennessee.

V John Shelby married Louisa Looney.

VI Mary Sheby, born 1734, died 1813; married Adam Alexander, born in Pennsylvania, 1728, died 11-13-1798.

VII Rees Shelby.

VIII ―――――, a daughter who married Joseph Chaplain.

The Shelbys are identified with the early history of Tennessee and Kentucky, and they share with the Seviers and the Isbells, the honor of having the greatest number or representatives in the Battle of King's Mountain. There

NOTABLE SOUTHERN FAMILIES

were seven Seviers, six Isbells and six Shelbys. By a peculiar coincidence also, the youngest soldiers in that famous Battle were of these families: James Sevier, aged sixteen, William Isbell aged fifteen, and David Shelby aged seventeen.

I MOSES SHELBY

Moses Shelby, son of Evan Dhu Shelby and Catherine Davies Shelby, joined the great tide of Southern emigration, and settled on Caldwell's Creek, in the Eastern part of Mecklenburg County (now Cabarrus County) North Carolina, in 1760. His will is on record in Mecklenburg County. Some think he was married twice as he mentions in his will "wife and six children". His children were:

1 Thomas Shelby, who married Sarah Helms.
2 Mary Shelby, born 1746, died 1822, married 1768 Oliver Wiley.
3 Evan Shelby married Susan Polk Alexander.
4 Moses Shelby, married ————.
5 Eleanor Shelby, married ———— Caruthers.
4 Margaret Shelby, born 1772, died 1838; married Oliver Harris, born 1763, died 1833.
7 Rachel Shelby.
8 William Shelby.
9 John Shelby.
10 Isabella Shelby.
11 Catherine Shelby.

Children of Thomas Shelby and Sarah Helms:

The only known child was Sarah Ellen Shelby, married James McLarty, born in Mecklenburg County, North Carolina, and died in Douglas County, Georgia. The only known child of Sarah Ellen Shelby McLarty was Catherine McLarty, married Charles Shelby Polk (their Shelby grandfathers were first cousins). She was born in Mecklenburg County, North Carolina, in 1817, died in Douglas County, Georgia, in 1905.

Children of Evan Shelby and Susan Alexander:

The only known child was Mary Shelby, married Thomas Polk about 1786, died about 1842.

This couple had issue:

(1) Shelby Polk, married Winnifred Colburn. He emigrated to Tennessee in 1813 and died about 1847, leaving issue: Esther; Headley; Thomas; William; Shelby; Mary; Eliza.

SHELBY

(2) Andrew Marshall Polk, married first to Miss Carraway, had issue: Thomas J.; James K.; married second, to Lorena Autery, had issue: L. L. Polk, of Raleigh, North Carolina.

(3) Thomas Shelby Polk, Fourth, married Sarah Brooks. Had issue: William; Andrew; Marshall. The latter two sons were killed in the Confederate service.

(4) Jobe Polk, died unmarried.

(5) Hannah Polk, married first, Mr. Sides, issue: Hannah; second, Adam Long, issue: Thomas; Henry; Adam and several daughters.

(6) Dicey Polk, married Francis Colburn; emigrated to Tennessee.

(7) Patsy Polk, married William Crittenden; emigrated to Tennessee.

(8 Mary Polk, married Aaron Little. She died in 1862 leaving ten chldren.

(9) Elizabeth Polk, married Richmond McManus.

Descendants of Mary Shelby and Oliver Wiley

Evan Shelby Wiley, born 1783, died 1825, married in 1804 Mary McCaleb, (born 1786, died 1840). He emigrated to Alabama, and was a farmer and miller near Courtland. He had a son, James McCaleb Wiley, born Cabarrus County, North Carolina, March 12th, 1806, died Troy, Alabama, 1878. He married first, April 19th, 1827, Elizabeth Duckworth. Married second, November 15th, 1843, Cornelia Appling. Married third, January 3rd, 1875, Rebecca Covington Wales. Issue by first wife: Rhydonia Wiley, James Horatio Wiley, Thomas Walter Wiley, and Henry Clay Wiley. Henry Clay Wiley, was born at Clayton, Alabama, on October 4th, 1840, and resided at Troy, Alabama. He married first, in 1861, Henrietta Worthy. Issue by first wife, Henrietta Worthy Wiley, Lizzie, Rhydonia Ophelia. Henry Clay Wiley married second, Ophelia Worthy, sister of his first wife, and had issue: Henrietta, Walter and Harry. Children of James McCaleb Wiley, and Cornelia Appling Wiley: (1) Ariosoto Appling Wiley, born at Clayton, Alabama, November 6th, 1848, died at Hot Springs, Virginia, June 17th, 1908, married Mattie A. Noble at Montgomery, Alabama, November 6th, 1877, and had issue: Noble James Wiley of the United States Army. (2) Oliver Cicero Wiley, born at Troy, Alabama, January 30th, 1851, died Troy, Alabama, October 18th, 1917; married at Troy, June 25th, 1874, Augusta Murphy, and had issue:

Oliver Lee Wiley, married Mary Graham McKellar. James McCaleb Wiley, married Mary Adelaide Bailey. Lois Wiley. married Marshall Bibb Folmer, Julia Lamar Wiley, married James T. Brantley.

II BRIG.-GEN. EVAN SHELBY

Evan Shelby, son of Evan Dhu Shelby and Catherine Davies Shelby, was born in Wales in 1720 and died in King's Meadow, now Bristol, December 4, 1794. He married first, Letitia Coxe, daughter of David Coxe of Maryland, who was born in 1723 in Maryland and died September 6, 1777, and is buried in Charlottesville, Virginia. He married second, Mrs. Isabella Elliott in the State of Franklin, now Washington County, Tennessee.

There is not much mention made of Gen. Evan Shelby's second marriage, but the following paper was found among the papers of Gov. Isaac Shelby, who was his father's executor:

"I now certify, to whom it may concern, that I performed the ceremony of marriage between the late Gen. Evan Shelby and Isabella Elliott (widow of James Elliott), when I acted as one of the associate Judges of the assumed state of Franklin.

"Given under my hand, this 14th day of Nov., 1779.

"Signed: Jno. Anderson

"Witness: J. A. Thompson, J. Shelby".

A daughter, name unmentioned, was given land on account of this certificate.

Brig.-Gen. Shelby was first appointed Captain of a Company of Rangers in the French and Indian Wars. He was Captain in the Provincial Army and personal friend of Gen. Washington, being with him at Great Meadows and Ft. Necessity. He was also in Braddock's expedition. Led the advance of the Army under Forbes, which took Ft. Duquesne in 1758.

In early life he was interested in the fur trade in Mechilmacinack, on the Great Lakes.

In 1756 he was a resident of Maryland and Potomac County. In 1772 emigrated to Fincastle County, Virginia. In 1774 he commanded a Company under Dunmore and Lewis against the Indians. He served at Point Pleasant. In 1776 he was appointed by Gov. Henry of Vir-

SHELBY

ginia as Major in the army of Col. Christian against the Cherokees. In 1777 he was appointed Colonel of a Sundry garrison exposed on frontiers of Virginia. In 1779 he led an expedition of 2000 men against the Chickamauga Indians, for which service he was thanked by the Continental Congress. Later he was appointed Brigadier General in the State Militia.

After the French and Indian wars he moved his family from Maryland to Salem, on the Yadkin River, in North Carolina, and in 1765 removed to Southeast Virginia. It was supposed at that time to be in Virginia, but the survey of 1779 showed his land to be in North Carolina. This property was in what is now Sullivan County, Tennessee, and he called it "Sapling Grove". He also owned land in Burke's Garden Farm, Tazewell County, Virginia. Brig.-Gen. Shelby is buried at Bristol, Virginia.

His descendants have as a maternal ancestor, Opechancanoe, said to be a brother of Powhaton, the Indian Chief. Powhatan died in 1618 and was succeeded by Opetchapan, who was old and was deposed by Openchancanoe. The tradition in the time of Beverly was that Openchancanoe was not the real brother of Powhatan but a stranger from Mexico or some South-western county. He made his last attack on the white people and was killed April 14th, 1644, when nearly one hundred years old. He had a granddaughter, Nicketti, whose daughter married Nathaniel Davis in 1618. This couple had a son, Robert Davis, who was the grandfather of Letitia Coxe, wife of Brig.-Gen. Shelby.

Brig.-Gen. Shelby and Letitia Coxe Shelby had the following children:

(1) Susannah Shelby, born 1746, died young.
(2) John Shelby, born 1748, married Elizabeth Pile.
(3) Isaac Shelby, married Susannah Hart. He was born in Maryland in 1750, married in Maryland in 1783, died in Kentucky, July 18, 1826.
(4) Evan Shelby born in 1754 in Maryland, was killed by Indians, January 15, 1793. He married his first cousin, Catherine Shelby, daughter of his uncle, John Shelby.
(5) Moses Shelby, marred Elizabeth Neil.
(6) James Shelby, killed by Indians in Lincoln County, Kentucky, in 1786.
(7) Catherine Shelby married Captain James A. Thompson, of Washington County, Virginia.
(8) Sarah Shelby, married Ephraim McDowell.
(9) Rachel Shelby, married Michael Leggett.

NOTABLE SOUTHERN FAMILIES

(2) *John Shelby*

John Shelby married Elizabeth Pile.

(3) *Isaac Shelby*

Isaac Shelby, of Maryland, born 1750, died 1820, married Susanna Hart, 1783 (born 1763, died 1826).

Isaac Shelby was born in Hagerstown, Maryland, December 11th, 1750. At the age of twenty he was elected deputy sheriff of Frederick County, Maryland, but moved in 1771 to the present site of Bristol, Tennessee.

His first essay at arms was as Lieutenant in a Company commanded by his father in the Battle at the mouth of Kehnawa, on the Ohio River. He came South and settled in Washington County. When the line was surveyed between North Carolina and Virginia, it placed him in North Carolina, which circumstance induced Gov. Caswell to appoint him Colonel of Militia of Sullivan County (afterward Tennessee). He served as a member of the North Carolina House of Commons, then moved to Kentucky and was a member of the Constitutional Convention in that state and afterwards, was elected first Governor of Kentucky. He gave the signal for the attack on Ferguson at King's Mountain and was one of the heroes of that celebrated battle. In 1782 he returned to Boonsville, Kentucky, and married in 1783, Susanna Hart. Was elected member of the Convention in Kentucky to obtain separation from Virginia. In the War of 1812 he commanded twelve Kentucky regiments in the Battle of the Thames. Died in Lincoln County, July 18th, 1826.

The children of Gov. Isaac Shelby and Susannah Hart Shelby were:

1. James, married Mary Pindell.
2. Sarah, married Ephraim McDowell.
3. Evan, married Nancy Warren.
4. Thomas Hart, married first, Mary McDowell; second, Mary Bullock.
5. Susannah.
6. Nancy, married Samuel K. Nelson.
7. Isaac, married Maria Warren.
8. John, died unmarried.
9. Letitia, married Col. Charles Stewart Todd.
10. Catherine, died young.
11. Alfred, married Virginia Hart.

A long and distinguished line comes through these children of Governor Isaac Shelby and Susannah Hart Shelby.

SHELBY

4 Evan Shelby

Evan Shelby, son of Evan Shelby and Letitia Coxe Shelby was a famous soldier like his father; served with him in Chickamauga campaign in 1779 and took conspicuous part in the Battle of King's Mountain at which he was Major of his brother Isaac's regiment. When Gov. Isaac Shelby came to Cumberland as Commissioner of bounty lands and pre-emptions in 1783, this Evan came with him and settled in West Fork of Red River, some distance to the West of Clarkesville, Tennessee. As he was returning on the 18th of January, 1793, from the Falls of the Ohio, in a large canoe laden with salt and other supplies, he was fired upon and killed by a party of Indians near the mouth of Cassey's Creek, in Trigg County, Kentucky. His gun, sword and other property were taken by the Indians. He married his first cousin, Catherine Shelby, and they had only two children, Isaac and Priscilla, who married Mr. Jeffries.

(Another authority gives the two children as Priscilla and Eleanor, the latter married to William Caldwell, junior).

After he was killed these children were reared by Maj. Smith in the Fort. A monument is erected to Evan Shelby at Knoxville, Tenn. There is a tradition in the family that he and his wife separated. Priscilla Shelby married in Tennessee, James Jeffries, and went to Mississippi, a widow with several children, as did her brother, Isaac. A granddaughter of Mrs. Jeffries, Mrs. Priscilla Metcalf, who lived with her grandmother, is still living, aged 87, at Metcalf, Mssissippi. The descendants of this brother and sister live in Mississippi.

The honor of receiving the Sword from DePeyster at the end of the Battle of King's Mountain is claimed for this Evan Shelby.

5 Moses Shelby

Moses Shelby, son of Brig.-Gen. Evan Shelby inherited also the military and patriotic spirit of his father. He served also with him in the Chickamauga campaign in 1779 and was wounded at King's Mountain, for Gov. Isaac Shelby, himself, says so in a letter (now in print), to John J. Crittenden, stating that Moses lay near King's Mountain three months recovering from a wound in the thigh. He was a Captain in the regiment commanded by Isaac Shelby,

NOTABLE SOUTHERN FAMILIES

at King's Mountain; was the trusted messenger between his brother Isaac and Col. Campbell, two of the leaders in the campaign against Col. Ferguson. He moved from Clarkesville to New Madrid, Missouri, where he died, September 17, 1828. Authentic records seem to credit him with two wives. One was Miss Renfro, and another record states he married Elizabeth Neal, who was born April 1, 1763, and died September 19, 1897.

6 James Shelby

James Shelby, son of Brig.-Gen. Shelby commanded a company during the whole of Col. Christian's campaign in 1776; was a Captain with Gen. George Clark, and was killed by the Indians in Lincoln County, Kentucky, in 1786.

9 Rachel Shelby

Rachel Shelby, daughter of Evan Shelby and Letitia Coxe, married Michael Leggett. Their children were:

1 Rachel Leggett, who married Thomas McCrory. They had, Sally McCrory, married Thomas Hiter, and Charles S. McCrory, married Martha Douglas Caldwell.

Eleanor Shelby

Eleanor Shelby was married in Mecklenburg, North Carolina, to John Polk, brother of Captain Charles Polk (who also married an Eleanor Shelby, daughter of Thomas Shelby, son of Evan Dhu Shelby). John Polk was a Captain during the Revolution and in his late years moved to Tennessee, where he died. It is thought that his wife died also in Tennessee. She was given land in Southwest Virginia as a daughter of General Evan Shelby. As her name is not given in the list of General Shelby's children by his first wife it is probable that she is the daughter by the second marriage to Isabella Elliott. Her children were:

(1) Charles Polk, married Margaret Baxter. Charles Polk served in the Revolution and was called "Civil Charlie" Polk. Had issue: John; Jennie; Andrew; William; Charles; Cynthia; Isaac; Alfred. He died in San Augustine County, Texas, in 1846-47. Born January 18th, 1760.

(2) Taylor Polk, married Jency Walker; had issue: Benjamin; Taylor; James; Cumberland; William Walker; Alfred; Warnell. Taylor Polk emigrated to Arkansas.

(3) ―――――――.

(4) John A. Polk, born in Charlotte, North Carolina, 1762,

SHELBY

died in Leon County, Texas, 1849; married Elizabeth Oldson about 1789. He was in the Revolution under his father. Had issue: Benjamin D. A.; Nancy; Evan; Robert; Elizabeth; John (Jackie); Armstead; all born in Tennessee. The son Evan Shelby Polk left son Judge John Polk, who had a daughter Jane, who married ———— Larvy. Evan Shelby Polk also had a son named Charles Polk, who died in Madison County, Arkansas, in 1919, leaving a son, Elmer Polk.

III THOMAS SHELBY

Thomas Shelby, son of Evan Dhu Shelby and Catherine Davies Shelby, settled on Caldwell's Creek in the Eastern part of Mecklenburg County, North Carolina, now evidently Cabarrus County, in 1760. He died at the beginning of the Revolution and left four sons, one was named Thomas Shelby, and was a private in Captain Charles Polk's Company, in 1776. His children were:

(1) Jacob Shelby, untraced; lived in Union County, North Carolina from 1787 to 1790; was in the first United States census from Fayette district, Anson County, North Carolina.

(2) Thomas Shelby, married ————. United States census for 1790 from Fayette district, Anson County, North Carolina, about 1785. She was left a widow in 1829 Charles Polk, junior, born in Mecklenburg County, North Carolina. Only known issue: Eleanor Shelby, married and emigrated to (now) Douglas County, Georgia, in 1835 with her four children. Died in 1852 in Campbell (now Douglas) County, Georgia; buried in the Watson grave yard.

(3) A son unknown.
(4) A son unknown.

V JOHN SHELBY

John Shelby, son of Evan Dhu Shelby and Catherine Davis Shelby, served with his brother, Brig.-Gen. Shelby, at the Battle of King's Mountain. He and Louisa Looney Shelby had issue: (1) John Shelby, junior, married Elizabeth Brigham; (2) David Shelby born about 1763 in Virginia, married Sarah Bledsoe; (3) Evan Shelby; (4) Thomas Shelby; (5) Isaac Shelby; (6) Louisa Shelby, married William McCrab; (7) Catherine Shelby, married Evan Shelby III; her cousin.

NOTABLE SOUTHERN FAMILIES

David Shelby

David Shelby, son of John Shelby and Louisa Looney, was born about 1763 in Virginia. He was the ancestor of a family which has been prominent in America and England. David Shelby was also a King's Mountain hero though he was only a lad of seventeen. He served in Isaac Shelby's Regiment. He moved to Sumner County, Tennessee, and was Clerk of the Court until his death in 1822.

He married Sarah Bledsoe, daughter of Anthony Bledsoe. George Bledsoe was the first of the Bledsoe line traced in America. He lived in Northumberland County, Virginia. His will was probated there July 23, 1704. The only child on record was Abraham Bledsoe, who after marrying settled in that part of Orange County which was later embraced in Culpepper County. Among his children was Anthony Bledsoe, born in (then) Orange County, Virginia, 1733, married about 1760 to Mary Ramsey, of Augusta County, who was born in 1734. Col. Bledsoe was killed by the Indians at Bledsoe's Creek, Sumner County, Tenn., on July 20, 1788. His widow died in Sumner County in 1808. Their children were, Abraham, born in Virginia about 1762; Thomas Sarah, Anthony, junior, Isaac, Henry Ramsey, Rachel, Polly, born in Virginia 1780; Betsy, Prudence and Susan.

Sarah Bledsoe was born in Virginia in 1763, came to Sumner County, Tennessee, in 1781, the same year she married David Shelby, and died March 11, 1852. They had issue:

  1   John Shelby, born May 24, 1785.
  2   Anthony Bledsoe Shelby, born Jan. 15, 1789.
  3   Philip Davies Shelby, born March 7, 1791, died May 27, 1799.
  4   Priscilla Shelby, born March 8, 1793.
  5   Lucinda Shelby, born March 24, 1795.
  6   James Shelby, born July 13, 1797; died Aug. 28, 1797.
  7   Nellie Shelby, born Jan. 14, 1799.
  8   David Davies Shelby, born July 15, 1801, died Aug. 2, 1805.
  9   Orville Shelby, born Jan. 21, 1803.
10   Sarah Bledsoe Shelby, born Jan. 21, 1806.
11   Albert Shelby, born May 25, 1808.

  1   John Shelby, son of David and Sarah (Bledsoe) Shelby was the first white child to be born in what is now Sumner County, Tennessee, on May 24, 1785. He received

SHELBY

a liberal education, then went to Philadelphia, where he studied medicine and where he married Anna Maria Minnick. After his return to Tennessee, he located on a large tract of land on the east side of the Cumberland River.

He was the founder of Shelby Medical College, afterwards merged into the medical department of the University of Nashville. He was the prime mover in the company, which built the first suspension bridge at Nashville. He was one of the founders of St. Ann's Episcopal Church. It was for him that Shelby avenue was so named. He was a warm personal friend of Sam Houston and other men of prominence of his day. His residence stood near the centre of Woodland street, directly in front of the present residence of Hon. A. V. Goodpasture. Had children:

Anna Shelby.
Priscilla Shelby.

I. *Anna or Ann Shelby*

Ann Shelby (in one place name given Anna, on other Ann), daughter of Dr. John and Anna Maria (Minnick) Shelby. Married Washington Barrow, who was born in Davidson County, Tennessee, Oct. 5, 1817. He was a lawyer by profession, and a man of affairs. He was the first President of the Nashville Gas Company. He was Minister to Portugal from 1841 to 1844 and a representative in Congress from 1847 to 1849. Was for a time editor of the Nashville Banner. Was State Senator in 1860 and 1861. Was identified with the Confederacy during the War Between the States. Was arrested by order of Andrew Johnson but soon afterwards was released by order of the President. Died in St. Louis, Oct. 19, 1866. Had children:

John Shelby Barrow.
A daughter, who died young.

John Shelby Barrow, son of Washington and Ann (Shelby) Barrow, married Miss Margaret Armstrong. Had children:

A daughter, who died young.
John Shelby Barrow, junior.

John Shelby Barrow, junior, son of John and Margaret (Armstrong) Barrow, married a daughter of Col. Hal Claiborne, of Nashville. They reside in New York. Their children:

John Shelby Barrow, Third.
Washington Barrow.
Ann Barrow.
Clayton Barrow.

NOTABLE SOUTHERN FAMILIES

Priscilla Shelby's Descendants

Priscilla Shelby, daughter of Dr. John and Anna Maria (Minnick) Shelby. Married David Williams of West Tennessee. Had children:
John Shelby Williams.
Joseph Minnick Williams.
Anna Minnick Williams.

1 *John Shelby Williams and his Descendants*

(1) John Shelby Williams, son of David and Priscilla (Shelby) Williams, married Mattie Sevier, daughter of Hon. Ambrose H. Sevier, formerly a Senator from Arkansas. Had children:
David Shelby Williams.
Juliette Sevier Williams; died young.
Maude Johnson Williams.
Anna Fassman Williams.
Ambrose Sevier Williams.

David Shelby Williams, son of John Shelby and Mattie (Sevier) Williams, married first, May Lawson McGhee, of Knoxville, daughter of Col. Charles McGhee.

Maude Williams, daughter of John Shelby and Mattie (Sevier) Williams married Robert P. Bonnie, of Louisville, Kentucky. Have children:
Shelby Williams Bonnie.
Mattie Sevier Bonnie.
Robert P. Bonnie.

Anna Fassman Williams, daughter of John Shelby and Mattie (Sevier) Williams, married Wentworth P. Johnson of Norfolk, Virginia. Children:
Wentworth P. Johnson, junior.
Shelby Williams Johnson (a daughter).
Three children died in infancy.

(2) *Joseph Minnick Williams*

Joseph Minnick Williams, son of David and Priscilla (Shelby) Williams, married Nov. 13th, 1860, Emily D. Polk, daughter of General Lucius Polk, of Maury County, Tennessee. She was born March 29th, 1837. Had children:

1 Henry Yeatman Williams, born Hamilton Place, Nashville, March 29th, 1863; married Louise Pitcher, March 8th, 1894. Residence, San Antonio, Texas.

2 J. Minnick Williams, junior, unmarried; born February 8th, 1866.

SHELBY

(3) Lucius Polk Williams, unmarried; born November 1867.
4 Nannie M. Williams, born July 1870, died April 9th, 1890.
5 Eliza Polk Williams, born April 1872, died July 3rd, 1891.
6 Priscilla Shelby Williams, born at Ashwood, Tennessee, January 4th, 1878; married George S. Briggs, March 7th, 1901. Had issue:
George Shelby Briggs, born March 7th, 1902, at Norfolk, Virginia.

(3) *Anna Minnick Williams*

Annie Minnick Williams, daughter of David and Prisilla (Shelby) Williams, married Frank Fassman, of New Orleans. Had children:
Maria Shelby Fassman, married Mr. Brook, has one child.
Anna Minnick Fassman, married Rev. J. G. Shackelford; has one child.

Anthony Bledsoe Shelby

Anthony Bledsoe Shelby, son of David and Sarah (Bledsoe) Shelby, was born in Sumner County, Jan. 15, 1789 He married Marian Winchester, daughter of Stephen Winchester. He studied law, and after practicing at Gallatin for some time, removed to Texas and assisted in gaining independence for that state. He was one of the Justices of the Supreme Court of the Republic of Texas, and was prominent in other ways. Later he removed to Mississippi and settled at Brandon where he died about 1855. His children were:
Sallie Shelby, born in Sumner County, May 10, 1812.
David Shelby, born Sumner County, May 7, 1814.
Marian Jane Shelby, born July 31, 1816; died Sept. 6, 1817.
Priscilla Kate Shelby, born July 15, 1818.
Annie W. Shelby, born July 10, 1820; died Aug. 27, 1821.
Julia Winchester Shelby, born July 15, 1822.
Stephen Winchester Shelby, born July 22, 1824; died July 15, 1828.
Winchester Bledsoe Shelby, born Jan. 18, 1827.
Lucinda Henderson Shelby, born Dec. 31, 1829.
Mariah P. Shelby, born Nov. 10, 1831.

NOTABLE SOUTHERN FAMILIES

Bennett Henderson Shelby, born March 24, 1834.
Antonette Marian Shelby, born Nov. 16, 1834, died young.
Nelson Shelby, died in 1838.

Sallie Shelby and Her Descendants

(1) Sallie Shelby, daughter of Judge Anthony Bledsoe and Marian (Winchester) Shelby, born in Sumner County, May 10, 1812, married Dr. Miles Seldon Watkins, of Mississippi. Had children:
Selden Watkins.
Leigh Watkins.
Marian Shelby Watkins.
Erskin Watkins.
Nettie Shelby Watkins.
Fearn Watkins. No information.
Leigh Watkins, son of Dr. Miles Selden and Sallie (Shelby) Watkins, married Willie Kearney, of Madison County, Mississippi. Had children:
Mary Leigh Watkins.
Leigh Watkins.
Mary Leigh Watkins, daughter of Leigh and Willie (Kearney) Watkins, married Wm. H. McCulloch, of Ferguson, Missouri. Had children.
Erskin Watkins McCulloch.
Eizabeth Zane McCulloch.
William H. McCulloch, junior.
Marian Shelby Watkins, daughter of Dr. Miles Seldon and Sally (Shelby) Watkins, married William Ewing Ross, of Madison County, Mississippi. Had children:
Willie B. Ross.
Marian Shelby Ross.
Sally Shelby Ross.
Watkins Ross.
James B. Ross.
Willie B. Ross, son of Wm. Ewing and Marian (Watkins) Ross, married Lillie Pearros, of Jackson, Mississippi. Have child:
Willie B. Ross.
Willie B. Ross, son of Wm. Ewing and Marian (Watkins) (Shelby) Watkins, married Alice Petrie, of Jackson, Mississippi, where they now reside. Had children:
Rosa Farrar Watkins.
Marian Shelby Watkins.
Erskin Watkins, junior.
Herbert Petrie Watkins.

SHELBY

Alice Petrie Watkins.
An infant who died young.
Rose Farrar Watkins, daughter of Erskin and Alice (Petrie) Watkins, married Calvin Wells, junior, a lawyer of Jackson, Mississippi. One child:
Alice Petrie Wells.
Nettie Sheby Watkins, daughter of Dr. Miles Seldon and Sally (Shelby) Watkins. Unmarried. Resides in Jackson, Mississppi.

(2) *David Shelby and His Descendants*

David Shelby, son of Anthony Bledsoe and Marion (Winchester) Shelby, was born at Gallatin, May 7, 1814; married Mary T. Bouldin, Jan 13, 1837. Had children:
Anthony Davies Douldin Shelby, born Oct. 10, 1845.
David D. Shelby, born Oct. 24, 1847; married Eason Davis in Huntsville, Alabama, August 8th, 1872; no issue.
Maria Bledsoe Shelby.
Marian Winchester Shelby; no information.
Yancy Howard Shelby; no information.
David Shelby, son of David and Mary T. (Bouldin) Shelby, was born Oct. 24, 1847; married Aug. 8, 1872, Annie Easton Davis. In 1882-86 he served in the Alabama Senate, was appointed Judge of the United States Court, Fifth Circuit, 1899. Resides in Huntsville, Alabama. No children.

Maria Bledsoe Shelby

Maria Bledsoe Shelby, daughter of David and Mary T. (Bouldin) Shelby, married May 14, 1871, Samuel Pleasants. Had children:
Nellie S. Pleasants, born May 2, 1872.
Marian Shelby Pleasants, born in March, 1874.

Marian Shelby Pleasants

Marian Shelby Pleasants, daughter of Samuel and Maria Bledsoe (Shelby) Pleasants was born in March 1874. Married Rev. Oscar Haywood, Aug. 1896; died in 1898; no issue.

Priscilla Kate Shelby and Her Descendants

Priscilla Kate Shelby, daughter of Judge Anthony Bledsoe and Marian (Winchester) Shelby, was born in Sumner County, July 15, 1818; married J. G. P. Hammond, of Mississippi. Had children:
Eli Shelby Hammond.
F. McLaren Hammond.
Priscilla Hammond.

NOTABLE SOUTHERN FAMILIES

Eli Shelby Hammond

Eli Shelby Hammond, son of J. C. P. and Priscilla Kate (Shelby) Hammond, was born at Brandon, Mississippi, April 21, 1838. Served in the Confederate army, then studied law and practiced until 1878, when he was appointed United States District Judge for West Tennessee, and served to his death, Dec. 17, 1904. He married Jan. 13, 1864, Fannie Davis. Had children:
I Patty Hammond.
II Orlando D. Hammond.

I Patty Hammond, daughter of Judge Eli Shelby and Fannie (Davis) Hammond, was born in Ripley, Mississippi, June 6, 1868. Married Dr. George W. Jarman, son of Prof. George W. Jarman, who was for many years President of the S. W. B. University at Jackson, Tennessee. Residence, No. 54 W. 76th St., New York. Have children:
George Wallace Jarman.
Shelby Hammond Jarman.
Martha Shelby Jarman.

F. McLaren Hammond and Descendants

F. McLaren Hammond, son of J. C. P. and Priscilla Kate (Shelby) Hammond married Mary Mayes. Had children:
Cora Hammond.
Ferdinand McLaren Hammond.
Mary Hammond.
Harry Hammond.

Cora Hammond, daughter of McLaren and Mary (Mayes) Hammond, married Wesley Owen. Residence in Texas. Has children. No information.

Ferdinand McLaren Hammond, son of McLaren and Mary (Mayes) Hammond, married and has children. No information.

Mary Hammond, daughter of McLaren and Mary (Mayes) Hammond, married and has children. No information.

Harry Hammond, son f McLaren and Mary (Mayes) Hammond, married and has children. No information.

Priscilla Hammond

Priscilla Shelby Hammond, daughter of J. C. P. and Priscilla Kate (Shelby) Hammond, married J. M. Scruggs of Byhalia, Mississippi, Oct. 19, 1864. Had children:
Frances Lynn Scruggs.
James Merriwether Scruggs.

SHELBY

Francis Lynn Scruggs, daughter of J. M. and Priscilla Shelby (Hammond) Scruggs was born at Jackson, Tennessee, July 25, 1865. Married J. Hancock Robinson, in Holly Springs, Mississippi, August 24, 1886. They reside in Washington, D. C. Have one child:
Shelby Goldsborough Robinson, daughter, born July 8, 1888.
James Merriwether Scruggs, son of J. M. and Priscilla Shelby (Hammond) Scruggs, married Lillie Whitney, of Memphis, where they have a home. Have children:
Whitney Scruggs, daughter.
James Merriwether Scruggs, junior.
Nolan Fountaine Scruggs.
Julia Winchester Shelby, daughter of Judge Anthony Bledsoe and Marian (Winchester) Shelby, was born at Gallatin, July 15, 1822. Married Mr. Ware, a lawyer, of Jackson, Mississippi. Had children:
Winchester Bledsoe Ware. Died young.
Winchester Bledsoe Shelby, son of Judge Anthony Bledsoe and Marian (Winchester) Shelby, was born at Dixon Springs, Tennessee, Jan. 18, 1827. He served in the Confederate Army, with the rank of Colonel. Married Margaret Alexander. Had children:
Bledsoe Alexander Shelby, merchant, St. Louis, Missouri; no information.
William H. Shelby, merchant, St. Louis; no information.
Edwin Shelby, insurance agent, New Orleans; no information.
David Shelby, lawyer in Oklahoma; no information.
Had daughters also:

Priscilla Shelby

(4) Priscilla Shelby, daughter of David and Sarah (Bledsoe) Shelby was born in Sumner County. Married Henry L. Douglass, a native of Sumner County. He was a merchant of Vicksburg, Mississippi, where he died in 1854. Their daughter was:
Priscilla Douglass.
After the death of his wife, Priscilla Shelby, Henry L. Douglass married Miss Alcorn, sister of Governor Alcorn, of Mississippi. After her death he married Mrs. Jane Crabb, mother of Henry Crabb of Sonora fame. Colonel Douglass was one of the largest merchants in Vicksburg and was owner of the first cotton compress in Mississippi.
Priscilla Douglass, daughter of Henry L. and Priscilla

NOTABLE SOUTHERN FAMILIES

(Shelby) Douglass, married Dr. Robert C. K. Martin, who was born in Nashville, Aug. 9, 1808. After receiving a classical education he graduated from Franklin Medical College, Philadelphia, with distinguished honors, then successfully practiced medicine for approximately forty years, winning eminence in his profession, and was noted for his philanthropy.

He died in Nashville, Feb. 9, 1872. Had children:
Bettie Martin.
Mary Shelby Martin. Never married.
Alice Martin.
Henry Douglass Martin.
Player Martin. Never married.
Robert C. K. Martin, junior.
Maria Martin.
Shelby Martin. Never married.

Bettie Martin

Bettie Martin, daughter of Robert C. K. and Priscilla (Douglass) Martin, married W. C. Butterfield. Had children:
William Butterfield; unmarried.
Robert Butterfield.
Nellie Butterfield; unmarried; resides at Little Rock, Arkansas.
Robert M. Butterfield, son of W. C. and Bettie (Martin) Butterfield, married Miss Phones of Little Rock, Arkansas, where they reside. Children:
Joseph Phones Butterfield.
Bettie Martin Butterfield.

2 Alice Martin, daughter of Robert C. K. and Priscilla (Douglass) Martin, married W. H. Hart. No issue. After the death of Mr. Hart she married John Lannahan.

3 Henry Douglass Martin, son of Dr. Robert C. K. and Priscilla (Douglass) Martin, married Lizzie Nichols. No issue.

4 Robert C. K. Martin, son of Robert C. K. and Priscilla (Douglass) Martin, married Sarah Shelby Anderson. Resides in Nashville. Have one child:
Bettie Martin, unmarried.

5 Maria Martin, daughter of Dr. Robert C. K. and Priscilla (Douglass) Martin, married W. C. Butterfield, who had previously married her sister, Bettie. Had children:
Bettie Butterfield; unmarried.
Duncan Butterfield; unmarried; resides in Nashville.

SHELBY

Eleanor or Nellie Shelby and Her Descendants

Nellie Shelby, daughter of David and Sarah (Bledsoe) Shelby was born in Sumner County, at Spencer's Choice, Jan. 14, 1799. She married Gen. Robert Desha, son of Robert Desha. Gen. Desha's mother was, before her marriage, Eleanor Wheeler, who was a daughter of Joseph Wheeler, a Captain in the Revolutionary War. He served as a Captain and a Brigadier-Major in the War of 1812. He was a representative in Congress from Tennessee from 1827 to 1831. He was for some time a merchant in Gallatin and later removed to Mobile, Alabama, where he conducted a flourishing business until his death, Feb. 8, 1849. Their children were:
Caroline Desha.
Phoebe Ann Desha.
Julia Desha.

I Caroline Desha, daughter of General Robert and Nellie (Shelby) Desha, marred first, Robert Barney; second, Lloyd Abbott. No. information.

II Phoebe Ann Desha, daughter of Gen. Robert and Nellie (Shelby) Desha, married first, Robert Barney; second, Mobile, Alabama. Had children:

(1) *Alva Erskin Smith*

Alva Erskin Smith, daughter of Dr. Murray Forbes and Phoebe (Desha) Smith, was born in Mobile, Alabama. Married first, William K. Vanderbilt of New York; second, Oliver H. P. Belmont, who was born in New York, Nov. 12, 1858, son of Augustus Belmont; educated at the U. S. Naval Academy, and served two years in the Navy; then resigned. Was for some time a member of the banking firm of August Belmont & Company. Elected to the 57th Congress as a Democrat. Died in New York, June 8, 1898. She has children:
Consuelo Vanderbilt, born in New York, March 2, 1877.
William Kissman Vanderbilt, born in New York, Oct. 26, 1878.
Harold Stirling Vanderbilt, born in New York, July 6, 1884.   K

Consuelo Vandrbilt, daughter of Wm. K. and Alva Erskine (Smith) Vanderbilt, was born in New York, March 2, 1877. Married first, Nov. 6, 1895, Charles Richard John Spencer Churchill, Duke of Marlbrough. Has Children:
John William Churchill, Marquis of Blanford.
Ivory Churchill (Lord).

NOTABLE SOUTHERN FAMILIES

She re-married in 1921.
William Kissman Vanderbilt, junior, son of Wm.. K. and Alva Erskin (Smith) Vanderbilt was born in New York, Oct. 26, 1878. Married April 1900, Virginia Fair. Has children:
Muriel Vanderbilt.
Consuelo Vanderbilt.
William Vanderbilt, Third, married Rachel Littleton.
2 Mary Virginia Smith, daughter of Dr. Murray Forbes and Phoebe (Desha)) Smith, married first, Fernando Yzanga; second, W. G. Tiffany, of New York.
3 Florence Smith, daughter of Dr. Murray Forbes and Phoebe (Desha) Smith married Gaston De Fontenilliat. Had children:
Renee Fontenilliat.

(9) *Orville Shelby and Descendants*

Orville Shelby, son of David and Sarah (Bledsoe) Shelby was born in Sumner County, on January 21, 1803. He married Caroline Winchester, daughter of Gen. James Winchester and soon thereafter removed to Lexington, Kentucky. His children were:
Joseph Orville Shelby.
Carrie Shelby.
Isaac Shelby.

I. Joseph Orville Shelby

General Joseph Orville Shelby, son of Orville and Caroline (Wnchester) Shelby, was born at Lexington, Kentucky, in 1831. Received a liberal education and engaged in mercantile pursuits. Removed to Waverly, Missouri, in 1850, and commenced the manufacture of baled rope. Soon afterwards the Kansas trouble broke out, and he returned to Kentucky, where he organized a company for territorial service. When quiet had been restored he returnd to his rope factory. At the breaking out of the War Between the States he raised a company of cavalry and entered the Confederate service with the rank of Captain. In 1862 he recruited a regiment, of which he was chosen Colonel, and was given command of a brigade of which his regiment formed a part. In March 1864, he was commissioned a Brigadier General, and later a Major General. Shelby's Brigade was one of the most famous commands in the Confederate service. Gen. Shelby was a born leader of men. Brave, daring, chivalrous, and knew not the meaning of the word fear. He was the idol of his men and was to the Trans-Mississippi department what Forrest was to the East.

SHELBY

No braver man than 'Old Joe Shelby', ever drew a sword". In 1893 he was appointed United States Marshal by President Cleveland, and held the office until his death, February 13, 1897, at his home in Adrian, Missouri.

· Joseph Orville Shelby, married 1858, Betty Shelby; had issue:
1 Orville Shelby; lived in Oklahoma.
2 Joseph Shelby; lived in Kansas City, Missouri.

II *Carrie Shelby*

Carrie Shelby, daughter of Orville and Caroline (Winchester) Shelby, married Henry Blood; had children:
Henry Blood; dead.
Lawton Blood; No information.
May Blood.
Laura Blood.
Olga Blood; no information.
Maud Blood.

May Blood, daughter of Henry and Carrie (Shelby) Blood, married a Mr. Walsh. Resides in New York. No information.

Laura Blood, daughter of Henry and Carrie (Shelby) Blood, married a Mr. Walsh.

Maude Blood, daughter of Henry and Carrie (Shelby) Blood married Harold Sanderson, manager of the White Star Line of Steamships of Liverpool. He was lost at sea.

III. *Isaac Shelby*

Isaac Shelby, son of Orville and Caroline (Winchester) Shelby, a younger brother of General Joseph O. Shelby, was born in Lexington, Kentucky. Removed to Missouri. He served in the Confederate Army as color-bearer in Gordon's Brigade, in the Trans-Mississippi department, and was distinguished for his daring. No other information.

10 *Sarah Bledsoe Shelby and Descendants*

(10 Sarah Bledsoe Shelby, daughter of David and Sarah (Bledsoe) Shelby, born in Sumner County, Jan. 21, 1806. Married Dr. Thomas Fearn on Feb. 26, 1822. Died May 22, 1842. Dr. Fearn was a son of Thomas Fearn and was born in Pittsylvania County, Virginia, Nov. 15, 1789; died Jan. 16, 1863. Her children were:
Mary Eleanor Fearn.
Sarah Fearn, married Hon. William S. Barry, Columbus, Mississippi; both dead.
Kate Fearn.
Ada Fearn.

NOTABLE SOUTHERN FAMILIES

Maria Fearn.
Bernice Fearn.
Lucy Lee Fearn.

I. Mary Fearn

Mary Fearn daughter of Dr. Thomas and Sarah Bledsoe (Shelby) Fearn, married Gustavus L. Mastin. Had children:
Arabella Mastin; never married.
Thomas Mastin.
James Mastin.
Frank Mastin; never married.
Sallie Shelby Mastin.
Gustavus L. Mastin, junior.

1 Thomas Mastin, son of Gustavis L. and Mary (Fearn) Mastin, married Mary Irby Bate, daughter of the late Senator William B. Bate, of Tennessee. Resides in Grand View, Texas. Their children:
Bate Mastin.
Mary Eleanor Mastin.
Julien Mastin.

Mary Eleanor Mastin, daughter of Thomas and Mary Irby (Bates) Mastin married John Stevens Douglass.

2 James Mastin, son of Gustavus L. and Mary (Fearn) Mastin, married Mattie Tutwiler of Alabama. No issue.

3 Sallie Shelby Mastin, daughter of Gustavus L. and Mary (Fearne) Mastin married Eugene Bucknor. No issue.

4 Gustavus L. Mastin, junior, son f Gustavus L and Mary (Fearn) Mastin married Lucy Matthews. Had children:
John Mastin.
Sallie Shelby Mastin.
Clara Mastin.
Lucy Mastin.
Frank Mastin.

II Sarah Fearn

Sarah Fearn, daughter of Dr. Thomas and Sarah Bledsoe (Shelby) Fearn, married Colonel William F. Barry. Had children:
William Shelby Barry.

William Shelby Barry, son of Colonel William F. and Sarah (Fearn) Barry, married first, Bernice Steel, a first cousin. Had one child:
William Shelby Barry, junior.

SHELBY

III *Kate Fearn*

Kate Fearn, daughter of Dr. Thomas and Sarah Bledsoe (Shelby) Fearn married in 1848, Colonel Matthew Steele. Had Children:
Thomas Steele.
Sallie Steele.
Eliza Steele; never married.
George Steele; never married.
Robert Steele.
Bernice Steele.
Matthew Steele.
Tracy Steele.
Katy Wille Steele; never married.

Thomas Steele, son of Col. Matthew and Kate (Fearne) Steele, married Lovie Strode. Had children:
Shelby Steele.
Kate Steele.
May Steele.
Sallie Steele.
Stella Steele.
Bernice Steele.
Matthew Steele, junior.
Annie Steele.

2 Sallie Steele, daughter of Col. Matthew and Kate (Fearn) Steele married John Newman. Had one child:
Robert E. Newman.

3 Robert Steele, son of Col. Mathew and Kate (Fearn) Steele married Tillie Weaver. No issue.

4 Bernice Steele, daughter of Col. Matthew and Kate (Fearn) Steele married William Shelby Barry, her first cousin. Had one child:
William Shelby Barry, junior.

5 Matthew Forney Steele, junior, son of Col. Matthew and Kate (Fearn) Steele is a Captain in the U. S. Army, Sixth Regiment of Cavalry. Married Stella Folsom. No issue.

6 Tracy Steele, son of Col. Matthew and Kate (Fearn) Steele married Courtney Crutchfield. Have children:
Tracy Steele, junior.
William Steele.

NOTABLE SOUTHERN FAMILIES

Second marriage, Josephine Holliquest. Had one child: Josephine Barry.

IV Ada Fearn

Ada Fearn, daughter of Dr. Thomas and Sarah Bledsoe (Shelby) Fearn married first, Dr. George Steele; had children:
Anna Steele.
Fearn Steele.
Married second, Judge Hook.
Anna Steele married Mr. Edgar. Had children:
Annie D. Eager.
Fearn Eager; died young.
Fearn Steele, son of Dr. George and Ada (Fearn) Steele, married Sadie ———. Had one child:
George Steele.

V Maria Fearn

Maria Eliza Fearn, daughter of Dr. Thomas and Sarah Bledsoe (Shelby) Farn, June 25, 1855 married Col. William W. Garth, of Huntsville Alabama, who served on the staff of Gen Longstreet during the War Between the States. He was born in Morgan County, Alabama; pursued classical studies at Lagrange and at Emory and Henry College, then studied law at the University of Virginia. Commenced practice at Huntsville. Elected a representative in Congress in 1888, and served one term as a Democrat. Had children:
Winston F. Garth.
Winston F. Garth, son of Col. William Willis and Maria Eliza (Fearn) Garth, married Lena Garth, a cousin. Had children:
William Willis Garth, junior.
Alice D. Garth; unmarried; lives in Huntsville, Alabama.
Maria Fearn Garth.
Horace Everett Garth.
William Willis Garth, junior, son of Winston Fearn and Lena Garth, married Louisa Dodsworth. Have one child:
Lena Garth.

VI Lucy Fearn

Lucy Lee Fearn, daughter of Dr. Thomas and Sarah Bledsoe (Shelby) Fearn, married George Miller; no issue.

VI MARY SHELBY

Mary Shelby, daughter of Brig.-Gen. Shelby married Adam Alexander of note in connection with the Mecklen-

SHELBY

burg Declaration of Independence, and still further known in North Carolina history for his military services during the Revolutionary War. He was born September 28, 1728, in Pennsylvania, of Scotch-Irish parentage. They had issue: (1) Evan Shelby Alexander, graduate at Princeton 1787, was a lawyer and a member of the Ninth Congress from Salisbury District, North Carolina, in 1808-9, died in 1809 unmarried; (2) Isaac Alexander; (3) Charles Taylor Alexander. (Three of the Taylor sisters of Carlisle, Pennsylvania, married Alexanders, ancestors of the North Carolina Alexanders; another sister, Margaret Taylor, married William Polk, and this couple were the progenitors of the Southern line of the Polk family in North Carolina). (4) Sarah Alexander; (5) Mary Alexander. The oldest married Caoain John Springs. There are many descendants of Isaac and Charles Alexander, and the Springs living in that section of North Carolina now.

VANCE

The ancestry of any family or person goes back in such a multiplicity of lines it is hard in any case to trace the predominate strain.

One may however, trace with fair degree of certainty the origin and various changes in the name the family bears.

Most interesting to study in such a way is the name Vance. In ancient Province, Baux, in Normandy and England, Vaux, De Vaux, De Vaus, or its Latin form De Vallibus, we find that in Scotland it takes the spelling Vans (pronounced Vanse), and in Ireland and America we have it spelled as pronounced, Vance.

It is one of the most ancient names whose history has been traced. Playfair in his Baronetage of Scotland says: "The Vance family combines within itself the blood of some of the most ancient names of European genealogy, the present representatives being by paternal descent heirs male of Lord Vaux, Vaus or Vans of Direlton Castle, East Lothian, a noble race, numbered amongst the magnates Scotia as early as 1244 and are indubitably descended from the same general stem as the noble houses, now extinct, of Vaux of Gilliesland, Brevor and Harrowden in England, all of Norman descent at the time of the Conqueror".

Though not elevated to the peerage this family has been from the first of the rank of the first of the order of Barons, holding their estates "in capite" by Royal Charter; conferring on their possessors all the rights and important privileges of free baronies, according to the most extensive use of the word in Scottish law, "It has been the custom," he continues, "of genealogists back to Charlemagne." This, however, is impossible in this case as the family actually deduce their paternal descent by the most authentic documents to a period of still greater antiquity, their ancestors holding them a very distinguished rank, their principal residence being the Castle of Baux, situated on an elevated rock near the City of Arles, where the ruins may yet be seen.

There have been many conjectures as to the rise of the family of the ancient Barons of Baux, but the Norman historians (who certainly must be considered the best authorities of their times), are decidedly of the opinion that they are a branch of the Visigothic Balti, a race which boasted having given a long line of monarchs to the Western Goths, with the formidable name of Alaric at their head.

This was in the year 500 of the Christian Era, but the first of particular record, is Rollin, or Gorsallin de Baux, settled at Baux in Provence 800. He married Herrinbuck, daughter and heiress of William, Sovereign of Count of Orange and niece of Bertha, wife of Emperor Charlemgne.

In 929 Bertrand de Baux of Provence, went to Normandy by invitation of the Duke of Normandy. In 1096 Raoul de Vaux of Normandy, bore the same arms as Vaus of the house of Provence.

On the continent of Europe the de Vaux family have been Dukes of Andrea, Princes of Joinville, Taranta and Alta Mara, Sovereign Count of Orange and Provence and Kings of Vienne and Arlis as well as Lords de Vaux of Normandy. Hubert de Vaux or de Vallibus, was the eldest son of Harold, Lord de Vaux of Normandy, who went over with William, the Conqueror, in 1066 and was as first lord of Parliament for the Barony of Gilliesland.

This Hubert was ancestor of the Lords of Ruthvine, Ker, and Home as well as the Earls of Bothwell. All of these families bear the quartered arms of Vaux.

It is many centuries since the noble house of Vaux in England became extinct and the peerage remained in abeyance until 1838, when it was revived in the person of George Mostyn, Esq., heir male to Mary, sister of the last Lord Vaux of Harrowden.

However, according to Playfair, the male line was carried by Johannis Vaux who settled in Galloway, married an heiress and obtained the lands of Branbarroch in Scotland.

Barnbarrouch House, located in the Parish of Kirkimer near the town of Wigton, is said to be one of the most beautiful in the country. The present owner, with whom the writer has corresponded, is James Vans-Agnew, twenty-

VANCE

first laird of Barnbarroch. He quarters the arms of Vans with those of Agnew. All children except the oldest son bear the name Vans. On the stone above the door of the house the Vans arms are cut in the stone with the date 1433 and initials J. V. & E. K.

Rev. John Vans, first of the name of Ireland, whose will filed 1662, in the records of Dublin Castle bears on its seal the arms of Vans of Barnbarroch, was a grandson of Sir Patrick Vans and Margaret Kennedy, his wife, granddaughter of King Robert III, of Scotland.

From this John Vans, the Vance families of North Ireland and America trace their descent.

Some years ago Mr. William Balbrinie, of Glasgow. at the request of an older brother living in Melbourne, who had been granted the right to assume the name Balbirnie-Vans, undertook to trace the history of the Irish branch of the Vance family.

He had access to a family history drawn up by his uncle, George Washington Vance (born 1790, died 1825), and one written previous to 1825 by one of the lairds of Barnbarroch. He visited the family in Scotland and Ireland and was given much assistance by Sir Bernard Burke, Ulster King at Arms, and other prominent genealogists.

The result of his labors, the Vance book published 1860, contains, no doubt, all the authentic data in regard to the family in Ireland up to that time.

The Vance family in America are practically all descended from the Irish family of that name. I have been endeavoring to connect up some of the family groups with those Mr. Balbrinie mentions as coming to this county.

The account of George Washington Vance says "a daughter of John Vance (my grandfather), married Andrew Jackson, of Magherfelt, who emigrated to America and there gave birth to Andrew Jackson, the general, late president of the United States, of whom it is written he is the bravest soldier and wisest statesman that ever ancient or modern history recorded'.

"Andrew Vance, fourth son of John, also emigrated to America and there became the founder of a family; one of his sons was an officer in the American war and was killed in action fighting under Washington. A descendent of his was member of Congress from North Carolina in 1824".

I give his statement in full: Mr. Vance, whose father was first cousin to Andrew Jackson, was named for Geroge

NOTABLE SOUTHERN FAMILIES

Washington, probably on account of his father's inability to carry thrugh his plan to come to America, and the family were, no doubt, in correspondnce with relatives here. The statement in regard to Jackson's mother's name is accepted by O'Hart and other authorities but for some reason Jackson's biographers here have never credited him with any prominent ancestry, much being made of his rise from a common family. His mother's father was John Vance, son of Launcelot Vance, son of Rev. John Vans of Ireland".

Another family that of Hugh of Gortwood 5, Thomas 4, George 3, Patrick 2, Rev. John 1, also has a record of several members who came to America. Patrick, son of Hugh, came to America unmarried. This Patrick had a brother also named Hugh who had five sons, four of whom followed their uncle to America. They were John, who located in Baltimore and had two sons, Patrick who had two daughters, Thomas of Baltimore and Hugh, who married a Miss Corscaddon, of Donegal, and emigrated to Pittsburg.

The Scotch-Irish began coming to this country from North Ireland early in seventeen hundred. They were urged to come to avoid persecution at home and large manors were granted along the frontier to various persons who agreed to bring a certain number of settlers. James and William Vance had grants in Beverly Manor in the Shenandoah Valley.

It seems well to put down for use of any one interested a few of the Vance groups who were here early, even if the connection between the groups is not clear.

The Virginia Vances came first to Lancaster and Chester Counties in Pennsylvania and from these with William Hoge, or Hogg, a relative of Andrew Vance, to form the first settlement in the Shenandoah Valley. These Scotch Presbyterians were there as early as 1736.

I. James Vance who married in Ireland 1734, Mary Gamble Glass names in his will, filed Frederick County, Virginia, 1754, his brothers William and David, and sons William and Samuel. One branch of the Ohio Vances descend from this Samuel.

II. Maj. William Vance (1718-88), was in Augusta County, Virginia, 1742 and 1756 and 1758 was engaged in the Indian wars with his brothers John and Patrick, M. D. This Patrick, according to the family records of his descendents, was directly descended of Rev. John Vans.

Major William Vance with his son Joseph and his nephew John (son of John), moved to Washington County,

VANCE

Pennsylvania, 1778. They were the founders of Vance's Fort at Cross Creek, Pennsylvania, where many of the name were born. A full account of their descendants may be found in the County History on file with the Washington County Historical Association.

III. Charles Vance was in Piqua, Pennsylvania, 1739. His sons John, Alexander and Joseph located in Ohio. (See Alexander Genealogy, Portifield Genealogy and Hayden's History of Virginia).

IV. David Vance of Frederick County, Virginia probably, a grandson of Major William, left according to his will filed 1768, the following children. David, married Sarah Quimby (see Quimby Genealogy), John, Joseph Colvill, Mary, Ann, (married Joseph Vance). Martha married Solomon Vail and Jeanette married Miles Wilson. Joseph Colville born March 24, 1759, son of David, went to Kentucky in 1788 later moved to Ohio. His sons were John M., who located in Illinois, William, Wilson, Moses, and Joseph who was one of the early Governors of the State of Ohio (1836.)

ALEX FRANKLIN VANCE
Son of Joseph Colville Vance

Alexander Franklin Vance (of Urbana, Ohio), married Mary Rebecca Ward and had thirteen children among whom were:

Joseph Colville Vance married Emily Patrick and had two sons, namely, Joseph MacArthur Vance (married Grace ———— and had two sons, Joseph Colville Vance, died in infancy, and Duncan MacArthur Vance), and Harry Vance (married Augusta Reid and has no children).

2 John Corwin Vance (living in Chattanooga) married Edith Price and has two daughters, Elizabeth (married Burleigh Annis and has a daughter, Vance Annis), and Esther Vance (married Richard Renner and has no children.

3 Henry Caldwell Vance, married ———— and had a son Marion, and a daughter Margaret.

4 Frank Vance married Mary Jamison. Their daughter, Louise Vance, married Senator Charles Brand.

5 Ella Vance, unmarried, now living in Urbana, Ohio.

V. Col. Samuel Vance lived in Augusta County, Virginia. His children were: Rachel married Hamilton, 1786; 2 James married Marshall; Margaret married Cockerill, Betsy, Sarah Patsy, Benjamin married Margaret Lindsay, of Kentucky, and James.

VI. John (1736-1823), married Jane Black. He had brothers David, Arthur, Samuel and Joseph C. His children were James, born 1760, John 1762, Elizabeth 1765, Andrew 1768, Samuel 1769, married Blackburn, Joseph 1772, Ester 1786, Christian 1778 and John 1783.

VII. Samuel Vance married in Ireland, Margaret Laughlin. Children: 1 Samuel, born 1784, married Elizabeth Brown (a descendant of King Robert III). He died at Clarkesville, Tennessee, 1823. Their children were Morgan, William, Samuel, Elizabeth married Topp, and Margaret married Childress. 2 Robert, 3 John, 4 David (of North Carolina), 5 James, 6 Elizabeth, 7 Sarah and 8 Margaret Abram married Alice Gale Armstrong.

VIII. Patrick and brother John, who had large estates along the Falling Spring near Chambersburg, Pennsylvania. The mansion house of these brothers still stands. They were direct descendants of Rev. John Vance. Patrick left no issue. John had a son John from whom George Vance Johnson descends.

IV. Hugh Vance of Boston, born 1699, married Mary Pemberton. Children: John, William married Clark, Ebenezer and Samuel.

X. Samuel Vance, whose father born on the High Seas, and lived in Baltimore County, Maryland, married Agnes (?) —————— of English Quaker stock. Samuel had four brothers: 1 David, whose children were Robert, Samuel, and daughters who married Clymr, Thompson and Rittenhaus; 2 Joseph, who lived in Pennsylvania; 3 William, 4 James, 5 Jonathan married Baxter, 6 Betsy and Mary. Two brothers, according to family traditions, settled in the "Carolinas." Samuel born Baltimore County, Maryland, 1762 and married Oct. 14, 1798 at Bel Air, Maryland to Mary Ann Waters, born March 29, 1779 was 14 years old when the Revolution started and served for a short time when about 17. His four brothers also served and his father erected an arsenal and gave powder to the State of Maryland. The mother, however, remained loyal to Great Britain. Samuel was educated at University of Baltimore and also learned the wheelwright trade. He traveled through New York and Lancaster Counties, Pennsylvania, buying horse hair, from which seives were then made. After marriage, however, he followed teaching exclusively. He died March 1, 1843 at Connersville, Ind.

VANCE

The four children of Samuel and Mary Waters Vance were, Elisha and Elijah, twins, born in Harnerd County, Maryland, 1801. Eli, born Feb. 5, 1810, Washington County, Pennsylvania, died young. Eliza, born Jan. 21, 1813, died young.

Elijah Vance had two daughters who left no issue. He was a lawyer and prominent in the early history of Ohio, being a member of the first constructional convention, and serving several times in the legislature.

Elisha, twin to Elijah, came down the Ohio to Cincinnati about 1820 on a flat boat, with Alexander Vance, a distant relative, who was a potter by trade and who located near Cincinnati. Elisha lived in Butler County, Ohio, and Connersville, Indiana, where he died. He was a lawyer and prominent in politics. He married in Butler County, Ohio, 1820, Mary, daughter of Samuel and Katherine De Moss Harper, born in Virginia, 1776. Her grand parents were John De Moss (Dumas) and Martha (La Huff) De Moss and Marsh (?) and Elizabeth Warren Harper. Elisha Vance died July 5, 1864 and his wife April 22, 1882. They had ten children, namely:

1 Samuel Warren, born Aug. 5, 1821, Warren County, Ohio, died Feb. 14, 1910; married in Connersville, Indiana, July 1, 1868, Adelaide Weaver Whittaker. Their children were, Portia, born April 17, 1869, married Dec. 1, 1895, Wm. C. Hanson. Has one child, Warren, born Sept.1 0, 1897; address, South Bend, Indiana; (2) Mary Harper, born Aug. 4, 1871, died April 1873; (3) Charles Francis, born June 7, 1874, married Rachel Griffin; (4) Coleridge Shelby, born March 11, 1876, married Lon Klein, address, Brdgeport, Illinois; 5 Galen Abernathy, born Dec. 25, 1877; 6 Teresa, born July 4, 1879, died July 22, 1882.

2 Benjamin Franklin, born June 1882, married Rebecca Fry. Children: Hattie, Sarah, Lillie, Lucy, Ida and Samuel.

3 Judge Elijah Milton Vance, born Butler County, Ohio, Aug. 6, 1825, died in St Louis, April 25, 1912. He was a lawyer and editor, prominent in Democratic politics. He campaigned with the father of Willaim J. Bryan, whom often entertained at his home. He stumped the state of Illinois with Douglas against Lincoln. He married first, ——— Sawyer; second, at Janesville, Wisconsin, June 8, 1860, Mary Jane, daughter of Rev. Aurora Callender and his wife Mary McMichael and granddaughter of Nathaniel and Oliver Kellogg Callender. She was born in Ravenna, Ohio, Nov. 16, 1833 and died in Seattle, Feb. 1, 1820. Their

NOTABLE SOUTHERN FAMILIES

children were: Edward Sawyer (by first wife —— Sawyer), born Aug. 14, 1855; 2 Maud, born April 1, 1860. died Feb. 15, 1864.

3 Milton Callender, born Nashville, July 13, 1863, married at Osceola, Missouri May 14, 1895 to Frances Russell. Children: Louis Whaley, born April 12, 1891 at Osceola, Missouri, and Edward Milton, born Dec. 2, 1898, and died in service Oct. 2, 1818.

4 Alice, born June 8, 1872 at Clinton, Missouri; married St. Louis, Oct. 21, 1900, Edward Nelson Robinson, son of George Woodford and Cornelia Beckwith Robinson. Children: Mary Ruth, born June 22, 1901 at St. Louis; Morton Jourdan and George Nelson, twins, born St. Louis, May 23, 1903; Margaret Helen, born Feb. 27, 1907, St. Louis.

5 Mary Harding Vance, born Nov. 5, 1875 at Clinton, Missouri.

IV. Katherine Demoss, born Connersville, Indiana, Aug. 23, 1878, married 1851 —— Trabor. One child, Harry, born Nov. 28, 1852.

V. Flora A., born Dec. 15, 1830, Connersville, Indiana, married Sept. 7, 1851 to John Gregg. Children: Horace, and Mary married Horace Flora.

VI. Mary, born April 15, 1833; married Maj. McIlevain who was was killed in War Between the States, June, 1864. She died 1867.

VII. Josephine, born Aug. 5, 1835; married Dec. 28, 1871 at Mt. Vernon Illinois, to —— Hoskins. Children: 1 Mary Rebecca, born at Jackson, Tennessee; married Rev. James Hawkins. Their children are Ruth and Dorothy. Elisha Vance, born Dec. 1, 1874 at Kansas City, Kansas; married to Leenie Price who died leaving children William and Andrew. He married, second, Margaret Wright

VIII. Van Roland, born Fayette County, Indiana, June 4, 1838, died single at Columbus, Ohio, Sept. 14, 1906.

IX. Robert Burns, born Connerssville, Indiana, Feb. 11, 1845, died single, Feb. 15, 1918.

X. Alice Hibbard, born Oct. 26, 1842, at Connersville, Indiana, died single Oct 28, 1908.

William Kirkpatrick Vance

William Kirkpatrick Vance, son of Patrick 8, (Patrick 7, Hugh 6, Hugh 5, Thomas 4, George of Raneel 3, Patrick 2, Rev. Jhn Vans 1) was born March 2, 1780 at Lexington, Virginia; married in Washington County, Tennessee, Keziah, granddaughter of Charles Robinson, prominent in

VANCE

early Tennessee history, daughter of his son, Charles Robinson, junior. He died 1852 at Kingspart, Tennessee. His children were Charles Robertson, James Harvey, Maria, died young; David G., died in Georgia; William Nicholas, Catherne, Patrick H. Caroline married Craighead or Craignoyes; Harriet married Thornton; Susan married Patton; Keziah married Dr. Herndon of Kentucky.

James Harvey, son of William Vance, born Jan. 4, 1811, Greeneville, Tennessee, married Aug. 26, 1832 at Warm Springs, North Carolina, Jane Sevier (daughter of Valentine Sevier and Nancy Dinwiddie Sevier), died July 7, 1893 at Kngsport, Tennessee. Children:

I. Charles Robertson, born Aug. 22, 1833, Jonesboro; married Oct. 16, 1860 Margaret Newland. They had:
  (a) James Isaac, born Sept. 25, 1802, Arcadia, Tennessee; married Dec. 22, 1886 at Yorkeville, South Carolina, Mamie Stile Currell. Children: Margaret, William, Agnes, Ruth, James, junior, and Charles R.
  (b) Rev. Joseph Anderson Vance, Nov. 17, 1864.
  (c) Charles R———.
  (d) Margaret, Jan. 20, 1877.
  (e) Rebecca, Jan. 20, 1877.
II. Maria C., married Rev. John King, Leesburg, Virginia.
III. Auna Elizabeth, died young.
IV. Keziah, died single.
V. James H., married Fasten Padlock.
VI. Wm. K., married Fannie Miller, Union City.
VII. Nannie, died single.
VIII. Joseph, married Mattie Fain and had James F., and Charles R.
IX. Jennie.

Patrick, son of William K. Vance, married Elizabeth ——— and had John, James, David, William, Robert, Sarah, married Campbell; Elizabth, married Davis; Jean, Mary, Joseph, and Smuel.

William Nicholas Vance, M. D., son of William K. born Nov. 12, 1814 at Greenville, Tennessee, married Sarah Ann Netherland and died Nov. 12, 1875. Children: Keziah R., Mary H., Samuel N., Charles S., Alice, William K., Ida, Jennie and Robert.

Willim K., son of William N., born May 27, 1852 at Bristol, married Susan M. Dorit. Children: Frederick, William K., David and Douglas D. Address, Bristol, Tennessee.

NOTABLE SOUTHERN FAMILIES

Captain David Vance

Captain David Vance born 1745 in Frederick County, Virginia, moved in 1775 to Burke County, North Carolina, where he taught school and became a surveyor. He served at King's Mountain nd probably also at Ramsons, Musgrove Mills,, Cowpens and Valley Forge. He was a member of the House of Commons 1786-91, then removed to Bumcomb County and in 1797, was one of the commissioners for running the line betwen North Carolina and Tennessee, and became a Colonel of the militia. He died about 1820. Some authorities give him as the son of Samuel and Margret Laughlin Vance, others as son of Samuel and Miss Colville, others as a son of Andrew, as brother of Samuel (born 1762), brother of Joseph Colville Vance, etc. Either would indicate him to be descendent of the Irish family of Vans, as he no doubt was, the name David being common in all branches of the fmily.

David Vance married Priscilla Brauk and lived about nine miles north of Asheville, North Carolina, on Reeves or Reems Creek. The place of burial is upon a beautiful knoll selected by him as a place from which to rise on the resurrection day. The D. A. R's. have erected a monument over his grave. There is also a very handsome monument to his memory in the Public Square at Asheville, North Carolina. Besides his wife he letft sons Samuel, David and Robert and daughters Jean, Elizabeth, Sarah married McLean, Priscilla married George Whitson, Celia married Benjamin Brittain. Samuel and the daughters except Elizabeth, moved to East Tennessee and settled on lands provided for them along the Duck River by their father. Mrs. Mary Burdett, of Austin, Texas, is descendent of Samuel.

Jane or Jean, daughter of David and Priscilla Vance was born Nov. 1777, near Asheville, North Carolina, and married Aug. 24, 1796 to Hugh Davidson. She died Jan. 12, 1858 near Wartrace, Tennessee. Children of this couple were:

1 William Mitchell, born Aug. 21, 1797; married July 6, 1837 and died March 6, 1877. One child.

2 Priscilla, born July 6, 1799; married Jan. 2, 1821, died Aug. 20, 1840. Ten children.

3 Margaret M., born Oct. 18, 1801; married Nov. 1, 1832, died April 21, 1868. Four children.

4 David V., born Nov. 20, 1803; married Jan. 22, 1829, died Nov. 3, 1869. Nine children.

VANCE

5. . Angeline, born July 26, 1806; married Dec. 24, 1824; died Aug. 16, 184—. Nine children.
6 John J., born July 26, 1808; married Dec. 3, 1833; died Oct. 12, 1897. Eleven children.
7 Sarah Eliza, born April 25, 1810; died Dec. 2, 1810.
8 Samuel Leander, born April 19, 1812; married three times; died Dec. 13, 1870. Five children.
9. Hugh Lawson, born April 17, 1814, marred twice; died April 30, 1889. Two children.
10 Robert Brauk, born March 12, 1817; married twice; died Oct. 3, 1900. Two children.
11 Eliza Jane, born June 3, 1819; died Sept. 18, 1822.
12 Martha Ann, Dec. 16, 1822; married Dec. 24, 1840; died March 3, 1857.

John Quincy Davidson, son of Hugh and Jean Vance, born June 26, 1808; married Dec. 3, 1833, Susan Hord, and died Oct. 12, 1879. They had eleven children, namely:

1 Mary Jane, born Nov. 14, 1834; married May 5, 1865. Nine children.
2 Rufus Edmund, born Aug. 3, 1836; married Sept. 25, 1862; died 1908. Ten children.
3 Hugh Albert, born Jan. 8, 1839; married July 30, 1885. Two children.
4 Samuel A., born Nov. 15, 1840.
5 William, born Aug. 20, 1842.
6 Susan Agnes, born March 12, 1844; married Nov. 15, 1866. Nine children.
7 James Mitchell, born Sept. 6, 1849.
8 Harriet, Sept. 13, 1851; married Oct. 3, 1871; died June 25, 1917. Eight children.
9 Coleman Lawrence, March 1855; married July 6, 1892.
10 Robt. V., born March 26, 1858; married Oct. 14, 1884. Four children.
11 Harriete E., daughter John and Susan, born Sept. 13, 1851; married Oct. 3, 1871 to Joseph Oliver Arnold and died June 25, 1917; had 1 Leonla Arnold born Nov. 14, 1872; married June 5, 1899 at Wartrace, Tennessee, to Dr. John Lane Walker. Children:

Elizabeth, Feb. 26, 1901.
Perry Arnold, Aug. 7, 1902.
Leola, Aug. 1, 1905.
Lydie Lane, Sept. 16, 1908.

NOTABLE SOUTHERN FAMILIES

Elizabeth, daughter of David, and Mary Priscilla B. Vnce married first, William Mitchell Davidson, and second, Samuel Davidson. The Asheville, North Carolina family descend frm this couple.

Robert Brank, son of David and Priscilla Vance was a member of congress 1824 and 25 and was killed in a duel n the latter year.

David, son of David and Priscilla Vance, born Jan. 2, 1792, died Jan. 14, 1844. He married Jan. 1825, Mira Margaret Baird, born Dec. 22, 1802 and died 1878. They had:

Laura Henrietta, born April 13, 1826.
Robert Brank, April 24, 1828.
Zebulon B., May 13, 1830.
James Noel, Feb. 10, 1833.
Anna Edgeworth, April 25, 1836.
Sarah Priscilla, Jan 4, 1838.
David L., Jan. 10, 1846.
Hannah Moore, Aug. 10, 1842.

Zebulon Baird Vance, born Buncomb County, North Carolna. May 13, 1830 and died April 14, 1894. He married Harriet Newell Epsy and second Mrs. Florence Martn.

He had two sons and three daughters. He was Colonel of the 25th North Carolina Regiment. He was elected Governor of North Carolina. He was one of the most brilliant men who ever sat in the Senatorial Halls, adding to his intellectual ablilty a ken and ready wit. He had four sons. One Thomas M. Vance is a prominent lawyer and politician living in Olympia, Wasihngton.

Robert Brank Vance, brother of David, was Brgadier-General in Confederate Army and member of Congrss several terms. He married Harriet McIlroy and had four sons and two daughters.

Vance in the Colonial Wars of Virginia

Vance, Andrew—Hennings Statutes, Vol. 7, p. 216.
Vance, John—Augusta Records, Vol. 1, p. 518.
Vance, Patrick—Hennings Statutes, Vol. 7, p. 191.
Vance, Samuel—Hennings Statutes, Vol. 7, p. 216; Vol. 8, p. 129.

Vance, Thomas—Hennings Statutes, Vol. 7, p. 198.
Vance, William—R. G. Thwaitlers, Dunmore's Wars, p. 412.

VANCE

Vance in the Revolutionary War
Who Served in Virginia.

(From Revolutionary Soldiers of Virginia—State Librarian's List).

Vnce, David—Illinois Papers, D. 48; Rom. 15.
Vance, Hadley—Conquest of the Northwest, 2:849.
Vance, James—(Washington County), Secretary of War, 135; Nen., 2 205.
Vance, John—(Ensign) R. C.
Vance, Joseph—(Pitts) 50; Saffell 263; War 4, 284, 386.
Vance, Robert—(Captain) Ar. C. L. 26. Aud acct. VII, 214.
Vance, Robert—(Lieutenant) Heitman 408.
Vance, Robert—(Pitts) 16; War 4, 68.
Vance, William—(Captain) Heitman 408.
Vance, William—Illinois papers, D. 156.

Patrick Vance was appointed third surgeon in Christian's Campaign at Camp Lady Amtler, Oct. 20, 1776.—"Hstoric Sullivan," Page 63.

WEAR

The Wears came from Ulster, Ireland. They reached Augusta County, Virginia, by way of Pennsylvania as did many of the Augusta County, Virginia, early families.

In April 1719, Robert Wier was one of the settlers in Nutfield, near Haverhill, Massachusetts, (but in New Hampshire) under the leadership of James McKee. It is probable that this Robert Wear was the father of Robert Wear, who later was established in Augusta County, Virginia, and was the father of Col. Samuel Wear.

The settlement of Nutfield was thought to be in Massachusetts, but the general court of May, 1719, decided that it was in New Hampshire. James Gregg and Robert Wear, in behalf of the Scotch-Irish settlers at Nutfield, asked the Governor and Court assembled at Portsmouth, New Hampshire, for a township ten miles square. They and others obtained a deed from Col. John Wheelwright. Londonderry, New Hampshire, was then incorporated in June, 1719. It voted to give a lot to each of the first comers, "which is the number of twenty" Robert Wear is one of the twenty. To Robert Wear and his wife, Martha Wear, a daughter, Elizabeth Wear was born in 1723.

A Robert Wear was Commissioner in Antrim County, Ireland, 1717.

Few names have been subjected to such varied spelling as that of "Wear". Wier, Weyr, Weer and Ware are a few of the variations. The early recorder's orthography conformed only to the sound of a name and there its nicety ended. Quite often a family accepted the change without protest, for to the pioneer, public records were more vital than the mere differenc of a letter or two in the spelling of his name. The families of Colonel Samuel Wear and his brother, John Wear, seem to have preferred "Wear". There are several romantic stories accounting for that preference.

A later family, spelling the name "Weyr", settled in North Carolina shortly prior to the Rvolution. The Virginia family of which the Tennessee family was a branch, spelled the name Weir as many of the descendants do to this day

While it is possible that the family name is a corruption of the Anglo-Saxon word DeVere, Mrs. Louise Wilson Reynolds, attributes its origin to the Gothic "Wehren", to check or from the kindred Anglo-Saxon "Wer", which, literally transcribed, means "To defend, to protect". From the latter we receive the word "Weir", a dam.

A family of Scotch, "Weirs" was established in Ireland in 1664 by the Rev. John Weir, who, with James Adair and several other ministers was sent into Ireland "to administer the covenant to all of the officers and soldiers and Protestants in Ireland".

The Rev. John Wear may have been the father or grandfather of Robert Weir, or Wear, of Nutfield, Massachusetts.

As early as 1690, we find in the City of Brotherly Love, Charles Weir asking for "ye thirty foot lot on ye river's bank adjoining Richard Wall and Timothy Clements".

Charles Weir received the lot; he also is recorded as one of the first attorneys of Philadelphia.

An early line of Pennsylvania Weirs, with branches in Cumberland County, is thought to have descended from Charles Weir; the names bear a marked dissimilarity to those in the Robert Wear line.

Robert, John and William Weir were the founders of the Bucks County, Pennsylvania, "Weirs". They are believed to have come from Massachusetts about the year 1737, and to have been sons of Robert Weir, of Nutfield. In that case their mother was Martha and their sister was Elizabeth, a name frequent in the family to this day.

(Col. Samuel Wear named his eldest daughter, Elizabeth).

John Weir married Elizabeth Holmes, September 3, 1737. No record has been found of the marriage of Robert or of William Weir.

Since no line has been found in Pennsylvania for some time prior to the Revolution that could be credited to John Weir, and as subsequently such a line does appear in Virginia, we are led to the belief that John Weir emigrated to Richmond before Robert Weir purchased land in the Borden grant in 1752.

WEAR

Robert Wear, Father of Col. Samuel Wear

In 1752, a deed is recorded to Robert Wear and John Cunningham of eight hundred and thirty-three acres in Borden's Tract, Augusta County, Virginia, and in 1754, Borden's executors deeded 240 acres to Robert Wear and his wife, Rebecca.

It is evident therefore that Robert Wear and his wife who was Rebecca ———, were settled in Augusta County, Virginia about 1752. This Robert Wear must have been born about 1715. His marriage to Rebecca ———, took place about 1740. One of their sons, John Wear, was born in Bucks County, Pennsylvania, October ———, 1742. Samuel Wear, the other son of whom we have record, was born in Augusta County, Virginia, 1753. Robert Wear was living in the year 1789, and at that period was probably about seventy-four years old. To Robert and Rebecca ——— Wear were born at least two sons, John and Samuel, and possibly other children whose names have not been preserved.

Near the year 1792 there were residing in Greene County, Tennessee, Thomas Wear, John Wear, junior, Hugh Wear, Thomas Wear and Saumel Wear. The name Robert Wear appears on Colonel Wear's company for the year 1785, but there is no evidence that he owned land in the county. Whether he was the father or a brother of Colonel Samuel Wear can only be conjectured.

The pioneer family of Wears was not large. Hugh and John Wear, junior, are supposed to have been sons of John Wear, senior, a supposition based on the fact that they resided near or adjoining the farm on which John Wear settled after his reomvel from Washington County into Green County. This farm, on the Nollichucky river south of Greeneville, is now known as the Devault place.

Thomas Wear in 1783 resided between Greeneville and Newport; his wife was named Elizabeth. Of Thomas Wear nothing more is known.

One of the above Wears, unfortunately the historians do not give the name, was killed at the Battle of Etowah, April, 1793.

Two Wear marriages are recorded in Greene County, namely:

Margaret Wear to Hugh Cunningham, October 8, 1792.
Jane Wear to Thomas Lovelady, October 14, 1796.

NOTABLE SOUTHERN FAMILIES

John Wear, Son of Robert Wear

John Wear, son of Robert Wear and brother of Colonel Samuel Wear and referred to in the early records of Washington and Greene Counties as "John Wear, Gentleman," was born in Bucks County, Pennsylvania, October, 1742, and died in Sevier County, Tennessee, at the age of ninety-two years. He was about ten years of age when his father emigrated to Borden's grant, Augusta County, Virginia. Among other contemporary families who had emigrated from Pennsylvania to Augusta County was that of Blackburn.

General Samuel Blackburn, was a distinguished officer of the Revolution, one of the most beloved friends of General Washington and one of the pallbearers at Washington's funeral.

John Wear married in Augusta County, Virginia, Nancy Blackburn, a daughter of Benjamin Blackburn and a sister of General Samuel Blackburn.

John Wear emigrated, with his brother, Samuel Wear, to Washington County, Tennessee, about the year 1778. He purchased the plantation adjoining that of John Sevier and here he resided for several years. A rock in the river known as "Wear's Rock" is supposed to mark the spot of an accidental drowning of some member of his family, but tradition does not relate further details.

John Wear served under his brother, Colonel Samuel Wear, at King's Mountain and was a soldier under General Nathaniel Greene at the "Surrended of Yorktown," as his pension papers show, mentioning also Col. Wear's presence at Yorktown. He is also reputed to have had much of the prowess which distinguished his brother in Indian warfare. He was a man of culture and intelligence and was one of the early magistrates of both Washington and Greene Counties. After the marriage of his daughter, Margaret Wear, to John Wilson. In 1792, John Wear moved into Greene County. He purchased one of the first town lots surveyed in the town of Greeneville, but resided on his farm, then called a "plantation," which lay below the old Greeneville College in a lovely valley on the river, and which for many years has been owned by the DeVault family.

Other friends may have failed in their allegiance to John Sevier, Governor of Franklin, but Samule and John Wear were faithful to the end. A laconic record once to be found

WEAR

on the books in the Greeneville court house, in the beautiful faded chirography of its clerk, General Daniel Kennedy, has in it not a little pathos:

"On this day of February, 1789, John Sevier and John Wear rode into court and took the oath thus subscribed in such cases".

The oath in question being that of renewed allegiance to North Carolina.

This was after the fall of the heroic little state of Franklin in which Sevier and the Wares had been leading siprits.

In November of the same year, without a competitive rival, John Sevier was elected to represent Washington District, North Carolina, in the United States Congress.

John Wear and his wife, Nancy Blackburn Wear had children:

Elizabeth Wear, married James Gray.

Phoebe Wear, married George Matthews.

Susan (?) married ——— Bird.

Hugh Wear.

George Wear.

Benjamin Wear, died between 1835 and 1839.

Margaret Wear, married John W. Wilson, 1792. She died between 1835 and 1840.

Nancy Wear, married Thomas Alexander.

General Samul Blackburn, of Virginia, dying without issue, Margaret Wear was one of the many nieces according to the terms of his will, among whom his large estate was divided.

At the date this legacy was received, a witness in court, Valentine Sevier, son of Governor John Sevier, testified to years of intimate friendship with John Wilson and his wife, Margaret Wear Wilson, and stated "that when a boy, with his father's family, he had attended the celebration of the wedding of Margaret Wear to John Wilson in Washington County".

Margaret Wilson's name has come down to her descendants as a woman possessing many charms and virtues. She was a full cousin of both Gideon Blackburn and of his wife, and the former always made his home with her when his pastoral duties brought him to Washington and Greene Counties.

Margaret Wilson was the mother of several children.

NOTABLE SOUTHERN FAMILIES

Mrs. Louise Wilson Reynolds has inherited Margaret Wear Wilson's Bible, which gives the eldest son, John Wear Wilson, as born September 10, 1793. John Wear Wilson was a soldier under General Andrew Jackson at the Battle of New Orleans. He was twice married, first to Isabella Rankin, and second, to Sarah Holt.

The eldest daughter, Nancy Wilson, was named for Margaret Wilson's mother. She married Thomas Lee.

COL. SAMUEL WEAR

Robert Wear, the father of Samuel Wear and John Wear (whose history has just been given), purchased land in the Borden Tract in Virginia in 1752, and on that property, in 1753. Samuel Wear was born. His older brother, John Wear, was born in 1742, in Bucks County, Pennsylvania, before the family left that state.

Samuel Wear began the military life which he was to follow always in 1777, when he was appointed ensign in the Augusta Militia. As he lived near John Sevier, and as both were young officers in the Augusta Militia, it is believed that their intimate friendship began in their early youth. It lasted throughout their lives and they pursued careers singularly similar. It is believed that John Sevier's removal to the "Mountains" now Tennessee, influenced that of his friend. They were together in all the adventurous life of early Tennessee and served in the Indian campaigns, at King's Mountain and other battles and later in the War of 1812. They each married twice and each named a son for the other, Samuel being a name frequently borne in the Sevier connection to this day; John Wear being equally familiar. John had been a frequent name in the Wear family, as is evidenced in the foregoing record, but Samuel is not apparent in the Sevier records before the birth of Governor John Sevier's son who was named Samuel.

In 1778 Samuel Wear married in Augusta County, Virginia, Mary (sometimes called "Polly") Thompson, daughter of William Thompson and Elizabeth Lyle Thompson (see "Notable Southern Families, Volume I, for the Lyle record).

The children of Samuel Wear and Mary Thompson Wear were:

I. Elizabeth Wear, born October 4, 1780, who married Robert Armstrong, Third. (See Armstrong Family, "Notable Southern Families, Volume I).

II. Robert Wear, who married Lucretia Thomas.

III. Rebecca Wear, who married John Witt.
IV. Samuel Wear, Second.
V. John Wear, who married first, Susannah Mullendore, and married second, Sarah M. Patty.
VI. Mary Wear, who married Colonel Simeon Perry.

Colonel Samuel Wear, after the death of Mary Thompson Wear, married Mary Gilliland, daughter of John and Elizabeth Gilliland and had children:
VII. Diana Wear, who married David Johnson.
VIII. Pleasant M. Wear, who married Tryphena Tipton.
IV. Margaret Wear, who married D. B. Cummings.
X. Minerva Wear, who married John Guthrie.

Colonel Wear served in public life for half a cenury. He removed with John Sevier from Augusta County, Virginia, to the "Mountains" some time after his marriage in 1778 to Mary Thompson and before the Battle of King's Mountain, October 7, 1780, when he was already a resident of the mountain country.

Samuel Wear, after making a choice of land for his new home, about five miles from Sevierville, on the west side of Little Pidgeon River, returned to Virginia for his family, leaving a negro slave named Frank to take care of the place and raise corn.

His daughter, Elizabeth Wear, was born in Augusta County, Virginia, October 4, 1780.

The other children of Samuel Wear seem to have been born in "the mountains'" in what is now Tennessee.

Colonel Wear served in the War of 1812 as a Colonel. He died April 3, 1817 and is buried within a mile of Henderson Springs, Tennessee. He willed his entire property to his second wife until his youngest child should become of age.

Samuel Wear was a captain in the Battle of King's Mountain and one of the organizers of the historic band which in the Battle of King's mountain put the enemy to route and practically ended the Revolutionary War.

His participation in King's Mountain is proved by every early Tennessee history and hundreds of documents. He was also present at the surrender of Yorktown, and this is attested by the pension papers of his brother, John Wear.

Samuel Wear's participation in all the early life of Tennessee and the various governments which preceded the state is well known. He was an ardent Indian campaigner, quite as enthusiastic and as successful as John Sevier, and Ramsey's is full of his achievements.

He was a clerk of the State of Franklin and Colonel of its militia. He was a member of the first legislative body ever assembled in Tennessee, the first Franklin convention. He was a member of the first Tennessee Legislature also and a member of the committee which made the constitution of the new state.

He was for many years clerk of the County of Sevier and he served in the War of 1812.

He lived to a good old age and is described by Lyman Draper in "Heroes of King's Mountain" as being tall, fully six feet in height, dark-complexioned and possessed much energy of character.

His descendants are all eligible to the Societies of the Revolution and the Societies of 1812.

The place selected by Samuel Wear for his home is known to this day as "Wear's Cove".

He and two young sons were fired upon by a party of thirty savages on one occasion. Again on June 19, 1793, a band of Indians entered "Wear's Cove," cut down the growing corn, stole one horse, killed ten and destroyed the mill. Col. Wear with a party of neighbors pursued the maurauders and at Tallahassee a battle resulted in which sixteen Indians were killed and four taken prisoner.

In 1784, Col. Wear was elected "deputy to the convention to deliberate upon public affairs". The convention met at Jonesboro, August 23, 1784. At that convention, the first ever held in what is now Tennessee, was born the State of Franklin.

When the State of Franklin had become a fact after that "deliberation upon public affairs", its new Governor, John Sevier, appointed Samuel Wear, Clerk of the County Court of Sevier County, and Colonel of the Regiment. In the summer of 1786, he was appointed one of the Commissioners to negotiate a treaty with the Indians. The conference between the Commissioners and the Indians lasted four days and ended at Coyton, August 3, 1786.

Old Tassel and Hanging Maw were present at Chota Ford for this treaty. The land claimed by the Commissioners included the Island in the Tennessee at the mouth of the Holston and from the head of the Island to the dividing Ridge between the Holston, Little River and the Tennes-

WEAR

see, which had been transferred to the settlers by North Carolina.

After the short life and fall of Franklin, Governor William Blount called an election which was held in December, 1793, and Samuel Wear was elected a member of the first Assembly of the Territory of Tennessee (representing the County of Jefferson). The Assembly was called to order in Knoxville, February, 1794. He was one of the committee of five appointed by this Assembly to draft an address to Congress. In this address the people of the Territory of Tennessee demanded a declaration of War against the Creeks and the Cherokees.

His name is found continually in the early records of the Territory and the State and he was a member of the first Tennessee Legislature after the Territory passed into a State. He was a member of the Committee which wrote the first Constitution.

In the War of 1812 he was a Colonel, though that title had already been bestowed upon him during the brief life of the State of Franklin. He died April 3, 1817, on his plantation and is buried within a mile of Henderson Springs, near Sevierville, Tennessee. He was survived by his second wife. His will, which is recorded, left all his property to his wife until his youngest child should come of age.

I. ELIZABETH WEAR

Elizabeth Wear, eldest child of Samuel Wear and his first wife, Mary Thompson Wear, was born October 4, 1780, a few days before her father's participation in the Battle of King's Mountain. She was born in Augusta County, Virginia, though her father had removed to the "Mountains" before that date, returning shortly after the King's Mountain Battle to accompany his wife and daughter to the new home.

Elizabeth Wear married Robert Armstrong the Third. Their children were:

(1) Drury Payne Armstrong, married Amelia Houston.

(2) Addison Wear Armstrong, married Nancy McMillan.

(3) Mariah Armstrong, married John Brooks and James McMillan.

(4) Rutelia Armstrong, married Thomas Gillespie Craighead.

(5) Charlotte Perry Armstrong, married Samuel Armstrong and Henry Baldwin.

(6) Robert Horace Armstrong, died young.
(7) Margaret Cunningham Armstrong, married Samuel Hannibal Love.
(8) Dialthea Perry Armstrong, married Pleasant M. Love.
(9) James Houston Armstrong, married Ann E. Park.
(10) Malinda Armstrong, married Samuel Morrow.
(11) Samuel Thompson Armstrong, died young.
(12) Betty Armstrong, died at birth.

Elizabeth Wear was accustomed to the somewhat exciting life of a soldier's household, as she was the daughter of the stalwart Samuel Wear. She must, therefore, have been resigned to Robert Armstrong's career which was also that of a soldier and Indian fighter. It is related in the family annals that on one occasion (1819), Robert Armstrong returned from a campaign against the Indians to find his wife and new born babe dead and a little son, Robert, lying dead beside them. The little boy had probably been exposed in some way during his mother's illness. Elizabeth Wear and Robert Armstrong the Third, and these two little children are buried on the place upon which they lived, now known as the Bounds place, on the river a few miles above Knoxville.

For the descendants of Robert and Elizabeth Wear Armstrong see Armstrong Family Vol. I Notable Southern Families.

II. ROBERT WEAR

Robert Wear, son of Col. Samuel Wear and his wife Mary Thompson Wear, was born 1781, after his father and mother had moved from Augusta County, Virginia, to the new country. He married Lucretia Thomas. Their children were:

(1) Louisiana Wear.
(2) Eliza Wear.
(3) Betsy T. Wear.
(4) Albert G. Wear, who died young.
(5) Mary Thompson Wear, or Polly as she was called.
(6) Erskine Haywood Wear.
(7) Malvina Wear.
(8) Gilbert N. Wear.
(9) Letitia Wear.
(10) Isaac D. Wear.
(11) Lucinda D. Wear.
(12) Lucretia A. Wear.

WEAR

(13) Robert H. Wear.
(1) Louisiana Wear, born 1803, died 1890; married John B. Tipton. Their children were:
Lucretia Tipton (who married Robert L. McNutt and had no children);
Lavinia (who married William H. Dawson and had John B. Dawson who married Phoebe Steed and had children; William R. Dawson, who married Bettie Elmore and had Eva L., Charles E. and Edna E. Dawson; Sarah L. Dawson, who married Frank Beals and had Frank and Daisy Beals, and married second, David Simpson and had Jessie Simpson; Mary L. Dawson (who married Lewis A. Hunt and had Charles F., Lewis and Gladys Hunt).
Marshall C. Tipton who married Sarah J. Dawson and had Mary Elizabeth Tipton (who married Henry C. Cobb and had Frank S., Robert C., Lena, Edgar, Charles and Margaret Cobb); Louise Tipton (who married Preston P. Sooy and had Frank Sooy, and married second, D. L. Edmonson); Marshall Alexander Tipton (who married Laura A. Shelterly and had Bettie C., Frank, Maude and Marshall).
Elizabeth Tipton married John C. Wilkey.
Amelia M. Tipton married Hugh L. McNutt and had Lucretia McNutt (who married Archibald Hitch and had Robert E., Sadie D., William B. and Lina Hitch); and Mary E. McNutt (who married Samuel P. Clark and had Hugh M., Lula and John Thomas Clark).
Sarah T. Tipton married Elbert S. Cobb and had Mary (who died young), Lena (who died unmarried), Arty (who married Andrew B. Montgomery and had Frank M., Myrtis, Arty and Joseph Montgomery), Aurelia (who married Lonnie M. Wimberly and had Dora C. Wimberly), Malvina Lee (who married Joseph Reagan and had Madge T. Reagan), Rachel (who married William W. McCormack and had Clifford died young and another son), and Eva (who married Bennett White).
Malcom M Tipton married Amanda Rider and had no children.
Jonathan N. Tipton married Eliza Jane Blair and had nine children: John Blair Tipton (who married Addie Anderson); Henry F. Tipton (who married Daisy Belle Wilson); Malcom M. Tipton (who married Alma W. Mayo); Cora E. Tipton; Robert F. Tipton; David D. Tipton; Laura E. Tipton; Edgar E. Tipton and Pearl E. Tipton.
Gilbert H. Tipton married Martha Nelson and had Sid-

ney N. Tipton (who married Elbridge Gerry Mayo), John B., Hope M., Nelson, Lawrence P. and Bessie A. Tipton.

Caswell T. Tipton married Evaline Montgomery and had Samuel H., Robert O., Edgar B., Nina L., Frank C., Horace C. and Lou Annie Tipton.

Henry T. Tipton married Mattie T. Tipton and had Louise, Lula, John H., Nellie, Lucy, Malcolm and Henry Tipton.

(2) Eliza Wear, daughter of Robert Wear and Lucretia Thomas Wear, married Michael Girdner and had seven children:

Lorinda Girdner married John W. W. Dearmond and had James M., Mary E., Lucretia Adeline, Haywood, Robert B., Allen J., Samuel, Catherine L., Sarah T., Herman W.

Eliza Jane Girdner married William A. Audau and had Henry A. Audas, Ella A. Audas, Mary C. Audas, Elizabeth J. Audas, Maria E. Audas, James W. Audas, Lorenzo D. Audas and Richard M. Audas.

Alexander Augustus Girdner married Nancy VanBidder and had Eliza H., Asenath Ann and Nancy Augustus.

Lucretia Malvina Girdner married John Audas and had J. Thomas., Michael, Martha Jane, Samuel R., William Henry, Isaac D., James B., Charles H., Haywood, John M. and Lucretia Audas.

Leonidas Haywood Girdner married Mrs. Asenath M. Lowery and had Robert T., D. Richard, Bettie, Amanda, Lillie, William Haywood, Charles E. and Hattie.

Maria Louise Girdner married Joseph Lowry Meek and had Katie C., James G., Charles W., Nancy E., Susan E., Martha J., Minnie F., Joseph F. and Amanda E. Meek.

Mary Emiline Girdner married Hugh Hamilton Craig and had William G., James B., Ann Eliza, John H., Samuel H. and Robert C.

(3) Betsy T. Wear, daughter of Robert Wear and Lucretia Thomas, married Creed Fulton and had Ferdinand Fulton and Aurelia Fulton; both died young.

(5) Mary Thompson Wear, daughter of Robert Wear and Lucretia Thomas Wear, married James A. Gallegher and had Ella (who married Zophar Case), Louisa (who married James Shrader), and Lee Albert Gallagher (who married Antoinette Holly.

John Albert Gallagher married Kate H. Gillman and had Leo and Victor; married second, Lina Catherine Gillum and had Catherine.

(6) Erskine Haywood Wear, son of Robert and Lu-

cretia Thomas Wear, married Rachel E. Morrow and had two daughters Lucretia Penelope Wear and Margaret E. Wear Lucretia Penelope Wear married Anderson L. Carson and had several children who died young and Mary Alice Carson (married Hugh L. Isbell, Addie Roselia (married James Hightower), Lillie Lucrelia Carson (married Anderson R. Tallent), Anderson L. Carson (married Alice Newman).

Margaret E. Wear married John A. Hull and had Alice May (married Lenry F. Lieb), Mary E. Hull (married Henry F. Hughes), Lillie C. Hull (married John Irvine Hostetter), Nannie Morrow Hull (married Charles W. Barnes).

(7) Malvina Wear, daughter of Robert Wear and Lucretia Thomas Wear, married James W. Lea and had:

Mary L. Lea (married Robert K Byrd).
Myrtele A. Lea (married Denning).
Albert T. Lea married Virginia A. Darnell and had a son, Albert Eugene Lea, who married his cousin, Deborah Wear.

(8) Gilbert N. Wear, son of Robert and Lucretia Thomas Wear married Margaret A. Strain and had James H., Nancy L., Susan Jane, Margaret M., Martha L., Robert T., Mary L., Eliza W.; and married second, Mary A. Wilson, by whom he had the following children: William C., Elbert N., Oscar Lowe, Mary, Julia A., Eugenia, Emma, Gilbert L., Viola, Howard T. Gilbert N. Wear had twnty-three children by his two wives. Some of them died young and are not enumerated in this list.

(10) Isaac Decatur Wear, son of Robert Wear and Lucretia Thomas Wear married first, M. A. Blankenship, by whom he had Elizabeth L. and Robert T.; married second, Susannah A. J. Shelton by whom he had John M., Talbert B., Louisiana A. and Susan D.; and married third, Susanna Isbell, by whom he had no children.

(11) Lucinda Jane Wear, married William Singleton.
(12) Lurcetia A. Wear, married Thomas Harvey.
(13) Robert H. Wear.

III. REBECCA WEAR

Rebecca Wear, third child of Col. Samuel Wear by his first wife, Mary Thompson Wear, was born 1787. She died 1836. She married in 1807, John Witt. They went from Tennessee to Fayetteville, Arkansas, Crittendon County, to reside. They had eight children, namely: Robert Witt, William Samuel Witt, John Witt, Elizabeth Witt, Caroline Witt, Margaret Witt, Charlotte Witt, Malinda Jane Witt.

Robert Witt, son of John and Rebecca Wear Witt, born about 1808, married about 1829, Sarah Wallace and moved, it is said, to Fort Smith, Arkansas, where he died. They had two children.

William Samuel Witt, son of John Witt and Rebecca Wear Witt, was born about 1801. He married first, in 1832, Mary Dennis and had two children: Elizabeth Witt (who married ——— Cheston and had a daughter that married George Trapp); William Jackson Witt, born 1845, died 1893, (who married Catherine V. Gardner, daughter of William Gardner and Matilda Robbins Gardner. Their children were William Samuel Witt, Mary M. Witt (married William Hobbs Watson of Hot Springs, and has a son, William Hobbs Watson); Lillian Mae Witt, Frederick Witt, and Miles B. Witt).

John Witt son of John Witt and Rebecca Witt married Lillian Harrington.

Elizabeth Witt, daughter of John Witt and Rebecca Wear Wear Witt, married William Lewis and went to the Indian Territory to reside. They had four children, two daughters names unknown, and Maggie Lewis (who married ——— Davis, lived in Vincent, Arkansas, and had a son, Perry Davis), and Joseph Lewis, who married in Hot Springs, Arkansas, and went to Indian Territory to reside.

Caroline Witt, daughter of John Witt and Rebecca Wear Witt, married Isaac Crabb. Nothing further is known of her.

Margaret Witt, daughter of John Witt and Rebecca Wear Witt, married Oliver Wallace and had four children, among them Houston Wallace.

Charlotte Witt, daughter of John Witt and Rebecca Wear Witt, married ——— Berry. She left no children.

Matilda Jane Witt, daughter of John Witt and Rebecca Wear Witt married first in Vincent, Arkansas, ——— Locker and had Frances Locker; married second, ——— Edwards and had Josephine Edwards; married third Berry Lack and had no children by him. Frances Locker married Thomas Smith, of Vincent, Arkansas, and had Adolphus Smith, Charles Smith, Katie Smith and Ethel Smith. Katie Smith married William Craven. Josephine Edwards, the only child by Malinda Jane Witt's second marriage, married James Brown and had one daughter named Cleveland Brown. Matilda Jane Witt, married third Berry Black but had no children by this marriage.

IV. SAMUEL WEAR, JUNIOR

Samuel Wear, son of Col. Samuel Wear and Mary Thomson Wear, married and lived in Alabama.

It is believed that he married Sallie White, as a marriage record in Knox County, Tennessee, September 26, 1811, is of Samuel Wear, junior, to Sallie White. His children were David Wear, Rebecca Wear and Mary Wear.

V. JOHN WEAR

John Wear, son of Col. Samuel Wear and Mary Thompson Wear, born about 1792, married Susannah Mullendore, and married second Sarah M. Patty. His children were: Mary Wear (who married first Isaac T. R. Ellis and married second George W. Waters); Musadora Wear (who married Maston E. Eslinger); Robert Wear (who married Matilda Ann Francisco); Lavater Wear (who married Martha Jane Meyers); Elizabeth Wear (who married first Alfred Baker and married second Enoch L. Waters); Malinda H. Wear (who married John Murray Marshall); John Wear (who married Julia L. Cabler); Thomas J. Wear (who married Mary Crowsen); Roten G. Wear (who married Sarah E. Stevenson); Creed F. Wear (who died unmarried); Diana Wear (who married Ezikel K. Hurst); Martha Wear (who married James M. Bird); Nancy Wear (who married John Caylor); Isaac D. Wear; Rebecca Wear (who married Bart Suttles); Josephine Wear (who married Nathan Meyers); Solly Wear (who married James A. Kerley); Malvina Wear (who married first Wyley Brickley, and married second Alfred Bolling); Letitia Wear (who married Willam Hatcher); and Pleasant A. Wear (who married Olive Bruce McCown).

VI. MARY WEAR

Mary Wear, sixth child of Col. Samuel Wear and his first wife, Mary Thompson Wear, was born 1795. She died 1821. She married 1801, Simeon Perry. Their children were:

(1) Caroline Frances, who married Drury H. Field and had Mary F. Field (who married Isaac Newton Jones and had John F. Jones, William I. Jones, Wood F. Jones and George A. Jones); Drury H. Field, junior (who married Laura A. Pearce and had John E., William H., and Susanna P.) John Edwin Field (who married Fannie S. Brown and

had Jesse B. Field and William R. Field), Carrie Eliza Field (who married Bradley Henry and had Surrey Henry, Thomas P., Henry and John M. Henry), Florence Field (who married John Wood Lindley), Eudora Field (who married first Daniel W. Hearne and married second William Boulware), and Mattie Lee Field (who married Gabriel M. Eddins).

James Monroe Perry, who married Mrs. Hannah Jackson Bruce, widow of Dr. Robert Bruce and daughter of Green Jackson. Their children were: Imogene and Horatio, (died young); Mozelle Perry (who married John G. Kirksey and had Imogene, Walter P., Kenmore V., Mozelle, Pauline, Hermance, Guy, Gertrude, and Ina); Deucalion Perry (who married Mattie Barnes and had Haile, Mozelle, and Hattie); Conrad Perry (who married Alice Barnes and had Stewart Estelle and Tempe), and Tempe Perry (who married Columbus Haile and had Tempe and Columbus who both died young, and Tempe and Elsie).

Colonel Samuel Wear married twice. His first wife, Mary Thompson, died in 1797. His second wife was Mary Gilliland. She survived her distinguished husband for more than twenty years, and according to descriptions left by her grand children, was a pretty, vivacious woman, fond of gaity and the center of an interesting group. Colonel Wear died April 3, 1817. As a Captain at King's Mountain, a Colonel in the War of 1812, and an important man in the community from every point of view, his widow had a station to maintain and she seems to have enjoyed maintaining it. Colonel Wear did not apply for a pension, nor did his widow. His means and hers, following his death, were ample. She lived until some time in the early forties, the exact date of her death not being known.

She had four children, namely: Diana; Pleasant M.; Margaret and Minerva.

VII. DIANA WEAR

Diana, probably the eldest child of Colonel Samuel Wear and Mary Gilliland Wear, married Dovid Johnson, who went to Missouri before 1840, being the first of the family to go there. He built and established the first Dry Goods store in Springfield, Missouri.

VIII. PLEASANT M. WEAR

Pleasant M. Wear, son of Colonel Samuel Wear and his second wife, Mary Gilliland Wear, was born October 12th,

WEAR

1802, in Sevier ounty, Tennessee. Pleasant M. Wear was Clerk of the Circuit Court of Sevier County from 1828 to 1838. He then served as a Major in the Seminole War in Florida. Some time in 1840 he removed with his family and slaves to Missouri, where for many years he was Clerk of the Court of Lawrence County. He died in Mount Vernon, Lawrence County, Missouri, January 7th, 1870. He married, before leaving Tennessee, Tryphena Tipton, daughter of Colonel John Tipton. There is an interesting story about this marriage. We know of the Sevier-Tipton feud. We know of the Sevier--Trpton friendship. A Wear boy and a Tipton girl were sweethearts. The Wears were opposed, probably the Tiptons also. The boy and girl were determined. They agreed to bury the subject of the inherited illfeeling and get married. This they did and loyally kept the agreement. This boy was Pleasant M. Wear and the girl Tryphena Tipton. She died in Mount Vernon, September 1st, 1863. He married for his second wife, Mrs. Naomi McFall. He had no children by his second wife. His children by his first wife, Tryphena, were: Malinda; Lavinia; Mary; Helen Mar; Margaret; Oscar; Lucretia; John Guthrie; Caswell Tipton; Pleasant M., junior; Alice.

Malinda Wear, daughter of Pleasant M. Wear and Tryphena Tipton Wear, was born November 27th, 1827. She died in the early part of December, 1862 in Fayetteville, Arkansas, as a result of exposure in that most severe of all winters, while attending wounded Confederate soldiers. She was married December 10th, 1845 to John Spiller Kimbraugh who was born in Louisa County, Virginia, July 5th, 1819, and died in Clinton, Missouri, May 16th, 1895. Their children were: Mary Katherine; Pleasant M., and Anna Nixon Wear.

Mary Katherine, daughter of Melinda Wear and John Spiller Kimbrough, was born in Springfield, Missouri, June 24th, 1850; died in Clinton, Missouri, August 28th, 1894; married in Clinton Missouri, November 16th, 1871, Harvey Wallis Salmon, who was born January 16th, 1839, Greenville District, South Carolina. They had five children:

Harvey Woodson Salmon, born March 18th, 1873, in Clinton, Missouri, married in Kansas City, Missouri, August 21st, 1905, Myra Quintilla Smith who was born August 12th, 1882 in Seattle, Washington. They had two children, Katherine Bush, born in St Louis, Missouri, August 11, 1906, and Elizabeth Kimbrough Salmon, born May 1st, 1910, in St. Louis, Missouri.

NOTABLE SOUTHERN FAMILIES

John Young Salmon, born August 28th, 1875, died January 26th, 1886.

Merritt Kimbrough Salmon, born in Clinton, Missouri, August 23rd, 1877. He was married in August, 1917, to Florence Estelle McLeod, of Michigan, and now resides in Los Angelese, California. They have no children.

Louis Salmon was born September 9th, 1879, at Clinton, Missouri and married June 7th, 1905 at Clinton, Howard Bailey, who was born in Georgetown, Kentucky, October 24th, 1861. They have no children.

Warren Davis Salmon, was born at Clinton, Missouri, January 2nd, 1882, died in St. Louis, Missouri, November 27th, 1916. He married Katherine Lindsey, March 19th, 1904, at Sedalia, Missouri. Their children are: Harvey Wallis, born Clinton Missouri, January 12th, 1905. Margaret Lindsay, born June 27th, 1909 in Clinton, Missouri.

Pleasant Wear, son of Malinda Wear and John Spiller Kimbrough, married Mary Brooks and had seven children, namely: Russell Wear, married; Katherine Salmon, married E S. Nolen by whom she had a son, Edwin Salmon Nolen; Maude; Pleasant Wear; Oscar; Susan and Allen Brooks.

Anna Nixon, daughter of Malinda Wear and John Spiller Kimbrough, married W. A. Davison, a lawyer of Jefferson City, Missouri. They have no children.

Lavinia, daughter of Pleasant M. Wear and Tryphena Tipton Wear, was born in Tennessee, July 17, 1829, and married Dr. Nicholas B. Hocker, April 7th, 1846. Their children were:

Katherine, (Mary T.), who was born January 3, 1848, married Henry George, January 15, 1867, in Mount Vernon, Missouri, and had two children: Sarah (Sallie), who married George King and had two sons, Paul and Charles, who live in Little Rock, Arkansas; Charles B. who died unmarried.

William Barnes, who was born November 13, 1850. He is unmarried.

Charles, born October 24, 1855, who married Thursa Bell, May 25, 1879, lives in Mount Vernon, and has two children: Clyde and Floss. Clyde married Andy McCanse, February 7, 1904, and to them were born three children: Harrell, McCanse and N. B. Floss married Henry Toliver, February 7, 1907.

Pleasant M., was born December 11, 1907.

Mary, daughter of Pleasant M. Wear and Typhena

WEAR

Tipton Wear was born in Tennessee, March 25, 1831. She married first Thomas Jefferson Cook, August 17, 1848, by whom she had one son, Thomas J., junior, She married second John W. Ween, by whom she had five children: Oscar Holmes, who married Catherine Reynolds, of Mount Vernon; Tipton, Jesse Wear, who married Minnie Barker, Sarah Tryphena, who married John Henry Brown, and to this union four children were born: Daniel Marion, Florence, Ophelia and Thomas, and William Woodson, who married Hattie Kirby (one child), Lelia.

She married third Thomas Stephens, by whom she had three girls, Frances Kate, born March 25, 1870, and married Jack Reynolds, died later in Coffeyville, Kansas, January 1889; Naomi Blanche, born August 29, 1872, married first J. A Miller, second S. K. Gibson; Lavinia Josephine, born May 15, 1868, married D. M. Fenton, November 10, 1892, and has one daughter, Freda Madaline, who married R. B. Harness and lived in Kansas City, Missouri.

Helen Mar, daughter of Pleasant M. and Tryphena Tipton Wear, was born December 27th, 1832, and died young.

Margaret, daughter of Pleasant M. Wear and Tryphena Tipton Wear, was born January 7th, 1835, died in infancy.

Oscar Wear, son of Pleasant M. Wear and Tryphena Tipton Wear, was born October, 1836; married Frances Brown in 1859. They had no children.

Lucretia Wear, daughter of Pleasant M. and Tryphena Tipton Wear, was born November 10th, 1838, and married Thomas Everett in 1854.

John Guthrie, son of Pleasant M. and Tryphena Tipton Wear, was born November 4th, 1840. He was a lawyer, a Confederate soldier, and Judge of the U. S. District Court of Southeast Missouri. He received the appointment from President Cleveland and served as Judge for sixteen years. He says that his father, Pleasant M., used to tell him of the change in the spelling of the name. Colonel Samuel, a patriot, had a break with members of the family who were for King George. In defiance of kings and "taxation without representation", he changed the "i" to "a" making Weir into Wear. John Guthrie Wear was married on November, 1865, to Miss Young: Their children were: Charles Young Wear, died in early manhood; Pleasant M., died young; Catherine, married William Dickey, and has one son John, married.

NOTABLE SOUTHERN FAMILIES

Caswell Tipton Wear, son of Pleasant M. Wear and his wife Tryphena Tipton Wear was born in Greene County, Missouri, June 25, 1842. He married Sarah Elizabeth Parrott, May 31, 1863, at Mount Vernon, Missouri. He died Jan. 23, 1921, at Placentia, California, and was buriled at Pawnee, Oklahoma, by the side of his wife who had died several years before him. The children were Oscar DeWitt Wear, who died young; Horace G. Wear who was born October 25, 1865 (married Nellia Kelly and had one child); Samuel Tipton Wear, born September 27, 1867; Frances Tryphena Wear, born December 11, 1869, died November 19, 1898 (married William C. Cherry and had one child who died young); Mary Eleanor Wear, daughter of Caswell T. and Sarah Elizabeth Wear, born Jan. 28, 1872, married Philip Dixon Sergent, at Mount Vernon, Missouri, Dec. 29, 1891. Their children are:

David Wear Sergent, born Oct. 23, 1893, and married Carrie Aline Wining, at Ashland, Oregon, Dec. 8, 1915.

Hilda Marguerite Sergent born Dec. 28, 1875, married Ernest Joseph Vaillancour at Ashland, Oregon, Feb. 18, 1920.

Mildred Dorothy Sergent, born June 22, 1897.

Mary Elizabeth Sergent, born March 3, 1899 married Ralph Wilber Swihart, April 23, 1921, at Vancouver, Washington.

Horace Caswell Sergent, born Nov. 4, 1902, married Violet Esther McCollum, July 16, 1921, at Kalama, Washington.

Mildred Clay Wear, born January 27, 1874 (married July 18, 1904, Charles E. Booth, married second, April 5, 1919, Arthur Hamilton Van Hays); Judson Pleasant Wear, born April 4, 1879 (married Myrtle Reese, July, 1901. She died October 2, 1904. Their only child died young); Judson Pleasant Wear married for his second wife, Dora Ellen Spears); William Victor Wear, born August 20, 1881, (married Ora Nelson, December 26, 1901. Their children are: Raymond Victor Wear, born June 22, 1903, and Mildred Eugenia Wear, born June 22, 1909).

Pleasant M. Wear, junior, son of Pleasant M. and Tryphena Tipton Wear, was born in Mt. Vernon, Missouri, February 29, 1848. He married and has a family and now resides in Vinita, Oklahoma.

Alice, daughter of Pleasant M. and Tryphena Tipton Wear, was born in Mount Vernon, Missouri.

February 29th, 1848. She married September 1st, 1869, Richard McFall, who died January 2nd, 1889, in MacDonald County, Missouri. Ten children were born to them:

Triphena, born October 9th, 1870, who married October 9th, 1887, Robert Boyd, and had one child: Nora, born September 20th, 1888 (married W. W. Henderson, 1905, and had one child, Louise, who was born in 1908).

Etta McFall, born February 27th, 1872; unmarried.

Oscar McFall, born March 1st, 1874, died November 9th, 1892.

Eurah McFall, born January 29th, 1876; died in infancy.

Gabriel A. McFall, born November 28th, 1878, married March 20th, 1904, Ethel Gillette and had three children: Almond G., June 18th, 1906, died Dcember 3rd, 1906; Byron, born January 17th, 1908; and Thyra, born July 7th, 1811.

Eleanor McFall, born March 27th, 1881; died in infancy.

Lawrence McFall, born March 27th, 1882; unmarried.

C. H. McFall, born August 26th, 1884; unmarried.

Caswell McFall, born October 25th, 1887.

Jesse G. McFall, born January 22nd, 1889, married in 1911 Andrew Bennett. Their children were: Harold Bennett, born Novmber 26th, 1911; William Bennett, born May 15th, 1914; Donald Bennett, born May 8th, 1917; Loleta Bennett, born January 1st, 1920.

IX. MARGARET WEAR

Margaret Wear, daughter of Colonel Samuel War and his second wife Mary Gilliland Wear, married the Reverend D. B. Cummings, who was sent as one of the first missionaries to the Indians after their removel to the Indian Territory. They had at least one child, Colonel Pleasant Wear Cummings, who commanded the 10th Missouri Infantry, C. S. A., and participated in the battle of Prairie Grove, in Arkansas, December 7th, 1862, Pleasant Mill, Louisiana, April 9th, 1864, and Jenkins Ferry, Arkansas, April 30th, 1864.

X. MINERVA WEAR

Minerva Wear, the youngest child of Colonel Samuel Wear and his wife, Mary Gilliland Wear, was born in Sevier County, Tennessee, October 20, 1807. She married John Guthrie March 29th, 1825. John Guthrie was born in Scotland and came from Richmond to Sevier County. He owned the Sweden Furnace. He built the first paper mill in the South. He owned the Holston Paper Mill, the Bright-hope Furnace, near Greenville, and the Middlebrook Paper Mill, at Knoxville. John Guthrie, at the reorganization of the University of Tennessee, was a member of the first Board of Trustees. His home in Knoxville was called Middlebrook (later owned by Major Webb). John and Minerva Wear Guthrie left Knoxville in the early forties. They went to Nashville, then to Columbia, Tennessee, where Minerva died June 4, 1844. John Guthrie died also in Columbia, Sptember, 1844. A son John Guthrie, junior, died about the same time, and the graves of the three lie a few feet from the graves of President Polk's father and mother. The children of John and Minerva Wear Guthrie were:

Franklin Guthrie, born 1827, died in infancy.
Catherine Margaret Guthrie, born June 11, 1830.
Mary Granger Guthrie, born 1833.
Helen Mar Guthrie, born October 21, 1835.
John Chavallce Guthrie, born 1838, died 1843.
Victoria Guthrie, born February 2, 1841, died 1908,
Martha Jane Guthrie, born February 24, 1843, died 1855.

On the death of their parents, the Maury County Court appointed guardians for the children: W. H. Mack, a Presbyterian minister, was the guardian for Catherine Guthrie; Major Gordon was guardian for Mary Granger Guthrie; Reverend W. M. Shemand was guardian for Victoria Guthrie. John Guthrie was said to be the wealthiest man in East Tennessee. Among other properties, his daughters inherited several negroes, some of whom lived until a few years ago. An interesting old court record of Maury County, Tennessee, dated 1849, gives a partial list of the darkies left to the children of John and Minerva Wear Guthrie, namely: Hannah, Leah, Sarah, Abram, Mary, Blount, Wesley and Jane.

Of the children of John and Minerva Guthrie:

Catherine Margaret Guthrie married Dr. Thomas White Kelton, of North Carolina parentage, born near Murfreesboro, Rutherford County, Tennessee. (For her descendants see Kelton Family).

Mary Granger Guthrie was born in 1833. She married Captain Samuel Rankin Latta of Dyersburg, Tennessee, in 1852. The marriage took place in Eaton, Tennessee, at the home of the bride's sister, Mrs. Thomas White Kelton, (Catherine Margaret Guthrie). Captain Latta was born in Pennsylvania in 1827, and was descended from the Revo-

lutionary family of Latta of that state. He came to Tennessee in 1850. He and Mary Granger Guthrie celebrated their golden wedding anniversary in the home in Dyersburg to which he had brought his bride. Captain Latta died 1911, His wife lived until September, 1922. Their children were:
John Guthrie Latta.
Kate Latta.
Mary Elinor Latta.
Sarah Latta.
Frank Latta.
Samuel Granger Latta.
Of the foregoing:
John Guthrie Latta was born in 1858. He married December 6th, 1882, Leonora Poland. Their children are: Leslie Latta, born November 13, 1883, in Marshall, Texas; married Harry B. Watkins in 1908. They live in Memphis and have the following children: Leonora, born August 6, 1908, died February 11, 1913; Harry B., junior, born September 3, 1910; Mary, born April 24, 1912; Jacquelyn, born September 28, 1914. (b) Nell Latta, born in Dyersburg, April 26, 1885, married H. C. Marley, in 1907. She lives in Memphis and has two children: John Hampton, born March 26, 1910, and Richard, born August 3, 1916. (c) Floy Letta, born May 6, 1892, married Robert J. Beasley in 1912. They live in Beeville, Texas, and have two children. Robert J., junior, born January 26, 1913, and Dorothy, born May 19, 1914.

Kate Latta was born in Dyersburg, October 17, 1858, and married T. C. Gordon, who was born in Jackson, Louisiana, on the 7th of May, 1856. To them were born six children: Mary Gordon, born April 26, 1880, in Dyersburg, Tennessee. She was married to J. P. Pelham on June 11, 1901, and had three children: Gordon; Mary; William. Winfield Osceola, born in Dyersburg, January 27, 1882. He has never married. Sadie Louise, born in Dyersburg, July 6, 1884, and died in Sisseton Agency, Dakota, December 11 1887. Kate Latta Gordon was born at Sisseton Agency, Dakota, May 7, 1887. She was married to Clark Tindall Jones, of Columbia, Tennessee, and had two girls: Harriett and Clark. Mr. Jones died in February, 1919. In September, 1921, Mrs. Jones married Doctor Wallace Wilkes, of Columbia. Samuel Latta Gordon was born in Dyersburg, August 22, 1889. He is at present a lawyer. He served as a Captain in the World War. Helen Marr Gordon, was born January 11, 1892. She married in Los Angeles, California, to J. Y. Johnston on the 15th of May, 1918, and died September 30, 1918.

Sarah Knott Latta was born February 12, 1862, and married November 14, 1888, William Madison Anderson and Martha Ann Holmes. Their children are:

Dr. Wm. M. Anderson, junior, born September 29, 1889. He married October 23, 1916, Nancy Lee Gossett, at Dallas, Texas, and they have one daughter, Sarah Catherine, born February 11, 1921.

Samuel Latta Anderson, born July 19, 1891, is a lawyer. He served in the World War. He entered the Training Camp, May, 1917; was commissioned Captain and assigned to Camp Travis, 165 Depot Brigade; served as company commander; battalion commander; regimental adjutant; assistant brigade adjutant. He was commissioned Major, September, 1919; Brigade Adjutant until December 22, 1919, when he received his discharge.
President of Court Marshall until discharged.

John Franklin Anderson, born February 19, 1921 married December 23, 1919, to Carrie Lucy Strain, and they have one son, Holmes Guthrie Anderson, junior, born November 3, 1920.

Granger Anderson, born July 27, 1895. He served in the World War. Entered the Training Camp 1917, was commissioned 2nd Lieutenant and assigned to the 345 Field Artillery; was made 1st Lieutenant later. He went to France, June, 1919, with the 90th Division, and served in the Army of occupation until ordered home. He married, August 20, 1919, Forest Richardson, and they have one child, Forrest Isabelle Anderson, born February 19, 1921.

John Franklin Anderson, born Fbruary 19, 1921.
He entered the |R. O. T. C. as a studen at Austin College, 1918, and went to Camp Arthur, Waco, Texas, 1918. He marreid August 14, 1919, Jewel Thomason, and has a son, John Franklin Anderson, junior, born May 27, 1920.

Robert Albert Anderson, born January 11, 1900; July 24, 1901.

James Rankin Anderson, born March 9th, 1802, is now a student. He entered the R. O. T. C. in Forrest Avenue High School and trained at Louisville, Kentucky, in the summer of 1919.

Mary Eleanor Latta, fourth child of Captain Samuel Latta and Mary Granger Latta, was born March 9th, 1864; married November 30, 1897, to John P. Grigsby, who was

WEAR

born April 4th, 1840. He was a gallant soldier in the War Between the States and died April 21, 1921. They lived in Dyersburg and had one child, Mary Granger Grigsby, who was born August 26, 1899. They live in the old Latta home.

Frank Wallace Latta, fifth child of Samuel Rankin and Mary Granger Latta, were born July 4th, 1866. He has for many years been Post Master of Dyersburg, holding that position during many political upheavals. He was married April 29th, 1891, to Pearl Willis Doyle, of Knoxville. Their children are: A son, born March 22, 1892; died in infancy. Stanley Doyle Latta, born May 11, 1893, served as a volunteer in the Navy through the World War. He was married on December 28, 1920 to Edna Moore of Clinton, Kentucky. He died February 5th, 1921. Samuel Rankin Latta was born April 3, 1896. He served as a volunteer in the Artillery throughout the war. John Hickman Latta, born December 10th, 1897, served as a volunteer during the latter months of the war. Evelyn Belle Latta, born October 24, 1898. Sadie Knott Latta, born January 22, 1906.

Samuel Granger Latta, son of Samuel R. and Mary Granger Latta, was born August 5,1871. He is a lawyer, being the senior member of the firm of Latta and Latta of Dyersburg, of which his son Franklin W. Latta is a partner He was married October 1, 1896, to Eveleen Pardoe and has the following children: Franklin Wallace Latta, who served in the World War in Aviation, married to Ruth Fumbanks, November 18, 1920, and has one child, S. Granger Latta jr. born September 4, 1921. Mary Latta, born May 29, 1899, married on January 19, 1919, to Homer Murphy Richards and has one child; Homer Latta Richards born February 15, 1920. Kate Latta, born August 9, 1901. Gordon Granger Latta, born September 30, 1903. Eveleen Latta, born June 15, 1905.

Helen Mar Guthrie, daughter of Minerva Wear and John Guthrie, married Dr. John Hocker, a brother to Lavinia Wear's husband, in Mount Vernon, Missouri. They died about 1870, leaving no children.

WILLIAMS

The Williams Family of North Carolina and Tennessee

One of the old and distinguished families of North Carolina and Tennessee is the Williams. The progenitor of the family was Nathaniel Williams, who was a native of Hanover County, Virginia. He had four sons and one daughter, namely:

I. Robert Williams.
II. Betsy or Elizabeth Williams.
III. John Williams.
IV. Nathaniel Williams, Scond.
V. Joseph Williams.

I. ROBERT WILLIAMS

Robert Williams, the eldest son of Nathaniel Williams, moved from Pittsylvania County, Virginia, Robert Williams was Adjutant General of the State of North Carolina and collected the only copy of the Acts of the Assembly. He married Sarah Lanier. They had seven children and possibly one more. The seven were: (1) Nathaniel Williams (who was Judge of the Superior Court of Tennessee); (2) Polly Williams (who married Matthew Cay, member of Congress 1797-1813); (3) Lucy Williams (who married Robert Call); (4) Patsy Williams (who married John Henry; (5) Sarah Williams (who married James Chalmers and lived in Halifax, Virginia, and was grandparent of General James R. Chalmers, member of Congress from Mississippi); (6) Elizabeth Williams (who married John Kerr, member of Congress, and had three children, namely: John Kerr, Second, who was also a member of Congress; Mary G. Kerr, who married her cousin,, Nicholas Lanier

NOTABLE SOUTHERN FAMILIES

Williams, and Martha Kerr, who married Dr. Frank Martin; and (second) Frances Williams (who married Thomas D. Conally of Tennessee. They had three children, namely: Rev. John Kerr Connally, who married Alice C. Thomas, daughter of James Thomas of Richmond; Mary E. Conally, who married James Turner Morehead, son of Governor J. M. Morehead of North Carolina; and Frances Conally, who married C. W. Guerrant of Rockingham, North Carolina). The other daughter of Robert Williams and his wife, Sarah Lanier Williams, who was the eighth child, is given by John H. Wheeler as also a "Frances," but it is improbable that two daughters would have reached maturity continually called by the same name. . She is given, however, as "Frances, the wife of General Barcilia Graves".

II. BETSY OR ELIZABETH WILLIAMS

Betsy or Elizabeth Williams, daughter of Nathaniel Williams, married ——— Hicks.

III. JOHN WILLIAMS

John Williams, son of Nathaniel Williams, First, born in Hanover County, Virgnia, in 1745; died in 1799. He was a Colonel of the Revolution and commanded the Minute Men from Hillsboro District, North Carolina. In April 1770, he was a member of the court which met at Hillsboro. He was one of the first Judges under the State Constitution in North Carolina, in 1777 He was a member distinguished for his sound judgment and common sense. He died in October. 1799.

He married Elizabeth Williamson and settled in North Carolina, Hillsboro District. They had two chidren, namely: Christopher H. Williams (who was a member of Congress from Tennessee 1837-1853, and Elizabeth Williams (who married General Azariah Graves. Their daughter, Henrietta Graves, married Judge Thomas Settle, First, and had two children, Thomas Settle, Second, and Fannie Settle, who married Colonel John W. Covington and had a daughter, Nettie Covington, who married P. D. Walsh of Rockingham, North Carolina).

Senator John Sharp Williams of Mississippi comes of this line. He is a son of Colonel Christopher Harris Williams and his wife Annie Louise Sharp Williams. John Sharp Williams was born in Memphis. He married Elizabeth Dial Webb.

WILLIAMS

IV. NATHANIEL WILLIAMS, SECOND

Nathaniel Williams, Second, son of Nathaniel Williams, First married ———— and had three children, namely: Robert Williams (who was appointed Governor of Mississippi by President Thomas Jefferson); Nathaniel Williams, Third; and Elizabeth Williams (who married ——— Baldwin of Louisiana).

V. JOSEPH WILLIAMS

Joseph Williams, son of Nathaniel Williams, the First was born in Hanover County, Virginia, and moved to North Carolina when he was eighteen years old. He settled near Shallow Ford, in what was afterwards Surrey County, before the Revolution. He was one of the delegates from Surrey to the Convention at Hillsboro in 1775, the other delegates being Robert Lanier, William Hall, Martin Armstrong, and Joseph Winston.

In 1776 he was appointed Lieutenant Colonel of the Surrey County Militia. Martin Armstrong was Colonel. Joseph Williams was distinguished for his enterprise, activity and patriotism. He was Clerk of the court of Surrey for many years and continued in that position until he died, at a ripe old age, in 1828. He married Rebecca Lanier of Granville County, North Carolina.

Their children were:

(1) Robert Williams; married Rebecca Smith.
(2) Joseph Williams; married Susan Taylor.
(3) John Williams; married Melinda White.
(4) William Williams; married Sarah King.
(5) Lewis Williams; died unmarried.
(6) Thomas L. Williams; married Polly McClung.
(7) Rebecca Williams; married John H. Wimbish.
(8) Alexander Williams; marred Catherine Dixon.
(9) Fannie Williams; married John P. Erwin.
(10) Nicholas Lanier Williams; marred Mary G. King.

Of the foregoing:

(1) General Robert Williams, son of Joseph Williams and Rebecca Lanier Williams, was born in Caswell County, and was prominent in the public life of North Carolina. He was a member of Congress from North Carolna 1797-1803, and in 1805 was appointed Commissioner of Land Titles in Mississippi by President Jefferson. He served for four

years. He married Rebecca Smith of Granville, North Carolina, and died in Louisiana.

(2) Joseph Williams, Second, son of Joseph Williams and Rebecca Lanier Williams, was Clerk of Surrey Court. He married Susan Taylor. They had three children, namely: Susan Williams (who married James R. Dodge and had: Richard Irwin Dodge, U. S. A., whose son was Frederick P. Dodge; Annie Dodge, who married Chalmers L. Glenn, and had James L. Glenn, Robert B. Glenn, and Edward T. B. Glenn; and Mary H. Dodge); Rebecca Williams (who married Frank Deaderick); and Midshipman John T. Wlliams.

(3) John Williams, the third son of Joseph Williams and Rebecca Lanier Williams, moved to Knoxville, Tennessee. Here he began to practice law. During the Seminole War he raised a troop of volunteers, after which he was made Colonel of the 39th Infantry, United States Army. In the Battle of the Horseshoe the 39th, under his command, is said to have borne the brunt of the battle. From 1815 to 1823 he was Senator from Tennessee. In 1825 he was appointed, by President Adams, Envoy to the Central American States. He died in Knoxville, August 7, 1837. He married Malinda White, daughter of General James White, and sister to Hugh Lawson White. He had three children, namely: Joseph Lanier Williams (member of Congress from 1839 to 1843); Margaret Williams (who married Chief Justice Pearson of North Carolina as his first wife: from this line comes Richard Pearson Hobson of Greensboro, Alabama); and Colonel John Williams, Second, (who married Rhoda Morgan and had three children, namely: John Williams, Third; Thomas Lanier Williams and Lizzie Williams. Of these: John Williams, Third, married Lizzie Nelson, daughter of Judge Thomas A. R. Nelson, of Knoxville, Tennessee, and had a daughter Mary Williams, who married —— Merriweather and lives in Washington; Thomas Lanier Williams married Isabella Coffin (see Sevier Family in Notable Southern Families, Volume I), and had Ella Williams who married William Gannaway Brownlow (see Brownlow Family in Notable Southern Families, Vol. I, and has no children; and Cornelius Coffin Williams, who marrid Edwina Dakin, and lives in St. Louis and has two children, Rose Isabella Williams and Thomas Lanier Williams, Second; Lizzie Williams, married Joseph W. Sneed of Knoxville, Tennessee, and had John Seed, Joseph Sneed, Lida Sneed, Eliza-

WILLIAMS

beth Sneed, Linda Sneed, who married Alex Brandeau, and William Sneed, who married Elizbeth Logan and had Joseph Logan Sneed, Elizabeth Sneed and Rebecca Sneed.

(4) William Williams, the fourth son of Joseph Williams and Rebecca Lanier Williams, was born about 1782, He graduated from the University of North Carolina in 1808 He was elected to Congress in 1815, and contiued to be a member of Congress during his life. He died while in Washington, February 25, 1842. He was unmarried.

(6) Thomas Lanier Williams, son of Joseph Williams and Rebecca Lanier Williams, was a twin brother of Lewis Williams, and was born about 1782. He moved to Tennessee and was Chancellor of Tennesse for many years. He married Polly McClung, daughter of Charles McClung and Margaret White, daughter of General James White of Tennessee. They had four children, namely: Rebecca Williams (who is said to have marrid a son of Governor Isaac Shelby of Kentucky); Malinda Williams (who married Chief Justice Napton of Missouri); Margaret Williams (who married John G. Miller, member of Congress from Missouri, and married as her second husband, H. W. Douglass of Nashville); and ——— Williams (who married Dr. J. Walker Percy of Huntsville, Alabama).

(Rebecca Williams, seventh child and first daughter of Joseph Williams and Rebecca Lanier Williams, married Colonel John H. Wimbish of Halifax, Virginia. They had one child, Rebecca, who married first Dr. Pleasant Henderson, and second Roger Q. Mills, member of Congress from Texas.

(8) Alexander Williams, who lived at Greeneville, Tennessee, seventh son of Joseph Williams and Rebecca Lanier Williams, was a physician. He married Catherine Dixon, only daughter of Colonel William Dixon.

(9) Fannie Williams, ninth child of Joseph Williams and Rebecca Williams, married Colonel John P. Erwin of Nashville.

(10) Nicholas Lanier Williams, tenth child and eighth son of Joseph Williams and Rebecca Lanier Williams, was born about 1800. He married Mary G. Kerr and had three children, namely: Bettie Williams (who married John A. Lillington; Joseph Williams (who married M. Lou Glenn, daughter of Tyre Glenn of Yadkin County, North Carolina, and had two children, Glenn Williams and Mary Williams); and Lewis Williams, who married Sarah A. Smith, daughter of Colonel William C. Smith of Anson County,

NOTABLE SOUTHERN FAMILIES

North Carolina, and had five children: Mary C. Williams, Eliza Helms Williams, William Smith Williams, Lena Pearl Williams and Lanier Williams.
From Tennessee Reports, Volume III, page 14.

CARTHAGE, 1816

Nathaniel Williams, officer in Colonial Line, March 7, 1786, grant for services, in Smith County Tennessee, on Cumberland River. Nathaniel died and left sons, Nathaniel and William Williams. The latter died unmarried, leaving Nathaniel Williams sole heir. He sold the land warrant in 1785 to Grafton Ireland.

Note: Another Williams of Revolutionary Service was Colonel James William, born in Granville County, North Carolina, 1737; died 1780 He commanded a regiment at King's Mountain and in other battles. At King's Mountain he was mortally wounded. He married Mary Wallace. Descendants of this Colonel Williams are Miss Caroline Williams Sproul of Abbeville, South Carolina, and Miss Mary Miles Jordan of Greenwood, South Carolina, and the Williams family of Alabama.

THE WILLOUGHBY WILLIAMS LINE

Colonel Wiloughby Williams of North Carolina was another distinguished officer of the Revolution. He served us "Commisary of Issues". He fought in many battles and was badly wounded at the Battle of Cowpens. Another authority says that he was killed in the Battle of Cowpens. He married Nancy Glasgow (after his death she married Governor Joseph McMinn of Tennessee, but by him had no children). Colonel Willoughby Williams left a son, Willoughby Williams, Second, who married Nancy Nicholls. They had a son, Robert Nicholls Williams. He married Mary Matilda Morgan, who is now living in Columbia, Tennessee. Their children were: Genevieve Williams (who married James Hillary Mulligan); Nancy Lee Williams (who married William Porter Morgan, and is now living in Columbia, Tennessee); Morgan Williams (of Greeneville, Florida); and Willoughby Williams, Third (who died November 23, 1919, in Nashville, Tennessee, leaving two sons).

Judge Joseph V. Williams of Chattanooga, is of a family which moved to the state of Tennessee more than a century ago from Maryland. James Williams (great-grandfather

WILLIAMS

of Joseph V. Williams), moved to Elizabethton, Tennessee, early in the year 1805; from Maryland where he had seen revolutionary service. Sometime before 1814, he died in Elizabethton. In that year his son, Jesse Williams, moved to Overton County, Tennessee, and after living there one year moved again, this time to White County, where he lived until his death. He married Elizabeth Tate of a well known Tennessee family, and their son, James Tate Williams married Matilda Wallace of an old revolutionary family. Their children were: Joseph V. Williams, and May Williams. Judge Joseph V. Williams moved to Chattanooga to reside, and married Annie Scholze. Their children are: Joseph V. Williams, junior, Robert Williams, Margaret Williams and Annie Gertrude Williams. May Williams, daughter of James Tate Williams and Matilda Wallace Williams, married J. T. Quarles, of Cookeville, Tennessee.

www.ingramcontent.com/pod-product-compliance
Lightning Source LLC
Chambersburg PA
CBHW031542300426
44111CB00006BA/146